Thackeray's Skeptical Narrative
and the 'Perilious Trade' of Authorship

In memory of Jane Law Fisher

Thackeray's Skeptical Narrative and the 'Perilious Trade' of Authorship

JUDITH L. FISHER

ASHGATE

Published by

Ashgate Publishing Limited
Gower House, Croft Road
Aldershot
Hants GU11 3HR
England

Ashgate Publishing Company
131 Main Street
Burlington VT 05401–5600
USA

Ashgate website: http://www.ashgate.com

Judith L. Fisher has asserted his right under the Copyright, Designs and Patents Act, 1988, to be identified as the author of this work.

British Library Cataloguing-in-Publication Data
Fisher, Judith L.
　　Thackeray's skeptical narrative and the 'perilous trade' of
　　authorship. – (The nineteenth century series)
　　1. Thackeray, W. M. (William Makepeace), 1811–1863–
　　Criticism and interpretation 2. Skepticism in literature
　　I. Title
　　823. 8

Library of Congress Control Number: 2001099682

ISBN 0 7546 0651 1

This book is printed on acid free paper

Printed and bound in Great Britain by MPG Books Ltd, Bodmin, Cornwall

Contents

The Nineteenth Century General Editors' Preface   *vi*

List of Illustrations   *vii*

Acknowledgements   *viii*

Texts and Abbreviations   *ix*

1   The Hermeneutic of Skepticism   1

2   The "Right Line I": Narratorial Collusion and the Perils of
    "Sternism"   44

3   A Version of a "Man and a Brother": Or, Character into Narrator   95

4   The Rebellious Text and the Resisting Reader   135

5   The Secret History of Henry Esmond   169

6   Infinite Isolations   205

7   "The Abode of Bliss and the Halls of Prismatic Splendour"   243

Bibliography   284

Index   292

The Nineteenth Century General Editors' Preface

The aim of the series is to reflect, develop and extend the great burgeoning of interest in the nineteenth century that has been an inevitable feature of recent years, as that former epoch has come more sharply into focus as a locus for our understanding not only of the past but of the contours of our modernity. It centres primarily upon major authors and subjects within Romantic and Victorian literature. It also includes studies of other British writers and issues, where these are matters of current debate: for example, biography and autobiography, journalism, periodical literature, travel writing, book production, gender, non-canonical writing. We are dedicated principally to publishing original monographs and symposia; our policy is to embrace a broad scope in chronology, approach and range of concern, and both to recognize and cut innovatively across such parameters as those suggested by the designations "Romantic" and "Victorian". We welcome new ideas and theories, while valuing traditional scholarship. It is hoped that the world which predates yet so forcibly predicts and engages our own will emerge in parts, in the wider sweep, and in the lively streams of disputation and change that are so manifest an aspect of its intellectual, artistic and social landscape.

Vincent Newey
Joanne Shattock

University of Leicester

List of Illustrations

1.1	Pictorial Initial, Chapter 13, *Vanity Fair*	32
2.1	Intratext, Chapter 6, *Vanity Fair*	64
2.2	Frontispiece, *Vanity Fair*, 1848	69
2.3	Intratext, Chapter 37, *Vanity Fair*	71
2.4	Intratext, Chapter 25, *Vanity Fair*	72
2.5	"False Gesture", M. Engels in Henry Siddons, *Illustrations of Practical Rhetorical Gesture*	75
2.6	"Menace", M. Engels in Henry Siddons, *Illustrations of Practical Rhetorical Gesture*	76
2.7	Intratext, Chapter 8, *Vanity Fair*	78
2.8	Intratext, Chapter 11, *Vanity Fair*	79
2.9	Cover, monthly number, *Vanity Fair*	88
2.10	"A Lecture on Soap-suds", December, 1844	89
3.1	Cover, monthly number, *Pendennis*	99
3.2	Title Page Illustration, volume 1, *Pendennis*	100
3.3	Pictorial Initial, volume 2, Chapter 27, *Pendennis*	129
3.4	Pictorial Initial, volume 2, Chapter 34, *Pendennis*	129
3.5	Decorative Harlequin, 1844	130
3.6	Pictorial Initial, volume 2, Chapter 35, *Pendennis*	130
6.1	"Gather ye Rosebuds while ye May", Chapter 18, *The Virginians*	234

Acknowledgements

I am very grateful to all the people who have encouraged and advised me in the process of completing this project. I could never have finished this book without the help of Peter L. Shillingsburg and John H. Fisher, both of whom patiently read and critiqued the manuscript. Mark Allen was tireless in his encouragement and helped me work through many of the theoretical issues about Thackeray's skepticism and its relation to the medieval tradition of skeptical fideism.

I am grateful to the Elizabeth Huth Coates Library for reproducing the illustrations and to Trinity University for academic leave to support the research and writing.

Many thanks go to Mrs. Belinda Norman Butler who as always is generous in her permission to cite unpublished material. I am also grateful to the University of California Press for permission to use material from my essay, "Image Versus Text in the Illustrated Novels of William Makepeace Thackeray", published in *Victorian Literature and the Victorian Imagination*, edited by Carol Christ and John O. Jordan (1995). I also thank the Huntington Library for their permission to cite the manuscript of "The Adventures of Philip" (HM 239).

And a special thanks to John Olmsted who introduced me to Thackeray.

Texts and Abbreviations

Catherine, Vanity Fair, The History of Pendennis, The Newcomes, and *The History of Henry Esmond* are volumes from the *The Works of William Makepeace Thackeray,* general editor, Peter L. Shillingsburg (*The Thackeray Edition Project*), published by Garland Publishing and the University of Michigan Press.

I have chosen these editions because their lists of variants and textual history allow me to refer to Thackeray's alterations in manuscript and the revisions made between editions. *The Virginians* and *The Adventures of Philip* are not yet available from the *The Works.* For these novels and all other works by Thackeray, I have used the *Biographical Edition* with introductions by Anne Ritchie Thackeray, cited by volume and page number in the text. Any essays by Thackeray not included in *Works* are cited individually.

Abbreviations:

C	*Catherine, a Story*
HE	*The History of Henry Esmond*
LPP	*Letters and Private Papers,* ed. Gordon Ray.
LPPS	*Letters and Private Papers,* Supplement, ed. Edgar F. Harden
N	*The Newcomes*
P	*The History of Pendennis*
Ph	*The Adventures of Philip*
RbP	*Roundabout Papers*
VF	*Vanity Fair*
Vir	*The Virginians*
Works	*The Biographical Edition of the Works of W. M. Thackeray*

1 The Hermeneutic of Skepticism

The Teller

> "Although we have seen Thackeray steadily, we cannot be said to have seen him whole".

Thus Robert Colby opens his penetrating study of Thackeray's *Canvass of Humanity*.[1] It is still true that Thackeray is known primarily for *Vanity Fair* – and perhaps *Henry Esmond*. Recent works such as John Reed's *Punishment and Forgiveness* and Micael Clarke's *Thackeray and Women* continue Colby's work of presenting Thackeray holistically, expanding upon George Saintsbury's comment that Thackeray's novels are "children of one family".[2] These studies are primarily thematic and contextual and, certainly, theme and context are important ingredients in Thackeray's unified work. But he is also rhetorically and stylistically all of a piece, and this recognizable Thackerayean presence, which Colby calls "Protean" (5), acts out a rhetorical intent that ties narrative technique and story together as mirror images of each other. Not only do his themes reappear within one story pattern re-dramatized from novel to novel, but each novel can be read holistically through the intra-relations between (to use Peter Rabinowitz's terms) the implied author and the "authorial" audience (the implied reader), the story and the "narrative" audience (the narrative reader), and what I will be calling the narrator and narratorial reader.[3]

My claim that one can read Thackeray "holistically" is ironic because such a claim refutes what this study will attempt to demonstrate: that Thackeray deliberately attempted to disrupt the reading process in order to thwart any stable interpretation. Perhaps a better term than holistic would be the phrase "continuous discontinuity" to describe the experience of reading a Thackeray novel. His upbringing and early training as an artist, parodist, and critic encouraged Thackeray to think skeptically about the possibility of arriving at absolute truths, not as a matter of belief, but as they could be expressed in language. For Thackeray, language was a system of conventions that depended upon an interpretive community for any stable meanings: change the codes or change the audience and the meaning changed. This skepticism developed into a suspicion of the egoism of the author as Thackeray achieved popular success and recognition with *Vanity Fair*.

Thackeray recognized early that the control of the Dickensian narrator who sees all, knows all, and tells all, could as easily direct readers to unethical as to ethical purposes. Dickens was flawed for Thackeray not just because he misused his narrative ability to over-direct his readers but also because he used his great skill to recreate the London underworld as a morally simplistic romance. In 1839, at the end of his notorious "Newgate" parody, *Catherine*, Thackeray speaks through his narrator, Ikey Solomons, to point out the ethical problem created by Dickens' narrative power:

> No man has read that remarkable tale of *Oliver Twist* without being interested in poor Nancy and her murderer; and especially amused and tickled by the gambols of the Artful Dodger and his companions. The power of the writer is so amazing, that the reader at once becomes his captive, and must follow him whithersoever he leads; and to what are we led? Breathless to watch all the crimes of Fagin, tenderly to deplore the errors of Nancy, to have for Bill Sikes a kind of pity and admiration, and an absolute love for the society of the Dodger. (*C* 132)

Dickens's unified, stable narrative voice (analogous with the sure and penetrating voice George Eliot would develop) could absorb the reader, remaking her into whatever image the author chose: here is both the lure and danger of authorship and reading for Thackeray. In modernizing romance, that is, combining contemporary settings with fairy-tale poetic justice, Dickens disconnected the structural elements of the romance genre from the actual ethical world of his setting and characters. If no one can read *Oliver Twist* "without being interested in poor Nancy and her murderer; and especially amused and tickled by the gambols of the Artful Dodger and his companions", then for whom, Solomons asks, are we really feeling sympathy? Fagin, Nancy, Bill Sikes, the Artful Dodger

> stepped from the novel on to the stage; and the whole London public, from peers to chimney sweeps, were interested about a set of

ruffians whose occupations are thievery, murder, and prostitution. A most agreeable set of rascals, indeed, who have their virtues, too, but not good company for any man. We had better pass them by in decent silence; for, as no writer can or dare tell the *whole* truth concerning them, and faithfully explain their vices, there is no need to give *ex-parte* statement of their virtues. (*C* 132)[4]

The very power of the unified Dickensian persona incorporates the reader into a world of oversimplified moral values inconsistent with the actualities of his contemporary setting. In contrast, Ikey Solomons rests the success of his story on the consistency between his narrative values, the values embodied in his characters, and the values of his fictional world:

it has been his attempt to make vice appear entirely vicious; and in those instances where he hath occasionally introduced something like virtue, to make the sham as evident as possible, and not allow the meanest capacity a single chance to mistake it.

And what has been the consequence? That wholesome nausea which it has been his good fortune to create wherever he has been allowed to practise in his humble circle. (*C* 132)

The "success" of Solomon's method has, paradoxically and designedly, resulted in critical failure; he has not "altogether failed" in his strategy because *Catherine* was abused by the newspaper critics as "one of the dullest, most vulgar and immoral works extant" (*C* 131). Thackeray's rejection of romantic idealization in *Catherine* develops in his subsequent work into specific narrative strategies designed to educate the reader into a self-awareness that rejects the narrative ethics of *Oliver Twist*. His response to the ability of omniscient narration to manipulate or control readers was to develop his skill at parody into an inconsistent multi-voiced narration that inhibits and undermines any consistent reader-identification.

James Phelan and Peter Rabinowitz have argued that we read at many levels inviting different identifications between reader and text. Combining Peter Rabinowitz's terms for audience with those James Phelan developed in *Reading People, Reading Plots* to describe the different facets of literary character allows me to extend the kind of reading Thackeray's audience experienced in a way arguably peculiar to nineteenth-century reading audiences. Phelan describes fictional characters as having "mimetic", "thematic" and "synthetic" components.[5] When we read as the "narrative" audience, we read "mimetically", as if the story were "real". This level invites our emotional connection to characters and basic responses to plot progression such as "what happens next". To move out of the story and read as the implied author, following his or her patterns of meaning, is to read "thematically". Thematic reading is our accumulating interpretation of underlying ideas and meanings of the story. Synthetic reading, also on the level of the implied author, is an even more abstract awareness of aesthetic artifices of textual construction such as patterns of symbol and image or structural features such as juxtaposition and parallelism in characters and events.

In addition to these kinds of reading, the first automatic and the second and third more self-consciously cultivated, nineteenth-century novels in particular (although not uniquely) ask us to join with the narrator and read the story as the narrator constructs, comments, and, occasionally, participates in it. This mid-level reading is most pronounced when the novel's story is subsumed under an "intrusive" or prominent narrative voice or, often in Thackeray's case, voices. If we understand this "narratorial" reading, then we can understand that such foregrounded narration as we find in Thackeray is not "intrusive", but, in fact, is the focus of the fiction. This subordination of story to narrator characterizes all of Thackeray's novels from the heavily ironic voices of Barry Lyndon and Ikey Solomons to the master-voice(s) of the "critic-as-narrator" in *Vanity Fair* to the arm-chair ironist of *Pendennis* into Pendennis, himself, whose own narration of the later novels increasingly dissolves the stories into explorations of the narrator's consciousness and the problems of interpretation.

If the values and tone of the narration are consistent with the values dramatized by characterization and plot-line in the story, readers will tend to respond with sympathy and identification and not, while reading, be conscious of their different levels of interpretation. But Thackeray, distrusting this hypnotic and seductive narrative magic, exploited these levels of reading to create multiple perspectives that are irreconcilable with each other, purposefully throwing the reader outside the text onto her own interpretive resources. These perspectives are embodied in his illustrations and in the contradictory sociolects used by the narrative presence and the characters. A sociolect is a presentation of a particular perspective recognizable in vocabulary (verbal and visual) and pronunciation (such as a character dropping her h's). Each language implies an ethical   standard for the user who manifests these ethics as evaluations of him- or herself, the other characters, and incidents in the novels. Each sociolect's frame of reference provides criteria that users apply to themselves and use to ex-plain characters' motives and to judge actions and speech as "good" or "bad" according to how well the characters under scrutiny fit the speaker's frame of reference. I use the term "sociolect" because these languages indicate class and class pretensions, are marks of gender, and use frames of reference that are conventions of representation. No sociolect belongs to an individual; all can be recognized as the language of a specific kind of community or tradition of representation, e.g.: public school, evangelical Christianity, classical mythology, painting, fairy-tale, "du monde", melodrama, romance, or classical myth. The characters' languages and the languages the narrator uses about them place them in specific worlds – which are not necessarily reconcilable with the linguistic worlds of the other characters. Thackeray's narrators are master-linguists. They use many sociolects, conflate sociolects, and enter into the linguistic world of all the characters without subscribing to a single sociolect. Henry Esmond is, we will see, an intriguing exception to this narrative game-playing.

Because the sociolects are by nature limited perspectives, their speakers often disagree in their interpretations, sometimes to the point of being incommensurable. Laura Pendennis could probably find no grounds upon which to base a conversation with Lord Steyne. And we see, for example, that Colonel Newcome's sociolect of Christian soldier does not allow him to understand Lady Kew's language of "du monde". But the narrative languages and commentary show us that each sociolect is a viable way of explaining and acting in the world: not necessarily a "good" way in terms of Christian ethics, but a viable epistemology.

The narrator weighs the languages equally and incorporates multiple sociolects into his own commentary as well as letting the characters speak for themselves. The consequence is often a "collision" between sociolects within the reader's interpretation. We cannot consistently read mimetically with any character or with the narrator. Thackeray's manipulation of his sociolects deliberately forces readers to move self-consciously among mimetic, narratorial, and thematic levels of reading. The more you read Thackeray, the more you become aware that his world is built from conventions of representation that readers and the characters experience as real. We want to believe what we read, but Thackeray's narrators and characters keep offering us irreconcilable interpretations. Consequently, we are thrown outside the text onto our own interpretive resources.

Thackeray's narrative presence is particularly tricky. His voices and stances make us aware of his contradictions even as they tell us they are "reporting" the "whole truth". His story is only a version (*Philip*) but yet it derives from sources outside the novel (*The Newcomes, Philip*). Sometimes the narrator changes his persona (*Vanity Fair*), sometimes he is interrupted by the "author" (*The Newcomes*) or an editor (*Henry Esmond, The Virginians*), sometimes he blatantly and playfully exploits his own reliability (*Philip*). His knowledge is simultaneously partial and complete (*Pendennis, Henry Esmond*); he gives up his story in despair (*The Virginians*); he gleefully tells us not to depend upon him but that he is telling us the truth (*Philip*). However, this maddeningly consistent inconsistency co-exists with rhetorical strategies which pull us into the narratorial world, not necessarily to believe any one narrative stance, but – if we are careful and wary readers – to play his language games with him. We can collude with the narrator to feel delight in our discomfort at his manipulation. Narratorial collusion seduces us into the pleasures of Thackerayean narration.

Both the narrative languages and the illustrations promote collision and collusion that participates in the larger modal conflict that increasingly undermines the conventions of plot and closure, narrative stability, and poetic justice as characteristics of the "novel". "We", the readers, may see, explain, and pursue the world as romance – easily discerned moral values and poetic justice – but realism – the need for money, a suitable marriage, and the facts of social hypocrisies that we all practice – adds a gray tinge to our rose-colored glasses. As Geoffrey Tillotson wrote about Thackeray's criticism of "idealism", what I am calling romance, in his novels: "All of us mix realism and idealism in our private philosophies, and most of us attend to the realism in the mixture as little as possible" (*View*, 173). In all the novels, Thackeray, self-consciously ironic, emphasizes the egoism of the narrator, his god-like perspective, in order to educate his reader out of belief and into self-reliant judgment.

Readers experiencing his narration as simply a meandering, unreliable consciousness have criticized all the novels, but especially *The Virginians* and *The Adventures of Philip*. From first publication to the present, for example, many readers have found these novels to lack "plot", because they find it difficult to read these novels mimetically. Thackeray's violation of the integrity of the narrator has also discomforted readers, leading critics to search for ways to explain the lack of narrative unity in the Thackerayean novel.[6] George Levine calls him a "realist" caught between the singleness of his vision and the knowledge that the "real" is many-visioned and unnameable.[7] Jack Rawlins suggests Thackeray was trying to write a realistic novel built on romantic conventions of form, but that the fictionality of his "realistic" text keeps interfering with the harmony of a romantic telling, wherein teller and tale are joined seamlessly.[8] Although Rawlins sees this alienation between modes primarily in *Vanity Fair*, it is even more apparent in *The Virginians* and *The Adventures of Philip*. This conflict is not, however, a failing but a deliberate effort by Thackeray to question whether or not language refers to any reality outside of its own codes of representation. Geoffrey Tillotson fixes Thackeray's narrative commentary as a "voice" of a community consciousness, aware of its own perplexities but able to connect through sympathetic self-awareness.[9] While Levine also sees Thackeray's commentary as a unifying voice and a source of authenticity, he assigns to that voice a more pessimistic role "to establish – within the central Victorian conventions of the author's responsibility to the audience – some kind of community to avoid the full potential anguish of our infinite isolation" (161). But to unify the narration and commentary simply by supplying a collective noun such as "community" ignores the fragmentary nature of any community and the self-conscious contradiction Thackeray always built between his particular "right line I" and the various masks the narrator dons.

Biographical interpreters often suspect that Thackeray responded nervously, if not in panic, to his own modernism. Winslow Rogers calls Thackeray "obsessed with the question of how to know and trust his feelings", and argues that Thackeray's allusions to the fictionality of his own fiction and his subversions of narrative conventions are "often not a balancing of opposed perspectives, not a creative irony, but rather a nervous retreat, closing off a discussion that has got out of hand".[10] Janice Carlisle finds that Thackeray's ironies and paradoxes stem from his uneasy relation with his audience: his distrust of them balancing with a desire for their approval.[11] Such psychological explanations rely on the traditional image of Thackeray as an ill-at-ease writer, uncomfortable with his profession and often rely on the publication of Thackeray's letters whose admissions of boredom and impatience with novel writing seem to link the wandering narratives to Thackeray's own unrest and dissatisfaction with fiction. However, Peter Shillingsburg's discussion in his study of Thackeray as a professional author, *Pegasus in Harness,* disabuses us of the notion that Thackeray was either inept or ashamed of his "trade", as he himself called it.[12] Moreover, the viability of this portrait of the angst-ridden artist is challenged by the stylistic fluidity and complicated rhetorical games of *The Virginians* and *The Adventures of Philip*. In the context of the *Roundabout Papers*, these late novels emerge as sophisticated versions of a constantly experimental and increasingly self-conscious hermeneutic of skepticism. Thackeray has been called a cynic, torn between satire and sentiment.[13] A cynic is a "person disposed to rail or find fault; . . . usually: one who shows a disposition to disbelieve in the sincerity or goodness of human motives and actions and is wont to express this by sneers and sarcasms: a sneering fault-finder" (*OED*). Such malcontentedness does not fit the Thackeray who described himself as a lay preacher in the famous ending of his *Book of Snobs* and who wrote to Mark Lemon that a writer's "profession is as serious as the Parson's own" (*LPP* 2: 281-82). His reputation during his life and after as a cynic or as caught between sentiment and satire derives from the absence of a simple homiletic or poetic justice in his works. Instead, his "lessons" are embedded in the ways his narrative techniques invite us to question ourselves and our world and to draw our own conclusions. Ina Ferris has made a similar argument exploring the "rhetoric of realism" in Scott, Thackeray and Eliot.[14] She argues that "realism" is a method of active reading (384) and that Thackeray's use of pronouns and his "characterized audience" (the audience inscribed within the text) moves readers inside his fictional world "to set reader, writer, and fictional world in a relationship of shifting but always mutual implication" in creating the fictional world (389, 387).[15] To go a step further, Thackeray's narrative consciousness invites a kind of reading which blends fiction and the "real". While Ferris argues that this kind of "active imagination . . . depends paradoxically on a prior submission" by the reader (385), ultimately the effect on readers is to encourage a reading that is skeptical of literal or surface statements. Instead, readers learn to make their own realistic fictions from their acts of reading his novels. The novels' narratorial collusions and hermeneutical collisions construct an authorial audience who reads skeptically and comically without becoming fatalistic or losing hope.[16] Thackeray's narrative games explore the ethical implications of the dialogic, multi-voiced modern novel.[17] Mikhail Bakhtin's study of "the dialogic imagination" is primarily a formal analysis of the techniques of dialogism. The stylistic analyst, he writes, studies "specific images of languages and styles; the organization of these images; their typology . . . the combination of images of languages and voice; their dialogic inter-relationship" (50). Wayne Booth and James Phelan look at the ethical effects such languages and narrative stances have in shaping a particular reader. Booth, in *The Company We Keep* extends rhetorical analysis into an ethical criticism that "attempts to describe the encounters of a story-teller's ethos with that of the reader or listener".[18] A hermeneutic of skepticism combines both stylistics and ethical criticism, exploring the ethics of actual intersections, collusions, and collisions among the languages of the novel and the ethical consequences of this dialogism for the characters, the narrator and his story (including the conflicting modes of romance and realism), and the narrator and the reader.

Thackeray's skeptical hermeneutic as manifested in his narrative practices and the kinds of stories created by these practices was designed to grapple with a specifically secular world. While Thackeray believed in God and the New Testament: ("I love and adore the Blessed Character so much that I don't like to speak of it, and know myself to be such a rascal that I don't dare") (*LPP* 2: 206), his letters showed that he felt God was an abstraction, not a being who meddled or manipulated human life in any way (*LPP* 1: 402-403). During one of his bouts of urethral spasms late in his life, he chastised his daughter Minny for "impugning Providence" on his account:

> A brick may have knocked a man's brains out: and a beam fallen so as to protect a scoundrel who happened to be standing under. The bricks & beams fell according to the laws wh. regulate bricks in tumbling – So with our diseases, we die because we are born; we decay because we grow. I have a right to say oh Father give me submission to bear cheerfully (if possible) & patiently my sufferings but I cant request any special change in my behalf from the ordinary processes, or see any special Divine *animus* superintending my illnesses or welnesses. (*LPP* 4: 128-29)

Consequently, he was almost dogmatically anti-dogmatic, insisting in a letter to his mother upon the multiplicity of point of view and belief: "We don't know what orthodoxy is indeed. Your orthodoxy is not your neighbour's – Your opinion is personal to you as much as your eyes or your nose or the tone of your voice. Objects make quite a different impression upon you to what they do upon any other individual" (*LPP* 1: 205).[19] John Chapman's diary records Thackeray's awareness of the unorthodoxy of his views: "I find that his [Thackeray's] religious views are perfectly free, but he does not mean to lessen his popularity by fully avowing them, he said he had debated the question with himself whether he was called upon to martyrise himself for the sake of his views and concluded in the negative" (qtd. in Shillingsburg, *Pegasus,* 31; diary in Beinecke coll.).

In his fiction, Thackeray's characters and narrators live as he experienced his own world, a "world without God" (*LPP* 2: 309). While Thackeray intended this statement to point to the moral laxity and selfishness of his characters in *Vanity Fair*, their moral condition must be understood as having resulted from the absence of a dominant system; that is, a world in which no one voice is *known* to be right.[20] "Living without God" entails living without an external and final arbiter either of action or language. Blind, or should I say "deaf", allegiance to any one cultural code alienates individuals and groups from one another. Ironically, Thackeray's characters can lose the sense of each other's humanity specifically because of the development of a human-centered world. "Living without God" means literally living without The Word. Thackeray's novels expose his narrative devices as pseudo Words, confronting readers with the falsity of their own expectations of resolution within the conventions of the novel and of moral certainty within their world.[21]

Thackeray's skepticism can be called "constructive" or "mitigated" skepticism as it develops in the seventeenth century as a *via media* between total (Pyrrhenic) skepticism and religious dogmatism.[22]   A mitigated skeptic, according to Richard Popkin, is "one who doubts that necessary and sufficient grounds or reasons can be given for our knowledge or beliefs; or one who doubts that adequate evidence can be given to show that under no conditions can our knowledge or beliefs be false or dubious".[23] So, instead of knowledge about a real nature of things, we can gain knowledge about "appearances, and hypotheses and predictions about the connections of events and the future course of experience" (Popkin 131). This "lesser" knowledge translates into Thackeray's concentration on the surface: material culture, speech, and aesthetic traditions.[24]

In the nineteenth-century, hermeneutics developed into the "higher criticism" of the Bible, used by German scholars to study the Bible to find the simple "truth".[25] The term connects 19th-century critical attitudes with 20th-century literary applications. In 1900, Henry Nash described the development of theological hermeneutics as the way to find wholeness and unity. It was both formal – rules of how meaning was established – and substantive – offering commentaries on passages. In its search for historical access to the transcendental, hermeneutics sought to reconcile religious faith with empirical science. By situating the Bible in history, criticism sought to find "the true nature of divine revelation" (Nash 14). Transcendental dogmas of divine inspiration and infallibility had isolated the Bible from human life, according to these Protestant critics, and so obscured its true revelation (Nash, chapter 3, *passim*). The pressure of "new facts" (Nash 59) from archaeology, geology, and biology spurred by the Protestant rejection of Papal infallibility encouraged biblical scholars to look for the "facts" in the Bible. Looking for the facts meant historicizing the scriptures and using the literal and ordinary as a door to the divine. Nash contextualized his history of theological hermeneutics within a history of the development of an overall "critical", or investigative, consciousness. Religious hermeneutics was itself a historical development, characteristic of a change in consciousness when the "individual" emerged and "Tradition" lost its automatic authority (Nash, chapters, 4-5).

Friedrich Schleiermacher's philosophical hermeneutics "concerned itself with the idea of the author as creator and of the work of art as an expression of his creative self".[26] Important for the development of hermeneutics as a secular tool for literary analysis was Schleiermacher's concept of "understanding" as an ongoing, constructive process not, as the Enlightenment argued, a simple decoding process (Mueller-Vollmer 9-10). Later thinkers such as Wilhelm Dilthey (1833-1911) extended this perspectival, historicized method of investigation into methods of interpretation related to pragmatism and positivism..Hans-Georg Gadamer and Richard Rorty develop the twentieth-century philosophical position into a general approach for literary studies which views a text not as "an autonomous object to be dissected but rather something to be addressed in dialogue by the reader that can readdress itself to the reader".[27] We can know and interpret if we know the codes and criteria for each symbol system. The historical, social, and psychological contexts of the text and those of the reader interact and change meaning, depending upon the specific contexts. Thus a literary hermeneutical approach is also historical and situational; Thackeray never offered a general or transcendental theory of truth but drew his readers into his world of multiple truths existing in and created by varieties of voices, often at conflict with each other.

Thackeray learned skepticism through his early reading and training as art student, reinforced by the death of his second child and then his wife's insanity. Prior to these tragedies, his early reading of the French eclectic philosopher Victor Cousin, Hume's *Essays and Treatises,* and his lifelong devotion to Montaigne's *Essays* (he owned three copies) educated him into the philosophy of mitigated skepticism.[28]   J. Russell Perkins suggests that Thackeray "was well aware, from his youthful visit to Weimar, of German biblical criticism" (80). Colby also notes Thackeray's possession of Isaac Watt's *Logic; or, the Right use of Reason* that advocated a "guarded skepticism". Watts wrote that "'The true method of delivering ourselves from . . . prejudice' . . . is 'to view a thing on all sides; to compare all the various appearances of the same thing with one another, and let each of them have its full weight in the balance of our judgment'" (qtd. in Colby 21). As a young man in Paris, Thackeray was strongly influenced by the philosophy of Victor Cousin. I do not want to repeat Robert Colby's valuable discussion of Cousin in *Thackeray's Canvass* (21-57), but I do want to stress Cousin's own emphasis on the process of inquiry "rather than on specific doctrines" (Colby 30), and his sense of this process as the multiple perspectives of many people as well as the fluid consciousness of the individual.

During the same years Thackeray was reading and listening to Cousin, his experience as a student of art reinforced his philosophical skepticism as manifested in the conventions of visual representation. His training as an artist in the studio of Henry Sass in London and in the ateliers of Baron Antoine Gros and Charles LeFond in Paris taught him that conventions of visual representation were simply that: conventions. His experience of the grandiose aspirations of Sass (caricatured as Gandish in *The Newcomes*) and the risqué romping of students and master in the Paris atelier of LaFond suggested just how suspect was the Romantic identification of art work with artist. His studio experience made him skeptical of Romantic expressionism even while his Romantic inheritance still encouraged him to find the artist in the art. Thackeray's art criticism, most of it written before the success of *Vanity Fair*, is full of his praise of painters as natural creators whose products flow from them as a bird's song from its throat. The most succinct expression of this organic view of creativity occurs in his text to Louis Marvy's *Sketches After English Landscape Painters.*[29]

The artist's mind communicates directly to the viewer by means of the painting: "We have scarcely ever seen a work by [Francis Danby] in which a . . . poetical beauty was not conveyed and in regarding which the spectator does not feel impressed by something of that solemn contemplation, and reverent worship of nature, which seems to pervade the artist's mind and pencil" ("Danby"). Thomas Creswick was a "composer singing his own airs with the most charming fresh voice" ("Creswick"). And in 1854 *The Newcomes* presents the natural artist whose temperament is his art in the character of J. J. Ridley. Ideally, then, visual art was a dramatization of the artist's consciousness, much as Romantic lyric poetry was a dramatization of the poet's consciousness. However, Thackeray's experience in the social world of arts and letters taught him early that artists could *pretend* their idealism so intensely that they could end up believing in their roles. In *The Newcomes*, for example, the artist "breaks out into *costume* naturally as a bird sings or a bulb produces a tulip" (*N* 1: 156; emphasis mine).[30] In *The Adventures of Philip*, the painter Andrea Fitch "was the most affected little creature, and, if you looked at him, would pose in attitudes of such ludicrous dirty dignity, that if you had had a dun waiting for money in the hall of your lodging-house, or your picture refused at the Academy – if you were suffering under ever so much calamity – you could not help laughing" (XX, 121-22). Side by side with the natural artist, J. J. or Creswick, then, is this oxymoronic naturally acting artist who teeters on the brink of hypocrisy. This potential collision between a true and a false artistic consciousness, both producing emotionally powerful works of art, underlies Thackeray's interest in the "ethos" of the artist – or, as it became in his exploration of the problems of self-representation, the egoism of the narrative presence. His philosophical skepticism increasingly focused on the techniques of his own art/trade of novel-writing, especially the lure of omniscient narration: that the narrator may believe in his own role-playing and forget that his story is only one version. Thackeray combined both eighteenth-century ideas of language as the "decoration" of the thought and Romantic ideas of language as "organic", inseparable from its meaning. His verbal and visual masks – conventions of linguistic and visual representation – offer not different versions of "the" truth or "the" character, but simply different versions, with no *a priori* anchoring meaning. All the viewer or reader can know are the particular conventions in use. A change in expression or code of representation will change the projected meaning. Changing the "outside" – the mode of representation or discourse – changes the "inside". Thackeray wrote Mrs. Brookfield in 1848 that a letter he had written her in French was:

> written by quite a different man to the English man who is yours respectfully. A language I am sure would change a man: so does a handwriting I am sure if I wrote to you in this hand [his slanting hand] and adopted it for a continuance my disposition and sentiments would alter and all my views of life – I tried to copy not now but the other day) a letter Miss Procter showed me from her uncle in a commercial hand and found myself after 3 pages quite an honest regular stupid commercial man . . . . How many people are you? (*LPP* 2: 439).[31]

This position that "the convention is all" is the literary theory (although Thackeray would not have called it such) that derives from mitigated skepticism. What is "there" is the representation – anything existing outside the expression of the version cannot be verified. But this private position was complicated by the exigencies of his public role as novelist and self-proclaimed lay-preacher. His skepticism cut the individual loose from traditional closed systems of values such as religion or aesthetic traditions, so the individual became responsible for his or her own judgment. But without transcendental principles, where does the individual find grounds for judgment?[32] To make matters more complex, there was no *a priori* private consciousness for Thackeray; he saw the individual always within culture, developing or displaying him- or herself by means of and within cultural codes so that no one could escape these systems, and in fact, the "individual" was shaped by the very systems Thackeray condemned for offering partial truth or outright falsity.

Like David Hume, Thackeray was concerned to make us understand that our very sense of stability and our methods of interpretation derive from our conventions of verbal and visual representation. His understanding that we are culturally constructed was the reason he concentrated on the external: appearance, performance, dress, language, manners, even where one shops or to what club one belongs. He has been criticized for a lack of Eliot-like psychological analysis, but the novels suggest that how we feel, what we believe, in other words what goes on inside, is explained by what goes on outside. Thus his "individual" is a social individual whose very imagination, as *Pendennis* shows, is constructed by cultural traditions that often contradict or undermine each other. His insistence upon sincerity and his attacks on humbug and sham derive from his understanding that since the "individual" exists as an actor; only one's intentions towards one's audience as expressed in one's public behaviors or products can determine one's integrity. The fiction produced from a hermeneutics of skepticism engages readers in an ethical process in which only their experience of the various versions can lead to ethical evaluations – there is no final comforting Dickensian narrative closure.

Paradoxically, the consequences of our interpretations are important because, as Thackeray insists, even though sociolects cannot represent any essential truth, we act upon such words as if they were true. While he was not completely Humean because he was neither atheist nor agnostic, Thackeray did not believe that foundational knowledge or certainty could be either found or presented in the conventions of language and visual representation.[33] My reading of Thackeray's distrust of traditions of representation is indebted to Sheila Delany's theory of the "skeptical fideism" of Geoffrey Chaucer, a writer much like Thackeray in his fascination with human nature and literary conventions.[34] Like Chaucer, Thackeray's skepticism was not agnosticism or cynicism but "a sense of the unreliability of traditional information . . . deliberat[ely] incorporate[d] into the style and structure" of the text"(2). R. D. McMaster's and John Loofborow's work demonstrates, as does Thackeray's expertise in parody and criticism noted by Colby and others, that Thackeray was very aware of traditional and contemporary cultural and literary codes.[35] Like Chaucer, Thackeray's works attempt "to establish for the artist a rhetorical and intellectual stance that can accommodate both traditional material and a skeptical approach to that material. From this point of view many of [the texts'] stylistic and structural features are neither inappropriate nor inconsistent. They are instead part of a coherent effort to portray a subject whose salient trait is ambiguity"(5). Thackeray, like Chaucer, had an intellectual position that could "accommodate traditional belief and the skeptical attitude toward belief that was the inevitable result of [his] logical investigations"(6).

Thackeray's situation differed from Chaucer's because of the increased demand for an "aesthetic of realism" as a norm for the novel. "Realism" in the fictional sense demanded a recognizable link between fiction and "life" – in material appearances, in the generation of and the connection between events, in narrative stance, and in character psychology. Since, the realistic novel still derived its basic plot structure from traditional romance, readers looked for a story providing ethical and moral certainty within a closed fictional world. While "realism" seems to convey a truth about the reader's world, romance suggests Truths that transcend any historical situation. Thackeray seemed to delight in emphasizing the uneasy conflation of romance and realism that characterized the Victorian novel. On the one hand he insisted that as a writer "this person writing [the narrator] strives to tell the truth. If there is not that, there is nothing" (*P* xvi). Thus, as he wrote, "a poker is a poker" (*LPP* 2: 288). But this attitude seems to collide with the actual writings that insist upon the trickiness of discourse and the artifice of art. We have elaborate games like the fable-frame in *The Newcomes* that disarms a critic looking for "reality" even as Pen the narrator (not Thackeray) insists he is telling the truth as he has observed and documented it from Clive's own letters and reports. Such an authenticating device seems to deny artistry as do narrative claims of partial knowledge or ignorance or lack of control over character. These conventions of mimetic narration coexist uneasily with narrative techniques such as talking overtly about the fiction as fiction or shifting between stylistic or generic modes to emphasize the artist's manipulation. The narrator turns from narrative prose to an ironic drama, for example, in chapter 9 of the second volume of *The Newcomes*, while the chapter's introduction claims archaeological accuracy for his "scene". An earlier instance, chapter 6 in *Vanity Fair*, demonstrates that changes in the expression changes the "facts" because the different modes of the silver fork and Newgate fiction must tell us different stories.

The playful claims for truth within overtly artificial scenarios centers our reading on the narratorial level. Phelan defines "voice" as a "social phenomenon", a collection of conventions; even the sense readers have of a personal connection to the writer is a matter of convention (*Narrative as Rhetoric* 44-46). Thackeray's intimate, informal, colloquial, yet relentlessly social voice claims that you cannot separate facts from the language which describes them, or separate the story from the consciousness which selects something as a fact. To divorce truth or the real from subjectivity – a "social" subjectivity – is impossible. As Phelan says, "All 'facts' exist within some framework to describe them".[36] To explain "what really happened" is to offer an interpretation of whatever happened. Thackeray's framework is always his awareness of the narratorial consciousness, both the power of that consciousness to create and the temptation to believe in the creation as something apart from the consciousness. His fiction is anti-Romantic even as he uses romance. He rejects the Romantic epiphany of Coleridge's "Eolian Harp" or Wordsworth's *Prelude* not the least because of the self-revelation required by epiphanic art and the consequent temptation of Romantic egotism. Thackeray's novels become increasingly suspicious of this narrative egoism, the narrative games implicitly denying that narration can present any experience that is separate from the narrating self.

His actual hermeneutical process recalls the process of Humean skeptical reasoning.[37] Hume states we start with two initial judgments, one derived from the nature of the object which is corrected by one derived from the nature of the understanding (in Thackeray's world, the particular sociolect or "language" conventions constructing a particular point of view). This correction automatically leads to "a new doubt deriv'd from the possibility of error we make in the estimation of the truth and fidelity of our faculties" (Hume, *Treatise*, IV, 1: 182). Such questioning continues *ad infinitum* until all certainty is gone.

> When I reflect on the natural fallibility of my judgment, I have less confidence in my opinions, than when I only consider the objects concerning which I reason; and when I proceed still farther, to turn the scrutiny against every successive estimation I make of my faculties, all the rules of logic require a continual diminution, and a last a total extinction of belief and evidence. (Hume, *Treatise* IV, 1: 183).

This could be Pendennis speaking in *The Adventures of Philip*, but it is Hume. And like Pendennis, Hume concludes that, although this disappearance of "truth" may be logically true, in daily living, "neither I, nor any other person was ever sincerely and constantly of that opinion" (1: 183). That is, we act as if we lived by stable truths and had a stable identity.

> If the relations involved in the fact of cognition are only those discoverable by observation of any particular portion of known experience, then such relations are quite *external and contingent* [ital. mine] . . . . Let us fix our attention out of ourselves as much as possible; let us chase our imagination to the heavens or to the utmost limits of the universe; we can never really advance a step beyond

> ourselves, nor can conceive any kind of existence, but those perceptions which have appeared in that narrow compass. This is the universe of the imagination, nor have we any idea but what is there produced. (*Treatise*, I, 2, 6: 67-68).

Consequently others' consciousnesses are unknowable – not just because we live in a world of our own perceptions but that any attempt to express our consciousness or describe someone else's must be in a conventional medium such as a language or image that is itself open to multiple interpretations. All we can know is an ambiguous external. Unsurprisingly, then, Thackeray often avoids interiority by his notorious "veil-dropping" on instances of emotion not susceptible to re-presentation and by avoiding questions of essence, or transcendental Truth.[38] Or, if he does represent a private scene, the narrator will often question his own accuracy. The narrator who asks, "Was Becky really guilty?" is not avoiding his story but showing us that such ambiguity is itself part of the "truth".[39] Even a stable voice such as the "armchair" narrator is countered or qualified by the authorial devices of editors and illustrations. Traditional narrative authenticating devices such as letters, rumors, and eye-witness reports from other characters offer direction beyond the narrator's control although within his awareness.[40] And from *The Newcomes* on, the actual narrative voice of Pendennis becomes increasingly self-contradictory and self-conscious, parodically undermining Pen's own narrative certainty. This unfixed method constantly questions the authority of the narrative "I" while these shifts engage readers in active questioning of their "placement" in the text.

Vanity Fair subsumes the narrative voices and shifts in persona under one critical master-voice, while highlighting the dangers of egoism, whether it be as author of a novel or of a life. Early in the novel, the Manager offers us a metaphor for how authors and actors write and act and how readers and theatre audiences read and respond. This metaphor shows us why we should be skeptical about reading even while we enjoy its effects. The middle novels, *Pendennis, The Newcomes,* and *Henry Esmond*, internalize the voices within one "I" and increasingly draw attention to the dependence of the story upon the narrating consciousness. *Pendennis*, usually acclaimed as Thackeray's most stable narration, nonetheless destabilizes reading by turning optical devices into narrative strategies. The "near/far" view and the "prism-vision" moves us in, out, and around in space and time. We follow Pen as he creates his imagination from literature and becomes the star of his own theatre, rapt in his own performance. His growth is from self-absorbed actor in *Pendennis* into Thackerayean narrator in *The Newcomes*. Pen flies his Pegasus in *The Newcomes,* mixing theatre, fable, realism to confuse our own sense of stable reading. By the time we get to *Philip*, the narrator has totally absorbed his story into his consciousness and the novel is cognition in action: an exploration into how outside facts become "stories" by means of the interpreter's available conventions.   This   protean narrator, immersed in traditions of representation – such as Spenserian romance, classical art, fables, fairy tales, religious discourse – epitomizes the "social individual" in three ways. The implied author dramatizes a world of colliding discourses and points of view in his characters and his story; the narrator is himself fragmented and extremely self-conscious about his narration; and, consequently, readers are forced to negotiate among the teller and his tale and their own interpretive practices.

Thackeray's narrative hermeneutic manifests itself in the two techniques of collision and collusion. His sociolects divide into two large groups, both fixed. That is, the languages all derive from stable frames of reference that their users can use to completely explain themselves and their world. In turn, these frames of reference derive from differing underlying authorities either implied or claimed by the languages. These two foundational authorities determine the range of the speakers' possible intentions. The first group conveys traditional affective values and rests on the transcendental Authority of Christian texts. Users of these languages, such as Helen and Laura Pendennis, organize everything and everyone according to a heiratic, seemingly non-manipulative, linguistic system.

The second group of languages constitutes the modern challenge to this fixed linguistic system. These languages are secular, often mercantile and openly manipulative, and always overtly (to the reader) conventional. They are the language of commerce, of the schoolmaster, of the rake, of the buffoon, of the sentimental writer, of the trained painter, of the clubman, of "du monde". "Truth" as a fixed, eternal, discernible value is replaced by "psychological effectiveness in social relations" because one's role is to achieve an end and people are a means to that end.[41] Single-sociolect users such as Barnes Newcome, Lady Kew, Dr. Firmin, or Blanche Amory are just as shaped by their language and unable or unwilling to move outside its particular system as are Laura and Helen.

Gradually, readers become aware that the choice of a sociolect is a necessary paradox. Each sociolect structures experience, allowing us to act with a purpose and to ascertain meaning. Such stability, however, can be shared only by those who belong to the proper interpretive community. Language thus simultaneously alienates and unifies us. The reader, forced to juggle the fixed experiences of the characters, acknowledges that their languages structure a reality for them. What one says creates a "meaning" in that it presents a self (not always intended by the speaker) that requires a responding role and this interaction is experientially real. Juxtaposition with each other, with the dramatic situation, with narrative commentary, and with the illustrations ironizes and so devalues all sociolects, but no one sociolect is shown to be completely false because many characters sustain their roles and act successfully (according to the ethos of each language). That is, J.J. Ridley, Mrs. Mackenzie, Barnes Newcome, Dr. Firmin, Rachel Esmond, Colonel Newcome, and Laura Pendennis use sociolects successfully. Their perspectives, as well as the literary sociolects used by the narrator, suggest that language projects a "self" onto the world and shapes reality to the requirements of that language.

Thackeray's criticisms of this fixed perspective, acted out in the stories and narrative games, are criticisms of what Rorty has called "mirror imagery", that what we see or say can somehow accurately reflect an essential world (12-13 and *passim*). In fact, Thackeray's many puns on "mirror", both in his illustrations and his prose, suggest the solipsism hiding within most discourse. The mirror only reflects our face, our perception of the world. The paradox, of course, is that conventions and traditional forms of representation do create communities of discourse that allow common values and interpretations.

Thackeray creates interpretive collisions by juxtaposing sociolects within characters' dialogue or moving from character dialogue to narrator-character discourse. A simple early example of such a collision is Michael Angelo Titmarsh's critique of a sentimental painting by Richard Redgrave, *Marriage Morning* (R.A. 1844).[42] While Redgrave's basic subject is a bride "taking leave of her mama after the ceremony", Titmarsh concentrates on the peripheral figures of the bride's father and sister. "The bride's father, a venerable, bald-headed gentleman . . . is trying to console poor Anna-Maria, the unmarried sister, who is losing the companion of her youth" (XXV, 426). The diction here is clearly that of sentimental cliché – a "venerable" father, the sister "losing the companion of her youth". This trite voice of the *Annuals* speaks directly to the over-sweet picture in an over-sweet voice: "Never mind, Anna Maria, my dear, your turn will come too; there is a young gentleman making a speech in the parlour to the health of the new-married pair, who, I lay a wager, will be struck by your fine eyes, and be for serving you as your sister has been treated" (XXV, 426). The language of sentimental romance ("young gentleman", "my dear", "fine eyes") collides with the code of the rake ("lay a wager", "serving you"). The sexual objectification of the rake's code subverts the idealism of the romance code, and the consequence is a fairly cynical exposure of the triteness of both languages. The romance-rake languages ask the reader to reconcile opposed attitudes and thus recreate the painting as a pastiche of clichés. By implication, the sociolects inhibit a positive response: what viewers will identify themselves with the voices Titmarsh offers?

When Thackeray expands this practice as the basis of characterization, the coherency of the fictional world begins to deconstruct. All these languages can be true if people (characters) act on them as true. Each sociolect defines, classifies, and provides a system of value, thus allotting roles and behaviors. But the premises of each group of languages are irreconcilable. Laura Pendennis could not explain Barnes Newcome's motivations and actions. Mrs. Twysden could not explain the Little Sister. All the sociolects are inadequate expressions of the moral variety of human life. Helen Pendennis or Barnes Newcome offers us views of the world that can explain their worlds – but cannot be reconciled to each other. This collision of sociolects is also manifested in the narration. His reflexive narration and protean narrative personae as well as his manipulation of traditional "authenticating" fictional devices constantly shift the narrator's proximity to the stories and involve us in a fascinating investigation into the nature of narrative ego.[43] These two collisions center on educating us into the "language game" as Rorty calls it (34).

The modal collision between romance and realism, particularly in the move from moral clarity and poetic justice to moral ambiguity, incorporate the stylistic collisions. All his novels could be romances disfigured by insistence on "realistic" characters, motivations, and plot structure. Or, all his novels could be "realistic", tainted by flights of sentimental fancy and motifs from traditional romance. In particular, Thackeray's self-conscious closures discomfort readers by forcing a parody of romance closure onto increasingly prosaic characters, making readers aware of their own fixed perspectives and cultural conditioning. These collisions thrust us out of the story so we cannot read as a narrative audience accepting the story and characters as "real". But we do read as the implied author wants us to, aware of the thematic and synthetic functions of the characters and of the artificial nature of story itself. We become multileveled readers in various ways: When we read characters whose perspective collides with their behavior or with the narrator's commentary, we read on the narrator's level, hearing the false or incomplete perspectives of the characters in, for example, Becky's speech about being a good woman "if only" she had ƒ5000, or Pen's "way of the world" speech, both of which are countered by the narrator. Or, the narrator may simply juxtapose alternate values as he does in chapters 22 and 23 (vol. 2) of *Pendennis* when complementary illustrations and dramatic scenes force us to compare the sniveling, deceitful baronet Altamont to the honest retainer Chevalier Strong. Michael Lund has developed Wolfgang Iser's theory of "revising reading", particularly Iser's analysis of *Vanity Fair*, in relation to all of Thackeray's major work.[44] The basic work of memory and anticipation (Lund 60) is in Thackeray particularly geared toward collision and contradiction, often only implied. Juxtaposition is a key structural element in Thackeray's mature style and exists from the beginning in the sometimes uneasy (deliberately so) relation between Thackeray's illustrations and his verbal text as well in larger narrative choices such as the Protean narrator in *Vanity Fair*, the editorial notes and narrative contradiction in *Henry Esmond*, the fable-frame in *The Newcomes*, the switch from editor to autobiographer in *The Virginians*, and the collision between pantomime and parable in *Philip*.

In contrast with authorial, synthetic reading, reading as the narratorial audience (colluding with the narrator) we accept the voice as real and the story as his vehicle and creation. The intimate I-you relation and the narrator's self-aware posturing draw us into his consciousness. His pronominalization can incorporate us into the narrative without us really knowing it. Blurring the line between author – text – reader, the "right line I" becomes "you" but "you" is never quite distinct enough to become a separate character. Even Thackeray's use of the "characterized audience", Mr. Jones in chapter 1 of *Vanity Fair*, for instance, is a unifying device. Mr. Jones is so obviously "not us" that we read with the narrator to make fun of him. If one way of defining realism is to define it as experiencing closeness between the narrative and authorial audiences, then "realism" in

Thackeray is our identification as his narratorial audience.

The Tale

As the multiple languages constituting narrative consciousness undermine any stable narrative ego, so does the ethics of self-representation and interpretation become a central theme through the focus on "choice" in the stories. The subtext of *Pendennis*, his choice between virtue and vice, is the key to all of Thackeray's novels. The choices of "virtue" and "vice" always operate within a given system of values which finds expression within a specific sociolect. Is a choice right if it is consistent with its sociolect? For example, in *Philip*, Pen's sarcastic explanation of Agnes Twysden's motives for jilting Philip and marrying Woolcomb does, despite the sarcasm, show us that her choice is well-grounded in her specific frame of reference that can be expressed by a consistent language. It would have been wrong for Agnes to marry Philip who is carefully put outside of "du monde" by the narrator and linked to Laura's transcendental system of religious values. "Choice" as acting out the demands of one's sociolect crystallizes the tension between the two groups of languages.

Thackeray offers a third language that tries to overcome this separation: the language of the aesthetic seems to integrate the transcendental into the cultural. The literary languages constituting the narrator's colliding values find their echoes in the women whom the narrator characterizes as embodying various aesthetic traditions. The aesthetic, subjective, and commercial unite in a precarious alliance between ideal and real in Thackeray's female characters as aesthetic love objects who must sell themselves in the marriage market. Thackeray's version of the "marriage market" derives from the art market that he knew in great detail. As his art criticism strives to make its readers into reverent buyers – that is, to purchase a work of art on the basis of aesthetic qualities that help you cultivate your senses of charity, love, and pity instead of buying art as an investment or sign of your aesthetic expertise – so Thackeray's men must marry women whose being encourages them to control their own narcissistic egoism. But paintings and women are commodities. Artists and writers construct art works; customs and mothers construct women. His conflation of women and commodity is a version of his identification of artist with artwork. But this identification demands an impossible unconsciousness from women in order to be gauged as "true" or "good" women. As a painting must be unaware of its status as a commodity so should a woman be unaware (or at least reject, as does Ethel Newcome) her status as commodity. One should not self-consciously sell oneself. If either artist or woman is a conscious self-promoter, they become prostituting predators, selling themselves to gain their own ends.

This aesthetic life choice is structured within a self-consciously flawed traditional romance.[45] The basic story, adapting the tradition of romance, follows a pattern of "descent", "struggle", and "ascent", deriving from Christian teleology and echoing Christianity's closed, stable, ethical universe.[46] Northrup Frye links the final pastoral vision of the Romance to the acquisition of a stable identity in an Edenic setting: "The closer romance comes to the world of original identity, the more clearly something of the symbolism of the garden of Eden reappears, with the social setting reduced to the love of individual men and women within an order of nature which has been reconciled to humanity" (*Secular Scripture* 149). Such is the romance fulfillment of *Nicholas Nickleby*, *Middlemarch, Our Mutual Friend*, and countless other Victorian novels, including Thackeray's world in which Clive, Ethel, Pen, and Laura can live next door to each other in the country, occasionally visited by Philip and Charlotte Firmin (and J.J.). But in Thackeray's version, the protagonists attain their identity through a self-conscious recognition that their "self" is cultural not natural. Thackeray rejected the romantic, organic, "expressive" self and its teleological unfolding by means of natural language and natural revelation in favor of the social individual who can use his roles to create community without falling into self-destructive narcissism or predatory solipsism. Each of his novels has image patterns and at least one subtext that emphasize the cultural influences directing this "growth". That is, the "realistic" bildungsroman is simultaneously written as a romance: Pendennis is Prince Arthur and the Redcrosse Knight of the *Fairie Queene*; Henry Esmond's "secret history" tells us of the manipulations of the Prince in disguise to conquer his kingdom; *The Newcomes* offers us a disquieting view of Fable-land; George Warrington is St. George whose brother, Prince Hal, never grows up; and *Philip* conflates pantomime with the parable of the Good Samaritan. These subtexts mock the readers' desire for an ideal pattern while they expose the protagonists' illusions.

Thackeray's basic story recounts the struggle of a naive protagonist like Pen or Clive to develop and control his cultural codes while being attracted to and manipulated by avaricious role-players like Becky and Blanche,

Barnes Newcome and Dr. Firmin. Since desire drives social role-playing, the player can become a solipsistic predator because he or she can reduce others to objects to be used. Such predators in Thackeray's fictional world define the relationship between themselves and others to their own advantage. One thinks, for example, of the pitiful letters from the swindler Dr. Firmin to Philip that victimize Philip by forcing him to play the role of loving son.

One alternative to predatory social relations is the Victorian idyll in the country: to withdraw from action and to emphasize the emotional empathy between individuals in a non-commercial world where the individual can be released from acting because neither action nor acquisition is required. The imagination can create empathy while the distance created by seclusion from the "world" protects the imagining self. However, the artist really cannot maintain such a balance because he has to sell his work and thus constantly imagine himself in relation to a buyer and a marketplace. Thackeray embodied the affective community in women such as Laura Pendennis whose private existence enables the protagonists to make ethical judgments that strengthen or uphold sympathy within the community. In general, the fictional Victorian affective community was made possible not by the poetic imagination but by the emotional direction of women: Laura and Rachel in Thackeray, Agnes for Dickens, and Dorothea for George Eliot (not to mention Mary Barton, Jane Eyre, Esther Summerson, Margaret Hale, and a host of others). But it is primarily in Thackeray's novels that we find this Victorian idyll undermined by its own dramatization.

Thackeray's version of the quest for this community follows a tradition of "skeptical" romance as described by Robert Unger:

> The execution of the worthy task for the sake of the true love is replaced by the willing exposure to an ordeal that consists precisely in uncertainty about whether there do [sic] exist a love beyond narcissism and a work beyond illusion that might take the individual out of himself and turn his self-division into empowerment.[47]

Thackeray's skepticism about the purity of desire for the ideal stems from, as Hillis Miller has noted, his sensitivity to "mediated" desire, worked out in *The Book of Snobs* that dramatizes in detail:

> Thackeray's extreme sensitivity to . . . the psychological
> mechanism whereby desire is never direct but always routed
> through the desire of someone else whose authority authenticates
> my desire. If he or she finds something desirable it must be worth
> having, but without the help of another I cannot tell what I should
> want to have or to do. (82)[48]

Since Thackeray's characters are products of their culture, their desires cannot be "autonomous" in the sense of being original to themselves. His protagonists want what the world tells them to want; unfortunately for them, they live in many worlds that offer them many choices. In Thackeray's skeptical romance, therefore, to pursue desire is to choose a role. The single greatest mediator for both characters and careless readers in Thackeray's fictional world is Romance itself, which schools men and women to see the world as a mirror of their desire but to disguise their solipsistic predation in the literary language of sentiment and idealism.

Thackeray's novels dramatize his skepticism about the possibility of a romantic sense of a "true" self most powerfully in their curious identification of successful maturation with self-effacement. Traditionally, the romance hero's quest is a metaphoric fall from an idyllic world of innocent vision to a demonic world of "a growing confusion of identity and restrictions on action" (Frye, *Secular Scripture* 129). Struggling to free himself from this confusion, he attains a state higher than his original innocence. However, Thackeray's version of the ascent is singularly unsatisfactory. The quest process is implicitly ironic because it is placed in terms of a descending movement of life from birth to death. Colonel Newcome becomes "as a little child" not a sage. Any linear development is implicitly denied by the circular movement of the protagonist back to the site of his youth, either literally as in Pen's and Harry Warrington's return to their mothers' homes, or symbolically as when Henry Esmond marries his foster-mother and builds a replica of Castlewood. Moreover, most of the protagonists are aware of the failure of this circular movement. His protagonists dwindle into husbands and fathers, most of them realizing the loss of their effective power even while they value their emotional community. Dobbin recognizes that his prize is not worth the struggle; Pen emerges as an explicitly unheroic narrator; Clive and Ethel only achieve their idyll in fable-land; Henry Esmond lives with a mysterious "bankruptcy of heart"; and Harry and Philip never do reach a level of self-awareness higher than they evince in their beginnings. It is characteristic of the latters' mediocrity that their involvement with the siren is the most obviously parodic to narrator and reader.

Pen exemplifies Thackerayean maturity in his narration in *Philip*, in which he as "master linguist" regulates his desires, recognizes his illusions, and chooses his own roles. Pen's realization at the end of *Pendennis* that Blanche's role need not dictate his, signals his ability to move among different sociolects. Henry Esmond experiences a more explicit epiphany when the beautiful Beatrix "desecrates" (382) his love by seducing the Pretender. Her willingness to use her beauty to buy power "reveals" the serpent beneath her beautiful surface:

> The roses had shuddered out of her cheeks; her eyes were glaring; she looked quite old. She came up to Esmond and hissed out a word or two: – "If I did not love you before, Cousin," says she, "think how I love you now." If words could stab, no doubt she would have killed Esmond; she looked at him as if she could. (*HE* 386)

This is Beatrix's "Second Appearance as Clytemnestra"; she shows her true sisterhood to Becky in her poison hiss and killing glance. And Henry's words suggest that he has seen his own delusion (whether we believe him is a matter for future discussion). Yet this ability to understand and use cultural codes entails a loss of idealism. Aesthetic compromises echo the life compromises made by Pen, Clive, and Henry, who produce "ordinary" novels, paintings, plays, and memoirs. These art works, which Thackeray's art criticism terms "mediocre", affirmed his skepticism of the Romantic artistic ego. Thackeray's marginalized narrators and editors make clear that telling the story is only possible to those who refuse to succumb to one version, but who nonetheless must experience the temptation of an ideal, transcendent vision.

The classic version of such enthrallment is, of course, the myth of Narcissus who traps himself in an infantile state of self-absorption and dies when he realizes his infatuation with his own surface.[49] Thackeray's masculine romance objectifies the Narcissistic gaze by projecting versions of the Self onto other characters, particularly women. Derek Brewer calls such self-projections "splits", "whereby one person may be 'split' into several" (21).[50] Romance depends upon such splits because its fundamental purpose is to trace the struggle of one protagonist who himself is a projection of an extratextual idea of a "self" (Brewer 23). To borrow Brewer's phrasing, the basic quest is to marry the princess and set up a home in her castle, free from parental influence. But in Thackeray's novels, the problem is to recognize the princess. Those who look and act like Princesses turn out to be reflections of the protagonists' immature desires that would, if attained, trap them in a state of child-like self-aggrandizement. While the false princesses lure the protagonists to self-destruction of one variety or another, the true princesses offer access to a language connecting the protagonist to a stable, transcendent order. Pen, Clive, and Henry live in worlds of conflicting codes without becoming Pyrrhenic skeptics because Laura and Rachel (and to lesser extents Ethel and Charlotte) act as linguistic moral-anchors. Although this development implies a mature, socially integrated identity, Thackeray's skeptical romance does not free the individual but ties him more fully to the maternal home. The mother is displaced, but not far enough for true maturity. With child-wives like Rosey and Charlotte come fairy-tale stepmothers like Mrs. Mackenzie and Mrs. Baynes. And even the "successful" marriages are severely marred by the suggestion of incest: Laura as Pen's "sister", and Rachel as Henry's "mother".

In quintessential Thackerayean style, the degree of mastery over the social codes the protagonist will have depends upon how far his childhood develops his aesthetic and emotional sensitivities– the very susceptibilities that tempt him toward narcissism. Thus true to romance conventions, the quest is worthwhile because it is dangerous, and this danger is self-generated. *Pendennis* establishes the archetypal youth of the Thackerayean protagonist. We first see Pendennis in an illustration and in the verbal text with his mother *within* a landscape painting, gazing outward from us and praying.

> At sunset, from the lawn of Fairoaks, there was a pretty sight: it and the opposite park of Clavering were in the habit of putting on a rich golden tinge which became them both wonderfully. The upper windows of the great house flamed so as to make your eyes wink; the little river ran off noisily westward, and was lost in a sombre wood, behind which the towers of the old abbey church of Clavering . . . rose up on purple splendor. Little Arthur's figure and his mother's, cast long blue shadows over the grass; and he would repeat in a low voice (for a scene of great natural beauty always

moved the boy, who inherited this sensibility from his mother) certain lines beginning, "These are they glorious works, Parent of Good; Almighty! thine this universal frame," greatly to Mrs. Pendennis's delight. Such walks and conversations generally ended in a profusion of filial and maternal embraces . . . . (2: 12)

"Arthur" grows up in the female bower, called by Spenser "the sacred noursery / Of vertue . . . [that] hidden ly / From view of men, and wicked worlds disdaine" (*FQ* VI.i.3). In this Eden, Pen learns from his mother how to interpret what he sees as a sign of what is not seen, the Invisible Love that knits a community together. Significantly, the illustration reinforces the outward direction of Pen's vision. Unlike George Osborne whom we see gazing complacently into a mirror (*VF* 104), Pen does not start out entrapped by his own reflection (Fig. 1.1). Henry Esmond also gazes outward at what he thinks, in his childish way, is also a manifestation of the Divine. He looks at Rachel "in a sort of delight and wonder, for she had come upon him as a *Dea Certe*, and appeared the most charming object he had ever looked on. Her golden hair was shining in the gold of the sun; her complexion was of a dazzling bloom; her lips smiling and her eyes beaming with a kindness which made Harry Esmond's heart to beat with surprize" (*HE* 6).

While Esmond also has a profound aesthetic sensibility and interprets Rachel as Love – that is, connects her surface beauty to her inner glow – the seeds of self-delusion are already present in his vision. "Dea certe" alludes to *Aeneid* I, where Venus first appears to her son Aeneas. Rachel doubling as Venus, Aeneas' mother, and also the goddess of love anticipates the entire novel, for Rachel is both mother and lover to Henry. Already the sexual elements of Henry's worship exist – as they have to because he is making a divinity out of a woman. He sees the "halo" the sun casts around her head, and Beatrix rightly laughs at him for praying to Mamma (*HE* 7). These two scenes present us with two kinds of sublime prospects that have different effects on the viewers. Pen sees in the landscape something greater than himself that is not a self-projection. His gaze is subjective but linked to a transcendental code of a spiritual community, taught by his mother who directs his language. Her literal language of Truth will conflict with the idealizing language of Romance Pen absorbs in his reading, but her interpretation of God for Pen offers an authoritative moral reference by means of a transcendental language: the sacred Word. Henry applies the same sort of interpretive gaze to a woman and reifies her as an idol: "To the very last hour of his life Esmond remembered the lady as she then spoke and looked, the rings on her fair hands, the very scent of her robe, the beam of her eyes lighting up with surprize and kindness, her lips blooming in a smile, the sun making a golden halo round her hair" (*HE* 7). Henry the narrator even calls her a "charming object". Henry also confuses religious and chivalric (romance) worship. She is angel and lady; he is priest and knight errant. He projects himself as a Christian knight, having a monastic sense of purity and martial training and a desire for life to be his self-sacrifice. His knowledge of Christianity is that of religion as romance, martyrs who perform miraculous deeds and resist death (*HE* 48-49). When Henry leaves Castlewood to go to University, he leaves as Rachel's knight errant.

> "And my knight longs for a dragon this instant that he may fight," said my lady laughing – which speech made Harry Esmond start and turn red: for indeed the very thought was in his mind that he should like that some chance should immediately happen whereby he might show his devotion – And it pleased him to think that his lady had called him "her knight", and often and often he recalled this to his mind, and prayed that he might be her true knight too. (*HE* 83)

Either as idol or Lady, Rachel is a reflecting surface, a parody of the "transparent" lady of romance who mirrors the potential moral perfection of the hero.

Both their stories start at sunset, Pen's with his mother, as has been quoted, and Henry's with his pseudo-mother, as he joins the Castlewood Esmonds to watch the sun set:

> They passed thence through the music gallery long since dismantled, and Queen Elizabeth's rooms in the clock tower, and out into the terrace, where was a fine prospect of sunset and great darkling woods with a cloud of rooks returning; and the plain and river with Castlewood Village beyond, and purple hills beautiful to look at. . . . (*HE* 8)

Thackeray's decision to introduce his two heroes in sunset suggests their capacity to yearn after an ideal and identifies that ideal with the maternal presence. That they gaze at the *sun*, an image of male power (in Pen's case it is God), defines these protagonists as capable of desiring masculine maturity. They are opened to this "prospect", however, by the guidance of a mother. Patricia Parker sees the "suspended" realm of twilight, just after sunset, as the "archetypal space of romance".[51] Why? Because, as the scene in *Pendennis* reveals, this blurred light, neither light nor dark, melts figures and objects into a unity, suggestive of the empathy between mother and child. Pen speaks the language Helen has taught him (the Lord's Prayer) as they stand together in the sunset. But this unity is already threatened by the protagonists' entry into masculine language. Pen has already started his conditioning in literary romance; Henry is already being educated by Father Holt.

The differences in the romance settings denote the differences in these two characters' quests. "Fairoaks" is a garden bower, directed by a pure "Alma" figure, Helen Pendennis. The Eden opposes "Clavering", taken from the Scottish dialect "to claver" which means to talk foolishly. Thus the meaningful Christian language of Helen (and then Laura) counters the foolish society chatter of Blanche. Pen's quest is circular; he leaves Fairoaks only to return with his sister/wife. Henry lives in a "Camelot", a suitable abode for the knight errant he wants to be for Rachel. The name "Castlewood" suggests the psycho-sexual tension at the heart of *Henry Esmond*. "In so far as the body obeys, protects, and nourishes the soul, it is a castle. In so far as its weakness clogs, annoys, and imperils the soul it is a forest".[52] "Castlewood" captures the conflict between desire and repression, which is Henry's battle. He is the hero in disguise, serving Isabella (the Crone) as page (*HE* 25) and Rachel as tutor. His illegitimacy symbolizes his lack of identity. The missing mother who should educate him in submission and temperance is replaced by a false mother who is really his wife – so that he never grows into a mature desire for a substitute for the mother. Henry's search is less for substitutes for the Mother than for the original unity with the maternal presence. Adding to the confusion of his sexual identify is that he is an orphan whose mother became a nun, and he is being trained by Father Holt, who as a priest acts as an asexual father. Holt is the owner of the phallus, the mark of difference, symbolized in his teaching Henry that most patriarchal of languages, Latin, but his phallus is, as signified by his office as priest, not potent. Holt's secrecy, his plotting, and his disguises suggest feminine intrigue while his sword-play and derring-do are masculine. Holt is neither father nor mother and yet

Fig. 1.1. Pictorial Initial, Chapter 13, *Vanity Fair*
Photograph courtesy of Elizabeth Huth Coates Library, Trinity
University

both Father and Mother, so the prohibition against Oedipal desire, which is introduced by the father, is not clearly marked.

Clive's sexual tensions are aestheticized as a conflict between two mistresses: Ethel and Art. His training as a painter makes his natural sensibility inherited from his father, exceptionally powerful, and he sees with a Keatsian sensual perception: "The view of a fine landscape, a fine picture, a handsome woman, would make this harmless young sensualist tipsy with pleasure. He seemed to derive an actual hilarity and intoxication as his eye drank in these sights" (*N* 1: 254). Clive's, Pen's, and Henry's youths set up the double danger of the romance quest. Their sensitivity to sign systems encourages them to read the world as symbolic and to project their own interpretations and desires onto others. Pen, Henry, and Clive are aesthetically inclined because they are directed early toward sympathetic receptivity by a maternal presence from whose transcendental language they are never absolutely separated: Helen Pendennis, Rachel Castlewood, and Colonel Newcome, respectively. This maternal presence is Thackeray's narrative solution to the problem of Romantic "natural" genius. Wordsworth's poet in *The Prelude* is first trained by his natural affinity with his mother who consequently incorporates the poet into the world by inculcating within the infant a feeling of "oceanic oneness" to use Freud's phrase:

> . . . blest the Babe,
> Nursed in his Mother's arms, who sinks to sleep
> Rocked on his Mother's breast; who, when his soul
> Claims manifest kindred with a human soul,
> Drinks in the feelings of his mother's eye!
> . . . .
> For feeling has to him imparted power
> That through the growing faculties of sense
> Doth, like an Agent of the one great Mind,
> Create, creator and receiver both.
> . . . .Such verily, is the first
> Poetic Spirit of our human life. . . .
> (*The Prelude*, 2: 234-38, 256-62)

The linguistic basis of Thackeray's filial-maternal bond emphasizes the constructed nature (oxymoron intended) of the feelings that will enable Pen, Clive, and Henry to produce any kind of valid art at all — validity defined as their ability to curb their own desire to manipulate their audiences for selfish purposes. But Thackeray's mothers are all flawed by their own egoism and by the intolerance produced by their sacred sociolects. As necessary as this influence is for the artist, it is just as necessary to grow beyond its limits into the multiple-voiced world of cultural codes. Correspondingly, in Thackeray's pattern, his "sirens", or the embodiments of these protagonists' narcissistic desires, manifest themselves as pure cultural constructions whose attraction is the illusion that their cultural roles are actually their natural being.

On the other hand, Rawdon Crawley, George Osborne, Harry War-rington, and Philip Firmin have little tendency to see aesthetically or idealize because they are strongly marked by faulty fathers and absent mothers. They have either been schooled in an exclusively masculine, public world (Rawdon and George) whose emphasis on class and money completely externalizes the self, or they do not have the capacity for imagination, a deficit which again can be blamed on the absence of someone to teach them the language of imagination and emotion (Philip, Harry). Philip's only mothers are his ineffective, biological mother and a displaced mother figure whose lack of maternal authority is indicated by her nickname "Little Sister". Significantly, Caroline Brandon (the Little Sister) is flawed both sexually and socially. She is a recovered "fallen woman" of the lower class, who cannot inspire Philip with any intense desire for the ideal. Without the benefit of the authoritative maternal vision, Rawdon, George, Harry, and Philip are easily susceptible to the alluring but palpably predatory visions of Becky, Lady Maria, and Agnes Twysden.

These "sirens" (Becky, Emily, Blanche, Ethel, Beatrix, Maria, Agnes) mirror the protagonist's self-aggrandizement by acting out his sexual desire and social ambition, but they are fatal attractions. The "angel-mother" (Helen, Laura, Rachel) mirrors the private path of virtuous domesticity, an "aesthetic of the mediocre". And the "child-woman" (Amelia, Rosey, Charlotte) mirrors the immature, self-absorbed spoiled boy at the heart of the protagonist. All these women are texts constructed by the narrator and open to the protagonists and our interpretations. But it is not so simple. Although the choice "should" be the angel-mother, the protagonist never clearly triumphs in this choice. He loses sometimes more than he gains, especially Pen and Henry Esmond. Moreover, Thackeray's most vibrant sirens, Beatrix and Ethel, defy their imprisonment within a male-defined tradition, and their defiance, discernible within the narrators' reactions, further undercut the ethical reliability of their creators, Pen, Henry, and Clive. So while the conventions of romance demand that the protagonists make a choice, realism determines that their choice is never satisfactory when it is made.

The tension between Thackeray's strong narrative presence that insists upon the power of the "I" and the narrator's insistence that this "I" is an unstable construction is the final challenge to narrative and ethical stability within his novels. The claim for "sincerity" in mimetic fiction rests on readers identifying the narrative voice with an essential self outside the text. The telling must be unforced, "natural", and spontaneous (a problem never completely solved by the high Romantics). But given Thackeray's social individual, such essentialism is impossible, for an artist does not re- present himself in his narratorial characterization; he creates a speaking- self fitted to its rhetorical task. Post-Romantic narration is an inescapably public performance of private self-revelation. Thackeray, in a diatribe about Sterne in *The English Humourists*, says he was aware that the artist in his generation must sell himself and that good art was a sincere selling of a genuine self. But if all cultural codes can create meanings, then what is sincerity and where is the genuine self? He distrusts Sternism and so uses Pendennis (and all his other pseudonyms) as a mask to free himself from his discourse, aware that the successful artist performs a role that only seems to be no role. One can, as Edgar Harden has written, know one's roles and fulfill them with "genuine feelings of sympathy and love, and thereby . . . bring a temporary end to human isolation".[53] The humility or at least modesty of this anti-egoistic acting can lead us to understand that the writing/reading/living ego tends to commodify, to humbug, to use one's position, brilliance, beauty for selfish and misleading ends, or to say "This is the truth". All are ways of dominating, claiming power over the reader. And, as Thackeray's fiction increasingly shows, the artist's ability to control his readers invites him into a self-destructive predatory relationship with his product and his readers – a relationship to which readers are only too eager to succumb. For, as Thackeray pointed out in "On a Lazy Idle Boy", novels are "sweets", loved by all healthy-minded people. But "as surely as the cadet drinks too much pale ale, it will disagree with him; and so, surely, dear youth, will too much [sic] novels cloy on thee" (XXII, 171).

Novels are so easy to devour that we fail to notice that we in turn are devoured by them and become prey to the implied author's visions. We become as "Alnaschar", one of Thackeray's favorite figures for the author/reader absorbed by self-aggrandizing visions. Alnaschar, the "Barber's Fifth Brother" in the *Thousand and One Nights*, acquires a cheap tray of glass to sell. He sets up the tray and falls to daydreaming about the eventual glory the wealth from the tray will bring. One fantasy leads to another, ending in Alnaschar reveling in marriage to the Vizir's daughter who submits to him, saying, "I am thy bondswoman". But, in his arrogance, Alnaschar spurns her: "Then I shake my fist in her face and kick her with my foot thus. So he let out with his toe and knocked over the tray of glass-ware which fell to the ground and, falling from the bench, all that was on it was broken to bits".[54] Getting lost in your interpretation leads to solipsistic disaster. If we read with the narrator, however, and not as subject to him, we can regain some control over the story by realizing "de te fabula", a third favorite Thackerayean metaphor: we are the story. If we follow Thackeray from *Vanity Fair*'s controlling critic's voice to Pen's self-ironic and self- parodic voice in *The Adventures of Philip*, we have moved from egoistic control to a dramatization of narrative games that leaves us to our own resources. If we can become "master linguists", we move away from the "infinite isolation" of being locked into one perspective (MacIntyre 32).

Colby says Thackeray struggles against skepticism (29), but in another view, the techniques and story and the multiplicity of voices all along the social scale (Colby 34) "sustain the conversation" (Rorty 378) to create a dialogue that offers a humane skepticism as a way of living in the world without god but also without becoming a predator. Colby points out that Cousin advocated viewing a subject from multiple sides to arrive at a "complete view" (51), but looking at Thackeray's oeuvre from this particular perspective, one sees that "complete view" is an oxymoron if applied to Thackeray because "complete" also implies "closed", or "fixed". His novels are negative in that they expose false systems of belief and the partial nature of any truth. The very nature of skepticism precludes a final purpose. But Thackeray certainly presented practical truths about the kinds of roles we could adopt in social relations. It was clear for him that ethical action was not learned through any transcendental system, but learned through one's own falseness, failures, and sufferings seen within the practice of ethical story-telling. Social individuals tell stories and act in others' stories. We can be the novel hero whose life is a process that is imperishable and forever renewing itself. Thackeray's texts dramatize a mode of understanding ourselves and our fellow social animals that teaches us to engage in dialogue with, but never resolve, the ambivalencies of modern life. His particular skepticism demands that we (and his characters) make moral decisions and choose actions without having absolute grounds upon which to base those choices. As readers we must interpret and evaluate. As characters we must act. Both readers and actors lack complete information and risk being based on misinterpretation. As Joyce Cary said, Thackeray "saw and grimly accepted a treacherous and insecure world where indeed there were love and goodness but no security for either" (Ray, *Age*, 430).

Notes

[1]   Robert Colby, Thackeray's *Canvass of Humanity* (Columbus: Ohio State UP, 1979), 6.

[2]   Micael Clarke, *Thackeray and Women* (DeKalb: Northern Illinois UP, 1995); John Reed, *Punishment and Forgiveness, Dickens and Thackeray* (Athens, OH: Ohio UP, 1995). George Saintsbury, *Thackeray: A Consideration* (London: Oxford UP, 1931), 244.

[3]   The terms "authorial" and "narrative audience" come from Peter J. Rabinowitz in *Before Reading, Narrative Conventions and the Politics of Interpretation* (Ithaca: Cornell UP, 1987), 20-29 and 93-96, respectively.

[4]   Geoffrey Tillotson argues that Thackeray came to understand while writing *Catherine* that literary character should mix virtues and vices, thus Catherine's character cannot be read as wholly good or bad. Tillotson goes on to suggest that Thackeray missed the real flaw in "idealist" writers such as Bulwer-Lytton and Dickens: "What was wrong with Dickens' Nancy was not her access of belated good-heartedness, but her acquiring refinement along with it" (*A View of Victorian Literature* (Oxford: Clarendon Press, 1978), 170-71. Thackeray rectified this error in later characterizations; for example, the lower-class "Little Sister" in *The Adventures of Philip* combines a strong will, practicality, and a great capacity for selfless love with bad grammar and no education.

[5]   James Phelan, *Reading People, Reading Plots* (Chicago: U of Chicago P, 1989), Parts I and II, *passim*.

[6]   See Marion Helfer Wajngot, *The Birthright and the Blessing. Narrative As Exegesis in Three of Thackeray's Later Novels* for her similar history of how critics have explained Thackeray's ambiguity (*Stockholm Studies in English XCI* [Stockholm: Almqvist & Wiksell International, 2000], 35-36).

[7]   *The Realistic Imagination* (Chicago: U of Chicago P, 1983), 136.

[8]   *Thackeray's Novels: A Fiction That is True.* (Berkeley: U of California P, 1974), 6. It is amazing that Rawlins should so expose the details and fail to see a system in Thackeray's narrative strategies.

[9]   Tillotson, *Thackeray the Novelist* (1954. New York: Barnes and Noble, 1974), chapters 1-3 are concerned with Thackerayean "oneness". See, for Tillotson's perceptive view of Thackeray's philosophy, *A View of Victorian Literature*, 152-186.

[10]   Winslow Rogers, "Thackeray's Self-Consciousness", *The Worlds of Victorian Fiction. Harvard English Studies 6,* ed. Jerome Buckley (Cambridge: Harvard UP, 1975), 149-150, 151. His conclusion reminds us of the way Titmarsh used Oliver Yorke, Mrs. Barbara, or self-ridicule to close his discussions of painting.

[11]   Carlisle, *The Sense of An Audience: Dickens, Thackeray, and George Eliot at Mid-Century* (Brighton, Sussex: Harvester Press, 1982), 120, 121.

[12]   Peter L. Shillingsburg, *Pegasus in Harness; Victorian Publishing and W. M. Thackeray* (Charlottesville: UP of Virginia, 1992).

[13]   See, for example, Lambert Ennis, *Thackeray: The Sentimental Cynic* (Evanston: Northwestern UP, 1950). Saintsbury called the cynic-sentimentalist debate a "duet contest of silliness" squawked by "parrots" (62).

[14]   Ina Ferris, "The Reader in the Rhetoric of Realism: Scott, Thackeray and Eliot", *Papers of the Aberdeen Scott Conference*, eds. J. H. Alexander and David Hewitt. (Aberdeen: Association for Scottish Literary Studies, 1983), 383-92.

[15]   The term "characterized audience" is from James Phelan, *Reading People, Reading Plots*, 135-41.

[16]   This view of Thackeray's shifting stances as deliberate and positive has become more prevalent since the advent of post-structuralist literary theory. J. Hillis Miller deconstructs *Henry Esmond* in *Fiction and Repetition* (Cambridge: Harvard UP, 1982), 73-115. R. D. McMaster's work on allusion in *The Newcomes* suggest that allusions in Thackeray's fiction "establish not a simple identity . . . but a set of interactive relationships where conventions are not only invoked but undermined or held in doubtful suspension. . . . The general effect is that of an infinitely debatable text in which interpretation draws attention to the process and problems of interpretation itself" (*Thackeray's Cultural Frame of Reference. Allusion in The Newcomes* [Montreal & Kingston: McGill-Queen's UP, 1991], 12). And Wajngot's study of Thackeray's retelling of biblical stories concludes that "the fictional method of retelling stories in various versions and guises goes hand in hand with the narratorial comments to produce the message that narrative is always a question of versions (36).

[17]   I will be drawing on Mikhail Baktin, *The Dialogic Imagination*, ed. Michael Holquist, trans. Caryl Emerson (Austin: U of Texas P, 1981).

[18]   Wayne Booth. *The Company We Keep. An Ethics of Fiction* (Berkeley: U of California P, 1988), 12. The title of Booth's work echoes Thackeray's ethical criticism of *Oliver Twist*.

[19]   Of course, the tragedy of Isabella's insanity dislodged any sense of knowable divine order in the world. He wrote to his mother, "Look at these unequal lots in the fortunes of men and see how completely circumstance (of personal disposition or outward fortune) masters all—and one begins to think of Vice and Virtue as here practised, with profound scorn or else with bitter humiliation and debasement" (*LPP* 1: 147). Gordon Ray's *Thackeray: The Uses of Adversity* traces the development of Isabella's malady and its effect on Thackeray's outlook (New York: McGraw-Hill, 1955), chapter 10.

[20]   This sense of the inaccessibility of Divine Authority has been traced, of course, by Hillis Miller in *The Disappearance of God* (Cambridge, MA: Harvard

UP, 1963). With no God to unify mankind in Himself, humans are caught in a solipsistic world that "mirrors back to man his own image" (5). These "mirrors" are Thackeray's sociolects.

[21] Two authors are particularly relevant to an examination of Thackeray's religious beliefs: J. Russell Perkin, "The Implied Theology of *Vanity Fair*", *Philological Quarterly* 77 (Winter 1998), 79-106, and John Peck, "Thackeray and Religion: The Evidence of *Henry Esmond*", *English* 40 (1991), 217-35. Perkin also notes the Bakhtinian nature of the narrative voice in *Vanity Fair* (83-84). Peck points out that "critics, by and large, regard [Thackeray] as either an instinctive sceptic or as a comfortable Anglican, with the kind of broad faith that could even embrace a degree of doubt" (217). Both critics uncover Thackeray's religious beliefs by looking for "implied" theologies. For instance, Perkin argues that the gaps in *Vanity Fair*, "something which is not narrated . . . . could be seen as an example of a negative theology, invoking an absent God, or at least a God who is only seen by indirection" (92). Peck sees in the politics of *Henry Esmond* an analysis of the shift from the absolute authority of Catholicism to the relativism and suspect values of individualistic Protestantism. For Peck, Thackeray is an "anxious author, for what he has to report on is a world where guidelines have gone" (224). And Peck locates this anxiety in the breakdown of what I would call the transcendental language of religion: "there is a corruption of language, in which words, particularly moral and religious words, are emptied of their original meaning" (224). Both arguments are compatible with my contention that Thackeray found any conventions of representation inadequate as expressions of Truth. Thackeray might have accepted Christian ethics, but he was skeptical about the power of art to represent the Christianity or Authority behind those ethics.

[22] Pyrrho, the Greek philosopher, coined the word skepticism to describe "one who doubts the possibility of real knowledge of any kind; one who holds that there are no adequate grounds for certainty as to the truth of any proposition whatever" (OED).

[23] Richard Popkin, *A History of Skepticism from Erasmus to Spinoza* (Berkeley: U of California P, 1979), 104.

[24] Thackeray's emphasis coincides with the Victorian empirical science that sought to find basic truths by starting with close observation of the physical. The most famous result of this process was, of course, Darwin's theory of evolution. Gillian Beer and George Levine have presented admirable studies of both the influence Darwinian thinking had on novel-writing and, more loosely, the general zeitgeist, or spirit of observation, speculation, and theorizing which allowed Darwinism and the kind of skeptical fiction Thackeray produced. Gillian Beer, *Darwin's Plots: Evolutionary Narrative in Darwin, George Eliot, and Nineteenth-Century Fiction* (London: Routledge and Kegan Paul, 1983). George Levine, *Darwin and the Novelists* (Harvard UP, 1988; Chicago: U of Chicago P, 1991).

His distrust of the conventions of representation should be seen also in the broader context of the politics of skepticism within whose ranks Michael Oakeshott included Spinoza, Pascal, Hobbes, Hume, Montesquieu, Burke, Paine, Bentham, Hegel, Coleridge, Calhoun and Macaulay ("The Fortunes of Scepticism", *Times Literary Supplement*, no. 4850 [15 March 1996]: 14). Oakeshott sees as the center of this tradition a political epistemology similar to Thackeray's aesthetic understanding. Political skeptics reject "the belief that governing is the imposition of a comprehensive pattern of activity upon a community and [consequently suspect] government invested with overwhelming power, and [recognize] the contingency of every political arrangement and the unavoidable arbitrariness of most" (14). McMaster also notes that Thackeray is writing during an age of "epistemological anxiety" (12).

[25] Henry Nash, *Higher Criticism of the Bible* (London: Macmillan & Co., Ltd., 1900), 66.

[26] Kurt Mueller-Vollmer, *The Hermeneutics Reader. Texts of the German Tradition from the Enlightenment to the Present* (New York: Continuum Publishing, 1985), "Introduction", 9.

[27] Wilfred L. Guerin, et. al., *A Handbook of Critical Approaches to Literature* (New York: Oxford UP, 1992), 297.

[28] See J. H. Stonehouse, *Catalogue of the Libraries of Charles Dickens and W. M. Thackeray* (London, 1935) for records of Thackeray's copies of Hume, Montaigne, and Locke.

[29] Thackeray held this image of the natural painter for most of his life, comparing them to birds and tulips in *The Newcomes* (1: 156). *Sketches After English Landscape Painters* (London: David Bogue, 1850). Not in the *Biographical Edition.*

[30] "Naturally" appears in the manuscript of *The Newcomes*; Thackeray revised it to "as spontaneously" in the first edition, as if he wanted to minimize his paradox (*N*, n2, 1: 156).

[31] This is not an idle sentiment; Harden's supplement to Ray's *LPP* includes Thackeray's two passionate letters to Kate Perry about Jane Brookfield written in French, the language of love (*LPPS* 1: 430-432).

[32] Linda Dowling asks just this question about "aesthetic democracy" in *The Vulgarization of Art* (Charlottesville: U of Virginia P, 1996). She argues that Shaftesburian "moral sense", specifically the aesthetic sense develops as a replacement for divine right in order to justify "a state deriv[ing] its authority from the consent of the people" (2).

[33] See Thackeray's review of William Tait's *Life and Correspondence of David Hume* in the *Morning Chronicle* of 23 March 1946, *Contributions to the Morning Chronicle*, ed. Gordon Ray (Urbana: U of Illinois P, 1966), 113-118. He found Hume "dangerous" because he was so eloquent a skeptic.

[34] Sheila Delany, *Chaucer's House of Fame. The Poetics of Skeptical Fideism* (Chicago: U of Chicago P, 1972).

[35] See McMaster's *Thackeray's Cultural Frame of Reference*. John Loofbourow. *Thackeray and the Form of Fiction* (Princeton: Princeton UP, 1964). And Thackeray's own *Novels By Eminent Hands* amply shows his own talent for parody.

[36] James Phelan, *Narrative as Rhetoric* (Columbus: Ohio State UP, 1996) 17.

[37] David Hume, *A Treatise of Human Nature*, ed. L. A. Selby-Bigge (Oxford: Clarendon Press, 1978; rev. ed. P. H. Nittitch, 1988).

[38] Richard Rorty, *Philosophy and the Mirror of Nature* (Princeton: Prince-ton UP, 1979), 190-91.

[39] I am indebted to conversations with Peter L. Shillingsburg for this understanding of Becky's "guilt".

[40] The nineteenth-century novel relied on such authenticating devices. Scott was particularly astute at this, using narrators, editors, locating his stories in apocryphal manuscripts. The practice of "editing", narrator as eye-witness, and autobiographical story was widespread. Thackeray used – and subverted – all such authenticating devices. See Elizabeth Segal, "Truth and Authenticity in Thackeray", *Journal of Narrative Technique* 2 (1972), 46-59, for an analysis of the motives for Thackeray's "misuse" of authenticating devices. Her conclusion accords with mine; that the "realism" in Thackeray is in the reader's experience of reading not in the text as given. Segal derives her argument from an earlier essay by Morton Bloomfield, "Authenticating Realism and the Realism of Chaucer", *Thought* 34 (1964), 335-58. Bloomfield argues that "authenticating realism", establishing "an air of truth or plausibility to a tale", is the *sine qua non* of "realistic" narrative, but does not require the contents of the narrative to imitate life (338).

[41] Alasdair MacIntyre, *After Virtue: a Study in Moral Theory* (South Bend: Notre Dame UP, 1981), 29.

[42] "May Gambols, or Titmarsh in the Picture Galleries", *Fraser's Magazine* 29 (June 1844), 700-17 in XXV, 419-445.

[43] I am adapting the idea of "reflexive" narration developed by Robert Siegle in *The Politics of Reflexivity, Narrative and the Constitutive Poetics of Culture* (Baltimore: The Johns Hopkins UP, 1986). Siegle argues that Thackeray's reflexive narration throws the reader "back upon his own philosophical resources to question not only the material itself, but the grounds of that material and the act of understanding it. The text presses hardest against a reader, perhaps, when it disperses conceptual grounds into the mere conventions of culture" (23).

44 Michael Lund, *Reading Thackeray* (Detroit: Wayne State UP, 1988), 60-61.

45 Derek Brewer notes that "the exigencies of the novel as 'true history' and 'autobiography,' imitating life as it seems actually to be lived on the surface" deforms the basically fairy-tale pattern of novels such as *Great Expectations* by forcing a pattern of cause-effect onto a romance structure. (*Symbolic Stories* [Totowa, NJ: Rowman and Littlefield, 1980)], 180).

46 See Northrup Frye, *The Secular Scripture. A Study of the Structure of Romance* (Cambridge, MA: Harvard UP, 1976), chapters 1 and 2 *passim*.

47 Roberto Unger, *Passion: An Essay on Personality* (New York: Free Press [Macmillan], 1984), 32.

48 "Mediated desire" originates with Rene Girard's *Deceit, Desire, and the Novel. Self and Other in Literary Structure*, trans. Yvonne Freccero (Baltimore: The Johns Hopkins UP, 1965).

49 Western literature seems almost obsessed with this problem. See Louise Vinge's *The Narcissus Theme in Western Literature*, trans. Robert Dewsnap (Lund: Gleerups, 1967). She catalogues over a thousand uses of the theme and I have encountered versions not included in her book.

50 This term, of course is common in psychoanalytic criticism.

51 *Inescapable Romance: Studies in the Poetics of a Mode* (Princeton: Princeton UP, 1979) 12.

52 John Erskine Hankins, *Source and Meaning in Spenser's Allegory: a Study of the 'Faerie Queene'* (New York: Oxford UP, 1971), 72.

53 "Theatricality in *Pendennis*", *Ariel* 4 (1973), 93.

54 *The Book of the Thousand Nights and a Night*, trans. Richard Burton (Burton Club: n. d.) 1: 338.

2   The "Right Line I":Narratorial Collusion and the Perils of "Sternism"

> It is very difficult for literary men to keep their honesty.
> We are actors more or less. (*LPP* 3: 13)

> To be greatly successful as a professional humourist, as in any other calling, a man must be quite honest, and show that his heart is in his work. (Thackeray, "George Cruikshank")[1]

In typical fashion, Thackeray used his most personal voice to alert his readers to the fact that this intimacy was a rhetorical and typographical construction:

> I should like to touch you sometimes with a reminiscence that shall awaken your sympathy, and make you say [I also] have so thought, felt, smiled, suffered. Now how is this to be done except by egotism?. . . That right line "I" is the very shortest simplest, straightforwardest means of communication. (XXII, 181)

Thackeray draws attention to the "I" as a *conventional* force, a representation of a symbol of a self. He showed himself fully aware of the difference in authority and intimacy depending upon the choice of narratorial pronoun.[2] Inaugurating William Ainsworth's *Ainsworth's Magazine* in 1842, Thackeray in his persona of Michael Angelo Titmarsh rejected the "editorial we" because "that simple right line I, which often seems egotistical and presuming is, I fancy, less affected and pert than 'we' often is. 'I' is merely an individual; whereas 'we,' is clearly somebody – 'I,' merely expresses an opinion; whereas 'we,' at once lays down the law".[3] This distinction derives from how readers respond to "we" and "I". While "I" supposedly has less *ex cathedra* authority, it creates another kind of authority in its seemingly intimate connection between individual writer and reader that suggests an empathetic identity between the writer and reader. As Bulwer Lytton wrote, "to make me feel, you must seem yourself to feel".[4] The writer creates a voice that at least "seems" to feel deeply about his subject; in turn, this genuine feeling invites a like response in the audience. The depth of the audience's response depends upon how closely they identify with the voice, and often the readers identify this voice with the author of the text. Arguably, the strong personal voice of the Eliot narrator, or Dickens' alter-ego voices of David Copperfield and Pip as well as Thackeray's playful *personae* of Titmarsh and Manager and his later second-self, Pendennis, were crucial marketing devices. People returned week after week, month after month, work after work not just to find out what happened next but also to participate in the "confidential talk between writer and reader" (*P* xv). But this powerful intimate connection opens the "I" to the dangers of authorial egoism: the temptation to dominate the discourse or to exploit the "I" for effect.

Lytton's dictum that the emotional response of the audience derives from their belief in the narrator's feelings is, of course, the keystone of Victorian "sincerity". Peter Gay in *The Naked Heart* has established just how preoccupied the Victorians were with self-scrutiny, self-revelation, and self-exposure.[5] The "narrator" developed in nineteenth-century prose fiction as a verbal construct that suggested an unrepresentable inner self, existing outside the frame of the text. Thackeray realized that creating a rhetorical voice that was authorized by its emotions (Rousseau's *Confessions*, of course, is the model for this presentation of the self) could lure the artist into a potentially destructive prostitution. The danger stems from the fact that self-revelation is accepted as "sincere" only if it is confirmed by public acceptance. The "right line I" with its concomitant "you" role for the reader creates an intimate writer-reader relationship that is based upon conventional signs of a personal relation. But the role-playing fundamental to narration makes any revelation of a "natural" or essential self impossible. The need to select and arrange words and, in Thackeray's case, create illustrations – that is, to produce a product that can be coherently consumed by an anonymous public – requires the writer to create a voice that suggests a "self" consistent with that particular narrative product. The sincere artist is not one who reveals himself, but one who plays a role so well suited to the rhetorical purpose (and the marketplace) that it suggests *no* role.

While the illusion of intimacy explicit in the "I-you" exchange implies that the narrator is revealing a essential self which lies beyond his language, the rhetorical success of the "I-you" relationship depends upon the implied author's ability to remain aloof from the textual "I" so as to be able to manipulate the semantic conventions of intimacy and self-exposure. Manipulation can easily turn into exploitation; Thackeray's experience in the literary and art worlds taught him it was all too easy to either present a self antithetical to the artist's real nature (Miss Bunion in *Pendennis*) or to act an ethos which exploited the audience (the narrator of *Oliver Twist*). But if the implied author does not maintain such distance, self-revelation can seduce the artist into Sternism: when the artist becomes the performer without even recognizing his falsity. I say "he" here, although Becky Sharp and Blanche Amory are brilliant female Sternes. If the artist is seduced by her rhetorical strategies, she can become an ego-invested performer, ultimately unable to control her representations of her "private" selves:

> A perilous trade, indeed, is that of a man who has to bring his tears and laughter, his recollections, his personal griefs and joys, his private thoughts and feelings to market, to write them on paper, and sell them for money. Does he exaggerate his grief so as to get his reader's pity for a false sensibility? feign indignation, so as to establish a character for virtue? elaborate repartees, so that he may pass for a wit? steal from other authors, and put down the theft to the credit side of his own reputation for ingenuity and learning? feign originality? affect benevolence or misanthropy? appeal to the gallery gods with claptraps and vulgar baits to catch applause?
>
> How much of the paint and emphasis is necessary for the fair business of the stage, and how much of the rant and rouge is put on for the vanity of the actor? His audience trusts him: can he trust himself? How much was deliberate calculation and imposture – how much was false sensibility – and how much true feeling? Where did the lie begin, and did he know where? and where did the truth end in the art and scheme of this man of genius, this actor, this quack? (XIV, 596)

Sterne's self-deceit resulted from having to sell *himself* as the aesthetic object; the artist becomes a performer. The term "artist", as Martin Meisel writes, "enjoins a respect for the integrity and honesty of the work, and a qualitative standard quite apart from fashion and the market. [The performer] acts from the disadvantage of dependence. It requires a success that entails cajoling an audience subject to fashion and providing the market, though the performer cannot afford to seem willing to go to any lengths for popularity".⁶ The "artist" thus remains distinct from his work that has its own existence as an artifact, while the performer's dependence on his audience can lure him to use himself to sell his work. From this latter situation arises the phenomenon of "celebrity": artists who sell their works by selling their "image". (One thinks of Byron's inadvertent celebrity here, and his consequent misfortunes.)   Sterne's exploitation of his own emotions violates the "ethical friendship" between the artist-as-perceived and the audience. Since the artist and critic must communicate either overtly or implicitly by means of the "right line I", they have the responsibility to "make of [themselves] the best 'character' possible, given [their] 'circumstances.'"⁷

Thackeray exploited this Romantic predicament: that while using yourself as your text or to rely on "the right line I" can open a door to a sincere relation with your audience, you also risk losing yourself in your text. He turned it against itself, making the narrator-performer tension central to his story and his relationship with his readers. We see inadvertent Sternism in the young Pendennis, Sternism at its most dangerous to artist and audience in Becky and Blanche, and Sternism brilliantly manipulated by the author [Thackeray] in Pen's narration of *Philip*. But Thackeray knew, as Titmarsh's comments suggest, that this "I" was also the most effective method to draw his readers into his world. In his early years as a critic of painting and literature, Thackeray used personal narration as his critical voice to dramatize critical judgments and his method of reading and seeing without sermonizing. As the pseudonym suggests, Michael Angelo Titmarsh taught the dangers of egoistic painting and egoistic seeing. Thus, even before *Vanity Fair*, Thackeray's methods and message were becoming reflexive. His critique of "theatricality" in painting, for example, uses narrative collusion to confront the reader with the dangers of egoism in the artist. The intimacy of Titmarsh's voice pulls the reader into his critical consciousness while that consciousness analyzes the "I-you" relationship between the painting and the viewer.

Theatrical painting is the visual version of Sternism in that it "shows off" the *artist's* virtuosity. Meisel points out that Thackeray "was troubled by the self consciousness of the performer, [but] . . .also deeply skeptical of the alternative ideals of performative art, such as sincerity" (322).

"Theatrical" art was self-conscious performance for the sake of "effect" (sensation without sense or sincerity; Meisel chapter 5). Meisel calls Thackeray "the deadliest enemy of the aesthetics of effect in England" (34), and Thackeray's attacks on theatricality in painting were his groundwork for his mature vision of the potential self-destructiveness of the theatrical human.

Theatrical skill is often formulaic mimicry; Titmarsh compares such imitative painting to a "boy's hexameters at school. Every lad of decent parts in the sixth form has a knack of turning out great quantities of respectable verse . . . but these verses are not the least like poetry, any more than the great Academical paintings of the artists are like great painting" (XXV, 460).[8] In "Picture Gossip", Titmarsh criticizes Charles Landseer's *Charles I before the Battle of Edge Hill* for having "all the parts and accessories studied and executed with care and skill, and yet meaning nothing" (XXV, 460). Thackeray elaborated upon this notion of meaningless clutter to explain both the vulgar taste of the *nouveau riche* Lady Clavering (*N* 1: 372) and the self-conscious artificiality of artist-performers like Blanche Amory and Becky Sharp, who arrange objects with an eye to their "effect" but with no sincerity. Artists can slide into theatricality if they lack a sympathetic awareness of the needs of their audience. Genre painting was often "arch", to use a common 19th-century term for comedy style. An "arch" actress such as Madame Vestris acted self-consciously, asking the audience to admire her cleverness. The common term for such self-conscious representation was "posing" which depended upon the audience's joining the actor in recognizing the humor or power of the actor's acting.[9] Thus in comparing Joshua Reynolds' and Thomas Lawrence's portraits of women, Thackeray found Reynolds' subjects "vastly superior" because the women are complete in themselves, "not anxious for applause", whereas Lawrence's "ladies are ogling out of their gilt frames, and asking for admiration" (VI, 530). Such posing was a self-conscious illusion whose coy awareness of itself pointed back to the cleverness of the painter. For example, Thackeray complained about James Harding, "if one may find a fault with Mr. Harding's works, it is that one is almost too conscious of the artist in his works. The effects are too palpable, the contrasts between light and dark too self-evident".[10] The "window" becomes a stage proscenium, the artist becomes the stage manager, and the viewer is deprived of a "real" subject and independent interpretation.

The metaphor of the painting as a "window" to suggest how we perceive linear perspective on a two-dimensional surface, goes back to "Book One" of Leon Batista Alberti's *De Pictura* (1435).[11] Thackeray based his own distinction between tableaux and windows on the role these metaphors offered the viewer. The theatrical tableau presented a frozen, posed picture that on stage stopped the action for a moment of viewer appreciation derived from the viewer recognizing the "staginess" of the scene. Instead of conspiring with the viewer, the window provided an "accidental" glimpse of a reality made static for a moment.[12] While the scene is still a self-conscious artificial design, the action or image does not seem to be "presented" at all, but is perceived as a momentary flash of an ongoing action that has its own integrity. Titmarsh demonstrates his sense of the "window" by creating for his readers an illusion of "before" and "after". Viewing a painting as a glimpse through a window is analogous to mimetic reading; one views the scene as "actual" and fills in the gaps to complete a reading. In both cases, the viewer is a voyeur instead of an expected audience, and the sense of voyeurism testifies to the artist's own self-forgetful absorption in the painting or the sincerity of the narrator. The illusion of reality is thus a reciprocal relation between viewer response and artistic presentation. A "real" subject puts the viewer in the role of accidental observer, just as Thackeray turned himself into a character in *Vanity Fair* "accidentally" to see Amelia at the opera in Pumpernickel (chapter 62). (He, of course, wreaks havoc with this convention, acting also as manager and immersed character.)

Scenes purporting to be "real" should have "none of [the] knowingness" of theatrical genre painting.[13]   Charles Robert Leslie's *Twelfth Night* transforms the farce of Sir Toby Belch encouraging Andrew Aguecheek to "Accost, accost!" (1.3) into a scene "joyous, frank, [and] manly".[14] Catherine being comforted by her maid (from *Henry VIII*) is "tender, and grave and naif" (EG 320). Both paintings create the illusion of window scenes because, ironically, Leslie's presentation is not dramatic:

> The great beauty of these pieces is the total absence of affectation.
> The figures are in perfectly quiet, simple positions, looking as if they
> were not the least aware of the spectator's presence, (a rare quality in
> pictures, as I think, of which little dramas, the actors, like those upon
> the living stage, have a great love of "striking an attitude", and are
> always on the look-out for the applause of the lookers-on), whereas

> Mr. Leslie's little troupe of comedians know their art so perfectly,
> that it becomes the very image of nature, and the best nature, too.
> (EG 320)

Painting, then, presents frozen acting that is so good, that is, so highly
developed in artifice, that it seems not to be acting. The non-theatrical
image is the visual evidence of the painter's ethos: the first suggests that
the second is "natural". (Similar non-theatrical acting characterizes Helen
and Laura's presentation of themselves as "natural" ladies.) The circularity
of this relationship is obvious; a non-theatrical painting testifies to the
successful ethos of the artist, and non-theatricality is evidenced by the
audience's ability to see and read mimetically.

Thackeray's critical analyses, however, teach his readers that "natural"
scenes are, nonetheless, constructed and controlled by the artist whose
design allows the critic to construct a controlling theme for and
corresponding analysis of the painting. Thackeray-Titmarsh appreciates
Leslie's painting from *Roderick Random* (RA 1846) as a specimen of
finely controlled art not as an image of "life":

> In this noble picture, every body is busied, and perfectly naturally
> with the scene, at which the spectator is permitted to look. Every
> single performer is a character and a comedy in himself, the minutae
> of which are somehow revealed to the looker-on by each
> countenance; and you acknowledge the effect of the whole by a
> replay of laughter . . . . [Leslie] ties you to all these grotesque ways
> by a certain lurking human kindness; and there is always felt (though
> not intended) in the midst of the fun a feeling of friendliness and
> beauty.[15]

"Is permitted to look" suggests a spontaneous, accidental site of viewing,
while "performer", "character", and "comedy" acknowledge the construction controlled by Leslie's theme of "human kindness". The
"naturalness" of which Titmarsh speaks is thus the non-intention of the
figures who, as actors of life, logically cannot perceive the theme that holds
them together. Thackeray was conscious of the paradox that to succeed, the
aesthetic object must convey the illusion that it is independent and "real",
although the success of the illusion depends upon overt patterning to create
a coherent design. While recognizing the painting as an illusion allows the
critic to interpret it without being overly directed by the painter, the illusion

can only spark the critic's imagination when the participants seem unaware either of an audience or their own artificiality.

The ability to perceive a scene as natural while admiring the controlling consciousness of the designer allows viewer-readers to see mimetically while maintaining enough distance to "use" the perception, that is, to also see thematically and synthetically. To lose oneself in the illusion is to be aware only of the depicted not of the depiction. Karlheinz Stierle argues that this "quasi-pragmatic" reception leads

> into an illusory realm beyond the picture itself. More precisely, however, this illusory realm is not located beyond the picture but in front of it, since the viewer has substituted his own imaginary stereotypes for the pictorial signs. In this case, the picture, like trivial literature, can restrict itself to immersing the viewer in his own self-produced illusion, which can be attained without very complex aesthetic procedures. The trivial painting and its pictorial vagueness, which can easily be replaced by stereotypes, is a good illustration of how reception can lead from the work of art into a purely imaginary world.[16]

This tautological reception, wherein the viewer replaces the object with a self-projection, is a modern theory of Sternism as a role for the reader. Stierle singles out "popular" novel as particularly guilty of this kind of illusion-making and calls such reading "non-reading" because the viewer-reader loses the text by transforming it into reality which is a narcissistic mirror (Stierle 86-87). Stierle's quasi-pragmatic reception describes how Thackeray's male protagonists, especially George Osborne and Arthur Pendennis, as well as minor characters such as Fanny Bolton, will produce self-deceptive interpretations. "Maturing" in Thackeray's novels means passing from quasi-pragmatic reading to more complex forms of reception, consciously employing the variety of activities entailed in "reading".

Thackeray's narrative personae counter the perils of Sternism by developing tactics that deliberately reveal the limits of the "I" and its parity with the audience's "you". In the art criticism, the paintings act as controlling factors; they exist outside the discourse in the various exhibits. That is, they are "stories" beyond narrative control. What Michael Angelo Titmarsh sees can be either corroborated or denied by the readers. Titmarsh invites us into egalitarian intimacy when, for example, his "I" reveals its own inadequacy, and its seeming powerlessness. This dramatic "I" seems to respond to paintings spontaneously without conscious role-playing. One consequence of this technique is our own sense of the narrator's sincerity: when the "critic" cannot interpret or describe, the "man" is palpably honest. For instance, Daniel Maclise's *Play Scene in Hamlet*

> is a noble poetic delineation of the awful story. Here I am obliged to repeat, for the tenth time in this letter, how vain it is to attempt to describe such works by means of pen and ink. Fancy Hamlet, ungartered, lying on the ground, looking into the very soul of King Claudius, who writhes under the play of Gonzago. Fancy the Queen, perplexed and sad . . . and poor Ophelia, and Polonius with his staff . . . . Fancy . . . a lamp in front casts a huge forked shadow . . . a shadow that looks like a horrible devil in the background that is grinning and aping the murder. Fancy ghastly flickering tapestries of Cain and Abel on the walls, and all this painted with the utmost force, truth, and dexterity – fancy all this, and then you will not have the least idea of one of the most startling, wonderful pictures that the English school has ever produced. (EG 320)

We move with Titmarsh into the painting, reading it "as if" it were real, then we move out with the "I", placed in front of the painting by suddenly being addressed as "you". Titmarsh's uncertain description suggests the inability of his language to recreate the painting, so suggesting the profundity of his response. It is an honest response just because it is beyond words. Titmarsh's public "I" draws us into its own idiosyncratic response, inviting us to empathize with it. Accepting the limitations of the critic's perceptions when they are couched in a dramatic, seemingly spontaneous response undermines "omniscient" interpretation while emphasizing the reliability of the interpreter. Titmarsh does not seem to "act;" he simply sees, and we accept his partial views because of the conventions of candor in his narrative relation with us.

When this trustworthy voice turns the painting itself into a drama, it can move us beyond mimetic seeing into flexible interpretation as in Titmarsh's reaction to a minor painting by Louis Trimolet, *La Prière*, reviewed in "On Men and Pictures".[17] He first re-sees the painting as a scene in the life of the family.

> A man and his wife are kneeling at an old-fashioned praying-desk, and the woman clasps a little sickly-looking child in her arms, and

all three are praying as earnestly *as their simple hearts* will let them. The man is a limner, or painter of missals, by trade, *as we fancy.* One of his works lies upon the praying desk, and *it is evident that* he can paint no more that day, *for* the sun is *just* set behind the old-fashioned roofs of the houses in the *narrow street* of the old *city* where he lives. (Italics mine; XXV, 369)

Not only does the dramatic present tense animate the painting, but Titmarsh has assumed a narratorial relationship to the subject. It is as if he is peering into a window and catching the family at prayers. Characterizing their hearts as "simple" and imputing cause-effect relationships subordinates the image to the subject-as-narrated. The man is a limner *because* we see an illuminated missal on the prayer desk. This assumed relationship charges the book with a particular human significance. If he is a limner, then we understand why he can no longer paint: *because* the sun has "just" set. If we had "seen" the painting earlier, we would have caught the limner finishing his day's work. The "as *we* fancy" includes us in his sample interpretation. Titmarsh creates "plot" here by establishing cause-effect relations between the parts of the painting – the family, the prayer book, the light of the sun, and the family's occupation – and these connections limit the kinds of interpretations that can be inferred from the whole.[18] The painting's meaning derives from Titmarsh's re-presentation of the painting as part of a dramatic continuum. The painting becomes self-reflexive; that is, its parts define each other to form a closed system. The pictorial signs' reflexivity depend upon Titmarsh's verbalized perception, which in turn depends upon the whole image for its process. It is a *stable* perception because the image and its reading create necessary and sufficient causes for each other, forming a closed system that contains and explains the image.

This holistic narrative "belongs" to Titmarsh because he has created the connections that make the parts cohere. And he is clear in the review, that he carries this story with him: "Indeed, I have had a great deal of pleasure in looking at this little quiet painting, and in the course of half-a-dozen visits that I have paid to it, have become perfectly acquainted with all the circumstances of the life of the honest missal illuminator and his wife, here praying at the end of their day's work in the calm summer evening" (XXV, 369). The phrase, "perfectly acquainted with all the circumstances of the life" suggests that he is constantly embroidering the basic story and, that the "pleasure" that he now feels derives from recognizing the painting as part of his own broadening narrative. This kind of interpretation encourages the viewer to recreate the painting as a sympathetic "other". It is possible to understand this mode of interpretation as projecting one's own desires onto the painting, in which case the object disappears into his interpretation, and Titmarsh is left looking into a reflection of himself. But if his story acts primarily as a sympathetic connection between Titmarsh and the figures in the painting, he can avoid (or disguise) solipsism. Titmarsh's perspective is stable because he can create an interpretation that makes his response cohere with the painting, but this interpretation is unfixed because he is conscious of the process and maintains enough control over it to create various readings. While this particular interpretation is both exclusive and satisfying for the critic, Titmarsh emphasizes that such holistic perceptions are never absolute – are never the only perceptions.

> Very likely Monsieur Trimolet has quite a different history for his little personages, and so has everybody else who examines the picture. But what of that? There is the privilege of pictures. A man does not know all that lies in his picture, any more than he understands all the character of his children. Directly one or the other makes its appearance in the world, it has its own private existence, independent of the progenitor. And in respect of works of art, if the same piece inspire one man with joy, that fills another with compassion, what are we to say of it, but that it has sundry properties of its own which its author even does not understand? (XXV, 369)

While Titmarsh may delight in embroidering the story of *La Prière*, he is aware *he* is doing the embroidering. His careful reconstruction of pictures as stories with themes shows his readers how to perform similar acts of self-conscious interpretation, moving from mimetic to thematic reading.

Thematizing paintings offers readers models of stable interpretations that are not dogmatic because they are only versions. The readers are on the same level as the critic because they could offer their own versions. Such egalitarianism develops into narrative collusion when the critic's language incorporates the reader into the critic's consciousness. The longer the reader reads the more the narrative ethos becomes her ethos. Two intricate examples from the art criticism dramatize the didactic effect of Thackeray's skill at the effortless confluence of "you" into "I". His discussion of Charles West Cope's painting, *Charity*, in "May Gambols" incorporates the reader into his critical process and uses this immersed reading of the painting to criticize the social hypocrisy of Victorian medievalism.[19]   The passage starts with a simple comparison between Cope's painting and Raphael in explicit contrast to contemporary imitations of Cimabue and Giotto. This contrast in pictorial styles enlarges into a contrast between the simplicity of sincere art, Cope and Raphael, versus the theatricality of formulaic art, as embodied in the Nazarenes and the Gothic Revival.

> And Mr. Cope has this merit, that his work is no prim imitation of the stiff old Cimabue and Giotto manner, no aping of the crisp draperies and hard outlines of the missal illuminations, without which the religious artist would have us believe religious expression is impossible. It is pleasant after seeing the wretched caricatures of old-world usages which stare us in the face in every quarter of London now – little dumpy Saxon chapels in raw brick, spick and span *bandbox* churches of the pointed Norman style for Cockneys in zephyr coats to assemble in . . . gimcrack imitations of the Golden Legend . . . stolen out of Norman missals – to find artists aiming at the Beautiful and Pure without thinking it necessary to resort to these paltry archaeological quackeries, which have no Faith, no Truth, no Life in them; but which give us ceremony in lieu of reality; and insist on forms as if they were the conditions of belief. (XXV, 431)

The complicated cumulative sentence, "It is pleasant . . . to find artists", extends the debate from pictorial style to a moral evaluation of different artistic intentions, which is based on how the products of these intentions influence the readers' lives. The neo-gothic artist cannot really feel the religious sentiments suggested by the tradition he imitates because they are embodied in imitations of outmoded religious forms. The image of a cockney in a zephyr coat "worshipping" in a Norman "bandbox" eloquently describes the inappropriateness of these "old" forms to the contemporary lifestyle by implying an equation between the "fashionableness" of the church and the coat. Just as cockneys affect this light, flyaway coat, so ecclesiastical architects affect a Norman style – a bandbox is a box for collars or hats. While this kind of triviality may be the essence of fashion in dress, it is hardly appropriate for the sacred purpose of a church. Moreover, Thackeray's use of the verb "stolen" to describe the artist's method of borrowing styles, and the term "gimcrack" to describe the result, implies that the revivalist artist is a conscious humbug. A "gimcrack" is both a flimsy, trivial thing and a "deceitful intent". Replacing "reality" with "ceremony", and "belief" with "forms", identifies the formula of the painting and the formula of the architecture with the moral hypocrisy of formulaic worship.

The pro-con structure of this passage reinforces the opposition between true and false art. Sentence one gives the reader the grounds for contrast: contemporary artists, one original, others imitators. Sentence two reacts to sentence one, and meliorates the criticism by telling us that the critic is not unnecessarily harsh but one who wants to be pleased. "It is pleasant after" switches "us" abruptly to the real object of criticism. The list of ugly artifacts reinforces the second half of the first sentence ("aping" is followed by "caricatures"); moreover, the number of details almost overwhelms the opening clause, increasing the reader's impatience for the completion of "It is pleasant" before she loses the sense of the sentence. The infinitive "to find" plunges the reader into a quick summary of the preceding architectural example and explains the moral significance of the stylistic flummery.

This syntactical structure moves between two belief systems and uses negative proof to slant the debate in favor of the style presented by Cope – and Raphael. The next paragraph blurs the line between the critic's interpretation and the reader's experience. Go, says "we", the critic, to the reader, across "Pall Mall to St. James Street . . . he will see the reason of our wrath" (XXV, 431). This reason, developed in the ensuing description of the Commission on the Fine Arts' "Exhibition of Decorative Works for the New Houses of Parliament", becomes not just the Gothic Revival but also the hypocrisy implicit in any faddish imitation of any style.[20]

> Here are all the ornamental artists of England sending in their works, and what are they? All imitations. The Alhambra here; the Temple Church there; here a Gothic saint; yonder a Saxon altar-rail; farther on a sprawling rococo of Louis XV. (XXV, 432)

Titmarsh attributes this focus on "every century except our own" to the influence of Sir Walter Scott, who "changed the character of novelists, then of historians, whom he brought from the study of philosophy to the study of pageantry", which then induced the artists to "fall back into the middle ages" (XXV, 432). This artistic trend accounts for what Titmarsh sees as the religious absurdity of Newman's high churchism which he typifies as an inappropriate if not insincere imitation of form: "until now behold we have Mr. Newman and his congregation of Littlemore marching out with taper and crosier and falling down to worship St. Willibald, and St. Winnibald, and St. Walberga the Saxon virgin" (XXV, 432). Thus we have come full circle: imitations of Giotto *do* materially affect those who try to use these empty forms as a way to revitalize faith. Art not only pervades life in pictures or ornamental exhibitions, but influences how we manifest our beliefs. Thus art helps determine the integrity of those beliefs, or, in other words, the expression (the outside) is the meaning (the inside).

At this point, however, Titmarsh interrupts his train of thought, before he becomes too overtly didactic or begins to claim too much for his associations. "But Mr. Cope's picture is leading the reader rather farther than a critique about exhibitions has any right to divert him, and let us walk soberly back to Trafalgar Square" (XXV, 432). The language here is interestingly ambiguous; the picture "leads" the reader, the critique "diverts" him, and the connecting "than" equates the two actions. The second clause, "than . . . him", should logically *restate* the first agent, not change the agent of the sentence. That is, the expectation in reading the sentence is that the picture is "leading" the reader "rather farther than a *picture* has any right to", not "critique". The shift identifies the picture with the critique. The "let us" of the final clause joins author and reader in the diversion, distancing Titmarsh from his own critique that has diverted both himself and his readers. The sentence gives us three clauses from three perceptions of what has just occurred: the inspiration by the picture, the resulting critique, and the effect on the spectator who occupies the same zone of contact as the "author" of the critique. This one sentence merges critic with reader by having the critic affected by his own discourse as if he were the reader.

The final example is from later in Thackeray's career, from his 1854 review of John Leech's *Life and Character*, in the *Quarterly Review* in which Thackeray uses a more elaborate method of narratorial collusion, especially in his pronominalization, to make his general critical point belong to his reader.[21] The five and a half page introduction overlaps the world of old and young to present the advent of middle-class values as cultural progress. The passage is a classic example of Thackeray's interpenetration of narration and interpretation. The opening intertwines the point of view of a child in Regency London with the "now" point of view of that child grown up, and the "now" point of view of *his* grandchildren looking at the past. The discussion focuses on the art available to children: the pictures on exhibit, the "shows" such as Mary Linwood's recreations of famous pictures in worsted, the story-books, and the graphic satires of Gillray and Rowlandson. The thesis is the paucity of visual entertainment for children and the morally suspect nature of much that had been available in the pre-Leech world.[22]   The underlying theme is the shift from old satiric art to "bourgeois humor". Leech "introduced [a] whole new genre of domestic satire which depended neither on verbal squibs or exaggerated drawing but on a greater naturalism of wit and draughtsmanship".[23]

Throughout the introduction, the critic uses the inclusive, critical "we", creating two possible critic-reader relations, as suggested in the first sentence: "We, who can recall the consulship of Plancus, and quite respectable old-fogyfied times, remember amongst other amusements which we had as children the pictures at which we were permitted to look" (XXV, 480). The comic, exaggerated claim of extreme age is one of Thackeray's characteristic narrative roles to suggest wisdom and distance from the vicissitudes of life. The "we" both establishes critical authority and invites a like segment of the audience to align themselves with him in his memories. However, those of the audience too young to do so are invited to hear the "history" of the narrator's – and of his fellow fogies' – childhood. The introduction then proceeds to give us an enormous amount of suggestive detail but little substantial information, which assumes that the reader is familiar with the writer's world. For example, the description of John Boydell's Shakespeare Gallery omits the names of the paintings and the first names of the painters. This elliptical style also creates the illusion of the child's reaction to these paintings. The "child" sees only "murky Opies, glum Northcotes . . . . there were Lear, Oberon, Hamlet, with starting muscles, rolling eyeballs, and long pointing quivering fingers. . . there was little Rutland being run through by Beaufort (Reynolds) gnashing his teeth, and grinning and howling demonically on his deathbed" (XXV, 480). At the end of this litany of bloody violence, even a reader unfamiliar with the paintings understands and sympathizes with the narrator's memory of his childhood reaction: "We did not like to inspect [the museum] unless the elders were present, and plenty of lights and company were in the room" (480).

The second memory, of Mary Linwood's gallery of classic paintings reproduced in worsted, pursues the same undercurrent of violence: "There were large dingy pictures of woolen martyrs, and scowling warriors . . . there was especially, at the end of a black passage, a den of lions, that would frighten any boy not born in Africa, or Exeter Change" (480). The same eye of the frightened child sees Benjamin West's private gallery, called in the essay simply "West's Gallery", Westminster Abbey, St. Paul's, the Tower, and the Royal Waxworks, this perspective incorporating, as the two opening descriptions, the adult narrator who generalizes from the remembered "child's" details.

When the introduction moves on to the children's books and the caricatures of the Regency, the narrator's comparison between then and now gradually moves his readers into dialogue with his descriptions. The style shifts to jolly, avuncular, exaggeration as in this comparison between past and present school conditions.

> We were flogged at school; we were fifty boys in our boarding-house, and had to wash in a leaden trough, under a cistern, with lumps of fat yellow soap floating about in ice and water. Are *our* sons ever flogged? Have they not dressing-rooms, hair-oil, hip-baths, and Baden towels? And what picture-books the young villains have! (XXV, 481)

However, when the narrator considers his (the Regency child's) comic engravings and illustrated satiric books such as Pierce Egan's Tom and Jerry series, his memories of childhood lose their fear and shift to delight – but are tempered by the adult's knowledge that Egan, perhaps, was not the most appropriate entertainment for children. Dr. Syntax "frolicking with rosy exuberant damsels" (481), and Tom, Jerry and Bob of Egan's *Life in London*, who drank too much, knocked down "Charleys" (watchmen), and "perpetrated a vast deal of boxing" (482) cause the narrator to pause and address the "grandchildren" for the first time:

> You are led to suppose [this is the first shift away from the inclusive "we"] that the English aristocracy of 1820 *did* dance and caper in that way, and box and drink at Tom Cribb's, and knock down watchmen; and the children of today, turning to their elders, may say, "Grandmamma, did you wear such a dress as that when you danced at Almack's? There was very little of it, Grandmamma. Did Grandpapa kill many watchmen when he was a young man, and frequent thieves' gin-shops, cock-fights, and the ring, before you

> married him? Did he use to talk the extraordinary slang and jargon
> which is printed in this book? He is very much changed. He seems a
> gentlemanly old boy enough now." (482-83)

The next paragraph moves back to the critical "we", an emphatic (because
italicized) *we*, to continue an account of caricature – Gillray's and Rowlandson's political satires during the Napoleonic Wars. A clear tension
exists between the enjoyment the adult critical "we" still finds in the
outrageous, sometimes "savage" satire (483) and the morality of exposing
the "we"-who-was-a-child to its impropriety: "we hated these vicious
wretches [Napoleon and the English "Broad-backed" Administration], as
good children should: we were on the side of Virtue and Pitt and Grandpapa.
But if our sisters wanted to look at the portfolios, the good old grandfather
used to hesitate. There were some prints among them very odd indeed; some
that girls could not understand; some that boys, indeed, had best not see"
(484). Thackeray moves in this passage from the child's position in the past
with *his* grandfather to the present where the "now" child reads this essay
with the child-turned-grandfather. The child-voice does not recognize the
impropriety, but the grandfather-voice surely does and acts: "We swiftly
turn over those prohibited pages" (484). This "we" is ambiguous – it seems
to equate the narrator with the grandfather of the Regency child as well as
with the Regency-rake-grandfather of the present child, which produces a
consensus among all generations of old fogies. The multi-voiced "we"
creates a shared concern for propriety that was frustrated in the past by the
absence of entertainment suitable for children. But instead of arguing the
position, Thackeray's dramatization has placed the reader in the ethical
dilemma.

The narrator now moves quickly from the "foul blows" of this old satire
to the "washed, combed, clothed" satire of today (484). The narrative "we"
includes the current "grandpapa" of the dialogue (the Napoleonic child and
Regency rake) with himself as the instigator of this change.

> But we have washed, combed, clothed, and taught the rogue [satire]
> manners; or rather, let us say, he has learned them himself; for he is
> of nature soft and kindly, and he has put aside his mad pranks and
> tipsy habits; and, frolicksome always, has become gentle and harm-
> less, smitten into shame by the pure presence of our women and the
> sweet confiding smiles of our children. (484)

This distinction between "humour" and satire recalls to the narrator George Cruikshank, who also acted as a link between past and present because his satires, while to the point, never offended.[24]   He is joined by a company of contemporary engravers and caricaturists who fill the book-shop windows with comic *and* morally appropriate picture-books (485).

This introduction places John Leech within the history of English caricature, which itself is placed within the larger history of the development of children's literature. Both "histories" depend upon the more significant development of moral "propriety" – and entail, in fact, an increased awareness of the distinction between "child" and "adult": a child is a separate being, not a miniature adult. This realization is evidence of progress in civilization from violent, brutal art and sensual, savage satire to good-natured comedy that every "young person" can enjoy without blushing. The development of the introduction, moving from then to now in terms of the readers' roles, makes them participate in this change and approve of the "progress".

The thesis of the opening history is particularly appropriate for Thackeray's analysis of Leech. After several pages outlining the analogous change of "Mr. Punch" from "earning a precarious livelihood by the cracking of wild jokes, the singing of ribald songs" to being "washed, combed, neatly clothed, and perfectly presentable" (486), Thackeray moves to his major focus which is an appreciation of Leech's middle-class family, the Briggs. The Briggs are comic exemplifications of the "we" who have developed from the children who enjoyed Gillray and Rowlandson. Thackeray's history thus shows the readers how they have grown into the audience for whom Leech draws. Reading about "we" has created a "we", "us", and "you" that Thackeray can now address from a moral, historic, and aesthetic common ground. The emphasis on community created by sharing this art, dramatized by the choice of pronouns and the situation of children reading this essay with their grandparents, emerges explicitly at the conclusion of the essay. No matter what biting humor may have been lost, what "we" have gained is a secure domestic community: "May we have more of [Leech's drawings]; more pleasant Christmas volumes, over which we and our children can laugh together. Can we have too much of truth, and fun, and beauty, and kindness?" (490).

As this analysis of Thackeray's introduction suggests, the personal history actually creates a common past that educates us into the specific sensibilities necessary to enjoy this art. One can appreciate Leech the more, perhaps, because his innate humor is also a sign of our cultural amelioration. Leech's art is a civilized pleasure. This significance derives largely from the context in which the narrator places Leech – the "happy ending" to a history of a deprived childhood. Thackeray's narrative process has created the moral significance of Leech's aesthetic.

These rhetorical techniques exemplify Thackeray's ability to use his narrative presence to incorporate his reader into his own critical judgment on a basis of seeming equality. An important part of this egalitarian process is the narrator's insistence on the "versions" that are his interpretations. The different voices offer the readers multiple perspectives of interpretation, which are stable but not fixed. This flexibility is controlled because it is bound to an independent object; that is, we can always test what we read by going to see the painting or buying Leech's caricatures. However, this rhetorical method evinces more skepticism about its narrative power when the narrator creates the object it interprets. *Vanity Fair* exploits the collusion between the narrative "I" and its implied and overt "you" to actually disengage the reader from the story, enabling him or her to read skeptically.

The voice of the "critic" in the novel subsumes its object, the story, into the critic's use of that story. The subordination of story to narrator is indicated in the subtitle of the novel, the original title: "Pen and Pencil Sketches". This title tells us not to expect a story independent of the narrator who makes and arranges these "sketches". The famous parody in chapter six, for instance, where the narrator rewrites his story as a Newgate adventure novel and then in the "genteel rose-water style" is framed by a controlling voice who labels and critiques the styles but who uses the styles to show us how any story is inseparable from the telling of that story. This voice finally rejects these purely literary voices because he knows nothing of the worlds referred to by these sociolects. This narrator's story can only be told in *his* language. The illustrations emphasize that choice of a language is not merely choice of "decoration" because the figures in the three intratexts bear no relation to the visual representation of the characters elsewhere in the novel (Fig. 2.1). Thus, this master-narrator suggests that fictional "realities" reside in complementary verbal and visual styles. The juxtaposition of the low-life and high-life modes, so inappropriate to the mundane events on which the narrator has focused, renders both styles absurd. So, the reader aligns herself with the common-sense of the master-narrator which is stabilized by this reader-identification. What stability exists in the narrator in *Vanity Fair* derives, paradoxically, from what Juliet McMaster calls an "outsider status",[25] still very much the directive voice of the art criticism. In fact, the passage from chapter six, criticized by George Henry Lewes as Thackeray's "magazine style", bears a resemblance to a *Punch* article of December, 1841, "Literary Recipes", which tells its readers how to "cook up" a fashionable novel, a sentimental novel, and so forth (39)[26]

The mechanistic structure of *Vanity Fair* also works to disengage the reader, emphasizing that the narrator uses specific dramatic events to exemplify his critical theses. *Vanity Fair* does not move of its own accord, "organically", by means of the desires and choices of the characters, but mechanically, as the narrator uses his shifting positions to point out parallels and lessons. John Lester's seminal essay on *Vanity Fair*'s "redoubling", Edgar Harden's analysis of the parallelism of plot movement, Peter Garrett's analysis of the characters (including the narrative roles) as "registers of experience", and Myron Taube's essay on contrast as a principle of structure in the novel attest to its mechanical construction.[27] The added puppet motif and his designation of himself as Manager of the Performance, the straightforward roles as "judge" who will "love" the good characters and "abuse" the "wicked and heartless" (72), and especially his direct addresses to the reader encourage a sense that an author is somewhere "out there", beyond his tale.

Nonetheless, this critical master-voice is self-conscious, aware of the fragmentary nature of his own telling, and truly protean in his shifting characterizations of himself. Early in the novel, he gives us a parable through which to understand his positionings as narrator and our possible roles as readers. In Chapter 8 the master-voice has disassociated himself from Becky's letters from Queens' Crawley, letters that uneasily mix sharp satire with hypocritical sentiment. He claims to be telling us the "truth as far as one knows it, whether one mounts a cap and bells or a shovel-hat" (72). But the sardonic truth of the jester and homiletic truth of the preacher are immediately questioned when the narrator implies that his "truth" is really the truth of *our* response, *our* belief in his obvious illusion.

> I have heard a brother of the story-telling trade at Naples, preaching to a pack of good for nothing honest lazy fellows by the sea-shore; work himself up into such a rage and passion with some of the villains whose wicked deeds he was describing and inventing, that the

wild wind tore the chimney-pots from the roofs of the old houses, and sent the tiles whirling and crashing through desolate streets. No soul braved that tempest—the watchmen shrank into their boxes whither the searching rain followed them—where the crashing thunderbolt fell and destroyed them—one had so been slain opposite The Foundling—a scorched gaberdine a shivered lantern a staff rent in twain by the flash were all that remained of stout Will Steadfast. A hackney coachman had been blown off his coach box in Southampton Row—and whither? But the whirlwind tells no tidings of its victim save his parting scream as he is borne onwards! Horrible night! it was dark pitch dark—no moon, No, no, no moon—Not a star: Not a little feeble twinkling solitary star. There had been one at early evening but he showed his face shuddering for a moment in the black heaven, and then retreated back.

One two three! It is the signal that Black Vizard had agreed on.

"Mofy! is that your snum?" said a voice from the area. "I'll gully the dag and bimbole the clicky in a snuffkin."*

"Nuffle your clod and beladle your glumbanions,"† said Vizard with a dreadful oath. "This way, men—if they scream, out with your snickers and slick! Look to the pewter room, Blowser—You, Mark, to the old gaff's mopus box—and I," added he in a lower but more horrible voice, "I will look to Amelia!"

There was a dead silence. "Ha!" said Vizard—was that the click of a pistol?"

. . . .

Or suppose we adopted the genteel rose-water style—The Marquis of Osborne has just dispatched his *petit tigre* with a *billet doux* to the Ladye Amelia.

* Captain, is that your voice? I'll light the candle and open the door in a minute.
† Hold your tongue, and stir your stumps.

The dear creature has received it from the hands of her *femme de chambre*, Mademoiselle Anastasie.

Dear Marquis! What amiable politeness! His lordship's note contains the wished for invitation to D— House!

"Who is that monstrous fine girl," said the *Semillant* Prince G—rge of C—mbr—dge at a mansion in Piccadilly the same evening (having just arrived from the omnibus at the opera.) "My dear Sedley, in the name of all the Cupids introduce me to her!"

"Her name, *Monseigneur*," said Lord Joseph bowing gravely, "is Sedley."

"*Vous avez alors un bien beau nom*," said the young Prince turning on his heel rather disappointed and treading on the foot of an old gentleman who stood behind in deep admiration of the beautiful Lady Amelia.

"*Trente mille tonnerres!*" shouted the victim writhing under the *agonie du moment*.

Fig. 2.1. Intratext, Chapter 6, *Vanity Fair*. Photograph courtesy of Elizabeth Huth Coates Library, Trinity University.

audience could not resist it, and they and the poet together would burst out into a roar of oaths and execrations against the fictitious monster of the tale, so that the hat went round and the bajocchi tumbled into it in the midst of a perfect storm of sympathy.

At the little Paris Theatres on the other hand you will not only hear the people yelling out *"Ah gredin, ah monstre!"* and cursing the tyrant of the play from the boxes, but the actors themselves positively refuse to play the wicked parts such as those of *infames Anglais*, brutal Cossacks, and what not, and prefer to appear, at a smaller salary, in their real character as loyal Frenchmen. I set the two stories one against the other, so that you may see that it is not from mere mercenary motives, that the present performer is desirous to show up and trounce his villains – but because he has a sincere hatred of them which he cannot keep down, and which must find a vent in suitable abuse and bad language.

I warn 'my kyind friends' then, that I am going to tell a story of harrowing villainy and complicated but as I trust intensely interesting crime. My rascals are no milk and water rascals I promise you – When we come to the proper places we won't spare fine language – no, no! But when we are going over the quiet country we must perforce be calm. A tempest in a slop basin is absurd. We will reserve that sort of thing for the mighty ocean and the lonely midnight – The present number will be very mild – others – but we will not anticipate *those*.

And, as we bring our characters forward, I will ask leave as a man and a brother not only to introduce them, but occasionally to step down from the platform, and talk about them. If they are good and kindly, to love them and shake them by the hand: if they are silly, to laugh at them confidentially in the reader's sleeve: if they are wicked and heartless, to abuse them in the strongest terms which politeness admits of.

Otherwise you might fancy it was I who was sneering at the practice of devotion, which Miss Sharp finds so ridiculous . . . . (72)

These parables illustrate the seductive power of narrative on both the teller and the audience. The opposed stories are not as clearly contradictory as they first seem. The immersed narrator earns his money honestly as a *story-teller* because his own immersion in his tale creates a similar absorption in his audience. But his story is "false" ("fictitious monster") and yet is truly good as a story. Is he jester or preacher? Neither perspective is clearly demanded because both jester and preacher can become absorbed in their discourse. The narrator switches grounds in the second story and hides the stage manager behind the actors who become absorbed in their acting to the extent that they confuse their roles with their lives. This honesty within dishonesty is similar to the Neapolitan story-teller because while their confusion is genuinely felt, there is no true identity between actor and role. The stage manager proper emerges ("My Kyind friends") to demonstrate his ability to manipulate his characters. In the first two cases, the narrator and the actors lose sight of the fact that they are the creators of the presentation. In the last instance, the narrator is the objective presenter of character.

These three modes – emotionally immersed creator, actor taken in by his role, and manager as conscious manipulator of story and language – appear as narrator, reader, and illustrator roles throughout *Vanity Fair*. The narrator's personal "I" dramatizes the story-teller who becomes so immersed in his tale that he forgets it is a story, while the generalized "I" of the critic puts us in the role of the Manager who evaluates his characters. The "I and my Julia" of chapter 9, who compares Aunt MacWhirter to Miss Crawley, is an absorbed actor-role which by its exaggeration is to be rejected by the reader. In contrast, the wonderful disquisition on "How to Live Well On Nothing a Year" presents a journalist "I", the Manager, who gives us the parable of "Jenkins".[28] We are to agree with this "I" and reject Jenkins. Aunt MacWhirter's nephew ("I and my Julia") is the teller turned actor, moving us to respond by the intensity of his response. His exhortation to the reader, "Is it so or is it not so? I appeal to the middle classes – ah Gracious powers!" makes this narrator a character and a reader (78). This "de te fabula" is visualized as the egoism of self-projection in the pictorial initial to chapter 13. George's mirror is the story's equivalent of the story's own relation to the gigantic "I" superimposing itself upon the mirror. But the "I" of "How to Live Well" is not this solipsistic teller but is "introduced to personify the world in general" and presents a common truth to be judged: "Many a glass of wine have we all of us drunk, I have very little doubt, hob-and-nobbing with the hospitable giver, and wondering how the deuce he paid for it" (322). Narrative statements such as "I remember one night being in the Fair myself . . ." (134) combine irony with immersion. Statements such as, "Becky has often spoken in subsequent years of this season of her life" (452) also suggest direct narrative involvement. To whom has Becky often spoken? Certainly not to Dobbin, so, presumably to our master-narrator. Thus a subtle inside voice connects teller to tale even while narrative poses, parodies, and journalistic digressions create the illusion of the stable voice as consistently outside the tale. This is not the standard distinction between "sentimentalist" (or moralist) and "ironist" (or satirist). Although the ironist is usually disengaged, the "personal" parables we are to take ironically are presented to us as if the narrator were caught up in his story. This distinction is one of perspective: how clearly the narrator sees himself as distinct from the story and thus sees the story as a story.

This critical consciousness keeps us from reading mimetically by reminding us he is writing a novel which can be simultaneously sermon and comedy, and at the same time he denies the story is of his making. The commentary in chapter 19, for example, inspired by Miss Crawley's final illness, uses her illness as a means of alerting readers to the conventionality of their reading.

> Sick-bed homilies and pious reflections are, to be sure, out of place in mere story-books, and we are not going (after the fashion of some novelists of the present day) to cajole the public into a sermon, when it is only a comedy that the reader pays his money to witness. But, without preaching, the truth may surely be borne in mind, that the bustle, and triumph, and laughter, and gaiety which Vanity Fair exhibits in public, do not always pursue the performer into private life . . . . O brother wearers of motley! Are there not moments when one grows sick of grinning and tumbling, and the jingling of cap and bells? This, dear friends and companions, is my amiable object – to walk with you through the Fair, to examine the shops and the shows there; and that we should all come home after the flare, and the noise, and the gaiety, and be perfectly miserable in private. (164)

Does the narrator make the fair through which we walk? Or does the fair exist outside of his consciousness? If the latter, what is the relation between the fair and the narrator's storybook?

Vanity Fair sophisticates Titmarsh's critical method in the narration's realization of the egoism central, necessary, to any public "I" which professes to speak for others. The narrator's assertion that "the world is a looking glass and gives back to every man the reflection of his own face" (*VF* 9) is qualified by Thackeray's description of the glass *he* turned outward as "warped and cracked" (*LPP* 2: 423). He advertised *Vanity Fair* as "brilliantly illuminated by the Author's own candles" (*VF* xiv).

Thus, although Thackeray's "motley fool" in the frontispiece to *Vanity Fair* looks at his own reflection, the external world, represented by the characters and story, is reflected *and* illuminated by the "lamp" of the author's own ego (Fig. 2.2). (This egoistic center is suggested by the crooked reflection of the clown's face.) Thackeray's mirror was "cracked" because he knew his imaging was only one perspective. Not only does a mirror show you an image in reverse, but, as the sketch suggests, the angle at which you hold it will determine what you see.

Thackeray's most literal "mirrors" were his own illustrations that he used to counter and comment on the text, often undercutting his narration. Such tension between the verbal and visual can encourage the reader to read thematically and synthetically, to promote skeptical reading, especially when created by a visual shock. The illustration introducing Lord Steyne in chapter 37 acts against the text so strongly that the reader becomes skeptical if not suspicious of the narrator (*VF* 335-36). In the first edition at the bottom of the recto page, the reader is treated to the glistening description of Becky cunningly arranged as an art work.

> The fire crackled and blazed pleasantly. There was a score of candles sparkling round the mantelpiece, in all sorts of quaint sconces, of gilt and bronze and porcelain. They lighted up Rebecca's figure to admiration, as she sate on a sofa covered with a pattern of gaudy flowers. She was in a pink dress, that looked as fresh as a rose; her dazzling white arms and shoulders were half covered with a thin hazy scarf through which they sparkled; her hair hung in curls round her neck; one of her little feet peeped out from[ ] (335)

The reader turns the page to finish the description – "the fresh crisp folds of the silk: the prettiest little foot in the prettiest little sandal in the finest silk stocking in the world" (336) – and to see what Becky is seeing: the leering, loutish Lord Steyne who has been introduced previously as her audience: "The great Lord of Steyne was standing by the fire sipping coffee" (Fig. 2.3). This illustration disrupts the narrator's tone by forcing readers to revise their perception. First, the shock at Steyne's appearance contrasts his brutal face with the "dainty" language of the picture of Becky. His visual reality reveals the "disguise" of Becky's art – a disguise that now seems obvious in the language itself. The overuse of diminutives and superlatives ("little feet", "prettiest little foot", "prettiest little sandal", "in the world"), the hackneyed simile "fresh as a rose", the slip in taste

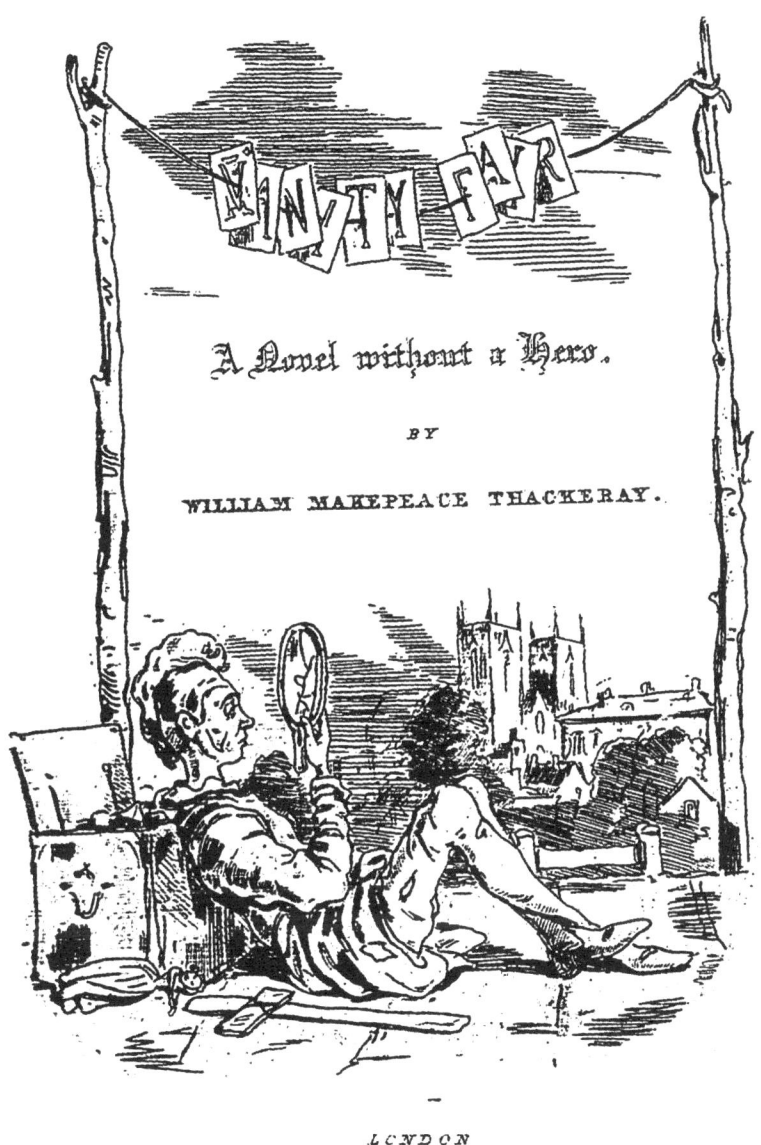

Fig. 2.2. Frontispiece, *Vanity Fair*, 1848. Photograph courtesy of Elizabeth Huth Coates Library, Trinity University.

suggested by the "gaudy" flowers on the sofa argue that the narrator intends for us to question the sincerity of this picture.

The juxtaposition of illustration and text encourages us to question the entire value of Becky's picture-making. If this is her preferred audience, what are her artistic intentions? Both Becky and Steyne are morally discredited by this juxtaposition: Becky by preening for a man like the one who is illustrated and Steyne by the nature revealed in the picture. In fact, Thackeray's use of the word "great" to describe Lord Steyne suddenly recalls Fielding's disassociation of "great" from "good" to describe Jonathan Wild – a definition Thackeray had used in "Caricatures and Lithography in Paris".[29] The instinctive revulsion readers feel against Steyne makes them reassess Becky's efforts and their own engagement in the process. Thackeray's illustration allows his readers to recognize how they, too, can be drawn in by Becky's art. A thinking reader is thus put on guard against Becky's machinations while being made aware of their potency.[30]

The narrator's own complicated attitudes toward Becky (and Amelia and Dobbin) develop within patterns of tacit comment between image and text that gradually provide the reader with a consistent counterpoint to the text by itself. In chapter 25 of *Vanity Fair*, Becky, Rawdon, George, and Amelia are at Brighton, and Becky and Rawdon are in the process of fleecing George (211-13). The intratext shows us George and Rawdon at cards with Becky standing at George's shoulder, gazing down with a sly smile (212) (Fig. 2.4). This simple illustration reverberates intriguingly with the text. On the previous page, the narrator has given us another suspect word-picture of Becky: "She was looking over her shoulder in the glass. She had put on the neatest and freshest white frock imaginable, and with bare shoulders and a little necklace, and a light blue sash, she looked the image of youthful innocence and girlish happiness" (*VF* 211). This Becky is depicted in the full-page illustration, "A Family Party at Brighton", opposite the intratext. Both text and illustration present a specific scene in which Becky's innocence is undercut by her knowing expression. The intratext, however, is a generalized representation of Becky watching "kindly" over George while he plays ecarté. This "kind" look is actually one of sly calculation. The text hints at its own disagreement with its illustrations when the narrator describes Becky as "fixing on a killing bow". Her "kindly" look is actually a "killing glance", as her bow is both hair ornament and weapon – also suggested by her too; he's shearing a Southdown. What an innocent mutton, hey? Damme, what a snowy fleece!"

Rebecca's eyes shot out gleams of scornful humour. "My lord," she said, "you are a knight of the Order. He had the collar round his neck, indeed—a gift of the restored Princes of Spain.

Lord Steyne in early life had been notorious for his daring and his success at play. He had sat up two days and two nights with Mr. Fox at hazard. He had won money of the most august personages of the realm: he had won his marquisate. It was said, at the gaming-table; but he did not like an allusion to those by-gone *freddaines*. Rebecca saw the scowl gathering over his heavy brow.

She rose up from her sofa, and went and took his coffee cup out of his hand, with a little curtsey. "Yes," she said, "I must get a watch-dog. But he won't bark at *you*." And, going into the other drawing-room, she sate down to the piano, and began to sing little French songs in such a charming, thrilling voice, that the mollified nobleman speedily followed her into that chamber, and might be seen nodding his head and bowing time over her.

Rawdon and his friend meanwhile played *écarté* until they had enough. The Colonel won; but, say that he won ever so much and often, nights like these, which occurred many times in the week—his wife having all the talk and all the admiration, and he sitting silent without the circle, not comprehending a word of the jokes, the allusions, the mystical language within—must have been rather wearisome to the ex-dragoon.

"How is Mrs. Crawley's husband," Lord Steyne used to say to him by way of a good day when they met: and indeed that was now his avocation in life. He was Colonel Crawley no more. He was Mrs. Crawley's husband.

About the little Rawdon, if nothing has been said all this while, it is because he is hidden up-stairs in a garret somewhere, or has crawled below into the kitchen for companionship. His mother scarcely ever took notice of him. He passed the days with his French *bonne* as long as that domestic remained in Mr. Crawley's family, and when the Frenchwoman went away, the little fellow, howling in the loneliness of the night, had compassion taken on him by a housemaid, who took him out of his solitary nursery into her bed in the garret hard by, and comforted him.

Rebecca, my Lord Steyne, and one or two more were in the drawing-room taking tea after the Opera, when this shouting was heard overhead. "It's my cherub crying for his nurse," she said. She did not offer to move to go and see the child. "Don't agitate your feelings by going to look for him," said Lord Steyne sardonically. "Bah!" replied the other, with a sort of blush, "he'll cry himself to sleep;" and they fell to talking about the Opera.

Rawdon had stolen off though, to look after his son and heir; and came back to the company when he found that honest Dolly was consoling the child. The Colonel's dressing-room was in those upper regions. He used to see the boy there in private. They had interviews together every morning when he shaved; Rawdon minor sitting on a box by his father's side and watching the operation with never ceasing pleasure. He and the sire were

looked as fresh as a rose; her dazzling white arms and shoulders were half covered with a thin hazy scarf through which they sparkled; her hair hung in curls round her neck; one of her little feet peeped out from the fresh crisp folds of the silk; the prettiest little foot in the prettiest little sandal in the finest silk stocking in the world.

The candles lighted up Lord Steyne's shining bald head, which was fringed with red hair. He had thick bushy eyebrows, with little twinkling bloodshot eyes, surrounded by a thousand wrinkles. His jaw was under-hung, and when he laughed, two white buck-teeth protruded themselves and glistened savagely in the midst of the grin. He had been dining with royal personages, and wore his garter and ribbon. A short man was his Lordship, broad-chested, and bow-legged, but proud of the fineness of his foot and ankle, and always caressing his garter-knee.

"And so the Shepherd is not enough," said he, "to defend his lambkin?" "The Shepherd is too fond of playing at cards and going to his clubs," answered Becky, laughing.

"Gad, what a debauched Corydon!" said my lord—"what a mouth for a pipe!"

"I take your three to two," here said Rawdon, at the card-table.

"Hark at Meliboeus," snarled the noble Marquis; "he's pastorally occupied

Fig. 2.3. Intratext, Chapter 37, *Vanity Fair*. Photograph courtesy of Elizabeth Huth Coates Library, Trinity University.

pretty little wife.

"I suppose she'll cry her eyes out," Becky answered. "She has been whimpering half-a-dozen of times at the very notion of it, already to me."

"*You* don't care, I suppose," Rawdon said, half angry at his wife's want of feeling.

"You wretch! don't you know that I intend to go with you," Becky replied. "Besides, you're different. You go as General Tufto's aide-de-camp. *We* don't belong to the line," Mrs. Crawley said, throwing up her head with an air that so enchanted her husband that he stooped down and kissed it.

"Rawdon, dear—don't you think—you'd better get that—money from Cupid, before he goes?" Becky continued, fixing on a killing bow. She called George Osborne, Cupid. She had flattered him about his good looks a score of times already. She watched over him kindly at écarté of a night when he would drop in to Rawdon's quarters for a half-hour before bedtime.

She had often called him a horrid dissipated wretch, and threatened to tell Emmy of his wicked ways and naughty extravagant habits. She brought his cigar and lighted it for him; she knew the effect of that manœuvre, having practised it in former days upon Rawdon Crawley. He thought her

Fig. 2.4. Intratext, Chapter 25, *Vanity Fair*. Photograph courtesy of Elizabeth Huth Coates Library, Trinity University.

calling George "Cupid". Becky is "betrayed" by the illustration that shows the reader a Becky hidden from the descriptions in the text.

Becky is consistently betrayed by Thackeray's depictions of her. In a brilliant touch of irony, Becky the expert actress (or mimic) is visually "shown up" by Thackeray's pen which transfers interpretive awareness to the reader even in the absence of overt irony in the text. The play between text and illustration warn the readers about the dangers of self-deception, "the dangers of creating from half-sight a self-flattering version of the world",[31] by constantly threatening to lure the reader into that very danger. As Jerry Williamson observed, the result is a reader who is trained to "distrust *all* surface appearances" (134).

The illustrations betray Becky both on the level of simple representation and in dramatic action. The end of the first number of *Vanity Fair*, chapter four, concludes with the illustration "Mr. Joseph Entangled". The pun appears in the text as "and before he had time to ask how, Mr. Joseph Sedley, of the East India Company's service was actually seated tête-à-tête with a young lady looking at her with a most killing expression: his arms stretched out before her in an imploring attitude, and his hands bound in a web of green silk, which she was unwinding" (32). The illustration ironizes the pun for the reader by the symbolic expressions of the characters. Borrowing from theatrical tradition, Becky's face resembles no. 32 in Henry Siddons *Practical Illustrations of Rhetorical Gesture and Action* (1822), "False gesture" (Fig. 2.5). Her slyness contrasts with Amelia's open, innocent face. But Jos is also typed by the fatuous complacency of his expression and posture that, by exposing his vanity, lessens our sympathy for him as victim of Becky's seduction. The illustration thus authenticates the satiric stance of the narrator. We see the Becky the satirist has been describing and consequently reject the judgment of the other characters who are taken in by her duplicity.

As *Vanity Fair* develops, however, the consistency of Becky's representation does not always accord with the text. Her face is drawn throughout the novel as either "False Gesture" or no. 29 in Siddons, "Menace" (Fig. 2.6). The uniformity of her expression in the drawings provides an independent piece of information for the readers, telling them not to be deluded by their own sympathy or to accept the narrator's many justifications of her actions, e.g., "that if she did not get a husband for herself, there was no one else in the wide world who would take the trouble off her hands" (*VF* 17). We see her first leaving school with this wicked smile and next in this scene at Sedley's. In the meantime the narrator has asked us to accept her as a "picture of youth, unprotected innocence, and humble virgin simplicity" (19). The term "picture" becomes suspect in light of the actual pictures. Obviously something is askew because the only Becky the reader sees is the conniving Becky as in chapters 7, 17, 36, 67. The consistency of Becky's representation would have reminded the reader in each monthly part of the character's "real" nature, but it would also have alerted Thackeray's readers to read passages as pieces of narrative irony that otherwise might not seem ironic. Becky's consistent, value-laden image allows readers to supply their own ironic rejections to other passages without explicit textual direction. Such ironic reading is only encouraged because so many characters (Miss Briggs, Lady Jane, Sir Pitt, Rawdon) are taken in by a face which readers are not allowed to *see* as either honest or attractive. This consistent representation suggests that to a discerning eye, Becky's nature cannot be disguised. In the intratext at the end of chapter 45 (408), while the text concentrates on Sir Pitt's fatuity, the illustration shows us Becky with an almost evil expression, her siren-mode indicated by her loose hair. The reader sees that vanity has made Sir Pitt almost literally blind. He cannot see the Becky we see although the composition emphasizes her "killing glance".

Becky is further betrayed when the illustrations present information she neglects. Just as Sir Pitt is blinded by his own lack of self-perception, Becky cannot see perspectives other than her own self-flattering one. Her two letters to Amelia in chapters 8 and 9 are undercut by the illustrations. Becky describes going into dinner when she first arrives at Queen's Crawley (69), but her letter obviously omits her scowling face and her scolding of the pupils she had met only a half an hour before (Fig. 2.7). The reader gets this missing information but Amelia does not; thus we are early alerted to Becky's selective perception. While Becky deliberately omits these details from her letter, her ignorance of Mrs. Bute's plot is just that – ignorance fostered by her own vanity. Noted also by Joan Stevens, the intratext shows Becky dancing with Rawdon while Mrs. Bute plays the piano (Fig. 2.8).[32] Becky's letter reports this as her triumph, while Mrs. Bute's face marks it clearly as *her* scheme. Thackeray emphasizes the irony by having Becky include her own drawings of her rivals. She has an acute eye, but no peripheral vision, so to speak.

The resulting irony of these shifts in proximity and attitude train us

Fig. 2.5. "False Gesture", M. Engels in Henry Siddons *Illustrations of Practical Rhetorical Gesture*. Photograph courtesy of Elizabeth Huth Coates Library, Trinity University.

Fig. 2.6. "Menace", M. Engels, in Henry Siddons, *Illustrations of Practical Rhetorical Gesture*. Photograph courtesy of Elizabeth Huth Coates Library, Trinity University.

to read consistently between the lines. As Garrett notes, "every comment or interpretation which the narrator introduces can exert only conditional authority. His formulations raise but cannot resolve the novel's issues; they must be tested against the implications of the novel as a whole" (109). Garrett's comment reflects the ordinary reader's impulse: we *want* there to be a "whole". Thus the process of reconciling narrative attitudes with visual images encourages the reader to infer a stable perception underlying image and text. Our interpretive struggles, thus, create a Voice that we never actually hear.

This silent Voice combined with the metaphoric commentary lodged in the pictorial initials suggests an "objective realism" underlying the rigorous satire and thus a perspective independent of the world it reveals. The very openness with which the narrator and illustrator choose scenes for contrast and comment suggests that the fictional world extends beyond the frame of the narrative "painting". The metaphoric pattern of comment in the pictorial initials, discussed by Robert Colby, J. R. Harvey, Joan Stevens, and Patricia Sweeney, among others, reinforces this sense of extension to the point of allowing our understanding to become the extra-textual interpreters. The Napoleon motif characterizing Becky, the recurring motif of church and home both align with and mock the narrative voice.[33] But the critical distance induced by such image-text play collides with the narrator's own experience of the story, most notably in chapter 62 when "on this very tour . . . I, the present writer of a history of which every word is true, had the pleasure to see them first, and to make their acquaintance" (563). On the surface, the eye-witness account is a traditional authenticating device, designed to make the story what Elizabeth Segal calls "an account of an actual happening" (50). The narrator did not invent the tale, no, he got it from Major Dobbin. Claims for first-hand knowledge and Ann Wilkinson's "Tomeavsian" way of knowing the world where truth of event "recedes behind Rumor" tend to collapse teller into tale.[34]

Corresponding to this involved narrator, is the "eye of sympathy" which visualizes a character's perspective to invite the reader to suddenly understand of a character's emotional state. Harvey, notes, for instance, that in chapter 21 of *Vanity Fair*, when Miss Swartz reappears as a possible match for George, Thackeray's intratextual illustration makes us see just as George does: "The drawing is not so assertive that the reader takes much notice of it before he comes to it in the text; but at the moment he does, he sees through George Osborne's eyes, and the imaginary world of the again to read a great pamphlet with which he was busy.

"'I hope you will be kind to my girls,' said Lady Crawley—with her pink eyes always full of tears.

"'Law Ma, of course she will,' said the eldest: and I saw at a glance that I need not be afraid of *that* woman.

"'My lady is served,' says the Butler in black and an immense white shirt-frill that looked as if it had been one of the Queen Elizabeth ruffs depicted in the hall; and so taking Mr. Crawley's arm she led the way to the dining room, whither I followed with my little pupils in each hand.

"Sir Pitt was already in the room with a silver jug. He had just been to the cellar: and was in full dress too, that is he had taken his gaiters off, and showed his little dumpy legs in black worsted stockings. The side-board was covered with glistening old plate—old cups both gold and silver, old salvers and cruet stands like Rundell and Bridge's Shop. Every thing on the table was in silver too, and two footmen with red hair and canary coloured liveries stood on either side of the side-board.

"Mr. Crawley said a long grace, and Sir Pitt said amen—and the great silver dish-covers were removed.

"'What have we for dinner, Betsy,' said the Baronet.

"'Mutton broth I believe, Sir Pitt,' answered Lady Crawley.

"'*Mouton aux navets*,' added the Butler gravely (pronounce if you

Fig. 2.7. Intratext, Chapter 8, *Vanity Fair*. Photograph courtesy of Elizabeth Huth Coates Library, Trinity University.

ily (she is a little black-faced old woman in a turban, rather crooked, and with very twinkling eyes)—and after the Captain and your poor little Rebecca had performed a dance together, do you know she actually did me

the honour to compliment me upon my steps! Such a thing was never heard of before—the proud Mrs. Bute Crawley, first cousin to the Earl of Tiptoff, who won't condescend to visit Lady Crawley except when her sister is in the County—Poor Lady Crawley! during most part of these gaieties she is upstairs taking pills.

"Mrs. Bute has all of a sudden taken a great fancy to me. 'My dear Miss Sharp,' she says, 'why not bring over your girls to the Rectory?—their cousins will be so happy to see them'—I know what she means. Signor Clementi did not teach us the piano for nothing—at which price Mrs. Bute hopes to get a professor for her children. I can see through her schemes, as though she told them to me: but I shall go, as I am determined to make myself agreeable—is it not a poor governess's duty who has not a friend or protector in the world. The Rector's wife paid me a score of compliments about the progress my pupils made, and thought no doubt to touch my heart—poor, simple, country soul—as if I cared a fig about my pupils!

"Your India muslin and your pink silk, dearest Amelia, are said to become me very well—They are a good deal worn now, you know we poor girls can't afford des fraiches toilettes. Happy, happy you, who have but to drive to St. James's Street and a dear mother who will give you anything you ask. Farewell, dearest girl.

"Your affectionate
"REBECCA.

"P.S. I wish you could have seen the faces of the Miss Blackbrooks (Admiral Blackbrook's daughters, my dear); fine young ladies, with dresses from London, when Captain Rawdon selected poor me for a partner!"

"Here they are. 'Tis the very image of them. Adieu, adieu!"

When Mrs. Bute Crawley (whose artifices our ingenious Rebecca had so soon discovered) had procured from Miss Sharp the promise of a visit, she induced the all-powerful Miss Crawley to make the necessary application to Sir Pitt; and the good-natured old lady who loved to be gay herself, as to see every one gay and happy round about her, was quite charmed and ready to establish a reconciliation and intimacy between her two brothers. It was therefore agreed that the young people of both families should visit

Fig. 2.8. Intratext, Chapter 11, *Vanity Fair*. Photograph courtesy of Elizabeth Huth Coates Library, Trinity University.

novel becomes visually precise in a moment of surprise, sudden movement and spontaneous response" (Harvey 93). The illustration breaks into a line of dialogue to evoke this spontaneity. Moreover, the line of text directly following the vignette – "is it *my* Amelia? Amelia that was at Miss P.'s at Hammersmith? I know it is. It's her, and – Tell me about her – where is she?" – conjures up an image of Amelia in contrast to Miss Swartz, creating sympathy for George's predicament as well as for Miss Swartz's good-natured but comic airs (182).

An intratextual illustration earlier in the novel works even more strongly to create sympathy for Amelia by allowing us to see what she sees when she visits George's house, before her father's bankruptcy . In chapter 12, we see the two Miss Osbornes and Miss Wirt. The text gives us their point of view: "And this day she [Amelia] was so perfectly stupid and awkward that the Miss Osbornes and their governess, who stared after her as she went sadly away wondered more than ever what George could see in poor little Amelia" (100). The reader, however, sees the unsympathetic, harsh faces that Amelia sees, automatically agreeing with the narrator's comment under the illustration, "Of course they did. How was she to bare that timid little heart for the inspection of those young ladies with their bold black eyes?" The illustration is, in fact, more hostile than the narrator; the "realistic" drawing showing just how unyielding Amelia finds the Osbornes. In chapter 24 both narration and illustration place us in the perspective of a specific character. The text reads, "Seeing young Stubble engaged in composition at one of the coffee-room" – and then we see Stubble just as Dobbin sees him (207). Stubble becomes suddenly less ridiculous, and the Major's sympathy is our own. In addition, this unexpected illustration of a minor character shifts our perspective from the main story to a peripheral theme, reminding us that the story of Dobbin and Amelia is not the *only* story possible. Even Becky is softened by the eye of sympathy. When we see Lady Southdown as Lady Macbeth in her nightcap in chapter 41 (373), we see Lady Southdown as Becky sees her and she *is* ridiculous. How could a mimic like Becky *not* satirize her? This ocular evidence softens Becky's later parody of her. The "eye of sympathy" evokes empathy that modifies our reading of the text by giving us a sudden understanding of how a character sees,

The poses of critical observer and immersed participant contradict each other. Each narrative pose becomes an obvious fabrication when it is contradicted by another narrative pose. The narrator as well as the illustrator become part of their own machine. How could the narrator have gotten the story from Dobbin when 15 chapters earlier "little Tom Eaves who knows everything" has told the narrator the history of the Steynes? Both claims are contradicted by the master-voice in chapter 15 who declares:

> If, a few pages back, the present writer claimed the privilege of peeping into Miss Amelia Sedley's bed-room, and understanding with the omniscience of the novelist all the gentle pains and passions which were tossing upon that innocent pillow, why should he not declare himself to be Rebecca's confidante too, master of her secrets, and seal-keeper of that young woman's conscience? (134)

Here the composition seems spontaneous, determined not by irrevocable past events but by immediate narrative desire. The stable master-voice is undermined by the voice's changing proximity to his tale while the reliable pattern of irony, contrast, and critical interjection keep implying a stable persona behind the various rhetorical stances. The narration becomes unreliable not in what it is telling but in the narrator's relation to his story and representation of himself.

The story in *Vanity Fair* mirrors this multi-vocal narration of skeptical egoism. The actual male protagonist in *Vanity Fair* materializes as three "splits" of a single figure, each acting out patterns based on specific qualities that contextualize each other.[35] George, the dandy, is egoist as commodity, the best dandy money can make. The "dandy" is the protagonist's first attempt to establish a public self. Thackeray's dandy is not a Beau Brummel dandy, who was conspicuous for his *lack* of visual display. Miles Lambert points out that Pendennis, George Osborne, and Clive Newcome are early Victorian dandies, modeled after real-life dandies such as Edward Bulwer-Lytton, Alfred D'Orsay, and Benjamin Disraeli. These dandies created themselves as elaborate art works, with colorful waistcoats and jackets, elaborate neckcloths and coiffures, and expensive toiletries.[36] They were determinedly exhibitionist and *individualistic* (Lambert 62). The dandy's transformation of himself into a decorative surface matches his infatuation with the siren. But at the same time, this manifestation freezes the protagonist, paralyzing him into his surface. George sees himself as a picture and has little understanding for any emotional connection. Love is a game, a pleasure for which one gambles

(106). He is the creation of his father (112) and thus has no insight into the sympathy engendered by the female:

> He was not, it must be confessed, very much cast down by good old Mr. Sedley's catastrophe. He tried his new uniform, which became him very handsomely, on the day when the first meeting of the creditors of the unfortunate gentleman took place. His father told him of the wicked, rascally, shameful conduct of the bankrupt, reminded him of what he had said about Amelia, and that their connexion was broken off for ever; and gave him that evening a good sum of money to pay for the new clothes and epaulets in which he looked so well. (*VF* 157-58)

George's interest in ornament illustrates the feminization at the heart of dandyism. By the 1830s, "gentlemen" were adopting a more sober dress; women decorated themselves as evidence of their husband's or family's wealth. Ellen Moers points out that Alfred D'Orsay either "enchanted or offended" by his "daring blend of the masculine and the feminine graces".[37] Like a woman, George is "created" by his father who pays for his display as a gentleman, usurping the female role of ornamental object. George's weakness for spending and self-display manifests a female form of economic behavior. His pride in his surface is a female quality, while his overweening sense of power is that of a master over a slave girl.

> ... old Mrs. Sedley, too greatly relieved, thought it was best to leave the young persons to themselves; and so quitted Emmy crying over George's hand, and kissing it humbly, as if it were her supreme chief and master, and as if she were quite a guilty and unworthy person needing every favour and grace from him.
>
> This prostration and sweet unrepining obedience exquisitely touched and flattered George Osborne. He saw a slave before him in that simple yielding faithful creature, and his soul within him thrilled secretly somehow at the knowledge of his power. He would be generous-minded, Sultan as he was, and raise up this kneeling Esther and make a queen of her. (*VF* 170-71)

Amelia is not decorative enough to reflect George's female/male vanity, however, and within a week of their marriage, he is falling under Becky's spell. While Rawdon wins money from him at cards, Becky "flattered him about his good looks a score of times .... She watched over him kindly at ecarté of a night . . . . She brought his cigar and lighted it for him; she knew the effect of that manoevre, having practised it in former days upon Rawdon Crawley. He thought her gay, brisk, arch, distinguée, delightful" (*VF* 212-13). Like the actual historical dandies, George is incapable of a genuine human connection. "The epitome of selfish irresponsibility, he [the dandy] was ideally free of all human commitments that conflict with taste: passions, moralities, ambitions, politics, or occupations" (Moers 13).

While George's life as a surface is the youthful narcissistic projection of the self upon the world, Dobbin's existence as only inner virtue embodies the mature feminized protagonist. His outer clumsiness, the ease with which others forget or discount his presence, and his homeliness all emphasize his metaphoric invisibility. He is invisible (as at Vauxhall) just as "real" ladies such as Helen and Laura are, but he *acts* the part of knight errant from the time he saves George from a beating at school (starting up, significantly, from reading the *Arabian Nights*) to forcing George to marry Amelia. He becomes a comfort and role model for his fellow soldiers by his integrity and bravery in battle, and rescues Amelia from the dragon of poverty (again, by forcing someone else – Jos – to take the responsibility he cannot). His clear perception directly contrasts with George's blinders of vanity. Dobbin always sees the serpent's tail beneath Becky's dress. At the opera in Brussels, Becky puts on one of her early performances as a fine lady, and, not quite mistress of the refinements, overdoes it. "She bustled, she chattered, she turned and twisted, and smiled upon one, and smirked on another, all in full view of the jealous opera-glass opposite" (*VF* 250). Dobbin reacts in disgust while George is "charmed" by the serpent:

> "What a humbug that woman is," honest old Dobbin mumbled to George, when he came back from Rebecca's box, whither he had conducted her in perfect silence, and with a countenance as glum as an undertaker's. "She writhes and twists about like a snake. All the time she was here, didn't you see, George, how she was acting at the General over the way?"
> "Humbug – acting? Hang it, she's the nicest little woman in England," George replied, showing his white teeth, and giving his ambrosial whiskers a twirl [the image of a melodrama villain]. "You ain't a man of the world, Dobbin," (*VF* 250)

Dobbin's lack of vanity gives him no surface upon which Becky's glance can play: "He never had had the slightest liking for her, but, on the contrary, had heartily mistrusted her from the very first moment when her green eyes had looked at, and turned away from, his own" (*VF* 595). But this clarity accompanies his dog-like attachment to an unworthy object. His fidelity is worthy of Lancelot, but his ideal is flawed. His "lady" is an overly romantic, self-deceptive woman who manipulates and abuses a love worthy of Redcrosse. Amelia's idolatry, clinging to the false image she has made of George, keeps her as a child – and as such Dobbin is willing to accept her (*VF* 538). He debases himself by worshipping an ideal that he knows is not worth the depth of his worship. Of course he does finally leave her, saying, "'I knew all along that the prize I had set my life on was not worth the winning; that I was a fool, with fond fancies, too, bartering away my all of truth and ardour against your little feeble remnant of love" (*VF* 608). Yet he comes back, and is the first in the long series of Thackeray's protagonists to settle for less than his desire. Thackeray describes Dobbin's success in purely literary terms: "Here it is – the summit, the end – the last page of the third volume . . . . Grow green again, tender little parasite, round the rugged old oak to which you cling" (*VF* 621). This language forces us to see that Dobbin's tarnished success is really the result of our own desire for a sentimental closure. His story is unsatisfactory if we read it either as romance or as realism. We are warned away from treating this text as Dobbin has imagined Amelia and Amelia has refashioned George.

In George and Dobbin, Thackeray gives us two ideas of the feminized male: the male coquette, absorbed in his surface, and the invisible, intuitive, pure womanly male. Rawdon represents the male aspect of the romance hero, the sexual desire that is awakened by the sexuality of Thackeray's aestheticized sirens. He is "a very large young dandy", says Becky (*VF* 89), whose exploits are quintessentially male: shooting, riding, swearing, fighting, drinking, betting, and hunting. He is inarticulate and extremely generous with his money and his love. His love for Becky is as generous and unthinking as the rest of his nature (*VF* 136). But his "brutish" character, which he owes to his masculine upbringing and environment, keeps him from being able to develop the clear-sightedness required to realize his delusion. Even Rawdon is gradually feminized, however, first by his love for Becky and then by his love for his son. He takes over the duties of the mother while he loses a public [male] identity. As he dwindles into "Mrs. Crawley's husband", (*VF* 337) he grows into a passionate father. Signs of his feminization are his growing attachment to Lady Jane, his sadness at Rawdy's departure for school, and finally, his replacement of Briggs as Becky's companion. Meanwhile Becky develops a very masculine indifference to his person and his moods:

> Becky burst out laughing once or twice, when the Colonel, in his clumsy, incoherent way, tried to express his sentimental sorrows at the boy's departure . . . . . He . . . would go and sit for long hours with his good-natured sister Lady Jane, and talk to her about the virtues, and good looks, and hundred good qualities of the child.
>
> . . . . It estranged Rawdon from his wife more than he knew or acknowledged to himself. She did not care for the estrangement. Indeed, she did not miss him or anybody. She looked upon him as her errand-man and humble slave. He might be ever so depressed or sulky, and she did not mark his demeanour, or only treated it with a sneer. She was busy thinking about her position or her pleasures or her advancement in society; she ought to have held a great place in it, that is certain. (465-66)

Ironically, Rawdon's union with the siren brings him that which "saves" him emotionally, even though it costs him his life. While his love for Rawdy develops the inner virtues essential to maturity, his equally sincere love for the serpent-woman allows her to drain him of the masculine will and strength which would allow him to survive his crisis. He leaves London for Coventry Island, "broken and sad" (*VF* 500), anticipating, perhaps even wishing for his death. In fact, Rawdon's end parodies the archetypal descent of the fallen woman: exile and death are the fruits of a sexual fall beyond the control of the victim.

The narrator's vacillating sympathy for his characters would seem to conflict with such sure control of the story as evidenced by the character patterns, commentary, and parody. Yet the rhetorical intents are the same. The narrator moves us in and out from event to significance, from his involvement in his story to an awareness of the artifice of all story-making, from Amelia's appeal to her silly selfishness or from Becky's "unfailing good humor" to her heartlessness. These movements from focus to distance, from isolated percept to perceptual patterns, paradoxically teach us a stable method of seeing, in a procedure that always forces us to look again. Thus, the narrator's conclusion, "Which of us is happy in the world? Which of us has his desire? or, having it, is satisfied?" (*VF* 624) follows logically from *Vanity Fair*'s phenomenological method that incorporates ambiguity and dissatisfaction into the readers' reading because nothing can be seen *definitively*. The critical ethos that enacts this system by assuming different voices and stances also assures us that final moral judgment is not possible precisely because we, on the outside, can see so variously. Only by shifting our own stances can we intuit what constitutes the truth of the story. And this truth has little to do with the story's events. The famous question of Becky's guilt is the most obvious example. What matters is our questioning of the event, our active reading, not whether Becky committed adultery.

Such openness has traditionally been called Thackeray's "ambiguity" (e.g. Peters 86; McMaster 8-9) that pushes the reader into "active participation in the moral chaos of [the] fictional world" (Wilkinson 387). However, *Vanity Fair* is not so much ambiguous or chaotic as it is dynamic; the narrative shifts push the readers into a consciousness of their own interpretive acts. Jerry Williamson argues in "Thackeray's Mirror" that a major effect of *Vanity Fair* is to educate the reader into "the peculiar fallibility of our expectations and perceptions"(134). Bakhtin's claims that "every literary work *faces outward away from itself*, toward the listener-reader, and to a certain extent thus anticipates possible reactions to itself"[38] describes the "ironist's" mirror that readers of *Vanity Fair* learn to turn on their world. However, the Fool preaching to other Fools on the title page of *Vanity Fair* does not suggest this sort of ironic control (Fig. 2.9). Donald Hannah describes him as "both puppet-master and one of his own puppets, pulled by the same strings, actuated by the same motives which animate his own figures" (126). But Joan Stevens has noted that the puppet motif was an afterthought in *Vanity Fair*, inserted as a frame after the novel was written. Without this frame, the Fool seems more puppet than master, especially when compared to a possible model for this engraving. A scene from the 1844 Pantomime, *Harlequin Crotchet* shows a clown lecturing "on soap suds" (Fig. 2.10). While not standing on a barrel, the Clown is elevated above the crowd and is on a washtub. The composition of the two engravings is similar. In general, the clown illustrations in *Vanity Fair* ridicule the assumption of any kind of narrative certainty. The clown balancing on the "W" in chapter 27, the clown leading the parade of clowns in chapter 40, and the clown on stilts being rocked by another clown in chapter 49 suggest both the narrative games of shifting perspectives and the partial knowledge that accompanies any single perspective. The initial to chapter 49 where the clown wears a Napoleonic hat links the narrator both to Napoleon and Becky, who failed because they tried to shape too much of the world in their image. This link is made explicit in the initial to chapter 18 where Harlequin meets Napoleon. More certain of authorial control is the initial to chapter 20, showing a boy and girl peering into a peep show, which suggests the writer's power to manipulate what the reader sees. The egoism of such control is clearly the focus of the narrative "I" accompanying George's absorption in chapter 13. These illustrations reinforce the narrator's clowning with us, as he changes character, parodies his characters and himself, and forces us to see in multiple perspectives.

Vanity Fair shows us that while subjective perception is an entry into "reality", it is never a definitive entry. When "Thackeray" takes off his mask in the drawing at the end of chapter 9, what voice are we seeing? His melancholic, uncertain gaze reappears metaphorically in the initial to chapter 37, where the clown balances the narrator's "I" on his nose. Or, is the clown balancing his own "I" on his nose? These illustrations in all Thackeray's self-illustrated novels make us aware that the narration is just one more "Tom Eavsian" way of knowing the world. Jones at his club in chapter 1, Rawdon and Dobbin reading letters we have just read in the text, the servants listening to Amelia play the piano (chapter 4), and Briggs and Firkin overhearing Sir Pitt proposing (chapter 15) parody both how the narrator gets much of his information and the way we make our own stories out of the bits and pieces we are given.

Taken as a whole, the multiple visual sociolects, the various patterns of commentary, the interpenetration of mimetic and metaphoric representation, and the self-consciousness of the acts of creation and interpretation engage the reader in multiple ways of seeing which tend to limit the truth-claims of any one perspective. The process of reading and seeing which forces the reader constantly to revise earlier reading and seeing compels readers to be aware of the process of their own consumption of the text, that is, the interpretive strategies they employ to create stable stories. *Vanity Fair* is not an ironic dialogue that invites relativism, however. Moral evaluations are certainly possible, and even demanded. We may not know whether Becky is an adulteress, but we can surely condemn her for lying to Rawdon and leaving him in debtor's prison. Our decisions in such cases become the "moral experience of the novel . . . largely a matter of the reader's decision as to where she wants to place herself among the various

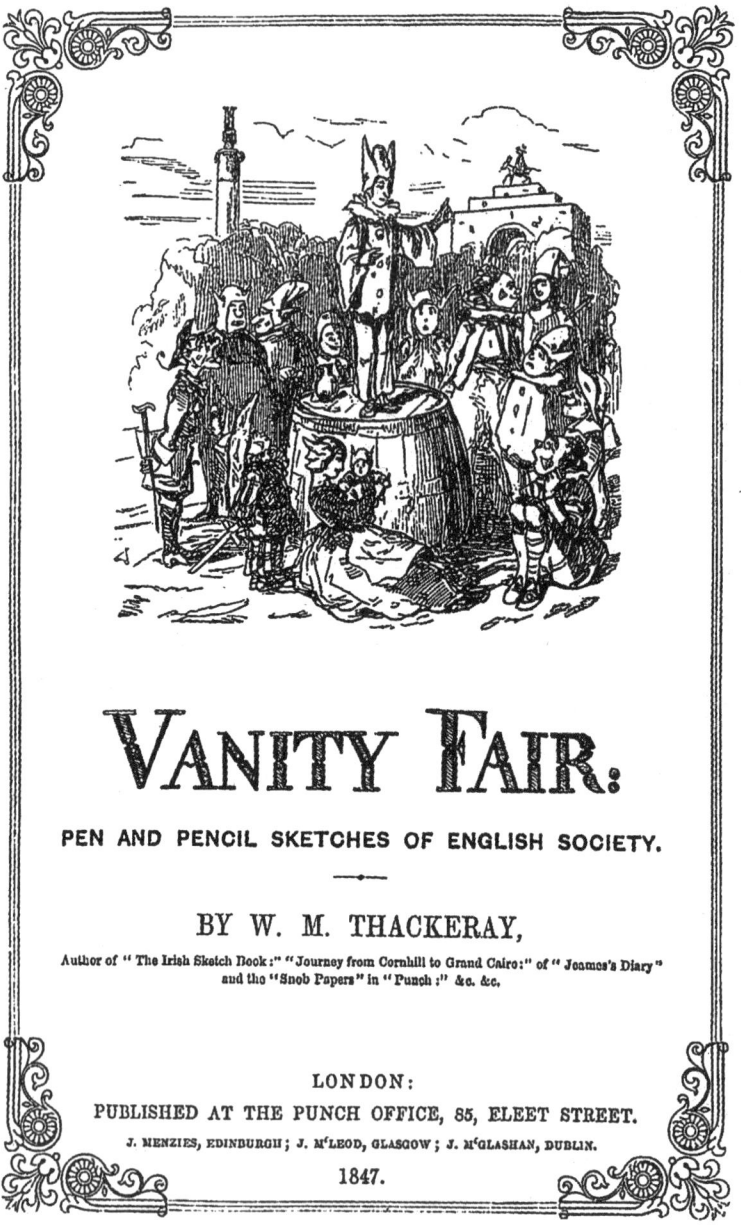

Fig. 2.9. Cover, monthly number, *Vanity Fair*
Photograph courtesy of Elizabeth Huth Coates Library, Trinity University

Fig. 2.10. "A Lecture on Soap Suds", December 1844
Raymond Mander and Joe Mitchenson, *Pantomime*
Photograph courtesy of Elizabeth Huth Coates Library, Trinity University

attitudes dramatized for him in the author's commentary" (McMaster 8-9). But how does a reader learn to negotiate among these narrative positions and move among the narrator's sociolects? Thackeray's next novel, *The History of Pendennis*, mixes the modes of kunstlerroman and bildungsroman to show us how a "man and a brother" grows from a solipsistic quasi-pragmatic reader into a Thackerayean narrator of his own life.

Notes

[1]   William Makepeace Thackeray, "An Essay on the Genius of George Cruikshank", *Westminister Review*, 34 (June 1840); in XXIV, 291.

[2]   In this understanding, Thackeray echoed Schleiermacher who conceived the author "not as a fixed substance", but as "something fluid and dynamic, something mediated, an act rather than a substance. It is the act from which the work originates. This authorial act constitutes itself in the creation of the work" (Mueller-Vollmer 11). Mueller-Vollmer's description is a more strictly hermeneutical way of describing Thackeray's rhetorical "I", the "speaking" I created by and for the specific act of writing.

[3]   William Makepeace Thackeray, "Exhibition Gossip", *Ainsworth's Magazine* 1 (June 1842), 319.

[4]   Edward Bulwer-Lytton, *England and the English*, (1833 rpt. Chicago: U of Chicago P, 1970), 189.

[5]   Peter Gay, *The Naked Heart, The Bourgeois Experience Victoria to Freud*, vol. IV (New York: W.W, Norton, Inc. 1995). Of course, the standard work on Victorian sincerity is Lionel Trilling's *Sincerity and Authenticity* (Cambridge, MA: Harvard UP, 1972).

[6]   Martin Meisel, *Realizations, Narrative, Pictorial, and Theatrical Arts in Nineteenth-Century England* (Princeton: Princeton UP, 1983), 347.

[7]   *The Company We Keep. An Ethics of Fiction* (Berkeley: U of California P, 1988), 166.

[8]   William Makepeace Thackeray, "Picture Gossip", *Fraser's Magazine* 31 (June 1845); in XXV, 446-464.

[9]   For more detailed description of Romantic and early Victorian acting styles see George Taylor, *Players and Performances in the Victorian Theatre* (Manchester: Manchester UP, 1989), especially chapters 1, 3, and 11.

[10]   "Harding", *Sketches After English Landscape Painters* (London: David Bogue, 1850).

[11]   A brief description of the original theory is in Louis Marin, "Poussin's *The Arcadian Shepherds*" in *The Reader in the Text*, ed. Susan R. Suleiman and Inge Crosman (Princeton: Princeton UP, 1980), 309.

[12]   See Michael Fried, *Absorption and Theatricality: Painting and the Beholder in the Age of Diderot* [(Berkeley: U of California P, 1980), 99, 131] for a discussion of the window/tableaux in the eighteenth-century. Tableau presentations, set, frozen scenes of crisis, were rampant on the early Victorian stage and the reciprocity between the pictorial and the dramatic was generally recognized. Jonathon Hill writes, for example, of Cruikshank changing his style of illustration from his usual caricature to a frozen tableau style in his

illustrations to William Harrison Ainsworth's *Jack Sheppard*. He realized that stage productions of the novel could (and did) use his illustrations as the basis for their dramatic tableau – it was free advertising for the novel. "Cruikshank, Ainsworth, and Tableau Illustration", *Victorian Studies* 23 (1980), 429-59.

[13]   William Makepeace Thackeray, "Royal Academy, Third Notice", *Morning Chronicle*, 11 May 1846 in *Contributions to the Morning Chronicle*, ed. Gordon N. Ray (Urbana IL: U of Illinois P, 1966), 150.

[14]   "Exhibition Gossip", *Ainsworth's Magazine* 1 (June 1842), 320.

[15]   "Royal Academy", *Morning Chronicle*, 5 May 1846 in Ray, *Contributions*, 145.

[16]   Karlheinze Stierle, "The Reading of Fictional Texts" in *The Reader in The Text*, 86-87.

[17]   William Makepeace Thackeray, "On Men and Pictures, A Propos of a Walk in the Louvre", *Fraser's Magazine* 24 (July 1841); in XXV, 369.

[18]   See Seymour Chatman, *Story and Discourse* (Ithaca: Cornell UP 1978), chapter 2 for a discussion of plot as the progressive limitation of options.

[19]   William Makepeace Thackeray, "May Gambols, or Titmarsh in the Picture Galleries", *Fraser's Magazine* 29 (June 1844); in XXV, 431-32.

[20]   The Commission on Fine Arts was started by Sir Robert Peel in 1841 to explore "how the Construction of the New Houses of Parliament can be taken advantage of for the encouragement of British Art" (Robertson 325). Their basic intent was to encourage "high art" with nationalistic overtones as the decoration for all rooms in the new Houses of Parliaments. The Commission held competitions offering premiums in the decorative arts, painting in fresco, and sculpture. In 1844, the competition in decorative arts opened at Crockford's Bazaar in St. James. Pseudo-medievalism predominated in household details such as doors, windows, doorknobs, and hat pegs. The Commission eventually abandoned decorative competitions, deciding to leave such details to the architects in charge of the projects. See David Robertson, *Sir Charles Eastlake and the Victorian Art World* (Princeton: Princeton UP, 1978), 327-44.

[21]   William Makepeace Thackeray, "John Leech, *Pictures of Life and Character*", *Quarterly Review* 96 (Dec. 1854), 75-86. The introduction under discussion runs from page 75 to page 81 in, XXV, 480-92.

[22]   An idea of the stringency of the child's life and the depressing possibilities for entertainment are in Ivy Pinchbeck and Martha Hewitt's *Children in English Society*, 2 vols. (Toronto: U of Toronto P, 1969) and Gillian Avery's *Nineteenth-Century Children: Heroes and Heroines in English Children's Stories, 1780-1900* (London: Hodder and Stoughton, 1965). In fact, Thackeray's Regency children had it better than he will admit; the market for children's literature exploded in 1742 with John Newberry. See Joyce Whalley and Tessa

Rose Chester, *A History of Children's Book Illustration* (London: John Murray, 1988).

[23] Simon Houfe, *The Dictionary of British Book Illustrators and Caricaturists 1800-1914* (London: British Library, 1978), 59. Houfe goes on to observe that Leech, like Cruikshank, was one with his audience, a "typical middle-class" Englishman and that his art appealed because it was like himself (60).

[24] Thackeray wrote of Cruikshank, "he has never used his wit dishonestly; he has never in all the exuberance of his frolicsome humour, caused a single painful or guilty blush" (XXIV, 319). The shift from satire to humor is explored at length in Thackeray's lecture, "Charity and Humour". Humour "is wit and love; I am sure, at any rate, that the best humour is that which contains most humanity, that which is flavoured throughout with tenderness and kindness" (XIV, 715).

[25] Juliet McMaster notes that most of Thackeray's early narrative poses are "outsiders" [*Thackeray: The Major Novels* (Toronto: U of Toronto P, 1976), 53]. I connect this, as she does not, to an overriding journalistic pose.

[26] Lewes' comment appeared in *The Athenaeum*, 12 August 1848, 794, and is noted in Robert Colby's "Historical Introduction" to *Vanity Fair*, 636.

[27] John Lester, "Thackeray's Narrative Technique", *PMLA* 69 (1954), 392-409; Edgar Harden, "The Discipline and Significance of Form in *Vanity Fair*", *PMLA* 82 (1967), 530-41. Peter Garrett, *The Victorian Multiplot Novel* (New Haven: Yale UP, 1980), 105, and Myron Taube, "Contrast as a Principle of Structure in *Vanity Fair*", *Nineteenth-Century Fiction* 28 (1963), 119-35.

[28] This chapter has an interesting precedent in *Punch* spoof of 1841 called "Wit without Money, or, How to Live Upon Nothing" by "Vampyre Horseleech, Esq". (38). It has the same emphasis on living on credit and other people's gullibility as Thackeray's presentation.

[29] "Caricatures and Lithography in Paris", IX, 142-165. Thackeray attributes to the satiric character Robert Macaire, a role originated in the play, *Auberge des Adrets* by Frederick Lemaitre, the same kind of "greatness" as Jonathan Wild (151).

[30] Of course, the ensuing conversation about the "moral sheepdog" and "shearing" Lord Southdown affirms the moral judgment of the reader.

[31] Jerry Williamson, "Thackeray's Mirror", *Tennessee Studies in Literature* 22 (1977), 133-53.

[32] Joan Stevens, "Thackeray's 'Vanity Fair", *Review of English Literature* 6 (1965), 33.

[33] Colby, *Thackeray's Canvass of Humanity*; J. R. Harvey, *Victorian Novelists and their Illustrators* (New York: New York: UP, 1971); Joan Stevens, "Thackeray's Pictorial Capitals", *Costerus* n.s. 2 (1974); Patricia Sweeney, "Thackeray's Best Illustrator", *Costerus* n.s. (1974); Catherine Peters,

Thackeray's Universe: Shifting Worlds of Imagination and Reality (Boston: Faber and Faber, 1987); Donald Hannah, "'The Author's Own Candles': The Significance of the Illustrations to *Vanity Fair*", *Renaissance and Modern Essays Presented to Vivian de Sola Pinto* (London: Routledge and Kegan Paul, 1966), 119-27. See also Judith Fisher, "Image Versus Text in the Illustrated Novels of William Makepeace Thackeray" in *Victorian Literature and the Victorian Visual Imagination*, Carol T. Christ and John O. Jordan, eds. (Berkeley: U of California P, 1995), 60-87.

[34] Ann Wilkinson, "The Tomeavesian Way of Knowing the World: Technique and Meaning in *Vanity Fair*", *English Literary History* 32 (1965), 371.

[35] Derek Brewer, *Symbolic Stories* (Totowa, NJ: Rowman and Littlefield, 1980), 51. This is a common term and concept in psychoanalytic writing.

[36] Miles Lambert, "The Dandy in Thackeray's *Vanity Fair* and *Pendennis*, an Early Victorian View of the Regency Dandy". *Costume: The Journal of the Costume Society* 22 (1988), 60-69.

[37] *The Dandy: Brummell to Beerbohm* (Lincoln: U of Nebraska P, 1960), 191.

[38] Bakhtin, Mikhail. *The Dialogic Imagination,* ed. Michael Holquist, trans. Caryl Emerson (Austin: University of Texas Press, 1981), 257.

3 A Version of a "Man and a Brother": Or, Character into Narrator

> Mr. Pendennis is the author of the book: and has taken a great weight off my mind for under that mask and acting as it were I can afford to say & think many things that I couldn't venture on in my own person now that it *is* a person and I know the public are staring at it. (*LPPS* 1: 589)

Deborah Thomas makes the point in *Thackeray and Slavery* that Thackeray's concluding description of Pen as "a man and a brother" borrows from abolition debates (*P* 2:372).[1] By accepting his own limitations and an "ordinary" life, Pen becomes a slave of sorts, in bondage to the conventionalities of life. But what kind of *narrator* will this make? *Pendennis's* narrator tells a story about how a dandy-performer grows up to be an artist who will use the conventionalities of life without becoming slave to them. Catherine Peters suggests that the "insider" persona of the narrator of *Pendennis* speaks in a more stable voice than the critic-voice of *Vanity Fair*:

> The narrative, instead of the bewildering multiplicity of voices of *Vanity Fair*, employs a single, reliable third person narrator. This deliberately sets a distance between reader and character, encouraging the reader to take on the role of an indulgent older relative or friend rather to identify with the central figure.[2]

However, to understand the distancing of the reader of *Pendennis* as simply the result of a "third-person" narrator oversimplifies the games Thackeray played with the conventional organization of a linear story and the parallel between the narrative techniques and Pen's own development into a novelist. While the narrator is reliable as a consistent voice, his multiple sociolects, his shifting proximity to his story, and the vagaries of his narrative knowledge never suggest a story outside of his narration. Jean Sudrann, Juliet McMaster, and Myron Taube have demonstrated that the "reminescential vision" or "armchair" perspective creates a coherent, far-distant point of view that, as Sudrann argues, actually creates the novel's subject matter.[3] But the distance of which Sudrann speaks is that of time, of memory. The narrator also zooms in and out of event as well as forward and backwards in time. *Pendennis* is not the story of Pen's life but the story of Pen's life as the narrator fits it into his own narrative consciousness. The events of Pen's life are inseparable from the narrator's presentation of them; there is little distinction between story and discourse. Sudrann argues that dramatic experience has no reality in *Pendennis*: "It is as though the moment lived is not the moment perceived and hence has no reality itself" (370). As *Vanity Fair* and the art criticism suggest, perception of reality is first a consciousness of oneself as a perceiving subject, which automatically reveals the arbitrariness of the "reality" perceived. Seeing *Pendennis* through time, or seeing Henry Esmond see himself through time, may create for us a sense of "design" (Sudrann 370), but such design is not automatically consequential or purposeful. The "pattern" of a life remembered depends upon the proclivities and selective memory of the central narrating consciousness, not upon Pen whose story mirrors this literally shifty narration in his own struggles with interpretation and his development from a passive reader into a narrator.

Pendennis sophisticates the critical method of *Vanity Fair*, wherein the narrator selects events from his story to illustrate his commentary. The shifts are more subtle here because both event and commentary are "interiorized" in our insider. His arbitrary pattern moves between "near" and "far" views in both time and space.[4] The actuality we see in a near view of a character or event shifts when the perspective lengthens or widens. This shift invites the reader to reassess and connect the moral and the physical nature of the object presented or even to question its existence. Just as the parable of the Neapolitan story teller, the French actors, and the Manager of the Performance in chapter 8 of *Vanity Fair* initiates the reader into how to read that novel, the narrator in *Pendennis* opens by dramatizing the perspectivism which will be this novel's major mode of narration and its primary ethical concern. Our first vision of Major Pendennis' perfect facade is, indeed, a picture of a perfect facade: "At a distance, or seeing his back merely, you would have taken him to be not more than thirty years old" (1: 2). Distance (which implies time because it takes time to move near or away) and position create one reality. This view, of course, does not hold when "by a nearer inspection . . . you saw the factitious nature of his rich brown hair, and that there were a few crow's feet round about the somewhat faded eyes of his handsome mottled face" (1: 2). The youthfulness seen from afar or seen from a limited position reveals itself as a disguise when seen closely and in full.

However, manipulating conventions of representation to create an image of something that exists only as that image is the method of any visual artist or novelist. In 1846 Thackeray complained of Turner that his pictures seemed wonderfully alive and real from a distance, "but on coming up to the picture, behold it was all an illusion".[5]   Similarly, the village of Clavering "looks so cheery and comfortable that many a traveller's heart must have yearned towards it from the coach-top" (1: 132). But, like Turner's paintings and the Major, this impression deceives, and the narrator reveals the deception as a function of perspective: "Like Constantinople seen from the Bosphorus; like Mrs. Rougemont viewed in her box from the opposite side of the house; like many an object which we pursue in life, and admire before we have attained it; Clavering is rather prettier at a distance than it is on a closer acquaintance" (1: 132). The near view reveals both physical dreariness and moral ugliness: gossiping, infighting, competition, and intolerance.

Such near/far views characterize story structure as well as individual descriptions. Chapters 1 through 15 dramatize Pen and his passion for Emily using short and long views. The narrative perspectives, his "time-telescope", as Michael Lund calls it, make us understand that Pen's genuine passion derives from his faulty vision (e.g. chapter 5; Lund 42).[6] The near view of Pen's own actions involve us in his emotional intensity while the far view contextualizes this immediate passion within his family history, literary conventions, and our own experiences of youthful infatuation. Through chapter 14, the novel develops as the reciprocal relation between Pen's infatuation and the narrative consciousness, including his knowledge of Pen's family history, that add dimensions to that story while "versionalizing" it. Helen's personal history, for example, parallels Pen's youthful folly, his father's history explains Pen's pride, Foker points up Pen's naiveté, and so forth. Neither near nor far view is complete without the other. Pen as the romantic 16 year old is potentially too ridiculous for us to ever accept him as our "brother", but the narrator's sympathetic yet piercing insight into the illusion at the heart of Pen's passion gives that passion a dignity as a mythic rite of passage: "He had found her; he had found what his soul thirsted after. He flung himself into the stream and drank with all his might. Let those who have been thirsty once how delicious that first draught is" (1: 52).

Moreover, the narrator's use of classical mythology incorporates Pen's love within a long-standing aesthetic convention and so disengages readers from fully immersing themselves in that love because we see that his love is itself a product of literary tradition.[7] The frontispiece of *Pendennis*, for instance, uses the traditional motif of the choice of Hercules (Fig. 3.1-2).[8] Pen is caught between siren and wife, and, reflecting the reality in the story that the lure of sexual passion is also the lure of worldly success (the crown and coronet). Pen enacts this metaphor early in the novel when he chooses to go to the play where he will become infatuated with the actress Emily Fotheringay instead of going home to his mother. The full-page illustration in chapter three, "Youth between Pleasure and Duty", replays the title illustration as Pen caught between the two kinds of men who will lead him into or away from temptation: Foker, the "man about town", and Dr. Portman, the vicar. The dialogue accompanying the illustration emphasizes the rite of passage embodied in this first choice.

> "I came up on Bishop's business," the Doctor said. "We'll ride home, Arthur, if you like?"
>
> "I – I'm engaged to my friend here," Pen answered.
>
> "You had better come with me," said the Doctor.
>
> "His mother knows he's out, sir," Mr. Foker remarked: "Don't she, Pendennis?" (1: 32)

What to Pen appears a one-time choice, becomes, as anticipated in the title page, the beginning of his long struggle to know that his pleasure *is* his duty.

Chapter 15 pulls back from this web to place Pen's love affair, so important and tragic to him, in the wider perspective of village life and of the readers. Reading with the narrator, we widen our own temporal and spatial visions. Picking up on the end of chapter 14, "Pen, as he rode home that night, actually thought about somebody but himself", the narrator asks us to think about somebody other than Pen – ourselves.

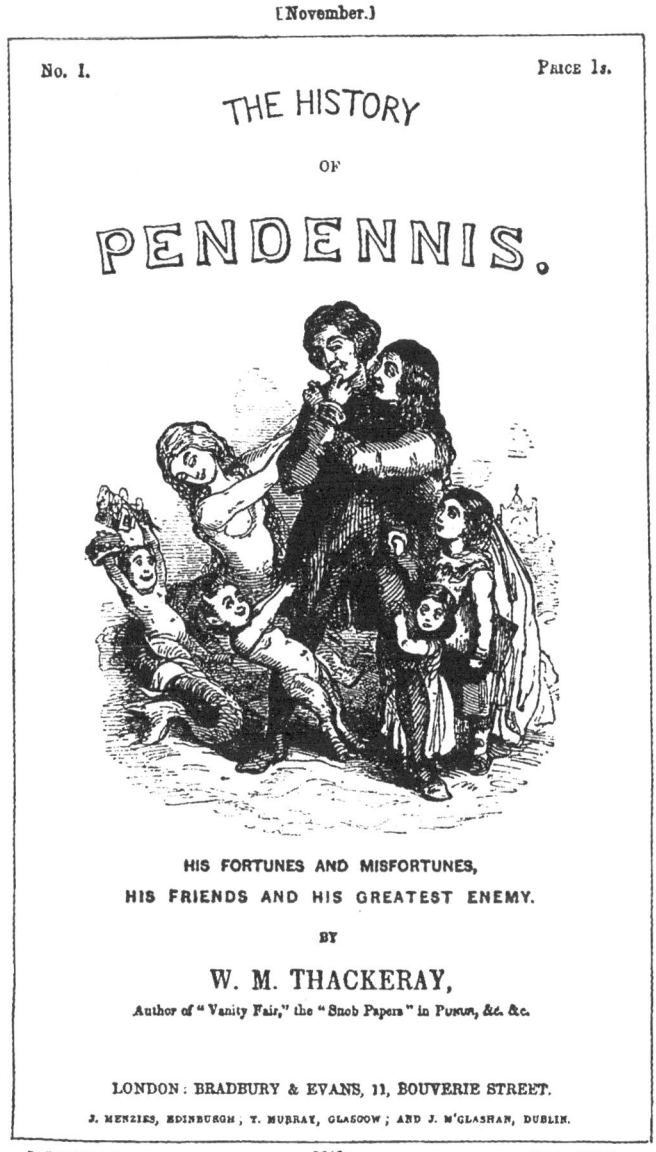

Facsimile of the Original Wrapper.

Fig. 3.1, Cover, monthly number, *Pendennis*
Photograph courtesy of Elizabeth Huth Coates Library, Trinity University

Fig. 3.2, Title Page Illustration, volume 1, *Pendennis*
Photograph courtesy of Elizabeth Huth Coates Library, Trinity University

> I suppose there is scarcely any man who reads this or any other
> novel but has been balked in love some time or the other, by fate
> and circumstance, by falsehood of women, or his own fault. Let
> that worthy friend recall his own sensations under the circumstances
> and apply them as illustrative of Pen's anguish. (1: 129)

Pen's experience becomes real to the reader insofar as the (male) reader
can remember his own passion. The readers apply the temporal long-view
heretofore applied by the narrator. Temporal distance is followed by
extension into space as we are asked to imagine "this very night in London
. . . the groans, thoughts, imprecations of tossing lovers . . . . I wonder what
a percentage of the male population *will* be lying awake at two or three
o'clock to-morrow morning" (1: 129). Once we accept the immediate story
as one version of general human experience, the narrator uses our
experience to suggest how Pen's story will complete itself: Pen "will
console himself like the rest of us" (1: 130) – not necessarily
complimentary, but true.

To incorporate this story into all stories, including the readers', suggests
that most stories remain unknown (and thus emphasizes the conventionality
of Pen's story). That our sympathy with Pen's intensity is a matter of
narrative choice is clear when he adopts (still in chapter 15) an impersonal,
descriptive mode to place Pen's story within yet a third context, the village
of Clavering. Seen from the distant view of the village, Pen's romance is a
titillating subject for gossip and ridicule; his secret joys and agonies can be
neither known nor felt, just as the dreariness of Clavering is invisible from
the coach top. This perspective from "The Happy Village" broadens out in
chapter 16 to again include the reader and human nature. The title, "Which
Concludes the First Part of this History", pushes us out of the story,
carrying the three perspectives of Pen as character, Pen seen in time by the
narrator, and Pen as seen in the context of the village.[9] Clavering's
ignorance of and thus insensitivity to Pen's real grief parallels Pen's
ignorance of and insensitivity to Smirke's private grief. Thus, chapters 1 to
15 suggest that:

> every man in the world, has his own private griefs and business, by
> which he is more cast down or occupied than by the affairs or
> sorrows of any other person. While Mrs. Pendennis is disquieting
> herself about losing her son. . . while the Major's great soul chafes
> and frets . . . while Pen is tossing between his passion and a more

>agreeable sensation . . . Mr. Smirke has a private care watching at
>his bed side. . . . How lonely we are in the world. . . .Your artless
>daughter . . . the honest frank boy just returned from school . . . .
>The old grandmother . . . O philosophic reader, answer and say, –
>Do you tell *her* all? Ah, sir – a distinct universe walks about under
>your hat and under mine – all things in nature are different to each .
>. . – you and I are but a pair of infinite isolations, with some fellow-
>islands a little more or less near to us. (1: 142-43)

This narrative comment questions its own narrative intent: if we are but
"infinite isolations" how can the narrator tell Pen's personal story? In fact,
the story (and Pen) are the narrator's creation as the narrator is the story's
voice – as in any fictional world. So "Thackeray's" assertion in the Preface
that in the confidential talk between writer and reader, the writer must tell
the "truth" acquires a curious ambiguity, especially in light of his own
confession that cultural conventions force him to "veil" certain truths of
manhood. The undulating structure of *Pendennis* from "zoom" shots to
"establishing shots" shows us just how temporary is any perception of truth
because it can only be a momentary perception. Focus on a specific scene
or character is always contextualized by a "long view". The narrator's
perspective withdraws from the immediate story in either "public" time, as
when he gives us the history of the Pendennis family or the Claverings, or in
"private" time as when he conjures up his own memory or appeals to the
readers'. Temporal expansions merge with spatial expansions where the
specific action or character line is seen as a distinct theme within a field of
vision. While this near/far technique develops from the critic's ironic use of
the story as developed in *Vanity Fair,* the commentary or larger view here
grows *from* the story; the story is a part of the narrative consciousness not
an external "object" for parody or comment. Moreover, the *Pendennis*
narrator does not subordinate his own voice under parodic roles distinct
from himself. The sociolects of classical mythology, the theater, and pastoral
romance are the narrator's "natural" frames of reference although still
intended to be recognized as literary formulae.

The illustrations in *Pendennis* complement the narration by supplying
alternate "truths" of characters, which emphasize the conventionality of their
desires and actions. The motif of children in the pictorial initials, for
example, undermines while it emphasizes Pen's egoism. Children symbolize
thoughtless desire, lack of foresight, as well as harmless innocence. Pictures
of children at play satirize Pen's introduction into worldly ambition

and his ignorance of the world in 1: 84, 1: 90, 1: 139, and 1: 161. A little boy straining to get a toy coach and horse from his mother introduces the Claverings and recalls the original title page where the imps accompanying Vice/Pleasure carry coach and horse (1: 209). Pen's apprenticeship to the world is symbolized by the "devil" teaching a boy how to pipe (1: 298) and a man teaching a boy how to skate (2: 22). The "devil" is both the Major teaching Pen his materialist philosophy and the printer's devil whose schedule becomes Pen's taskmaster. The ice or "surface" of society is, of course, slippery and laced with unexpected cracks. Pen's failure at Oxbridge is appropriately marked by a boy in a dunce cap with asses' ears sitting in a school room (1: 201).[10] These images of children trivialize Pen and automatically put the reader into a position of superior knowledge and power. The reader can either dismiss him or shift the blame for his actions to companions like Foker or his own ignorance.

As *Pendennis* proceeds, this perspectival method overpowers the thread of linear events. The long view of memory remains, of course, but it is not linear memory in the sense that event time in the story will meet the narrator's time as in an autobiographical novel such as *Jane Eyre* or *Henry Esmond*. Their sense of chronological connection correlates subjective existence – the life of one's perceptions and memory – with external existence – events or incidents. Autobiographical fiction demands some such connection because the reader must be able to accept the character as the teller by the end of the novel. The narrator of *Pendennis* denies the concept of character development, usually considered essential to any kunstler- or bildungsroman.

> We alter very little. When we talk of this man or that woman being no longer the same person whom we remember in youth, and remark (of course to deplore) changes in our friends, we don't, perhaps, calculate that circumstance only brings out the latent defect or quality, and does not create it. (2: 210)

So instead of presenting external events that cause psychological development, *Pendennis* focuses on Pen's performance on various stages and his growing mastery of various sociolects. He is first an unwitting, theatrical, actor, then a self-conscious performer in danger of believing his own performance, and finally, the Manager of his own Performance. It is difficult to get any sense of Pen maturing after he leaves for Oxbridge; he simply repeats his pattern of self-illusion, projection, and disillusion until he learns to recognize his own power to create illusions.

Thackeray's treatment of Pen's college career illustrates the kaleidoscopic narrative method. The narrator calls this period "a play" and a "Pantomime" (1: 160). He sets the stage for us by introducing college life, placing Pen in it, and then discoursing on various topics: Pen's taste, his dandyism, his growing academic idleness, and his gambling. This, the narrator argues, brings us closer to the "truth" of Pen's life than any series of events.

> As all this narrative is taken from Pen's own confessions, so that the reader may be assured of the truth of every word of it, and as Pen himself never had any accurate notion of the manner in which he spent his money, and plunged himself in much deeper pecuniary difficulties during his luckless residence at Oxbridge, it is, of course, impossible for me to give any accurate account of his involvement beyond that general notion of his way of life which we have sketched a few pages back. (1: 190)

If Pen cannot remember, then how should the narrator be able to create his subject's past? But of course, the detail about Pen's habits authenticates the narrator's wide view, and Pen's individual experiences dissolve into habitual actions. Consequently, Pen's history at Oxbridge seems ordinary, one of many, and this idea of "custom" is emphasized by the conventional chapter title, "Rake's Progress", and the pair of pictorial initials to chapters 19 and 20, marking Pen's rise and fall. What he feels is unique is placed for us as a *version*. Moreover, the narrator's associative structure of *Pendennis* is at odds with his claim that his information came from Pen. In part at least, this excuse for vagueness is a dramatic manifestation of the cultural restraint inhibiting the narrator. Juliet McMaster suggests that this overview indicates Pen's growth:

> In one sense experience is something as present and palpable as a physical sensation, like a cold shower or a kick in the shins; but such experiences, accumulated in time and reflected upon when the sensation is over, become remote and unavailable, and are replaced by that collective "experience" which goes with change in character. (73)

The memory in this case, however, is the narrator's, not Pen's. So any "change" (which the narrator denies) is *his*, evidenced in the finished form of his narrative-as-memory.

The narrator's complicated weave of reflection and scene absorbs Pen's life in London, dramatizing that life does not divide itself into crucial scenes. Pen is beginning his role as man-about-town under his friend Warrington's guidance. The chapter opens with an overview of London life as lived by Warrington, and moves further away from actual drama in the narrator's old-fogy perspective that sees both the intense joy and the transience of this period. He shifts the reader to Helen's and Laura's perspective – "I wonder what Laura and Helen would have said . . . ". – to ponder Pen and Warrington "carousing" (1: 299). He then zooms to the anchoring place/event: Pen's renewed acquaintance with the theatre manager Bows and Costigan in the Back Kitchen.

> Men serve women kneeling – when they get on their feet, they go away.
> That was what an acquaintance of Pen's said to him in his hard homely way . . . . (1: 300)

The seeming narrative generalization becomes a specific statement by Bows, and puts us in the Back Kitchen on a specific occasion. We are moved immediately out to a general view of the Back Kitchen, with the narrator remembering "many a time in my youth have I admired how Cutts the singer" moved his audience as singer and acted as landlord. This narrative memory concretizes into a dramatic event:

> . . . many a time in my youth have I admired how Cutts the singer . . . how Cutts the singer became at once Cutts the landlord . . . was calling, "Now gentlemen, give your orders, the waiter's in the room – John, a champagne cup for Mr. Green. I think, sir, you said sausages and mashed potatoes? John, attend on the gentleman."
> "And I'll thank ye give me a glass of punch too, John, and take care the wather boils," a voice would cry not unfrequently, a well-known voice to Pen, which made the lad blush and start when he heard it first – that of the venerable Captain Costigan . . . .
> The Captain's manners and conversation brought very many young men to the place. (1: 300-301)

We have no sooner fixed our sight on Pen hearing Costigan in a precise moment of time and space then we are pushed back out into a panorama of Costigan's fortunes since we last met him. The sense of the passage is that Costigan's life has been ongoing and Pen has happened into it. Costigan's presence at the Back Kitchen was not created *for* Pen. And the zoom back to the first meeting confirms this sense of accidental encounter: "It was in *one* of these moments of exultation [payday for Costigan] that Pen found his friend . . ". (emphasis mine; 1: 301). We then focus on this scene whose significance is only an example of the generality of Pen's experience: "Pen had many opportunities of seeing his early acquaintances afterwards . . ". (1: 303).

The two simplest conclusions to draw about this dizzying technique are that it is difficult to locate events in external time and that no event ever happens as a non-contextualized incident. The unlocatability of event is accentuated by Thackeray's sense of time as a spiral, again emphasizing the narrative consciousness. This technique, more evident in the later novels, spirals from event to past to present to future back to the same event. The focus on the Back Kitchen in chapter 31 circles back to Pen's mention of it in chapter 29 but the rest of chapter 31 pushes beyond this mention to introduce Pen to the publishing world. But we do not know that any of the actual scenes of chapter 31 (meeting, Bows, Costigan, Archer, etc.) had actually occurred at the time when Pen mentioned the Back Kitchen to Major Pendennis in chapter 29. This spiral structure combines with the near/far views. The intersections on the spiral are usually near views, anchors of dramatic events that vivify the narrative by their sense of precision. The far views of memory, panorama, and commentary sweep us from one intersection to another. Thus, the reader is caught in a fluid movement of narrative consciousness as it moves in, out, and around its subject.

A sense of simultaneity results from this technique. That is, while Pen is entering society and pursuing Blanche, he is also frequenting the Back Kitchen. To follow such multiple perspectives, the reader must read with the narrator's breadth of vision. But the narrator also uses the linear structure inherent in the novel form to present multiple perspectives on a "theme" which forces us to evaluate individual facets in light of each other. Unlike a near/far view which is hierarchical, the near view being interpreted in light of the far view, this "prism vision" offers us competing perspectives whose juxtaposition create their own context. The most significant prism vision runs from chapter 21 through chapter 26 in volume two, chronicling Pen's "bargain with the devil": his decision to marry Blanche Amory in order to gain a seat in Parliament. Chapter 23 is titled "The Way of the World" and is the thematic center of the novel. Here the worldly Pendennis pronounces his "man of the world", cynical philosophy. Taken in isolation, his relativism seems both logical and tolerant, but it follows chapter 22 where the Major has applied the Pen's utilitarianism to marriage, and we have been exposed to "the way of the world" in Sir Francis's gambling and cowardice. So Pen's philosophy seems inadequate; it does not justify the crass attitudes of chapter 22. In fact, the worldly philosophy of chapter 23 has no practical reference to the worldly conversations in chapter 22.

To ensure that we see the inadequacy of the language of "du monde" to describe such shabby actions as blackmail, gambling, and cowardice, the narrator gives us a parody of Pen's mercantile decision. Lightfoot, Sir Francis's valet, describes himself as doing precisely what Pen plans to do, marry a woman for her money and set up as a public figure: "She's old, but two thousand pound's a good bit, you see, Mr. Morgan. And we'll get the 'Clavering Arms' for very little" (2: 222-23). Pen will also get "Clavering Arms" of a sort when he takes Sir Francis' seat in Parliament. We must reject Pen's philosophical decision to "'take the world as it is'" because we have been presented with the distasteful reality of what "it" is. Like Warrington, we may acknowledge the existence of Altamont and Sir Francis, but which of us would liken our own codes to theirs or want to live among them? Moreover, chapter 24 makes it plain that Pen does not know what he is talking about, that this "philosophy" is an untested facade. What he sees as a modus vivendi allowing him to succeed in the world is also (unbeknownst to Pen) a sordid bargain based on Lady Clavering's (unintentional) bigamy and the blackmail by the Major (Pen's mentor in worldliness). This context suggests that Pen's primary ethical failure is not his assumption that he knows the world but that his so-called tolerance allows him to refuse to exercise his judgment:

> "who are we [says Pen] to measure the chances and opportunities,
> the means of doing, or even judging, right and wrong, awarded to
> men; and to establish the rule for meting out their punishments and
> rewards? We are as insolent and unthinking in judging of men's
> morals as of their intellects." (2: 235)

The narrator at first seems to acquiesce to Pen's philosophy by using it himself in responding to Pen:

> We are not pledging ourselves for the correctness of his opinions, which readers will please to consider are delivered dramatically, the writer being no more answerable for them, than for the sentiments uttered by any other character of the story. (2: 236)

But he follows his own statement of neutrality with a vehement rejection of Pendennis's relativism:

> To what, we say, does this scepticism lead? It leads a man to a shameful loneliness and selfishness, so to speak – the more shameful, because it is so good-humoured and conscienceless and serene. Conscience!   What is conscience? Why accept remorse? What is public or private faith? . . . If seeing and acknowledging the lies of the world, Arthur, as see them you can with only too fatal a clearness, you submit to them without any protest further than a laugh: if, plunged yourself in easy sensuality, you allow the whole wretched world to pass by you unmoved: if the fight for the truth is taking place, and all men of honour are on the ground armed on the one side or the other, and you alone are to lie on your balcony and smoke your pipe out of the noise and the danger, you had better have died, or never have been at all, than such a sensual coward. (2: 237)

Pen's skepticism at this point is not Thackerayean skepticism because Pen's fixed code of worldliness allows him to avoid acting. Readers have been trained by the narrator's shifting perspectives to see the versional nature of human experience and so distrust any single interpretation of an event or a person. Seeing the limitations of Helen's religious sociolect, the Major's worldly sociolect, or Blanche Amory's theatrical sociolect forces readers to exercise their own judgment. Understanding Major Pendennis' motives is not the same thing as condoning his actions. On the other hand, Pen at this point, has only moved from one perspective to another, from naive literary idealism to disillusioned cynicism. Right now, "living in the world without God", Pen is on the brink of losing the possibility of faith. When Pen asks, "What is truth", and demands to be "shown" it, we would like to refer him to the novel in which he is embedded. The multiple perspectives created by focalizing through Sir Francis, Lady Clavering, Altamont, Strong, Fanny, Sam, the Major, Pendennis, Warrington, Morgan,

Lightfoot, and Blanche create a web of experience in which judgment is imperative, at least for readers, if they are not to be caught in the web. Yet this same process demonstrates the impossibility of acquiring *enough* knowledge to judge definitively.

Thackeray's illustrations, appearing to be simple reifications of the text require similar reader judgment as the reader/viewer moves between text and drawing and between drawings. A clear example of this is a simple intertext of the Chevalier Strong blacking his boots in volume 2, chapter 23 of Pendennis (2: 227). On the same page he refuses to seek yet one more loan for Clavering because he has given his word to Lady Clavering: "the Chevalier said that he, at least, would keep his word, and would black his own boots all his life rather than break his promise". In this context, the drawing becomes an emblem of Strong's integrity, in sharp contrast to the intertext of Clavering begging money from Altamont in the previous chapter (2: 220). The essential characters of the two men are crystallized in these pictures that thus become "signs" of their moral quality.

Ultimately, *Pendennis* presents the reader with a tension between the supposedly stable voice of the armchair uncle and the multiple modes of seeing: near/far views in space and time, contrasting perspectives, parallel characters, "prism vision" created by sequences of events which force readers to revise even as they move forward. This dynamic balance is a paradigm for what Pen and the readers must learn: how to create and control their own interpretations. These specific narrative devices, as McMaster has noted, tend "to slide away from the substance of the vision to an evaluation of it and a consideration of its effect on the viewer" (20). Consequently, the narrative method invites readers to subjectivize for themselves the story already subjectivized by the narrator's method. Pen and the reader must learn to change their focuses (and thus interpretations) as time and space create new conditions for seeing. The shifting vision Pen has of Emily, Blanche, and Laura, which teach him to realize the self-delusion in his relationship with the two "actresses" and the real worth of Laura, parallels the reader's constant readjustment from criticism of to sympathy with Pen.[11] Pen must learn to re-see and re-read, while accepting that each convention offers a reality that he may *choose* to respond to.

The story of *Pendennis* interweaves with the narrative technique and illustrations not just by parallels in thematic and rhetorical intent but in its comparable emphasis on the telling and the tale as "versions". The story has strong connections to Book I of the *Faerie Queene*.[12] "Prince

Arthur's" quest is internal: to turn his propensity to create illusions into a linguistic mastery that allows him to become an interpreter of events for others. Pen – the significance of this nickname is obvious in this context – starts by projecting versions of himself upon his world to interpret it – the world is a mirror of his own literary delusions. The narrator emphasizes that these early versions of himself and his world are purely derivative and not under Pen's control. Pen's life is a romance quest because he reads it as such; that is, Thackeray displays for *his* readers, a reader seduced by a text. Nicknaming Arthur Pendennis "the Prince of Fairoaks" is only the narrator's most obvious directive to see Pen's story in the light of Spenser's Prince Arthur and his "split", the Redcrosse knight. Pen's falling in love with Emily Costigan, the "Fotheringay", signals the beginning of his life as a self-conscious being in search of a satisfying image, but this is a search for an image overtly constructed by literary tradition.

> Pen began to feel the necessity of a first love – of a consuming passion – of an object on which he could concentrate all those vague floating fancies under which he sweetly suffered – of a young lady to whom he could really make verses and whom he could set up and adore, in place of those unsubstantial Ianthes and Zuleikas to whom he addressed the outpourings of his gushing muse. (1: 27)[13]

Literary experience inspires passion whose intensity makes Pen mistake literary tropes for his subjectivity. This phase is a clear critique of the Byronic Romantic hero. His passion for Emily, an image unlike his mother, drives his entry into the symbolic order of language signified by his passionate turn to male poetic conventions, using his feelings as his text, thereby signaling the end of his union with his mother,. He recognizes Emily as an object to love by interpreting her as an aesthetic image. Writing is Emily. He can only experience his "love" as an imitation of his reading – Byron, Moore, and Scott. "He was as much in love as the best hero in the best romance he ever read" (1: 39). He has introjected himself into his texts and been consumed by their signs, fleshing them out with his own stereotypes, and the consequence is a blatantly (and comically) false interpretation or Stierle's "quasi-pragmatic" reading. Once one "surrenders" to self-projection as reception, one loses the text and "stereotypes of reading become stereotypes of practical and verbal action".[14] This surrender to types characterizes Pen's appropriation of chivalric and Romantic love into his own world of romance. The mechanical quality of Pen's passion is symbolized in Thackeray's comparison of Pen's "newfound" love to his father's watch. Both are created objects, separate from the self and manipulated by the desires of the self:

> And as, when three years previously, and on entering the fifth form at the Cistercians, his father had made him a present of a gold watch which the boy took from under his pillow and examined on the instant of waking: for ever rubbing and polishing it up in private and retiring into corners to listen to its ticking: so the young man exulted over his new delight [his infatuation with Emily]; felt in his waistcoat pocket to see that it was safe; wound it up at nights, and at the very first moment of waking hugged it and looked at it. (1: 39)[15]

The watch, not incidentally, "was a showy ill-manufactured piece", suggesting the crudity of Pen's first artistic self-representation. Just as Becky Sharp improves upon her performances, so will Pen as he becomes more aware that they are performances. At this point, Pen simply and unconsciously follows cultural tradition; he is unable to control and manipulate either his interpretations or his self-presentation because he sees them as "natural".

> He saw a pair of bright eyes, and he believed in them – a beautiful image, and he fell down and worshipped it. He supplied the meaning which her words wanted; and created the divinity which he loved. Was Titania the first who fell in love with an ass, or Pygmalion the only artist who has gone crazy about a stone? He had found her; he found what his soul thirsted after. He flung himself into the stream and drank with all his might. (1: 52)

The narrator contextualizes Pen's infatuation within literary traditions; that is, while Pen believes he is sincere, the narrator will not let readers see his love as existing outside culture. This pool of Narcissus reflects a delusive desire that can drown the desirer. Called by "Love" after seeing Emily act as Mrs. Haller in Kotzebue's melodrama, *The Stranger*, Pen is thrown into "fever and passion: wild longing, maddening desire; restless craving and seeking" (1: 39) – a type of Redcrosse's dream of lustful love (*FQ* I.i.45-47). Like Redcrosse and Narcissus, Pen does not *know* he is worshipping an illusion because his intensity is not illusory. He is the Neapolitan story-teller, unable to separate his story from himself.

Frederick Goldin argues that this initial fascination with the delusive "other" is really a pre-existing self-love, made visible in an object.[16] Pen not only has the predisposition to love but also already loves himself, so that he projects an image to realize that self-love. However, if the lover satisfies this love, he remains in a state of autoerotic narcissism, so the initial love object *should* fail in some way. The escapes from the failure of this image are three: to find an object that *is* the ideal, to see himself as the reflection of the ideal, or to cultivate in his inner life "something that never existed before and is not to be justified by its resemblance to anything" (Goldin 50). That Thackeray denies psychological development means that he must reject this third way of creating subjectivity. Thus Thackeray dramatizes the paradox of the artist: aesthetic value derives from the artist's intense absorption, but aesthetic quality depends upon a conscious control which automatically forbids the total immersion – or fixed perspective – necessary to *be* sincere as opposed to *appearing* sincere. While Redcrosse rejects the true Una as the false Una of his dream, Pen accepts the false Emily as his true Ideal Lady. Of course, Redcrosse is inadvertently right; the Una he rejects is actually Duessa. That readers know Redcrosse is right even though he does not argues that his virtue is instinctive. In contrast, Pen's dependence upon literary convention suggests that, for Thackeray, nothing is instinctive, that conventions of value construct our sense of internal values.

The illustrations generally from chapter 1 through chapter 14 illustrate Pen's unconscious conventionality as the interpenetration of life and acting. Thirteen of the 31 illustrations (pictorial initial, intertext, and full page) depict scenes of acting and life as "scenes." Pastoral merges with fairy-tale and theater to produce a visual subtext revealing the mediated nature of Pen's desire. Chapter 3 opens with an initial "A" depicting the lamp seller who sells Aladdin his magic lamp. Chapter 4, which gives us the history of Pen's infatuation with Emily, introduces itself with two actors in swashbuckle-garb, strutting on the boards. The initial to chapter 5, "Mrs. Haller at Home", depicts a panoply of fairy-tale and stage types: king, bishop, knights, and wizard.[17] And chapter 6, "Contains Both Love and War", opens with a pun on the chapter title. The initial is a large "C" that does indeed "contain" love in the guise of a Restoration rake and his ladylove. The visual dialogue suggested by this sequence communicates the magic of Pen's infatuation, and the glory to him of what he sees in the "magic" lamp of his own imagination, while showing the reader the illusion at the heart of the vision. Wishes granted by magic are illusions – dubious ones at that, if the expressions of the king and his court are any indication.

We move from the illustration of the fairy-tale stage types (chapter 5) to Costigan watching Emily act (chapter 5) to an 18th-century couple playing at love (chapter 6) to Emily in the character of Ophelia – whom Pen sees as Emily/Ophelia – to the full-page illustration, "A View from the Dean's Garden" in which Dean Portman and his wife watch, scandalized, at the love "scene" Pen performs with Emily. Their staginess is emphasized by the audience of the Portmans gazing at Pen and Emily in frame of the window, recalling the frame of the proscenium. This theatre of the real, with its unwitting audience, parallels the real theatre with its deliberate audience. How very appropriate for this romance! Pen, having absorbed romantic illusions from literature, acts them out as real emotions.

If we have any doubt how we are to "see" this scene, the stage cupid opening chapter 12, in which Emily breaks off with Pen, makes the reading clear. The illustrations ask the eye to superimpose the acknowledged illusion of acting over the self-conscious artifice of pastoral and impose both of those on the "real" actions of the story that can then no longer be taken as simple unconscious realism. Yet the story is "real", if the mimetic style and Pen's joy and grief have any power over the reader. In fact, the mixture of modes forbids any discernment of a single truth in Pen's emotions. The truth-in-falsity of Pen's infatuation speaks to the readers' own experience of theater and life: of acting that we as audience experience as real, and of a kind of reality that depends upon acting. While Pen genuinely feels his love and grief, his modes of expression falsify his emotions. His mad rides through the country, passionate poetry, and grandiloquent pronouncements are the stuff of hackneyed romance.

Nonetheless, acting out the conventions of romance signals the end of Pen's passive childhood. Love makes him feel "ever so many years older" (1: 4). Correspondingly, Helen, the pure mother, and the Major, the emblem of worldly desire, compete to direct his perception; each wants to save him from Emily but for different reasons. These competing advisors echo Book I, canto i of the *Faerie Queene*, with its pervasive emphasis on the proper advice: "the way to win / Is wisely to aduise" (*FQ* I.i.33). This advice, however, comes from Archimago, masquerading as the holy Hermit, so that "winning" contains a double meaning. Redcrosse and Una understand it to mean their winning through to the end of the quest, while Archimago means *his* winning over them. Such duplicity characterizes the Major's advice to Pen. Like Archimago, the Major's worldly wisdom teaches self-direction, and the disguise of each mentor personifies a type of "virtue" – holy hermit and successful man of the world. Helen and then Laura are the Unas who advise Pen to *avoid* error (I.i.13), which neither Pen nor Redcrosse can accept because to "quest", to "grow", is to "err" – the pun within "errant knight" should never be forgotten.

When Pen's love transforms his passive reading into active interpretation we have in miniature one theory of creativity. Pen immerses himself in the text to the point where the literary images are vivified in his own emotions, which he then, like the Neapolitan story-teller, projects upon the world around him. The resulting passion is now "genuinely" felt and can become the source of his own representation:

> He was biting a pencil and thinking of rhymes and all sorts of follies and passions. He was Hamlet jumping into Ophelia's grave; he was the Stranger taking Mrs. Haller to his arms . . . . Despair and Byron, Thomas Moore and all the Loves of the Angels, Waller and Herrick, Beranger and all the love-songs he had ever read, were working and seething in this young gentleman's mind, and he was at the very height and paroxysm of the imaginative phrensy. (1: 69)

Is this passion simply an imitation of his reading, however unconscious, or is this valid inspiration? The history of his consequent literary product suggests that perhaps there is no difference. *Leaves from the Life Book of Walter Lorraine*, a melodramatic historical romance Pen writes in the fever of his disappointed passion for Emily and his first infatuation with Blanche, is both trite and marketable.[18] The germ of marketability is the genuine feeling which spawned it, but the more mature Pen must craft the imitative outpourings while retaining the illusion of sincerity before it will sell.

Pen starts to grow into the artist able to manipulate his self-representations and his interpretations of others when he first self-consciously re-creates himself. He "takes his uncle's counsels to heart", counsels which play on his vanity and supposed status. The Major's flattery is designed to "open" Pen's eyes to see his own worth. Thus Pen cures himself of Emily by transferring his desire for the ideal onto himself, but this is not the transference Goldin suggests, of seeing the self as a mirror in which one can see the ideal. Pen's redirected gaze only entraps him the more because he becomes fascinated by his own surface. His poetry in chapter 15 is conscious self-romanticization, not grief. Pen's growth into narcissism accelerates in the all-male society at Oxbridge where Pen transforms his surface into a "butterfly" dandy, modeled on Bulwer-Lytton's Pelham:

> when he arrived for the long vacation, he brought more smart clothes; appearing in the morning in wonderful shooting-jackets, with remarkable buttons; and in the evening in gorgeous velvet waistcoats, with richly-embroidered cravats, and curious linen . . . . [he had] such a beautiful dressing case, with silver mountings, and a quantity of lovely rings and jewellry. And he had a new French watch and gold chain. (1: 172)

Now his watch is not the clunky heirloom from his father but the fanciful French decorative object. His reputation as a "man of taste" complements his dandyism. His taste runs to expensive paintings, books, and wine. And, like D'Orsay, Pen's dandyism is less a growth into mature maleness than feminization:

> He and his polite friends would dress themselves out with as much care in order to go and dine at each other's rooms, as other folks would who were going to enslave a mistress. They said he used to wear rings over his kid gloves, which he always denies . . . . That he took perfumed baths is a truth; and he used to say that he took them after meeting certain men of a very low set in hall. (1: 175)

Pen's dandy phase, like those of George Osborne and Clive Newcome, epitomizes the contradictions built into the quest pattern. It is at this stage that the protagonist thinks he yearns after an ideal when in fact he is projecting his own desires onto the desired object – progress is actually stasis. The dandy-phase of the protagonist is the public version of his private search for self through love; the costume and mannerisms are performances of status.

Thackeray's protagonists in general are insecure about their knightly rank or class as it derives from their fathers. Pendennis is a "Prince" whose status as a scion of "as old a family as any in the whole county of Somerset" (1: 6) has been undermined by the fact that his father was an apothecary.

Henry is "head" of his family, but his legitimacy is questioned first by himself and always by the world at large. Clive, another "young prince", has a father who is a black sheep, is descended from working class people, and loses the money that secures the modern kingdom. Philip's father is a social and moral fraud. Harry Warrington's status as Virginian Prince depends upon the supposed death of his brother, the real Prince. These dubious paternal lines lead the protagonists to define themselves through women – mothers, sisters, and lovers who, cannot, however, give them public recognition of their worth or true membership in the class of "gentleman" (Goldin 66-67). The purity of the invisible woman depends upon her remaining private, unsullied by the "world". Thus her valorization of the protagonist can only be private.

Pendennis' dandyism mirrors the theatricality and self-display we will see in Thackeray's sirens. Like the sirens, Pen runs the danger of becoming completely absorbed in his surface. Just as Becky signals her self-destruction through her lack of maternal feeling and Ethel saves herself by becoming a mother, Pen's trivialization of his literary talent threatens the male equivalent of female procreative passion: his aesthetic sense and genuine artistic ability. He degrades his former passion by turning it into Wertherian melodrama to increase his reputation. As he showed his friends his verses, "his brow would darken, his eyes roll, his chest heave with emotion" (1: 175). *Walter Lorraine*, although saleable, is never more than a stereotypical romance, filled with such purple passages as "'False as thou art beautiful? heartless as thou art fair! mockery of passion!' Walter cried, addressing Leonora; 'what evil spirit hath sent thee to torture me so?'" (2: 23). Pen's reputation at St. Boniface (1: 176) as a "tremendous fellow" man is founded on no achievement other than this self display which eventually inhibits his ability to act because he mistakes these displays for the substantial actions which would make him genuinely independent. He fails the examinations and overspends, and must return home.

Ironically, Pen's dandyism is part of his struggle to leave home. Fairoaks is the place of the "invisible women", Helen and Laura. But to be a man is to be seen in the world. When Pen leaves for London, after failing in his role as hero at St. Boniface, he carries with him two selves, one of which will be discarded for the other. The "dandy", continuing in its feminine, siren-like vein, is connected to Pen's social and monetary ambitions. "Prince Arthur" becomes the name of his better self. The virtue that will save him begins in vanity, an overvaluing of himself. This vanity is indicated in the title "Prince." But as Pen's immersion in the world opens his eyes to his powerlessness, he becomes only "Arthur", a dethroned prince who is contented with private life not public display. "Pen" is the public (and punning) name of the burgeoning writer, used by Warrington and the narrator. "Arthur" is the private name used by Laura to conjure up Helen's son.

Warrington identifies self-decoration of the dandy with effeminacy and sees the stasis bred by subsuming oneself into one's surface:

> "I don't know anything more wholesome for a man – for an honest man, mind you – . . . than a state of tick. It is an alterative and a tonic; it keeps your moral man in a perpetual state of excitement . . . a little necessity brings out your pluck if you have any, and nerves you to grapple with fortune . . . . You won't want new gloves and varnished boots, eau de Cologne, and cabs to ride in. You have been bred up as a mollycoddle, Pen, and spoilt by the women. A single man who has health and brains, and can't find a livelihood in the world, doesn't deserve to stay there." (1: 310)

As the dandy Pen starts to write, the "critic" develops, first as an arrogant slasher (1: 36). The "critical" eye encourages Pen to consciously separate himself from himself, an awareness that holds the key to his development.

The dandified Pen burns up in a conflagration of romance. The narrator constantly refers to Pen as "Arthur" and as mock-royalty (the "Prince of Fairoaks" [2: 82, 85, 90] the "Marquis of Fairoaks" [2: 86], "His Royal Highness" [2: 94, 95])   during the Fanny Bolton episode, which emphasizes his illusion of himself as a hero while hinting at the basic self-respect that will restrain him. Like Redcrosse, Pen finally is rescued by this "better" self, his Prince Arthur. His descent into Vauxhall, where he first meets Fanny, resembles the entrance to the third room of the House of Mammon in the *Faerie Queene*. To enter the Cave of Mammon, you must first go "through a darksome narrow strait, / To a broad gate, all built of beaten gold" (*FQ*, II.vii.40). To enter "the enchanted ground" of Vauxhall, one passes "through the black and dreary passage" to the "golden gate" where you must pay to enter" (*P* 2: 80). Fanny reacts to Pen and Vauxhall as if they were the same, admiring the glitter of both. She sees Pen as a knight out of *Walter Lorraine*. He acts the part of siren, kissing her, visiting her, and luring her to dream of an impossible union. His androgynous role fits his lack of identity. It is at this time that the narrator sees Pen as not fitting anywhere:

> In spite of his brag and boast to the contrary, he was too young as yet for women's society, which probably can only be had in perfection when a man has ceased to think about his own person, and has given up all designs of being a conqueror of ladies; he was too young to be admitted as an a equal amongst men who had made their mark in the world . . . . And he was too old for the men of pleasure of his own age; too much a man of pleasure for the men of business; destined in a word to be a good deal alone. (2: 93)

Fanny responds to Pen as Pen responded to Emily. She is seduced by her reading of both Pen's texts: his novel and his image. Mrs. Bolton, who has a theatrical background, unconsciously emphasizes the theatricality of their relation. She sees Pen as a "gentleman" visitor to the theatre (2: 98), while Pen envisions himself as the "grand seigneur" (2: 82). We are seeing another play, as Mr. Bows' diatribe makes clear:

> "And my belief is that you came to steal a pretty girl's heart away, and to ruin it, and to spurn it afterwards, Mr. Arthur Pendennis. That's what the world makes of you young dandies, you gentlemen of fashion, you high and mighty aristocrats that trample upon the people. It's sport to you, but what is it to the poor, think you; the toys of your pleasures, whom you play with, and whom you fling into the streets when you are tired? I know your order, sir. I know your selfishness and your arrogance, and your pride. What does it matter to my lord that the poor man's daughter is made miserable, and her family brought to shame? You must have your pleasures, and the people of course must pay for them. What are we made for, but for that? It's the way with you all – the way with you all, sir". (2: 109)

Bow's rhetoric comes directly from the melodramas and is no more true than Fanny's fairy-tale Prince Charming or the illustrations which cast this "romance" as pastoral daintiness. Chapter 8 in volume 2 depicts Pen as an 18th-century rake chucking a young girl under the chin. The rake's powdered wig, cane, and elaborate coat mark him a Georgian aristocrat seducing a country girl. The chapter title, "Monseigneur s'amuse" echoes the title of a Victor Hugo play, *Le Roi s'Amuse* (1832) about a self-indulgent king.[19] In this flirtation the innocence of fairy-tale belongs to

Fanny, depicted in the initial to chapter 10 (in volume 2) waiting in the window for Prince Charming. Like the young Pen, Fanny projects her desires onto an unworthy object. Fanny's vision of Pen as "His Royal Highness" (2: 94) and the nicety of Arcadian pastoral are undercut by Bows' unflattering theatrical version of Pen's flirtation. The "truth" lies, as so often with Thackeray, somewhere among the three modes – and neither Pen nor the reader knows precisely where. Arthur's struggle to avoid temptation contradicts Bows' version of the heartless aristocrat; Pen's vanity at Fanny's admiration makes her vision of Prince Charming ironic; and the genuineness of their attraction counters the artifice of the pastoral.

Pen's saving illness is caused by his resistance to his own sexual power. *He* is both the desired and desiring object. Resisting Fanny is resisting his narcissism. To seduce her would satisfy his vanity, but as Fanny's adoration makes clear, this is a vanity of the surface. To fulfill her stereotype is to be reduced to it. His fever burns away his fascination with the surface and releases him from his dandyism.[20] Significantly, there is a price to be paid. The fever burns away his hair thus eliminating a primary aspect of his dandyism. The loss of his hair also signifies his sexual repression. The pair of illustrations showing Pen admiring himself in his college robes (1: 167) and then ruefully gazing at his shorn head in a smaller, unadorned mirror visualize the contrast and loss. Both aesthetic and sexual energies are dimmed until he can reorient his quest.

This reorientation begins with a brutal measure, necessary to push Pen into maturity. When his mother invades his rooms to nurse him and brutally rejects Fanny, she repossesses Pen, attempting to trap him in a pre-sexual world. He must and does "kill" her, using Fanny as the weapon.[21] He attacks her doubt about his sexual restraint and Fanny's purity so violently that she has a stroke that causes her death. The Major is the catalyst for this scene, bringing Pen a letter from Fanny that Helen had suppressed. Thus, the man of the world reminds Pen that he possessed sexual desire, whether he had acted on it or not, and Pen lashes out at his mother. Her death scene re-enacts the first mother-son scene of the novel – mother and son saying the Lord's Prayer together (2: 189). But Helen's death also provides Pen with a new ideal. She becomes his icon of purity and repression literally embodied in Laura, who takes on the role of mother/sister (2: 190). To acquire the proper symbolic substitute for Helen will be to master his own desires, which once achieved will enable him to pursue writing as a *career*.

The ideal of repression changes the course of Pen's quest. Until this point, he has been mistaking material surface as an end in itself and thus his quest has been self-indulgent and narcissistic. The surfaces – Emily and Fanny's beauty, his own decoration – have blinded him just as his sexual desire has blinded him. The goal of self-discipline requires at least a curtailment of sexual desire, but desire itself reappears in his social ambition, a culturally acceptable form. *Self-consciously* pursued by the "critic" self, Pen's desire for power is marked by a cynicism that comes near to turning him into a predator. His pursuit of literary and then political success tempts him to use other people, such as faking an illness to flatter Mr. Huxter's medical skills (2: 269-70). Eventually, Pen would become unable to genuinely engage with anyone. Just as he repressed his sexual predatoriness so he must repress the social predator. Crucial to this period are the ongoing discussions between Pen and Warrington about the "best" way to live. His cynicism reflects the loss of faith that allows him to be seduced by ambition. While his growing critical eye enables Pen to see the falsity of the surface more clearly, as yet he has no substitute for appearance.

Pen's "romance" with Blanche corresponds with the cynicism that he mistakes for a mature, clear sight.[22] Blanche – the Duessa figure – dramatizes the displacement of sexual desire into social ambition. She has little sensuality and is a mass of artificial behaviors and costumes. Neither does he deceive himself about the nature of his "love". He is careful not to write any compromising letters (2: 258) and he deliberately uses the language of romance to disavow its possibility.

> "Is all life a compromise, my lady fair, and the end of the battle of love an ignoble surrender? Is the search for the Cupid which my poor little Psyche pursed in the darkness – the god of her soul's longing – the god of the blooming cheek and rainbow pinions, – to result in Huxter smelling of tobacco and gallypots? I wish, though I don't see it in life, that people could be like Jenny and Jessamy, or my lord and lady Clementina in the story books and fashionable novels. . . ."
>
> "Ah, Blanche," he continued after a pause, "don't be angry; don't be hurt at my truth-telling. Don't you see that I always take you at your word? You say you will be a slave and dance – I say, dance. You say, 'I take you with what you bring.' I say, 'I take you with what you bring.' To the necessary deceits and hypocrisies of our life

why add any that are useless and unnecessary? If I offer myself to you because I think we have a fair chance of being happy together, and because by your help I may get for both of us a good place and a not undistinguished name, why ask me to feign raptures and counterfeit romance, in which neither of us believe? Do you want me to come wooing in a Prince Prettyman's dress from the masquerade warehouse, and to pay you compliments like Sir Charles Grandison? Do you want me to make you verses as in the days when we were – when we were children? I will if you like, and sell them to Bacon and Bungay afterwards. Shall I feed my pretty princess with *bonbons*?" (2: 264-66)

This "realism" is the cynicism of chapter 23. While he is right to mistrust the literary language of romance, he is cynical to dismiss the possibility of genuine feeling. Pen's cynicism here debases the idea of love, accentuating the bargain in their romance. This commodification of love as literature to be sold debases both Pen and Blanche. And the fact is that the language of commerce more accurately defines their relation than does the language of romance. Pen's mercantile intentions are honest, but such intentions lead to cynicism because they interpret both himself and Blanche as non-human pieces of property. They are predators. Like Redcrosse, Pen fights his own Sansfoy, Sansjoie, and Sansloy – all within himself. His loss of faith in the purity of women, engendered by the loss of belief in Emily, leads him to commit himself to a joyless mercantile marriage that would be achieved by the crime of blackmail. His discussion with Warrington in "The Way of the World Chapter" illuminates the compromise Pen has made. In order to live the kind of active life he has described in 2: 63, he must become a utilitarian relativist.

Pen's ethical and aesthetic salvation lies in the above statement to Blanche, "'I always take you at your word'". Pen's personal and journalistic experiences have taught him that conventional modes of representation are non-referential constructs: Emily is not Mrs. Haller nor his Lady, and his criticism is a pastiche of jargon and superficial research. But his early life has left him with repressed belief in the possibility of meaningful signs. Pen had internalized Helen's spirit as his invisible icon— his repository of inner virtue.

All the lapse of years, all the career of fortune, all the events of life, however strongly they may move or eagerly excite him, never can

> remove that sainted image from his heart, or banish that blessed love
> from its sanctuary. If he yields to wrong, the dear eyes will look
> sadly upon him when he dares to meet them; if he does well, endures
> pain, or conquers temptation, the ever present love will greet him, he
> knows, with approval and pity. (2: 229)

However, Thackeray's placement of this passage undermines the effective power of moral vision in a world of present desire – the narrator says this just before Pen professes his cynical philosophy to Warrington, preparatory to selling himself for a seat in Parliament. Pen's memory of Helen cannot battle against his current political ambition; the invisible woman must appear. And it is at this juncture that Laura, with her "dazzling glance of calm scrutiny" (2: 278), re-enters to remind Pen of the boy whom Helen loved and to allow Pen to see the virtue Helen embodied. Laura, the repository of Helen's Word, the Lord's Prayer, points out the true quest. Laura marked out an alternative life for Pen as soon as he was sent down from Oxbridge, paying his debts with her fortune and then making Helen use the money she had saved to repay Laura to finance Pen in London so he could "be something, be worthy of his mother" (1: 253). Laura, the "country girl" (2: 278), presents Pen with the Ideal of the Victorian bower:

> "I would have you bring your wife to Fairoaks to live there, and
> study, and do good round about you. I would like to see your own
> children playing on the lawn Arthur, and that we might pray in our
> mother's church again once more, dear brother. If the world is a
> temptation, are we not told to pray that we may not be led into it?"
> (2: 286)

Now Pen can see Helen symbolized in Laura. His mother is recast as a substitute who urges him to realize his "better", i.e. private, self. Laura is characterized as is Una by a heavenly light: "Her angels face / As the great eye of heauen shyned bright, / And made a sunshine in the shadie place" (*FQ* I.iii.4). So Laura's beauty appears in "fair and trustful hand . . . bright clear eyes" (2: 281). Pen eventually recognizes his "angel" (2: 311) because she *acts* like an angel, vivifying in her appearance, behavior, and reminiscences the icon of Helen. They talk about Helen "often", Laura emphasizing the self-sacrifice of Helen's love (2: 284). Laura applies the yardstick of "goodness" to Pen's choice of career – inadvertently pointing out that going into Parliament would mean the sacrifice of his artistic ambitions. It might mean position, but his political activity would leave him no time to write and so would deny him the moral influence of the writer. Pynsent, a foil for this ambitious Pendennis, "is at the House all night; . . . always votes as he is told; . . . never speaks; . . . will never get on beyond a subordinate place; . . . [and] . . . is choked with red tape" (2: 285). Thus, Laura's "revelation" is that the position which *appears* so glorious actually subordinates the self to others' wills and, crucial to a would-be writer, *silences* the individual. Laura offers the alternative of "stop[ping] at home, and writ[ing] books – good books, kind books, with gentle kind thoughts, such as you have, dear Arthur, and such as might do people good to read . . . . I must not pretend to advise; but *I take you at your own word about the world*; and as you own it is wicked, and that it tires you, ask you why you don't leave it?" (emphasis mine; 2: 285-86). Laura undermines Pen's pose of blasé cynic by believing in a language of fixed truth just as Pen undermined Blanche's illusions of romance by taking her "at her word". Laura's "truth" is Truth because she acts out her language and the reference for both language and action is the transcendent image of Helen – female Christianity. She holds Pen true to his world by insisting that he offer to marry Blanche when they discover her father's existence (proof of her mother's bigamy) and the Major's blackmail. Laura's power comes from her willingness to sacrifice herself and Pen (by this time they know they love each other) that is, of course, to sacrifice their desire:

> "Her father's shame is not Blanche's fault, dear Arthur, is it," Laura said, very pale, and speaking very quickly . . . . "Are you not pledged to her? Would you leave her because she is in misfortune? And if she is unhappy, wouldn't you console her? Our mother would, had she been here. And, as she spoke, the kind girl folded her arms around him, and buried her face upon his heart.
> "Our mother is an angel with God," Pen sobbed out. "And you are the dearest and best of women – the dearest, the dearest and the best. Teach me my duty. Pray for me that I may do it – pure heart. God bless you – God bless you, my sister."
> "Amen," groaned out Warrington, with his hands upon his head. "She is right," he murmured to himself. "She can't do any wrong, I think – that girl." Indeed she looked and smiled like an angel. (2: 316)

Laura leads Pendennis to Faith in the same manner that Una leads

Redcrosse:

> Now when their wearie limbes with kindly rest,
>   And bodies were refresht with due repast,
>   Fair *Vna* gan *Fidelia* faire request,
>   To haue her knight into her schoolehouse plaste,
>   That of her heauenly learning he might taste,
>   And heare the wisedome of her words diuine.
>   She graunted, and that knight so much agraste,
>   That she him taught celaestiall discipline,
> And opened his dull eyes, that light mote in them shine.
>
> (FQ I.x.18)

The "sacred Booke" of Fidelia (*FQ* I.x.19) is a text that Redcrosse and Pendennis can read and believe *literally*. Gone is the disparity between sign and signified. Accepting her words as truth allows Pen to write his first piece of meaningful prose, his letter to Blanche in chapter 34. That is, this is the first piece he has written whose intent is for the good of his reader and not his own self-aggrandizement and which posits a reader who is not merely a consumer. He first presents himself to her in the language of romance because he knows that she shapes her world accordingly. The letter then repeats the scene in chapter 26 when Pen as a cynic rejected the facade of romance and saw their marriage as a financial and social exchange. But now his tone disparages neither of them and re-sees their marriage as an affectional union: "'I write gaily enough, for there is no use in bewailing a hopeless mischance. We have not drawn the great prize in the lottery, dear Blanche; but I shall be contented enough without it, if you can be so; and I repeat, with all my heart, that I will do my best to make you happy'" (2: 331). This textual "revision" is the mark of Pen's entry into Thackerayean authorship. He writes for the reader's benefit but is under no delusions about the limitations of his subject. Pen's ethos is now that of the sincere artist. His writing "gaily enough" signals his renewed faith in the possibility of, if not achieving the Good (the great prize in the lottery), at least of pursuing it.

This accomplishment is not without its price. Pen's final self-analysis when he is on his way to offer himself to Blanche, concludes that his ability to see multiple perspectives essentially isolates him; he understands the philosophy of "infinite isolations" voiced by the narrator early in the book. But he ungrudgingly accepts responsibility for himself and his actions in a world he sees as driven by chance. He will no longer sit on the balcony and smoke his pipe but come down to the ground and fight for the truth even while he is uncertain of it.

> "Ah me! you must bear your own burthen, fashion your own faith, think your own thoughts, and pray your own prayer. To what mortal ear could I tell all, if I had a mind? or who could understand all? Who can tell another's shortcomings, lost opportunities, weigh the passions which overpower, the defects which incapacitate reason? – what extent of truth and right his neighbour's mind is organised to perceive and to do? – what invisible and forgotten accident, terror of youth, chance or mischance of fortune, may have altered the current of life? A grain of sand may alter it, as the flinging of a pebble may end it. Who can weigh circumstances, passion, temptations, that go to our good and evil account, save One, before whose awful wisdom we kneel and at whose mercy we ask absolution." (2: 340)

Pen's self-contextualizing imitates the narrative method and signals his own beginning as a narrator. When Pen laughs upon discovering Blanche has transferred her affections to his friend Foker, he is refusing to play the role of brutal lover in which Blanche's lies to Foker have cast him. As he moves into narrator status, the laughter will no longer be "wild and loud" (2: 342) because it will be less personal. But here, his amusement over the meaningless letter Blanche writes in return to his proposal and the laughter denote his entry into a self-ironic vision beyond the *laissez-faire* skepticism of chapter 23.

The narrative – for the last time in a Thackeray novel – rewards Pen for this growth into skeptical fideism. Blanche is false to him so he is free to marry Laura, knowing he has acted faithfully. The reader is "rewarded" by this happy ending just as is Pen. The end of the story affirms his development into a narrator in that he acts on immediate perceptions as if they were real, but his long views intervene to keep him from clinging to an action or a perception when it is shown to be inadequate. Thus he can laugh at himself and Blanche because he maintains a stable sense of moral reality in Laura. He has, in fact, the best of both worlds: relativism and the ability, by means of Laura's code, to decide upon right and wrong.

This conclusion represents the integration of Pendennis's several selves. The weaker Pen, Redcrosse, has struggled through his delusions to fight the dragon of his own self-fashionings to win Una. "Prince Arthur", the egotist so deliberately named in the Fanny Bolton episode has been rescued by "Arthur" – his better nature. His final sacrifice demands an even greater regulation of self than with Fanny, because Pen must consciously choose to repress a love that he understands is superior to his previous desires and that would save him from his ambition for power. Significantly, Laura never calls him anything but "Arthur" when she re-enters the novel, and she achieves the ascendancy at their engagement: Pen's "heart is humbled by the prospect of his happiness: it stood awe-struck in the contemplation of her goodness and purity" (2: 348). Pen's inchoate dream of an ideal that he thought he had recognized "too late" (2: 311) has been realized. Luckier than Spenser's Prince Arthur, Arthur Pendennis gets to marry his Faerie Queene. Whether the idyll in the country is all that Laura promises it will be is another matter.

Cates Baldridge has argued that Pen accepts a bond of "silence" by the end of *Pendennis*.[23] The unspoken "but" in chapter 71, "the sceptic's familiar, with whom he has made a compact", "stands as the synoptic title for Pen's book of worldliness, a title that – while not revealing particulars – sums up the power that the still-hidden text possesses: that of undermining and cancelling every possible statement of Victorian orthodoxy with a corrosive, skeptical qualification" (Baldridge 506). But if Pen is to become a writer, he must find a way to speak – and to speak without being trapped, like Blanche, by his vision. The solution in *Pendennis* is to don the mask of Harlequin; the illustrations and text at the end of the novel align Pen with the critic-narrator of *Vanity Fair*. Similar to the fool and clown, Pen's status as narrator is the role of pantomime Harlequin even as he plays at his political ambitions.

This self-illusion is one that Pen is actually aware is all pretense: his campaign for the Clavering's seat in Parliament. While readers still know more than Pen at this point, for we know the seat is his because the Major has blackmailed Clavering, Pen knows that his election antics are acting. So the "consummate" hypocrisy of Pen "acting" to gain people's favor (2: 269) is not mimetic theatre but pantomime – that most extravagant and self-conscious form of theater which transforms "ordinary" life into fantasy. The initial to chapter 27 puts the traditional pantomime characters, Harlequin, Clown, Columbine, and Pantaloon at the hustings, entertaining an absorbed audience (Fig. 3.3). This initial dramatizes the conspiracy between actors and audience who know they act but both act the part of not acting. The narrator asks:

How is it that we allow ourselves not to be deceived but to be
ingratiated so readily by a glib tongue, a ready laugh, and a frank
manner? We know for the most part, that it is false coin, and we
take it: we know that it is flattery, which costs nothing to distribute
to everybody, and we had rather have it than be without it. (2: 269)

Pen's personal pantomime begins in the next illustration, an intratext
showing him "being a little unwell . . . the rascal took the advantage of the
circumstance to show his tongue to Mr. Huxter, who sent him medicines and
called the next morning. How delighted Old Pendennis would have been with
his pupil! Pen himself was amused with the sport in which he was engaged,
and his success inspired him with a wicked good humor" (2: 270). While
Pen has internalized the knowledge that "all the world's a stage", he still
imagines his role to be superior to others; he is not yet the melancholy fool.

An actor knowing that his role is a role may turn the role and play into
ridicule; however, if he sees the self-irony in his role, he becomes
"Harlequin", a brother wearer of motley. During Thackeray's life, the
pantomime began with a mock-realistic scene, with the major characters
wearing paper maché "big heads". The good fairy would descend, give the
big-head who was Harlequin a "magic bat"; Harlequin would then
transform himself and the other characters into the traditional pantomime
characters, and the "realistic" scene would be transformed into the
pantomime world. After the Harlequinade, all the characters assembled for a
grandiose final tableau in a fairy-tale world, called variously, the "Realms of
Bliss", or "Fairy Cave". *Pendennis* ends with a "Harlequinade" that marks
Pen's entry into the world of the ironist. The masked Harlequin of the
election in chapter 27 unmasks in chapter 34, easily recognizable as
Pendennis (Fig. 3.4). "Harlequin without his mask is known to present a
very sober countenance, and was himself, the story goes, the melancholy
patient whom the doctor advised to go and see Harlequin – a man full of
cares and perplexities like the rest of us, whose self must always be serious
to him, under whatever mask or disguise or uniform he presents it to the
public" (XIV, 423). The Harlequin Pen, whose costume echoes that of the
1844 Pantomime *Harlequin Crotchet and Quaver; or, Music for the
Million*, gazes questioningly at a masked lady as if asking her if she, too,
will unmask, and what will be revealed when and if she does (Fig. 3.5). Pen
has "unmasked" by recognizing the hollowness of his ambition and not

becoming bitter; his smile is now that of the melancholy Thackeray's at the end of chapter 9 in *Vanity Fair*. Paradoxically, Pen's entry into the clear-sightedness which will make him an author is through his recognition that although acting is inescapable, one can choose one's roles. His letter to Blanche contrasts her roles of vizier's daughter and Lady of Lyons with the more serious role of domestic realism – to recognize her limitations and be ordinary.

Blanche's inability to escape from her illusions, to see her parts as parts, is visualized in the initial to 2: 35. The lady has unmasked, but Harlequin has been superceded by Clown, recognizably Foker, who kisses her hand (Fig. 3.6). The next illustration offers, from Pen's point of view, a "discovery scene" from melodrama in which Pen finds Foker with Blanche. Pen's consequent laughter, the irony of his conversation with Blanche, and his willingness to let himself be "cast" as the villain demonstrate his control over his roles. It is appropriate that this Pen should become a "narrator" in 2: 37 to end his participation in this melodrama. He tells Lady Clavering about the last "discovery" scene in the novel, a full-page illustration titled "A Discovery", in which the romantic Madame Frisby discovers Colonel Altamont to be her husband Johnny Armstrong.

Pendennis's movement into the pictorial initials is a literal and symbolic move out of the boundaries of the verbal story and its events. Characters created by the narrator act within their sphere of knowledge; the initials offer perspectives unavailable to the characters and not always available to the narrator. Pen's self-discovery disqualifies him as "character", lifting him from the fixed perspective of those who do not know that they are "acting" in a story, to the detached, ironic perspective of narrator. *The History of Pendennis* introduces a complicated business of mask and being for the rest of Thackeray's novels for, in the later fiction, Pendennis unmasked will become Thackeray masked in *The Newcomes*, *The Virginians*, and *The Adventures of Philip*. It is significant that Pen plays the role of Harlequin and not clown. Harlequin has the Magic Bat that transforms other characters – just as the Manager controls his puppets and the narrator his story. Harlequin masked is an anonymous actor, subject to the story, but unmasked he will be the melancholy moralist who constructs the tale. A successful narrative mask presents to the readers a role that seems to be no role. In *Pendennis*, the mask is the avuncular arm-chair voice. The image "mask" suggests the stability of this role; the frozen features of a mask are analogous to the stable tone and repeated patterns of

Fig. 3.3. Pictorial Initial, volume 2, Chapter 27, *Pendennis*
Photograph courtesy of Elizabeth Huth Coates Library, Trinity University

Fig. 3.4. Pictorial Initial, volume 2, Chapter 34, *Pendennis*
Photograph courtesy of Elizabeth Huth Coates Library, Trinity University

Fig. 3.5. *Harlequin Crotchet and Quaver; or, Music for the Million*, December 1844
Raymond Mander and Joe Mitchenson, *Pantomime*
Photograph courtesy of Elizabeth Huth Coates Library, Trinity University

Fig. 3.6, Pictorial Initial, volume 2, Chapter 35, *Pendennis*
Photograph courtesy of Elizabeth Huth Coates Library, Trinity University

the near/far vision. The narrative strategy in *Pendennis* coheres through its very theatricality – playing a role that does not tell us it is a role but which must be a role by its very consistency in attitude, prose habits, and perceptual patterns. The narrative successfully performs what Pendennis grows toward: role-playing as "communion" (Harden, "Theatricality", 74). The narrative presence is one that constructs connections between itself and the readers; it permits communication. Like the narrator, Pen becomes aware of his role-playing and the ability of skillful manipulation of ones' roles in order to create communities. His languages can tell stories because he understands the referential conventions of different communities while being trapped in none.

Successful role-playing or narrating in *Pendennis* is self-conscious acting of roles chosen "to dramatize genuine feelings of sympathy and love, and thereby to bring a temporary end to human isolation" (Harden, "Theatricality", 93). To recognize that we are trapped in our interpretations is to be able to learn to adopt the perspective of others – to accept the roles they prepare for us and so join them without losing our sense of "self" which distinguishes us from the role. Narrator, reader, and character share the need to belong to a community without either manipulating the community to serve one's self or being appropriated by its conventions. This precarious balance is most clearly explored in the Thackerayean siren who is a metaphor for the text and in *Henry Esmond* where the right-line-I is narrator, mask, and story.

Notes

[1] Deborah Thomas, *Thackeray and Slavery* (Athens, OH: Ohio UP, 1993), chapter 4.

[2] *Thackeray's Universe: Shifting Worlds of Imagination and Reality* (Boston: Faber and Faber, 1987), 173.

[3] Jean Sudrann, "The Philosopher's Property: Thackeray and the Use of Time", *Victorian Studies* 10 (1967), 359-88. Myron Taube, "Thackeray and the Reminiscential Vision", *Nineteenth-Century Fiction* 18 (1963), 247-59, Juliet McMaster, *Thackeray. The Major Novels* (Toronto: U of Toronto P, 1971), 51-86.

[4] I use "arbitrary" here to mean "constructed" not "random".

[5] "The Exhibition of the Royal Academy. Second Notice", *The Morning Chronicle* (7 May 1946), *Contributions to the Morning Chronicle*, ed. Gordon N. Ray (Urbana: U of Illinois P, 1955), 148.

[6] Lund points out that Thackeray used two times to "mark the protagonist's growth: the time that measures the occurrence of events in the fictional world of the characters; and reading time, which measures the occurrence of events in the reader's world as he turns pages of the novel". Michael Lund, *Reading Thackeray* (Detroit: Wayne State UP, 1988), 48.

[7] In this balanced technique invites reader engagement and distanced evaluation, *Pendennis* is, I suspect, consciously criticizing Goethe's *The Sufferings of Young Werther* whose histrionics drew Thackeray's scorn. He wrote a satiric ballad parodying the novel which contrasts Werther's romantic passion with Charlotte's mundanity:
> . . . . So he sighed and pined and ogled,
>   And his passion boiled and bubbled,
> Till he blew his silly brains out,
>   And no more was by it troubled.
>
> Charlotte, having seen his body
>   Borne before her on a shutter,
> Like a well-conducted person,
>   Went on cutting bread-and-butter. (XXIV, 78)

[8] Thackeray changed the details of this design between monthly number and volume, toning down the explicit sexuality of the siren and Pendennis's own ambivalence. I have reproduced both versions.

[9] This is an example of how editing practices have undercut Thackeray's original designs. In the "cheap" edition of 1856, revised purely for profit, Thackeray had to cut out "approximately eighteen solid pages of text . . .along with the 179 illustrations" (Shillingsburg, "Introduction", 393). In this revision,

chapters 16 and 17 were elided and much of the village gossip omitted as "redundant". However, the gossip in the first edition serves to emphasize Pen's selfishness and the hidden motives from which we all act. It is worth a comparison between editions to see how this "streamlining" simplifies the kaleidoscopic narration.

[10] Catherine Peters notes the ass's ears (she refers specifically to the cover page of *Vanity*) refers to Carlyle's disparagement of the novelist writing a "Long-ear of a Fictitious Biography" ("Biography", 1832; qted in Peters 145).

[11] Juliet McMaster discusses Pen's development as it depends upon his ability to balance the competing perspectives of Helen and the Major (chapter 7). While these are two prominent perspectives, his encounters with Warrington, Fanny, Sam, even Bows, are also lessons in perception.

[12] Edmund Spenser, "*The Faerie Queene*", Poetical Works, ed. J. C. Smith and E. de Selincourt (Oxford: Oxford UP), 1969. Hereafter cited as *FQ* in the text.

[13] McMaster makes the point that *Pendennis* is about the development of Pen into an artist oriented precisely about perception (67). His infatuation with Emily is the early idealistic stage of his development while the romance with Blanche derives from Pen's mistaking cynicism for honesty (chapter 2).

[14] Karlheinze Stierle, "The Reading of Fictional Texts" in *The Reader in The Text*, ed. Susan Suleiman and Inge Crosman (Princeton: Princeton UP, 1980), 87.

[15] The diction in this simile aligns the gift of the watch *from the father* when the son moves into late boyhood with the conscious awakening of sexual desire in the adolescent. Keeping both watch and love secret, examining them in private, and "hugging", "rubbing", and "polishing" suggest the secret delights of masturbation.

[16] *The Mirror of Narcissus in the Courtly Love Lyric* (Ithaca: Cornell UP, 1967), 47-50.

[17] Edgar Harden has noted that this chapter title is emblematic of Pen's confusion between Emily and the roles she plays. As he points out, Pen goes to see "Mrs. Haller", the character in Kotzebue's *The Stranger*, not Emily Fotheringay. ("Theatricality in *Pendennis*", *Ariel* 4 [1973]), 75.

[18] The title is also a pun on Walter Deloraine, the hero of Walter Scott's *Lay of the Last Minstrel*.

[19] This play would have emphasized Pendennis's self-indulgence to a contemporary audience. *Le Roi S'Amuse* (*The King Amuses Himself*) was the source for Verdi's Rigoletto and a later English adaptation by Tom Taylor, *The Fool's Revenge* (1859). Hugo's melodramatic play focuses on a jester who abets his royal master's debaucheries. The jester's acerbic tongue alienates the courtiers who, in revenge, abduct a beautiful girl they think is his mistress but who is actually his daughter. Blanche, the victim, "submits" to the prince and ends by

dying to save him by drinking poison her father intended for her seducer.

[20]   A parallel exists between Pen's fever and Sir Guyon's swoon when he escapes from the House of Mammon (II.vii, 66).

[21]   Helen's sexual jealous intensifies the need for her death; she is in "rage" at being "dispossessed somehow of her son's heart, or that there were recesses in it which she must not or dared not enter. She sickened as she thought of the sacred days of boyhood when it had not been so – when her Arthur's heart had no secrets, and she was his all in all" (2: 173). This is not a mother who could ever resign herself to her son growing into sexual maturity.

[22]   Foker acts as a foil to Pen during this phase. As Pen grows more and more clear-sighted, Foker becomes more and more starry-eyed over Blanche. Thackeray makes this contrast clear in passages such as this one from after the ball at Gaunt House. In the early dawn, all flaws are revealed:

> Blanche smiled languidly out upon the young men, thinking whether she looked very wan and green under her rose-coloured hood, and whether it was the mirrors at Gaunt House, or the fatigue and fever of her own eyes, which made her fancy herself so pale.
>
> Arthur, perhaps, saw quite well how yellow Blanche looked, but did not attribute that peculiarity of her complexion to the effect of the looking-glasses, or to any error in his sight or her own. Our young man of the world could use his eyes very keenly and could see Blanche's face pretty much as nature had made it. But for poor Foker it had a radiance which dazzled and blinded him: he could see no more faults in it than in the sun. (2: 71-72).

[23]   "The Problems of Worldliness in *Pendennis*", *Nineteenth-Century Fiction* 44 (1990), 492-513.

4 The Rebellious Text and the Resisting Reader

[L]ove for an actress in nineteenth-century literature [explores] the aesthetic and metaphysical implications of the arbitrariness of signs – their lack of anchorage in either so-called reality or some equally elusive transcendental principle. The work of art – as it is figured by the actress as muse appears as an object of desire, but an illusory one, standing for an absolute object (or referent) that can only be elsewhere, or (more radically) irremediably absent.[1]

If a painter chose to join a human head to the neck of a horse, and to spread feathers of many a hue over limbs picked up now here now there, so that what at the top is a lovely woman ends below in a black and ugly fish, could you my friends, if favoured with a private view, refrain from laughing? Believe me, dear Pisos, quite like such pictures would be a book, whose idle fancies shall be shaped like a sick man's dreams, so that neither head nor foot can be assigned to a single shape.[2]

It is appropriate that it is Horace, one of Thackeray's favorite authors, who envisions the deformed text as a "lovely woman" whose nether regions are "a black and ugly fish" and so connects Thackeray's own texts to his sirens. Becky, Emily, Blanche, Beatrix, Ethel, Maria, and Agnes are all actresses, more or less self-defined as such, whose use their socially constructed sexuality for their own ends: either to "lure their victims" or to "secure a competency", depending upon the reader's point of view. The sirens are signs, texts, constructions of the not-so-idle fancies of the narrators, the male protagonists, and themselves. To love them is to love their reflection of you; to read them as texts is to project your own desires upon them. To an extent, any art work expresses the desires of its maker, even if those desires are hidden underneath terms such as "vision" or "inspiration". So an analysis of the contradictory nature and function of Thackeray's sirens offers an analysis of the narcissistic seduction of art for artist and audience, a central danger of post-Romantic aesthetics. True to Thackeray's description of writers as "actors", Pen, the incipient writer, first "performs" his writing for his friends at Oxbridge, turning his abortive love for Emily into a self-aggrandizing, Byronic one-man show.

> Pen had [a print of Emily] hung in his bedroom, and confided to the men of his set how awfully, how wildly, how madly, how passionately, he had loved that woman. He showed them in confidence the verses that he had written to her, and his brow would darken, his eyes roll, his chest heave with emotion as he recalled that fatal period of his life, and described the woes and agonies which he had suffered. The verses were copied out, handed about, sneered at, admired, passed from coterie to coterie. (*P* 1: 175)

While Pen's Sternism results in solipsistic theatrical performance, the narrative demonstrates the need for such intense experience despite the danger of self-delusion: Pen does publish *Walter Lorraine*, and it brings him a modicum of fame and fortune. A writer or a painter starts from his own vision: "a poet sets down his thoughts and experiences upon paper as a painter does a landscape or a face upon canvas, to the best of his ability, and according to his particular gift" (*P* 2: 24). Warrington, the rational skeptic, of course sees emotional "distance" as emotional prostitution, in that the artist replaces genuine emotion with emotion fabricated for, and only existing in, linguistic conventions.

> "That's the way of poets," said Warrington. "They fall in love, jilt, or are jilted: they suffer and they cry out that they suffer more than any other mortals: and when they have experienced feelings enough they note them down in a book, and take the book to market. All poets are humbugs, all literary men are humbugs: directly a man begins to sell his feelings for money he's a humbug." (*P* 2: 24)

Warrington understands the commercial exchange underlying Romantic subjectivity. He criticizes the transformation of language from spontaneous expression into the conventional formulae, which underlies the transformation of self into text. Since such distance allows the artist to craft feeling into art, implying that the language is the story, all post-Romantic artists are necessarily "humbugs" in his terms. And we have already seen in *Pendennis* that Pen's "spontaneous" outbursts derive from his reading of

Byron and Scott.

As Pen's verses inspired by Emily suggest, Thackeray's sirens, his linguistically and sexually seductive women are metaphors for literary texts and explorations into the delicate balance between using conventions of representation for selfish effect or to strengthen the bond of an interpretive community. At her best – or worst? – the siren is an "empty text", one that is nothing but conventions without extra-textual or intrinsic meaning and, as such, is open to interpretation. This neutral description develops positive and negative possibilities as Thackeray's sirens create themselves and as the narrators and protagonists try to contain them. By being all effect, to apply Meisel's term, Blanche, Becky, and Agnes risk completely alienating themselves from any community of meaning.   The more absorbed they become in their own performances, the less reference they have to anything outside their own conventions, and, consequently, the less meaning they have if one defines meaning as an *interaction* requiring a text and a reader, or a surface and an interpreter. Textual "meaning" can be identified with human identity: both are relational. As Barry Westburg puts it, "[n]o I exists without its thou".[3] When the sirens' performances and appearances slide into self-reference, they become texts incoherent to their readers. They no longer speak or display any sociolect; their languages become only their own, directed toward only themselves. But, while these solipsistic sirens are brilliant parodies of the egoism of the Romantic artist-turned-performer, they also embody and illustrate the danger particular to women of accepting the conventions of a cultural self-fashioning that insists on reading women by their surface. Thackeray's sirens are a paradox: generated from a mimetic aesthetic, they show us there is no mimesis in that aesthetic. But, paradoxically, this same emptiness can be a means to their survival, as Thackeray's (not his narrators') texts suggest if we read aware of the conventions that underlie these characters.

Blanche Amory becomes a consummate Sternist artist in *The History of Pendennis*. Her comically incoherent letter to Pendennis responding to his marriage proposal illustrates the disintegration of textual identity. The meaninglessness of her letter shows all the more sharply in its narrative context because the moment in the story is the crisis point for Pen and Laura. Will Blanche marry Pen and settle for an ordinary affection, thus trapping Pen in his self-sacrifice? Her letter cannot answer this question because she can no longer conceive of an "other" who needs to interpret her; she is trapped in a completely self-referential construction. What was a silly affectation of the language of "sentiment" in chapter 22 has become by chapter 72 language unable to communicate. Blanche's language has become, in effect, a pseudo-language, referring to nothing but her own chaotic fantasies of herself. She has emptied herself into random linguistic conventions with no regard for the responsive understanding of others. Her answer to Pen's final letter is a free-floating pastiche of cheap romance lines:

> . . . . I would have our two hearts one; but ah, my Arthur, how lonely yours is! how little you give me of it! . . . . Is life but a disillusion, then, and are the flowers of our garden faded away? I have wept – I prayed – I have passed sleepless hours – I have shed bitter tears over your letter! To you I bring the gushing poesy of my being – the yearnings of the soul that longs to be loved – that pines of love, love, love, beyond all! – that flings itself at your feet, and cries, Love me, Arthur!. . . . You treat me like a slave, and bid me bow to my master! Is this the guerdon of a free maiden – is this the price of a life's passion?" (*P* 2: 331-32)

These excerpts give some idea of the theatrical rant that constitutes Blanche's "communication". Blanche's disassociation from external events does allow her to transform Pen's proposal into a "betrayal" to justify her preference for Foker and his money: "'You flung me back with scorn the troth which I have had plighted! I have explained all – all to Mr. Foker'" (*P* 2: 343). But such callous manipulations of language are sporadic moments of control within a largely uncontrolled fantasy life. She does not feel that external realities, even her criminal father's reappearance (that for a short while make her mother seem a bigamist and Blanche, thus, illegitimate) have any effect on her (*P* 2: 366). What matters are her own desires, which, in fact, have no ability to structure an interpretable identity because they exist as self-directed posturings unregulated by any sense of a community of discourse. Blanche plays herself to and for herself and is immersed in her image. She is transfixed by her gaze into the mirror of self. Lacking any humility or recognition of kinship with others, Blanche's roles sustain a narcissism which devours her. To lose the understanding that to *play* a role requires awareness that one *is* playing a role and that "role-playing" implies an audience is to become insane, to be able to say "I am Napoleon" because your language loses any conventional referents. Thus, the narrator concludes that Blanche is only her random verbal expressions: "this young lady was not able to carry out any emotion to the full; but had a sham enthusiasm, a sham hatred, a sham love, a sham taste, a sham grief, each of which flared and shone very vehemently for an instant, but subsided and gave place to the next sham emotion" (*P* 2: 345). Blanche embodies the danger Pen courts when his Byronic despair over Emily or his later blasé cynicism develop into his projections of the world. Edgar Harden concludes that "what really exists at the heart of this circle of sham emotions is precisely nothing; at the center of the role, its motive and epitome, exists complete emptiness, for the self has been dissipated through a surrender to role-playing".[4]

Blanche's "emptiness" – because it is so conventional – entices Pen and Foker into Stierles' "quasi-pragmatic" reading. All the sirens, like Blanche, can be interpreted by any of the protagonists' mediated, that is culturally determined, desires: Pen's Romantic literary imagination then his rakish cynicism; Rawdon and George's oriental male vanity; Clive's bourgeois aestheticism; Henry's neoclassicism and need to worship and be worshipped. She lures others into a world of illusion either by meeting their own self-projections (George and Pen) or inscribing hers upon an empty field (Rawdon and Foker). A literal embodiment of the text, the siren is self and culturally authored, is written, in other words, by her own submission to cultural codes, by the narrator who places her within pictorial traditions of "high art", and by the protagonists who sometimes see with the narrator but more often function as self-deluding interpreters of her text.

The sirens' conflation of aesthetics and commercialism parodies the novel's dilemma: she only exists to sell herself, but her marketplace denies this reality it has forced upon her. So, too, the artist produces a narrator who creates an illusion of "reality" in order to satisfy the desires of his marketplace. Thackeray's own rejection of the visual sublime, exemplified in the works of Michael Angelo or Nicholas Poussin, with its power to sweep away the viewer, characterizes the sirens' threatening sexuality – which he never sees as natural but as culturally produced.[5]   She mirrors the protagonists' narcissistic desire to appropriate the world as their own creation. Her self-display invites harmful, self-absorbed belief. The narrators control her seductive power by subsuming the women under their [male] language of the conventions of art, and their descriptions control her intense effect even as they suggest for the readers that she is a dangerous artifact. The narrators are both attracted and repulsed by sirens such as Becky Sharp, Ethel Newcome, and Beatrix Esmond and this ambiguity conveys the necessary narcissism of the protagonists' desires, and the narrators' own attempts to control their texts.

> [P]aintings in romance function ambiguously as symbols of both the beloved and the romance of a work of art . . . Paintings in romance thus symbolize the endangered self – frozen, suspended, imprisoned, enthralled – and also the essential self – removed from the vicissitudes and contingencies of life, raised to a higher purity of being.[6]

But paintings are also actual objects, bought and sold in Thackeray's realistic world; they epitomize how the marketplace supposedly corrupts the aesthetic object and the admirer. So the objectification of the sirens as art works captures their position as objects to be bought and sold. For Thackeray an archetypal romance image – woman as art work – is also a contemporary *realistic* type – woman as commodity. I use the word "supposedly" because, as a close look at Beatrix and Ethel in particular show, in Thackeray's world, there is no "aesthetic object" separate from the "marketplace", thus the corruption exists in the perceptual tradition itself.

The tensions between the idealization of women in the romance tradition and the image of woman as artifact, decorated for display and sale, undermine the assumptions of both traditions. The narrators' conflicting descriptions of the siren and the women's inner vitality struggle against the annihilation of self that is implied by the entire metaphoric process. Emily Costigan, for example, seems to have the majesty and sublime presence of classical statuary:

> Her forehead was vast, and her black hair waved over it with a natural ripple . . . and was confined in shining and voluminous braids at the back of a neck such as you see on the shoulders of the Louvre Venus – that delight of gods and men. Her eyes, when she lifted them up to gaze on you, and ere she dropped the purple deep-fringed lids, shone with tenderness and mystery unfathomable. Love and Genius seemed to look out from them and then retire coyly, as if ashamed to have been seen at the lattices. Who could have had such a commanding brow but a woman of high intellect? She never laughed (indeed her teeth were not good,) but a smile of endless tenderness and sweetness played round her beautiful lips, and in the

dimples of her cheeks and her lovely chin. Her nose defied description in those days. Her ears were like two little pearl shells, which the earrings she wore (though the handsomest properties in the theatre) only insulted. She was dressed in long flowing robes of black which she managed and swept to and fro with wonderful grace, and out of the folds of which you only saw her sandals occasionally; they were of rather a large size. (*P* 1: 36)

Two voices speak in the above description. One is the voice of the art critic, while the other satiric voice consistently undercuts the classical allusions and the pictorial presentation. The icon is simultaneously created and destroyed. Emily's double physical appearance reflects her dual nature. She is not really conscious of her beauty, sees it, if at all, as a simple tool of her profession, and maintains the language and manners of her unaffected Irish nature. But she is also a trained mimic; she can use stage language and manners as props just as she wears the "pearl" earrings. Unlike Becky, Emily is not a true actress; that is, she has not the creativity to shape her own parts. She is the creation of the old man, Bows, and slips in and out of her parts as she does her costume. Unlike Blanche, Emily is not a sham but empty: she "has no heart and no head, and no sense, and no feelings, and no griefs or cares, whatever" (*P* 1: 128). She is a pure formula novel, unpretentiously presenting an illusion with no desire to fool the reader into mistaking her decorative surface for an essential self. Emily never thinks of intruding her stage parts into her own life; Pen is the one who translates her ignorance into charming innocence and simple humor.

Emily, although the first of Thackeray's "natural" sirens, parodies the later two, Beatrix and Ethel, both of whom are more dangerous, as suggested by their descriptions, because they are more conscious of their beauty and power, which is to say, that they possess their own surfaces and have not simply been "decorated". However, merely to say "dangerous" is to oversimplify. While Beatrix and Ethel may seem to be more genuine than Emily because their desires actively manipulate their appearance, this "sincerity", ironically, makes them predators because the cultural purpose of their surface is to use it to entrap the male. Pen is very clear in *The Newcomes* that Ethel cannot act other than she does (until her "conversion") because her upbringing schools her to choose to do so. This tension between objectification and agency is reflected in the narrators' varying attitudes toward the sirens. The narrator's condemnation of the siren's autonomous self-representation, such as Ethel's appearance at the ball at Baden or Beatrix making "mischief", contradicts his own construction of the siren as an object valorized by the male gaze which *demands her display* on stage, at balls, or in the parlor.

Beatrix and Ethel share similar visual tropes; both are likened to dangerous mythological figures; both are presented as too bright to look upon; and both employ the "killing glance". Even as a child Beatrix "could sing and dance like a nymph" and "had long learned the value of her bright eyes, and tried experiments in coquetry" (*HE* 94). The dark side of her enchantment is her ability to play one parent against the other and her "delight" in "the mischief which she knew how to make so early" (*HE* 94). Henry's enthrallment with her physical beauty as she grows wills his ignorance of her manipulative nature. When she is a "slim and lovely young girl" her cheeks blush with "roses", her eyes are "like stars shining out of azure. . .[her] waving bronze hair clustered about the fairest young forehead ever seen" (*HE* 105-106). But her demeanor is as "haughty" as she is beautiful, "such as that of the famous antique statue of the Huntress Diana – at one time haughty, rapid, imperious, with eyes and arrows that dart and kill" (*HE* 106). Beautiful but deadly while only thirteen years old, Beatrix is a type of "Artemis with the ringing bow and shafts flashing death upon the children of Niobe". Her "mischief" grows "more fatal. . . as a kitten first plays with a ball, and then pounces on a bird and kills it" (*HE* 106). Beatrix's mature beauty is almost more than the male eye can bear:

> She was a brown beauty; that is, her eyes, hair, and eyebrows and eyelashes were dark: her hair curling with rich undulations and waving over her shoulders; but her complexion was a dazzling white as snow in sunshine, except her cheeks, which were a bright red, and her lips which were of a still deeper crimson. Her mouth and chin, they said, were too large and full, and so they might be for a Goddess in marble, but not for a woman whose eyes were fire, whose look was love, whose voice was the sweetest low song, whose shape was perfect symmetry, health, decision, activity, whose foot as it planted itself on the ground was firm but flexible, and whose motion, whether rapid or slow, was always perfect grace – agile as a nymph, lofty as a queen – now melting, now imperious, now sarcastic, there was no single movement of hers but was beautiful. (*HE* 179)

Beatrix now combines sexual invitation as part of her aesthetic perfection; her "mischief" will likewise be seen as luring men to a kind of "death". And this, when "'not sixteen. . . one young gentleman is already whimpering over a lock of her hair, and two country squires are ready to cut each other's throats that they may have the honour of a dance with her'" (*HE* 188). She becomes the "fatal" object (*HE* 221), who "plies" young lords with "all the fire of her eyes" (*HE* 257). Beatrix's very vitality conflicts with Henry's classical description which attempts to freeze her into a statue female sexuality. How can an "object" be "fatal"?

We need to ask the same question of Pendennis' and Clive's characterizations of Ethel Newcome which pit a "natural" Ethel against a "social" Ethel. Most of the descriptions of Ethel come though Clive's aestheticized eyes that sublimate the siren's sexuality into the language of pictures. However, anyone familiar with Thackeray's attitude toward the sublime in "On the French School of Painting" or "On Men and Pictures", can easily see the sexual fatality generated by this "social" siren. Her natural beauty is evidenced by Colonel Newcome's identification of her with his lost love Leonore (*N* 1: 145, 187), by her own love of children, and her easy reclamation by Laura Pendennis. As she comes of age and enters society, we see her as Clive comes to see her, through his drawing. "He had made a thousand sketches of Ethel before a year was over; a year, every day of which seemed to increase the attractions of the fair young creature, develop her nymph-like form, and give her figure fresh graces" (*N* 1: 157). Her social conditioning shapes this innocent "nymph" into a calculating huntress who uses her natural beauty to capture a husband. Pen and Clive see this social Ethel as a cold, cruel Mayfair Diana:

> But those who had no cause to heed Diana's shot or coldness might admire her beauty; nor could the famous Parisian marble, which Clive said she resembled be more perfect in form than this young lady. Her hair and eyebrows were jet black . . . , but her complexion was as dazzlingly fair and her cheeks as red as Miss Rosey's own . . . . In Miss Ethel's black hair there was a slight natural ripple, . . . a ripple such as Roman ladies nineteen hundred years ago, and our own beauties a short time since, endeavoured to imitate by art, paper, and I believe crumpling irons. (*N* 1: 228-29)

During these adolescent days Clive can admire the cold virgin because he is not in love with her (*N* 1: 185); his neoclassical art training with Gandish inspires in him an "aesthetic passion" that develops during his visit to the Louvre. Writing to Pen, Clive compares the Venus de Milo and Ethel-Diana:

> "I had not been ten minutes in [the Louvre] before I fell in love with the most beautiful creature the world has ever seen. She was standing, silent and majestic, in the centre of one of the rooms of the statue gallery, and the very first glimpse of her struck one breathless with the sense of her beauty. I could not see the colour of her eyes and hair exactly, but the latter is light and the eyes, I should think, are grey. Her complexion is of a beautiful warm marble tinge. She is not a clever woman, evidently; I do not think she laughs or talks much . . . . She is only beautiful." (*N* 1: 203)

Of course this statue exists as an object for admiration, but Clive personifies the statue, presenting her as an ideal type of female beauty. Her lack of agency increases her beauty: Clive claims the Venus is only "more beautiful" because of the loss of her arms. Clive prefers this harmless passivity to Ethel's vibrancy:

> "[Ethel] has a great look of the huntress Diana. It is sometimes too proud and too cold for me. The blare of those horns is too shrill, and the rapid pursuit through bush and bramble too daring. O thou generous Venus!" (*N* 1: 203)

Clive's training makes him see Ethel as divinely beautiful, but when her humanity forces him to vivify his images, he creates an Ethel who is as much of a man-killer as Beatrix.

> "As for Ethel . . . . How she . . . looks at you from under those black eyebrows! If I painted her hair, I think I should paint it almost blue, and then glaze over with lake. It is blue. And how finely her head is joined on to her shoulders!". . . "She would do for Judith, wouldn't she? or how grand she would look as Herodias's daughter sweeping down a stair – in a great dress of cloth of gold like Paul Veronese – holding a charger before her with white arms, you know – with the muscles accented like the glorious Diana at Paris – a savage smile on her face and a ghastly solemn gory head on the dish – I see the picture, sir, I see the picture!" (*N* 1: 233)

Clive's conventional images of Judith and Salome, of course, identify Eros with Thanatos. His infatuation with her surface turns Ethel into a killer. Is it this deadly energy that keeps Clive from being able to paint her? He despairs at his inability actually to reduce Ethel to a frozen icon. "'You may paint her form, but you can't paint her colour; that is what beats us in nature'" (*N* 1: 253). But this same painterly drive leads him to admire Ethel's beauty just as "he worshipped . . . masterpieces of his art" (*N* 1:282).

When Ethel steps out of her frame, she fulfills the deadly nature that the male pictorial tradition assumes motivates her beauty. Angry at the revelation of her fiancé Lord Kew's youthful sexual exploits, and angrier still at the double standard which says she should neither know nor care about them, Ethel decides upon revenge in kind, but she displaces her sexual activity onto the brilliance of her surface. If her surface is what she is admired and valued for, then this is what she will use as a weapon against the system that insists upon that valuation. Accordingly, she appears at a ball not in her usual simple dress but in her court dress with hair elaborately done. She "astonished all beholders" and is, of course, admired as a display:

> Mr. Jones of England pronounced her stunning; the admirable Captain Blackball examined her points with the skill of amateur, and described them with agreeable frankness. Lord Rooster was charmed as he surveyed her, and complimented his late companion-in-arms [Lord Kew] on the possession of such a paragon. Only Lord Kew was not delighted – nor did Miss Ethel mean that he should be. She looked as splendid as Cinderella in the prince's palace. But what need for all this splendour? this wonderful toilette? this dazzling neck and shoulders, whereof the brightness and beauty blinded the eyes of lookers-on? She was dressed as gaudily as an actress of the Variétés going to supper at the Trois Frères. (*N* 1: 318)

Taking control of her presentation and flouting the tradition which can only approve of her if she is passive and seemingly unaware of her sexual beauty reduces her to an "actress" (prostitute). Her gaudy decoration tells her world that she *knows* what she is doing. Pen's attempt to diminish Ethel's dazzling appearance suggests that he fears the power of this self-conscious sublimity. Art objects should remain unconscious of their existence as objects to be viewed.

Pendennis accentuates Ethel's aggressiveness through his own development of the Diana motif. To Clive, Diana is the cold virgin, to Pen she is the active huntress. In London, as at the ball, taking control of her social self brings her notoriety; her pursuit of Lord Farintosh becomes a betting event for young society men (*N* 2: 64-65). She hunts for Lord Farintosh by hunting with him at his Scottish estate, although Pen blames her Aunt for most of the scheming (*N* 2: 67). Presenting Ethel as a modern huntress because she is a beautiful virgin makes readers recognize their own contradictory responses. "We" set these social standards of pursuit and conquest and yet condemn the women who fulfill the standards. Diana hunted for pleasure and meat – so do modern sirens whose "meat" is wealthy husbands. Paul de Florac reports a conversation with Lord Farintosh in which Farintosh is jocularly accused of being engaged to Ethel:

> "He laughs at the notion of an engagement. When one charged him with it of late at the club; and asked how Mademoiselle Louqsor – she is so tall, that they call her the Louqsor – . . . when one asked how the Louqsor would pardon his pursuit of Miss Newcome? my Ecossais permitted himself to say in full club, that it was Miss Newcome pursued him, – that nymph, that Diane, that charming and peerless young creature!" (*N* 2: 78)

In such a reported conversation, the juxtaposition of "pursuit" and "Diane" cannot be "Pendennis'" doing; this is the extra-textual Thackeray arranging for us to recognize that Ethel, having been cast as the mythical Diana, is only acting as a Diana of 1853 would. And yet she is condemned for following her "natural" bent by the same male society that created the pictorial tradition designed to contain her sexual power. The final reference brings the two Dianas together – Ethel *and* her aunt are the huntresses, but only Ethel is the Diana.

> Miss Newcome has been compared ere this to the statue of "Huntress Diana" at the Louvre, whose haughty figure and beauty the young lady indeed somewhat resembled. I was not present when Diana and Diana's grandmother hunted the noble Scottish stag of whom we have just been writing; nor care to know how many times Lord Farintosh escaped, and how at last he was brought to bay and taken by his resolute pursuers. Paris, it appears, was the scene of his fall and capture. (*N* 2: 142)

Both Diana images – the cold virgin and relentless huntress – imprison Ethel. The pictorial tradition values only her surface that is also her weapon. And she is accused of unseemly aggression and fatality to the male when she animates the image in which male pictorial tradition has imprisoned her. Ethel's overt aggression violates the "male-oriented convention . . . that the heroine of romance is supposed to carry out her tactics [winning the male] in low profile, that is, behave with due modesty". [7]

Pendennis's mixed reaction to Ethel, the tension between praise and criticism, reveals the inadequacy of the sociolects of classical and high art to contain a human being. He can praise her only in terms of metaphors that flatten the character into a static surface. Metaphor and symbolism derive their meanings from the breadth of associations and connotations possible in the language; thus the initial tenor can become the vehicle. The narrators' and protagonists' use of classical myth, the pictorial tradition of High Art, and motifs such as fairy-tale are actually attempts to replace these women with symbolic constructs, created and controlled by masculine language.[8] The inhumanity Thackeray saw in classical statuary is, in fact, the inhumanity of the interpreting system that freezes a human being into a decorative object.

But Pen, of course, does not invent this system; it is inherent in the language of pictorial metaphor. Neither does he invent his discomfort when his own object activates herself; Spenser also sees the siren, or false woman, as producing only deceit because she controls her self-representation:

> What man so wise, what earthly wit so ware,
> As to descry the crafty cunning traine,
> By which *deceipt doth maske in visour faire,*
> *And cast her colours dyed deepe in graine,*
> *To seeme like Truth, whose shape she well can faine,*
> *And fitting gestures to her purpose frame,*
> The guiltilesse man with guile to entertaine?
> (emphasis mine; *FQ* I.vii.1)

Another term for such a vivified "picture" (already used by Pen to describe Ethel) is "actress". While Thackeray does not let the male victim off the hook so easily as Spenser (being deceived by one's own masculine language of art does not make its male users "guiltilesse"), he shares with

Spenser this suspicion of the self-awareness necessary to the good performer. Becky and Blanche represent themselves not in the static poses of a traditional high or classical art but act in "scenes" such as Becky's presentation of herself before the fire to Lord Steyne. As actresses they question Steiner's definition of the pictured woman in romance as the "frozen self" because their active, mercurial façade disguises (and eventually erases) any sense of interiority.

Both Becky and Blanche are influenced by the French: Becky's mother was a French dancer and Blanche was educated in Paris. The Gallic emphasis on "manner" pervades their always active and sometimes witty imitations of the contemporary male images of women. The narrators' language place Becky and Blanche as contemporary *objets d'arts* not "timeless" pieces of high art. Becky's admiration of Jos, Rawdon, the younger Sir Pitt and Lord Steyne satisfies their vanity, and her own wit and ornamental appearance make her admiration valuable to the men. For Becky to speak to a man is to entrap him by his own susceptibilities. Her power early manifests itself in her attempt on Jos Sedley, when she actually gets him "*tete-à-tete* . . . looking at her with a most killing expression; his arms turned stretched out before her in an imploring attitude, and his hands bound in a web of green silk, which she was unwinding" (*VF* 32). This early success is followed by Becky's making herself indispensable at Queen's Crawley, playing backgammon with Sir Pitt, copying and correcting his ill-spelt letters, evincing interest in "everything appertaining to the estate":

> She was almost mistress of the house when Mr. Crawley was absent, but conducted herself in her new and exalted situation with such circumspection and modesty as not to offend the authorities of the kitchen and stables. . . She was quite a different person from the haughty, sly, dissatisfied little girl we have known previously, and this change of temper proved great prudence, a sincere desire of amendment or at any rate great moral courage on her part. (*VF* 81)

She also charms the younger Sir Pitt by reading his parliamentary pamphlets and intuiting his political ambitions:

> "You remain a baronet – you consent to be a mere country gentleman," she said to him . . . "Sir Pitt Crawley, I know you better. I know your talents and your ambition. You fancy you hide

them both: but you can conceal neither from me . . . I know what you want. You want to distinguish yourself in Parliament; every one says you are the finest speaker in England . . . . You want to be member for the County where with your own vote and your borough at your back, you can command anything. And you want to be Baron Crawley of Queen's Crawley, and will be before you die. I saw it all". . . . .

Pit Crawly was amazed and enraptured with her speech. "How that woman comprehends me!" (*VF* 403)

Becky has in fact created this ambition in Pitt by speaking of it. The essential difference between Becky and Blanche lies in the way their roles divide the conventional "missions" of women. Blanche is the consummate decorative object, designed to adorn an over-decorated parlor like a Christmas *Annual*. Becky adds to her visual lure the role of encouraging companion, the moral support for male ambition. She only becomes purely decorative in the presence of General Tufto and Lord Steyne who are too strong to need her support.

Blanche as "sylph" presents herself as a sentimentalized "romance", objectified as a porcelain figurine:

Blanche was fair, and like a sylph. She had fair hair, with green reflections in it. But she had dark eyebrows. She had long black eyelashes, which veiled the beautiful brown eyes. She had such a slim waist, that it was a wonder to behold; and such slim little feet, that you would have thought the grass would hardly bend under them. Her lips were of the colour of faint rosebuds, and her voice warbled limpidly over a set of the sweetest little pearly teeth ever seen. She showed them very often, for they were very pretty. She was very good-natured, and a smile not only showed her teeth wonderfully, but likewise exhibited two lovely little pink dimples, that nestled in either cheek. (*P* 1: 221)

She speaks French and English, writes poetry in French in her journal, "Mes Larmes" ("My Tears"), draws and dances. Laura, the "honest and generous country girl", had "never seen anything like *it* before; anything so lovely, so accomplished, so fragile and pretty; warbling so prettily, and tripping about such a pretty room, with such a number of pretty books, pictures, flowers, round about her" (emphasis mine; *P* 1: 221). This language presents Blanche as an animated "thing", a mechanical doll. She is "wrought by art and counterfetted shew, / Thereby more louers vnto her to call" (*FQ* II. vii. 45). True to the duplicitous nature of a Duessa, Blanche has a double life, signified in her double name. She is by birth "Betsy", having re-named herself "Blanche" while in Paris. Betsy is spoiled, ill-tempered, and brutal to her mother, brother, and maid. The "Muse", the narrator's alternate term for her, uses her supposed emotional fragility as an excuse for self-indulgence and cruelty that cannot be countered because it is administered "with a soft voice, and a well-bred simper" (*P* 1: 230). The narrator's excessive diminutives, his exaggeration of Blanche's daintiness, and the contradiction between the "sylph" and "Betsy" reveal her to be not just a false woman but a parody of male desire; she, like George Eliot's Rosamund Vincy, creates herself to be what she thinks men will want. Blanche has not internalized her role as much as has Rosamund; her bad-nature and increasingly deliberate manipulation of Pen and Foker do not allow us to excuse her by saying, "she doesn't know better". She may not know *better* but she does know *other* than her role as sylph – at least until the end of the novel.

Like the Homeric sirens, Blanche entraps by singing: to Laura, to Pen, and finally to Foker. When she first meets Foker, she is dressed in a "killing white silk dress" (*P* 1: 377) and "[makes] music for the young men. Foker was enraptured with her performance" and calls her a "nightingale". Blanche also uses her eyes as lures: "she gave him the full benefit of her eyes, – both of the fond appealing glance into his own, and of the modest look downwards towards the carpet, which showed off her dark eyelids and long fringed lashes" (*P* 2: 20). Blanche's skill is a lesser version of Becky's consummate art of conversation; she does have a genuine ability to manipulate men, even if Pen is never really taken in –because he is performing a similar role. The unconscious Foker is not only entranced by her singing but by her conversation that makes him the center of interest:

> And it was Blanche who, when the conversation flagged, and the youth's modesty came rushing back and overpowering him, knew how to reanimate her companion; asked him questions about Logwood, and whether it was a pretty place? Whether he was a hunting-man, and whether he liked women to hunt? (in which case she was prepared to say that she adored hunting) – but Mr. Foker expressing his opinion against sporting females, and pointing out Lady Bullfinch, who happened to pass by as a horse-godmother,

whom he had seen at cover with a cigar in her face, Blanche too expressed her detestation of the sports of the field, and said it would make her shudder to think of a dear sweet little fox being killed, on which Foker laughed and waltzed with renewed vigor and grace. (*P* 2: 69)

Blanche's very dexterity with language makes her "purity" suspect. Like "Blandina" (a possible namesake?), Blanche "when needed,. . . could weepe and pray, / And when her listed, she could fawne and flatter; / Now smyling smoothly, like to sommers day, / Now glooming sadly, so to cloke her matter; / Yet were her words but wynd, and all her teares but water" (*FQ* VI.vi.42).

Becky and Blanche also illustrate an essential conflict within the Victorian idea of female identity. On the one hand, as the non-visual characterizations of Laura and Rachel Castlewood (after smallpox) suggest, the good woman exists as an interior, stable, unseen identity whose language is at one with her intent and action. But on the other hand, in Victorian England, with its emphasis on manners and social etiquette, the social identity as "lady" or "gentleman", only exists through the exhibition of visual signs – dress, language, and manner. Thackeray tries to suggest that such ladylike self-representation is natural for Helen and Laura, but they are nonetheless very aware of the difference between their manners and those of Lady Clavering and Blanche. To choose to underdress, as do so many Victorian ladies (Helen, Laura, Rachel, Dorothea and Celia Brooke) is to fulfill Isabella Beeton's admonition in *The Book of Household Management* (1861) which sees over-dressing as what Thackeray presents it as – the sign of the nouveau riche.[9] The self-presentation of the true lady resembles the self-presentation of the true artist, such as Cruikshank, who creates a role that seems not to be a role. Ethel exemplifies just how delicate is this performance: when she dresses simply and seems not to use the power of her beauty, thus seeming to be unconscious of it, her pride and imperiousness appear "natural" to Clive and Pen. But when she evinces consciousness of her façade by decorating it, she is condemned as an actress. Barbara Hardy points out that one of Thackeray's motifs in *The Newcomes* – it is actually a constant in his work – is that "we act emotion until we cannot distinguish the act from genuine feeling".[10] Ethel is in danger of actually becoming nothing but the siren by acting as the siren; her surface may absorb her interior self.

Becky's most successful role parodies this dilemma. She is most believed by others when she is "acting" herself; that is, using the truth about her past and present to create a false moral identity:

> And in her commerce with the great our dear friend showed the same frankness which distinguished her transactions with the lowly in station. On one occasion, when out at a very fine house, Rebecca was (perhaps rather ostentatiously) holding a conversation in the French language with a celebrated tenor singer of that nation, while the Lady Grizzel Macbeth looked over her shoulder scowling at the pair.
>
> "How very well you speak French," Lady Grizzel said, who herself spoke the tongue in an Edinburgh accent most remarkable to hear.
>
> "I ought to know it," Becky modestly said, casting down her eyes. "I taught it in a school, and my mother was a Frenchwoman."
>
> Lady Grizzel was won by her humility and was mollified toward the little woman. (*VF* 453)

It is no accident that this scene occurs before the charades at Lord Steyne's in which her appearance as Clytemnestra betrays the deadliness of her siren-nature. The scene with Lady Grizzel is a safer example of Becky's ability to turn the truths of her life into the means of ingratiating herself with the upper classes. Lady Grizzel is "mollified", Thackeray is quick to point out, because Becky's humility satisfies her ladyship's own vanity. Of course this is just one of Becky's self-representations. When she invents her link to the Montmorencys (which she also uses to explain the quality of her French) or when she "forgot that there was no money in the chest at home – duns round the gate, tradesmen to coax and wheedle – no ground to walk upon in a word" (*VF* 427), her roles are (like Blanche's) more obvious to others. She uses the role of the "real" Becky to disguise her developing "real" self – the adventuress. Becky is wise to ground her acting in her experience because she can only imitate, not act, the grand lady. On her way to be presented at court her "demeanour [is] so grand, self-satisfied, deliberate, and imposing, that it made even Lady Jane laugh" (*VF* 427). Here Becky is overacting – if gentle Lady Jane laughs, Becky must be ridiculous; the part does not suit. But she has also played the "real" Becky when she explains away her diamonds as rented because of course she and Rawdon could not afford such jewels. Because this explanation is perfectly consistent with the "real" Becky, it acts as a successful lie, keeping the real source of the jewels, loot collected from Lord Steyne, hidden (*VF* 428-29).

The difference between Becky using her life as her material and Beatrix and Ethel acting out a masculine pictorial tradition is that Becky's calculating ambitions seem to give her greater control. We are less inclined to see her as trapped, which lessens our sympathy for her. But all three suggest the same parody of the sincerity of the artist who must present himself in his art work and yet remain sufficiently disengaged to avoid Sternism. And this parody suggests the siren-text's danger to a too-credulous reading public. When the siren occupies both the role of beauty and the role of moral agent, any successful acting or presentation of surface threatens Victorian moral ideology. By accepting such roles as realities, society could no longer offer trustworthy standards for its members. When Emily Costigan becomes Lady Mirabel, "fantasy – the belief that an ignorant actress is socially acceptable as a wife – having been exposed as an illusion suddenly becomes fact and yet retains its illusoriness; the fantasy creates a reality that yet remains fantastic. London society has its private reservations . . . but publicly it allows the role to define the person and thereby encourages her to simulate the part she has chosen by marrying Sir Charles Mirabell, that most 'theatrical man'" (Harden, "Theatricality", 77). Underlying this threat to social stability, to the sense of knowing who is who in society, is erosion of the private moral sense. If women are to be moral influences, even moral "regenerators" as Sarah Lewis argued in 1840, their public presentation of their interiority must be trustworthy.[11] But by "representing" themselves according to a code, are not even ladies like Laura acting? And, as Martin Meisel points out, "a woman who can act feelings cannot be *known* to have them or can dissemble those she has; on the other hand, to act feelings – those of a lover, a flirt, an adulteress, a murderer – is in some sense to have them, and to be what you act".[12] Meisel is suggesting that the surface can actually create the interiority: that Becky, for instance, behind the booth at Vanity Fair could actually become the respectable woman she imitates. Such a possibility, of course, denies the stability of the interior identity and certainly questions the spiritual authority of the domestic angel.

The problem is only a problem, however, if the acting is recognized as such – at least by the reader – and yet accepted as non-acting by other characters. To avoid such ambiguity, the narrators use text and image to "strip" the sirens of their façade, revealing a hideousness inside which denotes their moral corruption for having acted in the first place. While the revelations reveal the siren as hideous, the narrative suggests they are only necessary because *her* actions have undermined the narrative idealization. She has acted for her own satisfaction and in so doing she questions the narrative control of her as myth or picture. The narrative takes revenge for the sirens' destruction of narrative idealization by re-seeing her as a monster. I have noted how Henry Esmond finally "sees" the "true" Beatrix when he discovers her with the Pretender. Suddenly Beatrix is old and ugly because Henry finally sees that her ambition and sexuality are not simply pictorially "Titianesque" but active (and not for him). Beatrix returns the favor years later when, as Baroness Bernstein in *The Virginians*, she "strips" her niece, Lady Maria, telling Harry Warrington, "'She is forty-one years old. All her upper teeth are false, and she can't eat with them'" (XVIII, 170), which starts Harry wondering what *else* is false about his aged lady-love. The truth is, Maria had begun to reveal herself when she became ill in the carriage and her cheeks "continued to blush as it seemed with a strange metallic bloom: but the rest of her face, which had used to rival the lily in whiteness, became of a jonquil color. Her eyes stared round with a ghastly expression. Harry was alarmed at the agony depicted in the charmer's countenance; which not only exhibited pain, but was exceedingly unbecoming" (XVIII, 170). Once the façade has cracked, Harry's love erodes rapidly, leaving him trapped in his promise to marry her. As things work out, Maria recovers her façade and finally, very appropriately, marries an actor, which allows her to live out her romance.

Blanche also strips herself by clinging to her romance role in the face of Pen's discovery of her lie to him and her suppression of her knowledge of her mother's bigamy. Knowing this secret and not acting on it establishes Blanche's disdain for the sanctity of marriage, the core of female moral power. Her cry for "emotions", and that she would rather live with her real father the "pirate" (he is actually a forger and polygamist) alternates with savage accusations of Pen's cruelty, and pathetic appeals for his pity upon a "defenceless girl" (*P* 2: 345). Her romantic affection for her father is appropriate; like him, she has become a forger – of her own identity – as well as an incipient polygamist. Blanche travesties the essentialist self of the nineteenth-century woman, who was supposed to feel instead of know or to know by feeling, exemplified by Laura Pendennis' intuitions of others' moral natures.

Similarly, Becky hides her "hideous tail" (*VF* 577) beneath the water: this metaphor is reified in her mask. She smiles at the world, hiding the hag underneath. When Rawdon insists on accompanying her to parties to protect her (and his) reputation, she "was charmed with Rawdon's gallantry. If he was surly, she never was. He fell asleep after dinner in his chair; he did not see the face opposite to him, haggard, weary, and terrible; it lighted up with fresh candid smiles when he woke. It kissed him daily" (*VF* 472). The initial to chapter 63 of *Vanity Fair* shows us this ghastly sea hag, her killing glance now positively Medusan in its malice. All these revelations, Becky's most closely, echo a tradition of "stripping the siren" characteristic of romance. Duessa/Fidessa in *The Fairie Queene* is stripped on Una's order of her scarlet robe.

> Ne spared they to strip her naked all.
> Then when they had despoild her tire and call,
> Such as she was, their eyes might her behold,
> That her misshaped parts did them appall,
> A loathly, wrinckled hag, ill fauoured, old,
> Whose secret filth good manners biddeth not be told.
>
> (*FQ*, I.viii. 46)

In chapter 64 in *Vanity Fair,* Thackeray, like Spenser, claims his siren has been

> presented to the public in a perfectly genteel and inoffensive manner. In describing this syren, singing and smiling, coaxing and cajoling, the author, with modest pride, asks his readers all round, has he once forgotten the laws of politeness, and showed the monster's hideous tail above water? No! Those who like may peep down under waves that are pretty transparent, and see it writhing and twirling, diabolically hideous and slimy, flapping amongst bones, or curling round corpses. (*VF* 577)[13]

Both authors proceed to describe what they have said they will not. Duessa is bald, bereft of the long locks that entangle men. Her teeth and gums are rotten, her "dried dugs like bladders lacking wind" (*FQ* I.viii.47), but most significantly, like Becky the mermaid, Duessa is not human below her waist:

> Her neather parts, the shame of all her kind,
> My chaster Muse for shame doth blush to write;
> But at her rompe she growing had behind
> A foxes taile, with dong all fowly dight;
>   (*FQ* I.viii.48)

Similarly, in *The Purgatory*, Dante strips his siren, "exposing her as far down as the paunch" which exudes a horrible stench.[14] The very metaphor of stripping away a cover describes the linguistic process at the heart of this motif. These monsters have only deluded "us" because they have been clothed by the masculine voice in his symbolic disguises. The women underneath are again rendered invisible, however, by this revision of them as monstrous sex in yet another masculine convention. This language controls her sexual threat by making her sexuality nonhuman and therefore inaccessible to the narrator or protagonist. Her beastiality is another presentation of the masculine idea of *vagina dentata* that devours men.

Thackeray's narrators and Spenser connect the sexual monstrosity of the siren with her own mercantile ambition which makes her both a commodity and an acquisitive buyer. Duessa is stripped of "royall robes and purple pall, / And ornaments that richly were displaid" (*FQ* I.viii.46). Rawdon likewise strips Becky of her ornaments, tearing her diamond brooch from her breast. His search through her possessions identifies her secret sexuality with secret money, the symbol of commodities, earned by her commodity exchange of self with Steyne.

> Rawdon flung open boxes and wardrobes, throwing the multifarious trumpery of their contents here and there, and at last he found the desk. The woman was forced to open it. It contained papers, love-letters many years old – all sorts of small trinkets and woman's memoranda. And it contained a pocket-book with bank notes. Some of these were dated ten years back, too, and one was quite a fresh one – a note for a thousand pounds which Lord Steyne had given her. (*VF* 479)

Rawdon's stripping of Becky reveals not just her duplicity but the complete identification of her sexuality, the "secret desk", as a commodity. Becky resembles a fraudulent investment bank that shows a prosperous façade while at the same time its officers are stealing the depositors' money. She parades her small but exquisite house, parties, and ornamented self, supported by "nothing a year". She imitates the banker's public presentation of his social reliability through material ostentation, essential to inspire trust in his depositors.[15] Steyne's deposits of money to support her façade she secrets with a miser's lust, not so much to use the money as simply to have it. Her relations with objects and people are "entirely predatory . . . envying them, accepting them, showing them off, scrounging, and using them to please and solicit" (Hardy 103). She misuses Rawdon's investment of love and Ruggles' of trust by returning fraudulent "interest" (her pretended concern). But her world of commodity exchange succeeds through such fraud. She has financial "credit" (*VF* 397-98) only because her world gives her credit for being immoral. Her credit exists only because she is thought to be Steyne's mistress. But like the financial panics of 1825, 1836, and 1846-47 her speculations become wilder and wilder and finally explode. Without any genuine capital (moral principle) to back her up, no one will accept her when her social "credit" fails. And the irony is that her social credit fails because it is realized. That is, when Rawdon discovers her, society's belief in her immorality is confirmed, and her world disowns her. Such social credit has power only as long as it remains a supposition.

The final image of Becky in *Vanity Fair* suggests that the corruption of the market place extends to all male-female relations, not just conscious adventurers like Becky. She has the hoarding characteristics of the poverty-stricken, as when she tallies her "merchandise" in chapter 30, after Rawdon has ridden off to Waterloo. And her last two roles also link her successful merchandising with her sexual threat; in her "Second Appearance as Clytemnestra", she "kills" Jos Sedley, which brings her his insurance money, enough to set up as a respectable lady. Her role as maligned victim is her last; we see her selling her wares at a charity bazaar. She no longer has to hoard things because she has a "character" and the selling of things for charity is in fact a sign of that character. But the connotations of the bazaar would have reminded Thackeray's readers of the sexual exchange at the heart of Becky's respectable commerce. Gary Dyer points out that observers of early bazaars such as the one established in 1816 by John Trotter assumed that "the bazaars would naturally become sites of prostitution" (197).[16] The primary purpose of these early bazaars was to aid widows, especially war widows. Thus Becky has usurped Amelia's rightful position as widow, even though Amelia had been preserving her moral purity by remaining in private, never attending a bazaar and only attempting to sell her wares through a dealer. A Cruikshank print, "A Bazaar", published in 1816 emphasizes the sexual looseness of the bazaar, suggesting that customers and venders alike were for sale, as does an 1816 poem by John Agg ("Humphrey Hedgehog"), "The London Bazaar, or, Where to get Cheap Things", which accuses women working in bazaars of prostitution. Even when the "respectable" classes take over the bazaars in the 1820s, and they become Charity Fairs such as the one in which we see Becky, the sexual overtones linger. In Thackeray's illustration of Becky at the charity bazaar, as in his description of the siren, we cannot see below Becky's waist; she still hides her tail.

Despite the narrators' revelation of their monstrosity and sham, Becky and Blanche cannot be debased by the market place because they are of the market place, and thus their images as actresses and fancy *objets d'artes* coincide with their own intentions. They survive simply because they have no designs on the inner life of the domestic angel. Barbara Hardy points out, specifically in relation to Becky, but her comment is even more applicable to Blanche, that Thackeray's refusal to punish Becky and Blanche is not cynicism but a valid estimate of their emotional vacuity; "the faithless and heartless, the entirely corrupt, lacking any ideal, cannot suffer from lost desire" (36).

The romantic love at the heart of the domestic myth is antithetical to the calculation necessary to achieve successful domesticity.

> Warm friendship and thorough esteem and confidence (I do not say that our young lady [Ethel] calculated in this matter-of-fact way) are safe properties invested in the prudent marriage stock, multiplying and bearing an increasing value with every year. Many a young couple of spendthrifts get through their capital of passion in the first twelve months, and have no love left for the daily demands of after life. O me! for the day when the bank account is closed, and the cupboard is empty, and the firm of Damon and Phyllis insolvent! (*N* 1: 355-56)

The clash between the sociolects of love and investment discredit the idealization of both romance and social myth. Pendennis in *The Newcomes* and *The Adventures of Philip* repeatedly makes the point that Ethel and Agnes Twysden are educated to violate their modesty and hunt men. The "right" end to the pattern for the romance heroine is a marriage that reconciles her to, by integrating her within, the cyclical pattern of human life (Frye 80), seen in her sexual fulfillment and motherhood. However the violation of woman's proper nature in the siren's forced pursuit of men result in marriages that pervert this conventional closure. In *Philip*, Agnes marries a rich mulatto who beats her; they separate, and she lives a promiscuous life on the continent. Ethel almost marries a man whom she does not love and who is her mental and moral inferior. She is "saved" by Clara Newcome's elopement with Jack Belsize, the result of Clara's agreement to a mercantile marriage with Barnes Newcome – who also strikes her. Clara's fear has made her sacrifice her chance for power independent of men; instead, she transfers herself from one owner to another. But in this male mercantile world, women cannot transfer themselves; the object owned must be passive to remain an object of value. As a pathetic fallen woman, Clara's loss of value deprives her of even the identity of an object. Accepting one's sacrifice is more disastrous than using one's role to manipulate the market to one's own advantage, as do Becky and Blanche.

The collocation of images of these sirens inhibit the reader from settling on any stable interpretation of them: actress, nymph, goddess, Diana, sylph, prostitute, commodity, virgin-huntress, Niobe, Judith, painting – and ultimately slave. Ethel and her grandmother, Lady Kew, visit the Water-Colour Exhibitions, and Lady Kew is struck by a painting of William Henry Hunt of "one of those figures which he knows how to paint with such consummate truth and pathos – a friendless young girl cowering in a doorway, evidently without house or shelter" (*N* 1: 265). Someone has bought the picture of this pathetic young girl, as indicated by a green tag in the corner. Ethel sees herself as the painting and the girl in the painting and the Exhibition as a microcosm of her world:

> "I think, Grandmamma," Ethel said, "we young ladies in the world, when we are exhibiting, ought to have little green tickets pinned on our backs, with 'Sold' written on them; it would prevent trouble and any future haggling, you know. Then at the end of the season the owner would come to carry us home." (*N* 1: 265)

Ethel becomes the "friendless young girl" when she appears at dinner that evening "with a bright green ticket pinned in the front of her white muslin frock" (*N* 1: 265). The motif of portraiture pervading *The Newcomes* (e.g., 2: 45, 50, 91) links Ethel's prostitution of herself as a social artifact to

Clive's prostitution of himself as an artist when he becomes a portrait painter. While customers may choose to objectify themselves in portraits, neither Clive nor Ethel has any choice: Ethel's culture dictates her commodification, Clive's financial necessity dictates his. However, can Ethel be passive commodity, "friendless young girl", and imperious Diana? Pendennis insists that she is all these things as well as a Circassian slave girl.

> "The Circassian beauties don't sell under so many thousand purses," remarked Mr. Pendennis. "If there's a beauty in a well-regulated Georgian family, they fatten her; they feed her with the best *Racahout des Arabes*. They give her silk robes, and perfumed baths; have her taught to play on the dulcimer, and dance and sing; and, when she is quite perfect, send her down to Constantinople for the Sultan's inspection. The rest of the family never think of grumbling, but eat coarse meat, bathe in the river, wear old clothes, and praise Allah for their sister's elevation. Bah! Do you suppose the Turkish system doesn't obtain all the world over? My poor Clive, this article in the May Fair Market is beyond your worship's price."
> (*N* 2: 44)

These sociolects of classical and sentimental art, goddess and slave all apply to Ethel. Logically they should cancel each other out. Our ability to understand these irreconcilable definitions as we read implicates us in the system of double-think. Clive sees Ethel as the princess in the crystal box out of the Arabian nights (*N* 2: 83), and yet her virginal clarity (the "crystal") is marred by her active participation in her own sacrifice.[17] A woman making a "career" out of selling herself desanctifies her "nature":

> ... a girl of the world, *bon Dieu!* the doctrine with which she begins is that she is to have a wealthy husband; the article of Faith in her Catechism is, "I believe in Elder Sons, and a house in town, and a house in the country!". ... As you see a pauper's child with an awful premature knowledge of the pawn-shop, able to haggle at market with her wretched half-pence, and battle bargains at huxter's stalls; you shall find a young Beauty, who was a child in the school-room a year since, as wise and knowing as the old practitioners on that Exchange; as economical of her smiles; as dexterous in keeping back or producing her beautiful wares; as skilful in setting one bidder against another; as keen as the smartest merchant in Vanity Fair. (*N* 2: 66)

But, earlier in this passage (as elsewhere), Pen claims that she cannot help herself because of her "schooling" (*N* 2: 65). But he also declares that women are "naturally" flirts and manipulators, and those who are not are "monsters" (*N* 2: 79). According to this reasoning, Becky's hideous tail is a natural appendage. And yet, she is condemned when she follows her nature. Beatrix "naturally" grows from child-coquette to know "my face is my fortune. Who'll come buy, buy, buy! I cannot toil, neither can I spin, but I can play twenty-three games on the cards. I can dance the last dances, I can hunt the stag, and I think I could shoot flying" (*HE* 286).

The protagonists' and the narrators' confusion of nature and nurture and their ability to twist their imagery so as to condemn the sirens for both their nature and their nurture suggests their need to repress their own desires and rechannel them into nondestructive paths. They do not control the texts they produce; the symbolic systems they use threaten to turn back on them. As long as the *femme fatale* is symbolic she is an object of harmless, or relatively so, fantasy. But when she internalizes the symbolic attributes to become a fatal woman, she threatens the entire system of "confidential talk" between writer and reader (*P* xv). The fatal woman like the seductive text can appropriate the reader, turning a reader into prey for his or her own sentimental or illusory desires. Accordingly, the siren produces or threatens death in Thackeray's fiction. Both George and Rawdon are so touched by Becky that they cannot reclaim themselves. George, breaking his marriage vows, is quite appropriately killed "with a bullet through his heart" at Waterloo (*VF* 32). Rawdon exiles himself to Coventry and dies of a fever. Pen experiences two "fevers" of love, and the second, sparked by his self-restraint toward Fanny, is almost fatal. Beatrix's fiancé, Lord Hamilton, is killed in a duel by Lord Mohun, the same rake who killed Rachel's husband in a duel about Rachel's honor. Lord Kew in *The Newcomes* has a duel indirectly caused by Ethel's knowledge of his past, which results in a wound and fever.

But, by failing to regulate their desires, to, in fact, repress their natural coquetry, the sirens also endanger themselves. As texts produced from vanity out of cupidity, the sirens' willing sacrifice of themselves to their market can be a loss, not a gain, of independence. And it is doomed to frustration because this desire to satisfy themselves is an essentially masculine desire for active power – unassuagable for women. Beatrix is particularly self-destructive because she recognizes her ambition to be masculine:

> "I have been long enough Frank's humble servant – Why am I not a man? I have ten times his brains, and had I worn the – well don't let your ladyship be frightened – had I worn a sword and perriwig instead of this mantua and commode to which nature has condemned me . . . . I would have made our name talked about." (*HE* 286).

Beatrix takes the only female avenue toward power in the world of courts and society – first a wealthy, powerful husband, and, when that fails, the role of *mistress en titre*. Henry the narrator punishes her by imposing premature aging, loss of that beauty which was her selling point.

Ethel redeems herself in the narrator's eyes by experiencing the "fall" vicariously, through Clara's elopement, and by becoming financially independent as her grandmother's heir – inheriting through the female line. Ethel begins to become intimate with Laura (*N* 2: 203). On the very day of Clara's flight, Clara's daughter declares Ethel to be her mamma (*N* 2: 202), and with "pious resolve" Ethel accepts the trust (*N* 2: 202). To Laura she confesses her worldly career (*N* 2: 204-207). She acknowledges her ambition and willingness to sacrifice herself "for an establishment and a position in life" (*N* 2: 207). In her terms it would be slavery and unconditional obedience in exchange for social position (*N* 2: 207). She then confesses to Lord Farintosh: "'I never could make you happy; I know I could not: nor obey you as you are accustomed to be obeyed; nor give you such a devotion as you have a right to expect from your wife'" (*N* 2: 210). Her penance is to be accused by the women in her world as a justly jilted flirt (*N* 2: 212). Ethel dedicates herself to self-improvement so she may teach "her brother's orphan children" (*N* 2: 222-23). Eventually Ethel becomes a true domestic angel, able to see with the spiritual eyes of the pure woman. Clive had tried to teach her to see the world through the masculine version of transcendence: aesthetic vision. Laura has taught her to see through surfaces and to become invisible herself

> "I remember in the old days, when we were travelling on the Rhine – in the happiest days of my whole life – I used to hear Clive and his friend Mr. Ridley, talk of Art and of Nature in a way that I could not understand at first but came to comprehend better as my cousin taught me; and since then, I see pictures and landscapes and flowers,

with quite different eyes – and beautiful secrets as it were, of which I had no idea before. The secret of all Secrets, the Secret of the Other Life, and the Better World beyond ours – may this not be unrevealed to some? I pray for them all, dearest Laura – for those nearest and dearest to me, that the truth may lighten their darkness; and Heaven's great Mercy defend them in the perils and dangers of their night." (*N* 2: 269)

Ethel learns a different mode of signification when she abandons her preoccupation with her surface and aligns herself with the invisible, untranslatable Language of God. She sees "through" conventional systems and fixes her perception on an unknowable Truth – which can be Truth precisely because it is beyond representation. Very clearly, Ethel's reformation and Thackeray's suspension of the pattern by leaving her in a virginal state, mistress of her self sexually and materially, suggests that the siren saves herself only by repressing her predatory desires, especially when we compare Ethel's tranquility to Clara's miserable life, totally dependent upon Jack Belsize, isolated from friends and children, and tormented by guilt. Clara's is the demonic world of the sacrificial virgin who tries to rescue herself by giving into her desires (*N* 2: 194-95). (It is no accident that her surname is "Pulleyn", a variant name for a domestic hen.)

Perhaps the ultimate revelation of the cannibalism at the heart of the sacrifice of the virgin is Agnes Twysden in *Philip*, Thackeray's last completed novel and one in which, I will argue, he felt the professional security that allowed him to write what he wanted to write:

That dear girl [Agnes] is like a beautiful fragrant bower-room at the Star and Garter at Richmond, with honeysuckles mayhap trailing round the windows, from which you behold one of the most lovely and pleasant of woods and river scenes. The tables are decorated with flowers, rich wine-cups sparkle on the board, and Captain James' party have everything they can desire. Their dinner over, and that company gone, the same waiters, the same flowers, the same cups and crystals, array themselves for Mr. Brown and *his* party. Or, if you won't have Agnes Twysden compared to the Star and Garter Tavern, which must admit mixed company, liken her to the chaste moon, who shines on shepherds of all complexions, swarthy or fair. (XX, 269)[18]

Instead of a locked, secret desk, Agnes is a passive room, which can be entered at will, and the chaste moon of the modern huntress Diana is now openly revealed as promiscuous. Objectification as a painting or part of a pictorial tradition may freeze the woman into a surface and acting may imprison her in a series of behaviors, but they do not prohibit the possibility of a rebellious autonomy or an interior self; they merely suppress identity. But Agnes as a dining room is presented as the interior from which those she engulfs look out while they use her. This is not merely an image of the siren as prostitute, it suggests Agnes is empty of anything but desire. At their worst, the sirens embody *necessity*, the driving power of desire which overrides self-control and the awareness of others. This infinite appetite is the sublime turned mercantile, the yawning mouth of the libido fed by sex and money. The "intoxication" of the viewer who gets drunk on Poussin ("On the French School of Painting", IX, 56), the anthropophagic mermaid "revelling and feasting on the wretched pickled victims" (*VF* 577), the dog drowning in the pool out of greed for the bone already in his mouth in *The Virginians* (XVIII, 148), and the author and reader who cannibalize the text in *The Adventures of Philip* (XXI, 537) reveal life as a horrible cycle of predation wherein the act of predation also devours the predator.

Reading with the enthralled characters, we feel the seductive power of the siren. Reading with the narrator in *Pendennis*, we balance sympathy for Pen's passion with an amused, lofty understanding of his self-deception. But reading *The Newcomes* or *Henry Esmond* or *Philip* we can read with the implied author. Pen's and Henry's inconsistent treatment of their sirens invite us to read their texts skeptically. While stripping the siren suggests the narrator/protagonist sees through her seductive surface into a bestial non-human being, her monstrous appearance as hag or mermaid reminds us that in one myth of patriarchal society, women are "in their natural state, unacceptable, imperfect monstrous".[19] The violence of the narrators' language should also make us skeptical that these scenes reveal any "truth" about the women. The passages are truths about the narrators' needs to incorporate the women within the narrative sociolects and to control the seductive power of these texts that they (the narrator and protagonist) have created by re-imagining that seduction as horrifying and predatory. Because the women are literary characters as well as metaphors for texts, they have no existence outside the narrators' perceptions of them, and the inconsistency of these descriptions, especially the fluctuations between attraction and repulsion, admiration and triviality, should reinforce our sense that the language *is* the meaning – including any interpretations we might make from reading these contradictory portraits.

However, skeptical reading is a practice of reading that, while giving readers authority, does not free readers from the rhetorical conventions that produce that authority. Oppositional reading, defined by Ross Chambers as reading against the grain or surface of the text, strengthens existing systems by making them livable.[20]   Skeptical reading is like oppositional reading in that it is a process that creatively adapts "dominating systems to uses for which they were not intended", using the characteristics of power *against* the power and *for* one's own purposes (Chambers, *Room*, 9, 10). This kind of reading is a resisting reading wherein the reader, in this case a woman, capitalizes upon the multiple narratorial attitudes to appropriate the power of the text to control meaning.

Self-conscious sirens such as Becky, Blanche, Ethel, and Beatrix are skeptical readers of the cultural codes that construct and constrain them. They exploit their object position. They are not revolutionaries; in fact, their opposition strengthens the patriarchal system that condemns them. There is no chance that the marriage market will disappear simply because Ethel wears a green ticket. Becky can achieve her own booth in Vanity Fair because society believes its own myths of respectability. And Beatrix becomes a Baroness as a reward for selling herself to the Pretender. But these sirens do mitigate their captivity by exerting some control over themselves. The empty text, as epitomized by Blanche's letter, can achieve self-definition by subverting all conventions to her own purposes. Acting as mirrors of male vanity, narcissism, and especially the need to control by retaining the power of naming, the sirens use their seductive powers to take from the system, and since their powers are derived from the system, they cannot be ostracized. As Ross Chambers points out, "the disempowered seduce opportunistically and oppositionally" (*Room*, 222).

And Thackeray's (not the narrators') texts abet the sirens' opposition. He does not kill his seductresses, even the most fatal. They live with wealth, within or independent of British respectability and the constraints of domesticity. To be sure, the narrators deplore Becky's hypocrisy, Blanche's extravagant Parisian life, Beatrix's life as royal mistress and doyenne of the Castlewoods, Agnes Woolcomb née Twysden's rouge-ridden Continental existence, but the women are not depicted as any more miserable than respectable counterparts such as Amelia – and there is a certain allure to their self-sufficient risqué existence. Virtuous society may shudder and turn away, but one wonders whether Thackeray always did. The only really miserable women are Rosey Mackenzie Newcome, dominated by her mother and unloved by her husband (who nonetheless keeps her pregnant and kills her by it) and Clara who gave all for love – except her bourgeois mentality. Seen skeptically, then, the cycle of predation threatens only narrators, characters, and readers who fix themselves into its double-think and accept contradictory sociolects which disguise the predatory nature of human relations.

Notes

[1]   Ross Chambers, *Story and Situation: Narrative Seduction and the Power of Fiction* (Minneapolis: U. of Minnesota P, 1984), 78.

[2]   Horace, "The Art of Poetry", *Satires, Epistles, Ars Poetica*, trans, H. Rushton Fairclough, Loeb Classical Library (Cambridge, MA: Harvard UP, 1947), 451.

[3]   Barry Westburg, *The Confessional Fictions of Charles Dickens* (Dekalb: Northern Illinois UP, 1977), xix.

[4]   "Theatricality in *Pendennis*", *Ariel* 4 (1973), 88.

[5]   Thackeray systematically rejected three kinds of "sublime" art, each for a different reason. Classical art, especially statuary, he felt was so perfectly beautiful that it was "inhuman", above all human sympathy. "High" art of the Great Masters' tradition (Michelangelo and Poussin in particular) was painful to look upon because of its power which derived from an almost incomprehensible power of invention. About Michelangelo's "Last Judgment", Thackeray wrote, "How did he [Michelangelo] suffer the painful labour of invention? One fancies that he would have been scorched up like Semele, by sights too tremendous to bear" (IX, 47). This power runs through the art work to sweep away a viewer, affecting him like heavy drink or like a fever (IX, 55-56). As much as Thackeray privately appreciated such art, and his letters suggest that he was keenly sensitive, his public pronouncements recommend "mediocre" art, or "third rate" paintings. As this chapter suggests, so do the fortunes of his sirens suggest the protagonists are better off with "mediocre" women – at least this is the story on the surface. The third kind of sublime was exemplified by the work of Benjamin Haydon and John Martin in England and Jacques Louis David in France. This style Thackeray called the "theatrical historical" or "theatrical sublime" because he felt their work to be fundamentally sham, a collection of tricks and conventions designed to titillate the audience. See "Strictures on Pictures", *Fraser's Magazine* 17 (June 1838) in XXIV, 261-71; "A Second Lecture on the Fine Arts", *Fraser's Magazine* 19 (June 1839) in XXIV, 272-84; "On the French School of Painting", *Fraser's Magazine* 20 (Dec. 1839) in IX, 41-57; "On Men and Pictures, apropos of a walk in the Louvre", *Fraser's Magazine* 24 (July 1841) in XXV, 361-83.

[6]   Wendy Steiner, *Pictures of Romance: Form against Content in Painting and Literature* (Chicago: U of Chicago P, 1988), 48.

[7]   Northrup Frye, *The Secular Scripture. A Study of the Structure of Romance* (Cambridge, MA: Harvard UP, 1976), 79.

[8]   See Margaret Homans, *Bearing the Word: Language and Female Experience in Nineteenth-Century Women's Writing* for a discussion of the theory underlying this thesis (Chicago: U. of Chicago P, 1986), chs. 1 and 2.

[9]   For a more complete discussion of the role of manners and etiquette see Elizabeth Langland, "Domestic Ideology in the Victorian Novel", *PMLA* 107 (March 1992), 290-304.

[10]   *The Exposure of Luxury. Radical Themes in Thackeray* (Pittsburgh: U. of Pittsburgh P, 1972), 83.

[11]   Sarah Lewis, *Women's Mission* (London, 1840). One of many manuals for the Victorian woman, this was as influential as Sarah Ellis' publications in establishing the type of the morally superior domestic angel.

[12]   Martin Meisel, *Realizations, Narrative, Pictorial, and Theatrical Arts in Nineteenth-Century England* (Princeton: Princeton UP, 1983), 333.

[13]   In Book I, Canto ii, of *The Faerie Queene*, "Fraudubio", one of Duessa's victims, chances to see her in her real guise which is remarkably (or not so remarkably) like Becky the mermaid: "Her neather partes misshapen, monstruous, / Were hidd in water, that I could not see, / But they did seeme more foule and hideous, / Then womans shape man would beleeue to bee" (*FQ* I. ii. 41)

[14]   Dante, *Purgatory*. Mark Musa, trans. (Bloomington: Indiana UP, 1981), XIX: 32-33.

[15]   "The hallmarks of a banker's public character were an outwardly grave and calm aspect, and a shunning of personal ostentation. While maintaining a standard of living consonant with his status as a gentleman, he was careful not to allow himself to be tainted with the flashy vulgarity of the 'new men' of the age. In a highly hierarchic society, the maintenance of high social standing was essential to a sound public character". Norman Russell, *The Novelist and Mammon, Literary Responses to the World of Commerce in the Nineteenth Century* (Oxford: Clarendon Press, 1986), 75.

[16]   "The 'Vanity Fair' of Nineteenth-Century England: Commerce, Women and the East", *Nineteenth-Century Literature* 46 (1991), 196-222.

[17]   Northrup Frye makes the point that the image of the Princess in the crystal box is one of the most frequent romance analogues of symbolic fixing, 14.

[18]   Thackeray is just as frank in earlier in the novel (XX, 189) when he states his preference for prostitutes who display themselves as prostitutes over "your High Church or Evangelical Aspasia, the model of all proprieties, and owner of all virgin-purity blooms, ready to sell her cheek to the oldest old fogey who has money and a title".

[19]   Judith Fetterley, *The Resisting Reader* (Bloomington: Indiana UP, 1978), 26.

[20]   I am adapting the term "oppositional reading" from Ross Chambers, *Room To Maneuver* (Chicago: U of Chicago P, 1991), 7 especially and chapter 1, passim.

5 The Secret History of Henry Esmond

As there are a thousand thoughts lying within a man that he does not know till he takes up the pen to write, so the heart is a secret even to him (or her) who has it in his own breast. Who hath not found himself surprized into revenge, or action, or passion, for good or evil; whereof the seeds lay within him, latent and unsuspected until the occasion called them forth?

> *Henry Esmond* (139)

The heart is deceitful above all things and desperately wicked: who can know it?

> Jeremiah 17: 9

The thought that I have been made a fool of, is the bitterest of all perhaps – and a lucky thing for all it is perhaps that it should be so.

> Thackeray (*LPPS* 1: 429)

The History of Henry Esmond extends the intricacies of taking oneself as one's text. As the siren uses female accomplishments and dress to construct herself, so Henry uses the masculine mode of autobiography to write himself.[1] His narrative self interprets his younger self just as the narrator interprets both siren and protagonist. The consequence is a novel preoccupied with the possibilities and dangers of self-fashioning. The balance between Henry as narrator and Henry as character, emphasized by the shifts between first and third person, "have the effect of creating a character who is able to reveal his most intimate thoughts and feelings, but who also sees from the outside, describing himself, his appearance, virtues and failings as they would to an impartial narrator".[2] But a close reading of Henry's narration questions his "impartiality" to suggest the dangers of this nicely self-contained self construction.

The story of the unfolding of Henry seems stable because it is controlled by both private and public criteria. On the surface, Esmond's sense identity never vacillates. The somber child in the opening is already the melancholy man writing the memoir. As Henri Talon has argued, Henry's story is "the progressive realization of the ideal image of himself that he has ever cherished, the means of actualization of the ideal being loyalty to Rachel and her family and allegiance to the cause of the Stuarts".[3] The public story of the infidelity of monarchs and subjects offers an external code against which Henry can define himself as faithful to his own private allegiances. Henry is a Jacobite because Rachel is: "Had she been a Whig, he had been one: had she followed Mr. Fox and turned Quaker, no doubt he would have abjured ruffles and a perriwig, and have foresworn swords, lace-coats, and clocked stockings" (155). He parallels his privately inspired Jacobinism to the loyalty of the public and the unworthiness of the objects of their loyalty: "Ours is the most loyal people in the world, surely; we admire our kings and are faithful to them long after they have ceased to be true to us. 'Tis a wonder to any one who looks back at the history of the late family to think they kicked their crowns away from them, how they flung away chances after chances, what treasures of loyalty they dissipated, and how fatally they were bent on consummating their own ruin" (156).

That *Henry Esmond* locates public history in private lives is evident in the preface where Henry castigates heroic versions of history, preferring "History familiar" (4). The private views of history Henry gives us, Webb's quarrel with Marlborough, the bloody military campaigns, and especially the debauched Pretender, James Edward Stuart, suggest that the Henry who chooses to be a private gentleman is superior to his titular superiors.[4] Beatrix is the crucial intersection between public and private. She trades on her sexuality within the confines of her family, and when the Pretender abandons his public role as king for the private role of lover he loses his crown, and Henry loses his love for Beatrix. The Pretender's illicit desire for Beatrix is also proof of his lack of fitness for the monarchy. Public history is the consequence of private motives. The consistent character of Henry against the backdrop of the interaction between public and private life seems to give this novel a moral certainty unlike any other Thackeray novel.

But – and since *Pendennis* we know there is always a "but" – Henry's seemingly stable pattern has weaknesses. The interconnection among personal, family, and public histories enable Henry to disguise his subjective perception as objectivity. While Henry's story seems stable in its analogy to public history (a very eighteenth-century strategy), his narration subjectivizes the public history to make the analogy affirm his personal desires. Occasionally Henry is quite frank about how his emotions influence his judgment. For example, he tells us that his allegiance to Webb (312) and a sense of personal insult (245) motivate his hatred of Marlborough, but these confessions serve to substantiate Henry's code of faithful knight. He serves Webb, therefore he must be emotionally faithful to his service. He is much less overtly aware of the torturous paths on which his loyalty to his family leads him when that loyalty conflicts with his loyalty to himself and what he thinks he is owed. "Familiar" history may be truer to the human experience, but this private history makes history malleable by human desire – and Henry Esmond in *Henry Esmond* is all about desire.

Henry relies on one primary code to interpret his life, himself, and his world. His code of fidelity, of the Arthurian knight-errant, should allow Henry to sustain a stable identity that is affirmed by the definite roles it forces others to play.[5] But this code of fidelity is only one code, the one of which Henry is most conscious. He also uses, although he does not acknowledge it as such, the language of patriarchal power. The code of the "cavalier serviente" fits uneasily with the language of the family despot, and this tension aligns with Elaine Scarry's discussion of the many discrepancies and ambiguities in the novel, which concludes that Esmond's narration "violates the primary criterion of subjective truth, internal consistency"(7).[6] But reading these codes together suggests what Henry desires and how he achieves that desire.

What *does* Henry want? If, as *Pendennis* and the figure of the siren suggest, all art derives in part at least from the artists' desires/visions/inspirations this question when asked about an autobiography and autobiographer has three parts: First, what does Henry the character want in his life? How is his code of fidelity supposed to define himself and those around him? Second, what does Henry the narrator want to do for himself and thus to us (show us) in his autobiography? What motivates his writing and directs his construction of his roles for himself, other characters, and his readers? And, finally, can his autobiography actually *accomplish* his life's desire?

To put it simply, what Henry-character wants in life is power: power over others and power over himself. He wants to be esteemed as more noble than the system of nobility to which he finds himself legitimate heir.

(Rachel finally sees Henry as "too great" for the name of Castlewood [308].) On the isolated plantation in Virginia he is able to set up an undisputed absolute monarchy that is affirmed by the worship of women whose adoration establishes his own divine right of kings through the good woman's access to the Transcendental Symbolic Order of True Language. Early in the novel, Henry likens the husband and father to a king:

> For in our society there's no law to control the King of the Fireside. He is master of property, happiness, – life almost. He is free to punish; to make happy or unhappy; to ruin or to torture. He may kill a wife gradually, and be no more questioned than the Grand Seignior who drowns a slave a midnight. He may make slaves and hypocrites of his children; or friends and freemen; or drive them into revolt and enmity against the natural law of love. (109)

He also refers to wives as slaves and drudges (93).[7] Henry, however, will counter domestic tyranny by becoming a benevolent despot whose reward for his benevolence is adoration. His "Castlewood" is based neither on the old system of feudal inheritance nor the "new" system of bourgeois capitalism. He neither inherits nor buys the land, but it is "given" to him by Frank as a reward for Henry's stellar family role.[8] He is alienated, then, from both traditional and modern forms of masculine public life. Thrown back on his own subjectivity, Henry presents himself as a triumph of moral character. Beatrix, always sharp-eyed about Henry, sees that "of all the proud wretches in the world Mr. Esmond is the proudest, let me tell him that. You never fall into a passion; but you never forgive, I think. Had you been a great man, you might have been good-humoured; but being nobody, Sir, you are too great a man for me: and I'm afraid of you, Cousin – there – and I won't worship you, and you'll never be happy except with a woman who will" (304). His daughter Rachel, who takes over Henry-worshipping from her mother, tells us in an editorial note that Henry as king of his Virginian domain, "was obeyed eagerly by all under him; and my mother and all her household lived in a constant emulation to please him, and quite a terror lest in any way they should offend him" (362 fn). Rachel's intriguing combination of voluntary obedience and "terror" of disapproval captures the essential puzzle of Henry Esmond. At once the "proudest" man Beatrix knows, Henry is also "the humblest man" (362), one who inspires terror and adoration. Rachel's seemingly oxymoronic descriptions reflect the successful interaction of Henry's two codes in building an identity whose power cannot be denied because it is ethically impeccable. I stress "ethical", here, because the way Henry represents his life to his readers forces us to judge his *conduct* as without flaw; his self-analysis and the testimony of others provide almost insurmountable evidence for such a reading.

This over-determined reading points to the power Henry the narrator wants: power, over his past and his readers. "Henry" – not Thackeray – wants us to think Henry is a paradigm, that he has acted better than anyone else in his life so that he *deserves* to be monarch – if you have a private monarchy, its justification should be merit.   His autobiography is the romance of the hero-in-disguise coming into his own reign. First, of course, Henry the narrator holds power over us simply because we are the captive audience of his autobiography. His "subjectivity" is a textual production with no referent outside the text.[9]   More technically, Ross Chambers in *Story and Situation* discusses two kinds of textual authority which give narrators power over readers.[10] Narrative authority is informational; it is the teller's hold over the reader of simply knowing more than the reader, in the case of autobiographer, knowing everything more than the reader. Narratorial authority is the affective lure of the narrator; it is the voice which seduces us, which keeps us reading even as we know more and more of what is happening and so can see ahead to what will happen. When we read, the narrative authority gradually diminishes; the narrative gives up its information and readers acquire the ability to predict – the more formulaic the fiction, the less narrative authority. The exchange is between narrative authority and narratorial authority – we keep reading because of the second: "so long as the reader puzzles, narratorial authority remains intact" (Chambers 64).[11]   The exchange between narrative authority and narratorial authority becomes unbalanced in Thackeray's later novels, especially in *Philip* where Pen the narrator sacrifices narrative authority as early as chapter two when he assures us that Philip is alive, well, and happy at this very moment of writing/reading. In *Henry Esmond* the texture of Henry's narration keeps us puzzling about the events in his life and his voice, his own attitude toward and awareness of himself. This is an autobiography that does not want to "give up" anything, especially in its seemingly most self-revelatory moments.

But while the function of his autobiography for him is a self-fashioning in which the writer controls everything – in order to align narrator, protagonist, character, and action – the alignment is unstable in *Henry Esmond*. Neither Henry nor the other characters (especially Beatrix) can consistently flatten themselves into their appropriate roles. Psychological and emotional tensions burble up between the seams of his rhetoric of faith and service and rupture the surface, creating ambiguities of fact, feeling, and consequently reveal glimpses of a disturbing undercurrent in which Henry the knight is also Henry the manipulator. Like David, in *David Copperfield*, Henry has to seem passive to retain his virtue; therefore he presents himself as a victim: as an unacknowledged child, hungry for love, and later as a victim of his own passion for an unworthy *femme fatale*. But the disturbances imply another story wherein Henry has and uses power. These ruptures are subtle enough so as to have caused years of critical debate over intentionality – are they Henry's ruptures and thus also Thackeray's? Or, as I think, are they not Henry's ruptures – at least not entirely consciously – but Thackeray's? And do these ruptures reflect aesthetic uncertainty on Thackeray's part or act as subtle exploration into the character of the self-deceiving, desiring self – Thackeray had read *David Copperfield* whose inconsistencies are much less subtle and probably not of Dickens' intention. The brilliance of *Thackeray's* rhetorical games creates a voice that has the unconscious nuances and echoes we associate with our own humanity. "Henry" is words on a page; Henry's powerful first person narration seems to be a thinking consciousness. Thackeray uses the inherent untrust-worthiness (because conventional and ambiguous) of language to, in the words of Paul Jay, explore the problem of "how to use one medium – language – to represent another medium – being" (21).

Henry's "right line I" is destabilized by three kinds of ruptures: the internal inconsistencies and ambiguities noted in large part by Elaine Scarry, Marjorie Garson, and Hillis Miller;[12] the messages sent to us by the two Rachel-editors who break the continuity of Henry's self-presentation (eg. Rachel's quote of Henry's memory of Beatrix hints that he has not successfully eradicated his desire for her [xxviii]);[13] and his own "secret history" which shows him master of his fate even while he is bemoaning his "slavery" to Beatrix. For instance, as Scarry has shown, his actual information, even his description of Castlewood itself, is inconsistent and ambiguous. To ask of Henry Esmond "what really happened" is to be befuddled.   Ambiguity reserves narrative and narratorial authority for Henry, while Thackeray uses it to suggest psychological depth.[14] Readers experience both by shifting among mimetic, narratorial, and synthetic reading. If we read narratorially with Henry, we can believe he is an ethical paradigm. Such a reading is affirmed by reading with Henry the character instead of Henry the narrator, because this Henry is presented as a victim. But if we read skeptically, synthetically, outside the narrator, we can read Henry's own self-consciousness and read a secret history which re-presents Henry's merit as a form of power. His merit resides in his constant renunciation of his rights, which actually increases his power throughout the novel, finally justifying his private monarchy on the almost unanswerable feminized terms of sacrifice of self for others. Henry's power develops from, ironically, abjuring the power of public identity and private ego.

This sacrifice of self extends to the narrative technique. Henry disguises the egoism of the autobiographical "I" and its almost inevitable Sternism by de-centering his subject "I" into the character "he" and by marginalizing Henry's actions, making him an observer, or an incidental player.[15] Henry calls himself an "observer" in the Introduction (5) and what he is observing is the corruption and debasement of the king and aristocracy, those lives "that have noble commencements" (5). If we read "noble" as a pun here – as a mark of class and as a character trait – we see that Henry's observer status distances him from the degradation of the public system of nobility and his own degradation as a boy when he is page to the crone Isabella and seduced into popery by Father Holt.[16] He is consistently "Harry" and "he", and when an anti-Catholic mob hits him in the eye with a potato, he is "the little page" and "the poor little wretch" (30). But this same detachment also emphasizes what will be the focus of Henry's autobiography, the "he" as a specimen for analysis, an exploration of how the "little wretch" grew up to be monarch of all he surveys in Virginia.

Scarry and Miller have pointed out inconsistencies in the narration and between narration and story in *Esmond* that invite us to read Henry's narration ironically.[17] According to Miller, "In analyzing the lack of worth of all other people Henry unwittingly provides the reader with the tools by means of which to identify Henry's own lack of worth. What applies universally must apply to him too" (*Fiction and Repetition*, 99). Scarry notes that Henry's verbal patterns deconstruct their own assertions. For example, he is ambiguous about his age and the timing of his college career. It is impossible to really figure out when he is 14, 16, and 18; on the last page of chapter 7 he is 14 and on the first page of chapter 8 he is 16 with no explanation of the missing two years; he is "past sixteen" (78) when he goes to Cambridge and on his "last vacation" (89) which he calls his "third long vacation" from Cambridge he is suddenly "twenty-two years old" (107). If his first college vacation is in 1696 (96), how can his third be, as he says it is, in 1700 (105)? Scarry's essay demonstrates that "the novel is a tissue of small, almost imperceptible contradictions, each in isolation insignificant; collectively, devastating" (9). Ultimately, Scarry claims that Esmond cannot "preserve his world by committing it to the written word, for the instability is inherent in the structure of language itself" (21). Instead of becoming a self-conscious, master-linguist as does Pendennis, Henry's surface claims of a single truth designed to present a stable moral character fix his language, disguising his motives and feelings from himself, while his own narrative strategies disrupt these surface claims. As we read, becoming discomforted by the contradictions and unrealistic gaps in Henry's awareness, we grow to understand the painful narcissistic repression that allows Henry's stable sense of identity and underlies his increasing power. An ironic reading of Henry Esmond is not necessarily condemnatory of Henry, but skeptical of subjective truth as a "stable core of facts, feelings, and thoughts" (Scarry 41). In a passage that is tempting to read as a deliberate self-parody but is not acknowledged as such, Henry suggests an image of himself as narrator in the character of Father Holt:

> A foible of Mr. Holt's, who did know more about books and men than perhaps almost any person Esmond had ever met, was omniscience; thus in every point he here professed to know, he was nearly right, but not quite. Esmond's wound was in the right side, not the left; his first general was General Lumley; Mr. Webb came out of Wiltshire, not out of Yorkshire; and so forth. Esmond did not think fit to correct his old Master in these trifling blunders, but they served to give him a knowledge of the other's character, and he smiled to think that this was his oracle of early days; only now no longer infallible or divine. (223)

A difference between Holt's information and Henry's, of course, is that Holt is mistaken about material facts that can be verified, but because *Henry Esmond* is a fictional autobiography, we have no external frames of reference; we will never know how old is "past sixteen". Moreover, the bulk of Esmond's story is emotional and psychological analysis that can only ever be a matter of interpretation. The autobiographical mode filters everything through Henry's psyche and our knowledge that this is "fiction" makes this mode our only knowledge of Henry; therefore he is, unlike Holt, omniscient. Henry cannot be mistaken because there is no version other than *Henry Esmond,* and no point of view outside of Henry's.

The totalizing inherent in the mixture of genres makes the seepage, or what I have called "ruptures" more intriguing. Are these frictions ways of telling us what he does not/cannot tell us consciously? Garrett Stewart writes of Victorian fiction performing crucial cultural work in its ability to allow the individual reader privacy while joining readers by presenting "narratives that tell individual secrets over the signature and under the guise of otherness" (206). Henry's secret is open and closed. As do so many autobiographers, Esmond uses his past to create a heroicized self to justify his present situation. But Thackeray creates an autobiographer who, while master of all he surveys, also "suffers from some bankruptcy of his heart, which his spirit never recovered".[18] Henry writes his autobiography to create his unified, stable ego. Thackeray writes Henry writing his autobiography to affirm our egoism (we *all* see ourselves as monarchs of our world) while making ironic the ego's self-perception (we all see ourselves as *monarchs* of our world).[19] This double stance is inherently anti-Romantic: Thackeray denies the heroic vision of self in the act of creating a character who pursues and seems to achieve that vision. Henry's overt story hides a secret history in which the poor orphan emerges as deliberate manipulator. His self-descriptions and interpretations of his own and other's characters and actions demonstrate the triumph of moral power manifested in private behavior and character, over effective power as evidenced in public action (political, military) and being (rank, title). Reading his history synthetically reveals that Henry's narrative choices and languages hide or disguise his own exertion of power and manipulation to achieve his ends. The most profound flaw in the seamless union between the autobiographical narrator and his created self as text is what I am calling his "secret" history – present in event but almost absent from the narrative consciousness. Within the events of his life lies the story Henry wills himself *not* to tell. We should read *Henry Esmond* remembering Thackeray's words about painters: they do not recognize the children their own creative labor produce:

A man does not know all that lies in his picture, any more than he

> understands all the character of his children. Directly one or the
> other makes its appearance in the world, it has its own private
> existence, independent of the progenitor. And in respect of works of
> art, if the same piece inspire one man with joy that fills another with
> compassion, what are we to say of it, but that it has sundry properties
> of its own which its author even does not understand? (XXV, 369)

Henry starts from nothing and as nothing: "no servant though a dependent, no relative though he bore the name and inherited the blood of the house" (8). He is a male Cinderella, harshly treated by an unjust stepmother and speaking French better than English (19). He tells Rachel "how he had a father and no father; a nameless mother that had been brought to ruin, perhaps, by that very father whom Harry could only acknowledge in secret and with a blush, and whom he could neither love nor revere" (52). Complications start when he becomes aware of his own and others' sexuality; that is, he becomes consciously desirous to possess and to exert himself. In fact, the first use of "I" is in the context of his sexual relationship with Nancy Sievewright (62). As he develops from this point, the plot and characters, including the narrator, act out the autobiographer's attempt to establish himself as "legitimate" and to preserve control over his desires. Henry's story develops through a series of splits who act out his not-always-licit desires and who act as alternative identities: Lord Castlewood (Frank), Lord Mohun, the younger Frank, and the Duke of Hamilton exorcise Henry's demons for him. In the process, Henry legitimizes himself, becoming the true father of his family. Karen Chase sees Henry as "the involuntary agent who does not want what he causes and does not cause what he wants".[20] In contrast, it is possible to read Henry as only superficially involuntary, in part because his secret plot will ultimately justify the moral high ground his narrative self consistently takes. As we read with him and against him we see him acquire power by means of his secret, and consequently we are implicated in his own self-duplicity.

> "A serpent", echoed he; no sooner said
> Than with a frightful scream she vanished:
> And Lycius' arms were empty of delight,
> As were his limbs of life, from that same night.
> (305-308)[21]

At the end of Keats' *Lamia*, the philosopher Apollonius turns his "demon eyes" (l. 289) on Lamia who shrinks with horror into her true serpent-shape. Lycius, her young lover, sees her true shape, names her, and dies from losing her – a loss caused by his own insistence at displaying Lamia at a public feast. Until this point, Lamia has been the deadly siren, luring Lycius away from his friends and proper duties. Edward Bostetter comments that this conclusion overlays the siren with "the connotation of an ideal or dream love".[22]   Bostetter goes on to claim that "Lycius is ultimately responsible for the catastrophe by his desire to display her. Had he been willing to keep her to himself, he might never have lost her. The implication is plain that only through utter withdrawal from the world can visionary beauty and love retain reality" (161). Lycius and Apollonius are "splits" of one "self": the youthful idealist, susceptible to sexual desire, and the older skeptic who turns the cold eye of understanding upon his ideal, recognizes it as self-projection, and exposes it in order to save himself. This pairing anticipates the Old Ulysses in Thackeray's metaphor about "The Old Story" in *The Virginians*, who cannot hear the sirens sing any longer while "Young Telemachus was for jumping overboard" (XVIII, 149). *Henry Esmond* dramatizes the aging of Ulysses. Using himself as text, Henry the narrator, the Apollonius figure, analyzes his Lycius self, the youthful Henry in search of the ideal which will, by satisfying his desires, allow him to realize his ideal self. For, like the traditional knight errant, Henry wants to see in his Lady a mirror "which debases an ideal reality so that it may be seen by man in his mortal infirmity".[23]   From his first glimpse of Rachel as angel and goddess of Love, Henry finds in women both the motive and object of his quest for moral perfection. An Arthurian analogy would be apt, perhaps, if Lancelot sought the Grail and found it not a chalice but Elaine, the Lily Maid of Astolat, thereby achieving sexual, aesthetic, and moral satisfaction. Like the actual Lancelot, however, Henry's story one of loss, of the failure of the pursuit for the ideal. Yet, this loss is paradoxical, because it is also the means to his power.

It is clear in *Henry Esmond* that the sirens, first Rachel and then Beatrix, are simply the scapegoats, displaced images of Henry's own desires which are erroneously attracted to a mirror which reflects the inner qualities that make *him* the object worthy of adoration :[24] He could "no more help this passionate fidelity of temper than he could help the eyes he saw with" (293) – that is, his code of fidelity and his passion are natural to him and arise from his perception:

> . . . . when he returned after Blenheim, the young lady of sixteen, who had appeared the most beautiful object his eyes had ever looked on two years back, was now advanced to a perfect ripeness, a perfection of beauty such as instantly enthralled the poor devil, who had already been a fugitive from her charms. Then he had seen her but for two days and fled; now he beheld her day after day, and when she was at Court, watched after her; when she was at home, made one of the family party. (205)

In Dante's *Purgatory*, the narrator exhorts the pilgrim to cover his eyes when confronted by the Medusa so as not to be enthralled. John Freccero interprets this command as an order to protect the male mind from being "petrified" by its own desire for the surface that is, in fact, a mirror for the self. The Medusa threatens because she freezes the male in a narcissistic gaze:

> The search for the self which is the quest of the poet can only be accomplished through the mediation of the imagination, the Narcissus image which is at once an image of the self and all that the self is not . . . . Seeing the self in otherness and accepting the vision as true reduces the spirit to something alienated from itself, like a rock or a tree, deprived of consciousness. Like language itself, the image can only represent by pointing beyond itself, by beckoning the beholder to pierce through it to its ultimate significance. Idolatry in this context is a refusal to go beyond, a self-petrification.[25]

Henry-narrator fights his petrification even as he describes his character-self becoming enthralled. He constructs a life history that protects Henry from his own gaze (206-207). Of course, the idolatry of the eye, worshipping the surface as the substance, pervades *Esmond*. His worship for Rachel's divine appearance parodies her worship of Lord Castlewood's physical beauty. The shoulder notes in chapter 7 of the first edition identifies both as false religions: "My idol's idols", "priestess", and "Idol worship". Henry the narrator points out the unworthiness of Frank Castlewood; he is a dandy, drinker, hunter, and womanizer. When he tires of Rachel's worship, she looks "into her heart" and "perceives that the god of the honey-moon is a god no more" (57); that is, Rachel early achieves an "inner vision" which sees beyond the surface.

However, this very sequence of events – Rachel and Frank's estrangement, Rachel's love for Henry, Henry's flirtation with Nancy, Henry bringing smallpox to Castlewood, and then Henry being "expelled" to University offers a similar lure of the surface to the reader. While Henry's history of this crucial period *seems* clear, to accept it as such is to miss the point that while Henry seems to create a pattern, Thackeray is emphasizing the selectivity of Henry's perspective, suggesting that his pattern is not *the* truth, but *a* truth. In fact, Henry gives us a hint of this himself, writing a warning about perspectivisim: "We have but to change the point of view, and the greatest action looks mean; as we turn the perspective glass, and a giant appears a pigmy. You may describe, but who can tell whether your sight is clear or not, or your means of information accurate?" (202). Henry's observation applies to his public self, his military career and his feelings toward Webb and Marlborough. But, as Hillis Miller suggests, this warning is a tool we can apply to Henry's private life in which ambiguous dating and plotting allow Henry the narrator to retain control. We do not know exactly when and how the crises happen and how they are related. Four years at Castlewood, from 1691 to 1695, disappear between chapters 7 and 8 when Rachel's worship suddenly is revealed to have turned toward Henry – although he is only sixteen. The narrator compresses the length of Rachel's worship of her husband to emphasize its loss and identify that loss with her changed object of worship (Garson 420). The revelation of her new love for Henry coincides with the narrator's revelation of Henry's birth of sexual desire, signaled by his visit to Nancy Sievewright, the blacksmith's daughter.[26] Rachel's ensuing unaccountable outburst betrays both her jealousy and her unmotherly affection for Henry. Thus Henry becomes a desired object at the same time he becomes a desiring subject.

Garson's analysis of the relation between Henry and Rachel convincingly argues that Henry at least partially understands Rachel's love for him.[27] Garson argues that "the smallpox episode is the turning point in Henry's relation with Rachel because he suddenly understands the sexual nature of the attraction between them and is deeply shocked and shaken by the revelation. The Oedipal nature of both Henry's and Rachel's feelings, which is eventually clear to the reader, is made clear to Henry himself here in a flash of intuition from which he spends the rest of his life turning away" (427). However, all the "facts" of Rachel's estrangement from her husband Frank are uncertain. Henry offers not only dissonant scenes but dissonant stories. Henry narrator insists that Rachel stops worshipping Frank first and is superior to him (57-59) but acknowledges, even emphasizes, that she is jealous. But when he is 14 (and aware of sex), he has a fight with Bryan Hawkshaw who has said that Rachel is jealous and henpecks Frank (60). This story supports Frank's own version (101-102) that she is "frigid" and of an unforgiving nature. At one point (57), Frank has "broken away" from Rachel before the smallpox episode, and she has ceased to adore him. But later (102), Frank attributes their separation to the smallpox episode. This version we get after the smallpox episode when we discover, as possibly Henry has (he acknowledges her jealousy of him [72]), that Rachel loves Henry – so her coldness to her husband is at least partly accountable to her illicit passion for her 16-year-old "son". We also get a version that Frank and Rachel's estrangement occurred while Henry was at college (91-92). We must doubt her claim that Frank was the one who cast her away first (103). And we have to be skeptical that Henry does not *hear* Rachel's desperate love for him when he returns on one of his college vacations. She has once again flashed out in sexual jealousy, insulting Henry to diminish her own sense of guilt; Henry responds by asking her how he has wronged her to deserve her insults.

> "What wrong?" she said looking at Esmond with wild eyes. "Well, none – none that you know of, Harry, or could help – Why did you bring back the small-pox," she added after a pause, "from Castlewood village? You could not help it, could you? Which of us knows whither Fate leads us? – But we were all happy, Henry, till then." And Harry went away from this colloquy thinking still that the estrangement between his patron and his beloved mistress was remediable; and that each had at heart a strong attachment to the other. (104)

His belief in their reconcilability is unbelievable because this exchange occurs when he is at least 17 and has been aware of her jealous nature and alienation from Frank for at least three years. Equally unbelievable is Henry's claim that "he scarce knew how" he learned "the sad secret of his patron's household" (95), when he has just told us, and we have just read a sample scene as proof of it, that Frank uses Henry as his confidant. Moreover, we have been reading his minute analysis of their relation and disaffection. More curious is what Henry means by "secret" here. It is no secret that Frank drinks, gambles, and philanders; even Rachel knows that. It is no secret that she has become cold and aloof; she criticizes Frank in public. The only "secret" is that her disdain for her husband is coupled with her discovery of an object worthy of worship – Henry himself. Lord Mohun actually sees what Henry the narrator refuses to: a triangle of Rachel, Frank, and Henry (110).

So, we actually have three versions of their estrangement: first, before the smallpox episode, Rachel's jealousy and coldness have driven Frank into taking mistresses, and then she discovers her own mental superiority; second, the loss of her beauty due to the smallpox (itself a highly ambiguous result) has driven Frank away because he cares only for physical beauty; and, third, Rachel has come to love Henry before the small pox episode, realizes this love is illicit, and is consumed with guilt that manifests itself in attacks on Henry, first in response to his bringing smallpox into the house and later when she banishes Henry from Castlewood after Mohun kills Frank in a duel.   In all cases, our far-seeing, self-aware narrator does not appear to know Rachel is jealous when Henry flirts with Nancy Sievewright or that her anger at him is her deflected guilt for her illicit love. The coexistence of these versions suggest the resistance of "life into art". Life is not a clearly sequenced, single-cause-and-effect pattern.   These small discrepancies and ambiguities convey the multiplicity of lived experience. When we read with Henry as character or narrator we feel that we could straighten this out if we paid more attention or could find another record. But to recognize the places where the versions do not fit each other, the statements that do not quite convince, the all-too-appropriate metaphoric and symbolic overtones, is to recognize Thackeray's skillful dramatization of memory in action. Thackeray depicts how we do struggle to make stories out of our lives and how those lives resist our story-telling.

Henry's story requires that he remain ignorant to keep himself aloof from the degradation of an incestuous love. He will be worshipped for the character traits his story tells us he has. Only such deification will affirm his idea of himself. The "divine punishment" of small pox starts the process that will turn Rachel from siren into worshipper and Henry into an object which she *can* worship "safely". Rachel sends Henry away to Cambridge to prepare him for taking orders – her way of suppressing his desire and her own. And her loss of beauty changes her from alluring physical image to invisible angel:

> When the marks of her disease cleared away they did not, it is true, leave furrows or scars on her face . . . but the delicacy of her rosy

> colour and complexion were gone, her eyes had lost their brilliancy,
> her hair fell, and her face looked older. It was as if a coarse hand had
> rubbed off the delicate tints of that sweet picture, and brought it, as
> one has seen unskillful painting-cleaners do, to the dead colour. (69)

No longer a painting, an idealized surface, the siren disappears into the woman who "laid out her all upon her children" (75), becoming the archetypal "good" woman: "To be doing good for some one else is the life of most good women" (75). It is only when she has lost her beauty that Henry announces his desire to serve Rachel as her knight (83) – both have purified themselves of their potential vices: Rachel has lost the dangerous sexual beauty of Venus, and Henry's guilt at bringing the infection home makes him repress his own sexual desire. If Henry had not visited Nancy, that is, if his sexual desire had not awoken, Rachel might not have felt the jealousy that forced her to recognize the nature of her own love. And the physical symbol of this jealousy, the smallpox, would not have ravaged her and sent Henry off to University, meanwhile setting the stage for the death of Henry's first rival, Lord Castlewood. Of course, Rachel's loss of beauty is Henry's perception; he is the only character to see any disfigurement.[28] Henry defaces his own idol upon whom, as the novel develops, he will again bestow youth, fresh complexion and beauty. (Two years after the smallpox, Lady Sark sees Rachel's complexion as "a wonder of freshness" [99].) While Garson sees Henry's defacing of Rachel as "punishing" her for her erotic attraction to him (426-27), this uglification also acts as a defense for Henry, so that his desire can shift to the more aggressively sexual object, Beatrix. To love Rachel is to violate a taboo; to desire Beatrix is to become a man.

Enter Lord Mohun. When Henry returns from Cambridge for his third long vacation – in 1700, somehow 22 – *he* is a man (he wears a mustache) and Lord Mohun is in place as his "father's" friend.

> [Mohun] was a person of a handsome presence, with the *bel air*
> and a bright daring warlike aspect – which, according to the
> chronicle of those days, had already achieved for him the conquest
> of several beauties and toasts. He had fought and conquered in
> France as well as in Flanders; he had served a couple of campaigns
> with the Prince of Baden on the Danube and witnessed the rescue of
> Vienna from the Turk. (100)

Mohun is Henry's "dark split", the dark mirror of himself as male. Mature, active, aggressive, sharing the same Christian name and dark coloring as Henry, Mohun *pretends* virtue to attract Rachel. Mohun's pursuit of Rachel acts out Henry's repressed desire, and the duel that follows this pursuit acts out Henry's desire to rid himself of Lord Castlewood, the possessor of Rachel and Henry's rightful title.

In fact, Henry encourages the argument between Frank and Mohun by his "warnings" and meddling. He incites Rachel's anger toward Frank by acting as Frank's go-between between Frank and Rachel (103-104). Then Beatrix recognizes the Oedipal complications displaced onto Mohun when she says to the threesome, seeing Mohun's devotion to Rachel, "I think my lord would rather marry Mamma than marry me; and is waiting til you die to ask her" (110). The child speaks what should not be spoken, the son's desire for the mother. But Henry covers up this truth by immediately reconciling Frank and Rachel, assuring Frank of Rachel's virtue. However, this reconciliation has the effect of Frank throwing Rachel and Mohun together to prove his own trust and her virtue. Of course, Mohun is a hypocrite whose virtue is a mask designed to seduce Rachel, suggesting the hidden corruption of Henry Esmond's affection for his mother. Rachel actually conspires in her husband's death by responding to Mohun's overtures in hopes that she can "save" his soul and her husband's estate. Mohun's role as seducer allows Henry to almost guarantee that a duel will occur. Henry can virtuously "warn" Rachel against Mohun (113) and so manifest himself as her male protector for the first time. He then warns Mohun of Frank's jealousy (114-115), arousing the lord's *amour propre*. The crisis comes when Mohun accuses Henry of loving Rachel while both are driving in Mohun's carriage. Immediately after Henry's protestation that Henry worships Rachel as "'a devotee worships a Saint'" (116), the carriage crashes, throwing them both to the ground. This crash is the immediate cause of the duel: Frank reports to Rachel "Here's poor Harry killed, my dear" (117). Rachel screams and faints, an over-reaction that establishes her guilt no matter which "Harry" she thinks is dead. If it is Mohun, then she is guilty of an adulterous love, if Henry, then she is guilty of an incestuous and adulterous love – and Frank sees this truth that Henry rejects (125).[29]

When Mohun kills Lord Castlewood, he rids Henry of a rival for Rachel's hand and gives Henry his legitimacy. Before the duel Frank leaves Henry as heir to his estate and his position as Rachel's husband: "I leave my wife and you as guardians to the children" (124). He also appoints Henry as head of the house, saying, "By George, Harry! you ought to be head of the house" (124). As Castlewood dies, he confesses that Henry's parents were in fact married. While Henry represses his legitimate rank by burning Lord Castlewood's confession, this renunciation brings its first of many rewards when, in response to his sacrifice of public rank, Castlewood "anoints" him monarch: "My Lord Viscount sprang up in his bed and flung his arms round Esmond. 'God bl– bless. . . ". was all he said – the blood rushed from his mouth deluging the young man. My dearest lord was no more. He was gone with a blessing on his lips, and love and repentance in his manly heart" (131). Henry-narrator's use of Frank's formal title, "Viscount" sets the tone of this scene as a rite of passage, of Henry inheriting by means of blood tie and blood as holy sacrament everything that was – unrightfully – Frank's. Frank's death frees Henry from the private stigma of bastardy and the public subordination of becoming a dependant such as Tom Tusher (154). The wound in his hand, received during the duel, and Rachel's rejection of him punish him for his unlawful desire and rechannel his repressed agency into the active life of a soldier. But both wound and expulsion justify his desire for revenge on Rachel and his rage at his ignominious past position.

Volume two begins with Henry exulting in the power his secret knowledge brings him: "he had that in his heart which secretly cheered and consoled him" (135). His sense of secret authority increases throughout the novel: he begins to "feel an independency" (151), he "took a greater pride out of his sacrifice that he would have had in those honours which he was resolved to forego" (161). But this power is not simply the sense of self worth, it is power over others, those others whose very existence up until now inevitably reinforced his private shame.

> Should he bring down shame and perplexity upon all those beings to whom he was attached by so many tender ties of affection and gratitude? degrade his father's widow? impeach and sully his father's and kinsman's honor? and for what? for a barren title to be worn at the expense of an innocent boy, the son of his dearest benefactress. He had debated this matter in his conscience, whilst his poor lord was making his dying confession. – On one side were Ambition, Temptation, Justice even – but Love, Gratitude, and Fidelity pleaded on the other. And when the struggle was over in Harry's mind a glow of righteous happiness filled it, and it was with

grateful tears in his eyes that he returned thanks to God for that
decision which he had been enabled to make. (135)

Adhering to his code of faithfulness will, ironically, ensure his secret
power. Immediately after this reflection, Harry is visited in prison by
Rachel who accuses him of helping to murder Frank (which, in fact, he has
unconsciously done), accuses herself for her guilty love, and expels Henry
from his now-legitimate family. Rachel misinterprets his actions in the duel
as a failure of his chivalric duty to *her*: "'Why did you stand by at midnight
and see him murdered? Why did the traitor escape who did it? *You*, the
champion of our house, who offered to die for us?'" (136). She will, of
course, be punished for thinking Henry is unfaithful. Our experience of the
duel has already convinced us that Henry could do no more than he did;
Castlewood insisted on fighting. Rachel sees Henry as failing his
immediate duty to her, but failure is actually success for Henry because
Castlewood's death compels Rachel to release Henry, which allows him to
grow beyond her control. For the knight to achieve his "lady", Castlewood
must die, but for this knight to be worthy of the lady, he must not be the
actual instrument of death. Moreover, his secret knowledge of his
legitimacy which comes from this death spurs him into self-definition: "'If
I cannot make a name for myself, I can die without one. Some day when
my dear Mistress sees my heart I shall be righted; or if not here or now,
why, elsewhere: where Honour doth not follow us, but where Love reigns
perpetual'" (139). Henry here decides to exteriorize his "inner" self into
public mastery, but his recognition that he might have to wait to be honored
"where Love reigns perpetual" anticipates the failure of his quest as a quest
in this world. Nonetheless, Rachel's attack leaves Henry in a totally self-
justifying position: "And he had to bear him up, at once the sense of his
right, and the feeling of his wrongs" (141), his "wrongs" being Rachel's
"injustice" (145). As "victim", Henry is free to pursue his own course that
will lead him to total ascendancy within his family while still acting out his
code of fidelity.[30]
     The displacement of Henry's desire for Rachel and murder of Lord
Castlewood onto Mohun begins the paradox of paralyzed desire that
characterizes Henry's development. Henry learns to rechannel his desire
into language that will act for him. The first stage is to exploit his exile
from Castlewood as freedom from subordination to Rachel: he admits to
himself, "that to be Castlewood's chaplain was to be Castlewood's inferior

still, and that his life was but to be a long, hopeless servitude" (164). By becoming chaplain (staying "priest"), Henry would never have freed himself from Rachel's domination of him as a beloved child.[31] He never would receive the worship that would establish his public and private worth. The first "action" the free Henry takes is to use his renunciation to enforce his legitimacy and to *speak* this refusal in public before the old Marchioness (152). This first performance of chivalric renunciation wins him financial support and a military commission. Henry's subsequent career as a soldier is also recast in language as general descriptions of military campaigns. And his London life as a wit and unrequited lover for Beatrix also centers on words. He writes a play and constantly talks about his passion for Beatrix to Rachel. Diffusing action into words keeps both public and private selves "pure" until the story can integrate the public and private identities through the actions of the splits.

Henry achieves remarkably easy military success for one trained as a priest and a scholar. The narrator disposes of his first expedition to Vigo Bay in four pages (163-66) and gives Esmond a reputation for courage and ability on the fifth page (167). His initiation in the masculine world clears his eyes to see Rachel as "Goddess now no more, – for he knew of her weaknesses, and by thought, by suffering, and that experience it brings, was older now than she" (173). But their love cannot be realized until both come to it as they would the Grail, as an *agape* far beyond human desire. A most peculiar scene sets the stage for this development into platonic love. When Henry returns from his first military campaign, he returns, in triumph, to Castlewood. Here he will see beautiful Beatrix and fall in love – right after he has proposed to Rachel. She is wildly ecstatic at his return, weeping "wildly", smiling a "wild" smile, and seeing him now as a "deus certe": "I knew you would come, my dear, and saw the gold sunshine round your head" (175). The narrator would have us believe that this is the *first* time Henry realizes "the depth of this pure devotion" (176), but if the emphasis is on "pure", then the subtext becomes clear: both Rachel and Henry can now assure themselves that their love has no erotic overtones.[32] However, if this is true, why does Henry propose? He calls her love for him "True Love" and asks her to be "generous" to him (176) and come away to Virginia with him. If this is the love of which marriages are made, then his infatuation with Beatrix and subsequent confessions to Rachel seem conscious cruelty. But any sexual overtones in this proposal is denied by his describing her response as "a mother's sweet plaintive tone and look" (176). Very clearly Rachel confesses she has loved him sexually – it is her "Sin" – but now she loves him as a Sister or Mother (177). The very ambiguity of this scene implies that the narrator is either uncertain or concealing something, that something suggested by the last sentence in the paragraph in which Rachel is "Sister", "mother", and "mistress" (177).[33] Henry the narrator acknowledges the ambiguity of their relationship and implies its lack of passion. When he leaves after their reconciliation, "'twas difficult to say with what a feeling he regarded her [Rachel]. 'Twas happiness to have seen her: 'twas no great pang to part; a filial tenderness, a love that was at once respect and protection filled his mind as he thought of her; and near her or far from her, and from that day until now, and from now till death is past, and beyond it, he prays that sacred flame may ever burn" (191).

The "sacred flame", which Henry narrator feels (he uses the dramatic present "prays"), is the achieved *agape*, the fruit of Henry's battle between renunciation and active desire. Henry's relationship with Beatrix is an internal power struggle between his desire for emotional and moral autonomy and the enthrallment of his senses. He vacillates between slavery and devaluing that which enslaves him so as to exert some control over his passion. His love for Beatrix becomes more shameful as Henry's desire denudes him of power; his relationship with Rachel becomes more "innocent" as it is emptied of desire and becomes a matter of Rachel adoring him, without Henry having to make any return. Ultimately, Beatrix and Rachel will exchange roles in Henry's eyes, justifying the outcome of Henry-narrator's autobiography.

As Henry-character becomes enthralled with Beatrix's physical beauty, Rachel becomes his tormented confidante and mirror. He learns the humiliation of worshipping one who does not worship him, while he protects himself from any real encounter with Beatrix. He insists that his experience has made him "thirty years older" than Beatrix in "life" and even older than Rachel, distancing him from the one and preparing him for the other. In fact, when Henry sees Beatrix before she comes to court, she is sixteen and he is twenty-three; there is no real barrier to their marriage. He constructs barriers as his desire grows:

> Day after day he would seek his dear mistress [Rachel], pour insane hopes, supplications, rhapsodies, raptures, into her ear. She listened, smiled, consoled, with untiring pity and sweetness. Esmond was the

> eldest of her children, so she was pleased to say; and as for her kindness, who ever had or would look for aught else from one what was an angel of goodness and pity? After what has been said, 'tis needless almost to add that poor Esmond's suit was unsuccessful. What was a *nameless, pennyless* Lieutenant to do, when some of the greatest in the land were in the field? *Esmond never so much as thought of asking permission to hope so far above his reach as he knew this prize was* – and passed his foolish, useless life in mere abject sighs and impotent longing. What nights of rage, what days of torment, of passionate unfulfilled desire, of sickening jealousy can he recal! (emphasis mine; 206)

Henry protects himself from his passion with a shield of words, performing his love in front of Rachel – a variation on Pendennis's turning his loves into poetry. In fact, Henry runs away from his infatuation (221) until Beatrix is engaged. However, as he well knows, Henry's greatest prophylactic is his first act of self-renunciation. He is only "nameless" because he has chosen to be so. When Beatrix learns of his legitimacy, she whispers, "'O, why didn't I know you before?'" (309).

But to create himself as victim is to allow him to protect himself from his desire by devaluing Beatrix. Her eyes, capable of killing glances are paradoxically but "shining toys", "glittering baubles" (205). This woman is not worthy; not only will she not worship him, but her flaws render her an unfit priestess. While "to see her dazzled Esmond: he would shut his eyes and the thought of her dazzled him all the same" (249), at the same time he acknowledges her vanity and materialism.[34]

> Esmond's mistress [Beatrix] had a thousand faults besides her charms: she was flighty, she was false, she had no reverence in her character; she was in everything, even in beauty, the contrast of her mother, who was the most devoted and the least selfish of women – Well, from the very first moment he saw her on the stairs at Walcote, Esmond knew he loved Beatrix. There might be better women – he wanted that one. (249)

As Eve Sedgwick has noted, "what he defines as lovable in her is exactly the same catalog of traits that he defines as morally damning, and to which he holds out a contrast in her mother . . . so that his erotic servitude to her, compulsive as it feels, exists only on the ground of a more or less willed suspension of judgment, a judgment with which he is always free to threaten her and which he finally allows to descend on her with extraordinary punitive force".[35] Henry's passion demonstrates the allowed nature of female sexual power; sexual beauty has power only as long as it is allowed so by the male. Henry deprives Beatrix of her own sexual power when he comes to see her as simply that which a man will desire; that is, as desire itself (263). He knows that "expectancy", "hunger", and "desire" are stronger than "fond love of dearest friends" (what he feels for Rachel), "fruition", and "gratitude" (182). "There is some particular prize we all of us value, and that every man of spirit will venture his life for" (283). Love for Beatrix is neither love for a person nor a matter of her power at all: "'Tis a state of mind that men fall into – and depending on the man rather than the woman. We love being in love, that's the truth on't" (248).

The older Henry calls his younger self "Ulysses" and Beatrix "Circe"(293) – suggesting that older Henry now sees an element of bestiality in his youthful passion. His scorn for Beatrix, however, is a double-edged sword. Lessening her value by abuse and by attributing his desire to the male's need to pursue an ideal also degrades Henry. He is trapped by either an unworthy object or his own emotions. And if, as is very likely, Henry is trapped by both, his own desire for the ideal is degraded by his abuse of Beatrix. He risks sullying his knightly identity. Understandably, then, a rage underlies his passion and the "humiliation", "shame", and "defeat" he experiences at her hands (258). His desire is for "Dulcinea" (264, 284) who is also "the tail of a dirty fox" (263). Both images reduce the paragon of beauty to an illusion, suggesting that desire itself is the degradation because desire renders Henry helpless.

Henry will be able to act on this rage and restore his dignity by means of his secret power that grows as the secret becomes known. Paradoxically, publicizing this private knowledge is crucial for Henry's future because renunciation cannot win you moral authority unless everyone knows you have sacrificed for someone else's good. Henry acts as if he were "the Marquis of Esmond" before the Dowager Marchioness, and her startled reaction to his new self-assurance elicits his "confession" which in turn elicits her confession – that she had known of his legitimacy. His renunciation then wins her financial and social support. Her deathbed confession to Rachel reveals the secret to those who will worship him the most for his renunciation. He dubs himself "Head of the House" before Rachel who "flung herself down on her knees before him", crying "'Let me kneel – Let me kneel and – and – worship you'" (278). Then the "Knight of the Woeful Countenance" (263) becomes King when Rachel publicly acknowledges him as head of the family before the Duke of Hamilton (308). He tells Frank junior, "'I stand in the place of your father . . . and sure a father may dispossess himself in favour of his son'" (345). And, Henry calls Frank and Beatrix "the children" (278) even though he is still madly in love with Beatrix.

The Oedipal overtones of his passion for *Beatrix*, which indicates that Rachel and Beatrix are starting to change roles, are clearly evident in his false *Spectator* paper that mocks Beatrix, Henry casts himself as father (Oedipus) and lover ("Cymon") and Beatrix as mother and lover "Jocasta" (288-92).[36] Rachel, living in private, now is younger-looking than Beatrix (282) and designated for Henry as his wife: "'Mamma would have been the wife for you had you been a little older, though you look ten years older than she does'" (304).[37] Once Rachel and Beatrix have exchanged roles, and Henry's status is secure, the crucial duel between Lord Mohun and the Duke of Hamilton arrives to free Henry from sexual and social ambition. When Mohun kills Hamilton and is forced into exile, they symbolically destroy those parts of Henry that actually could possess Beatrix. The Duke of Hamilton is a split of Henry's public self, the titled aristocrat he would have been if he had claimed his birthright. He could then have married Beatrix and fulfilled the sexual desires symbolized by Mohun. The duel destroys this "public" aspect of Henry and acts out his revenge on his dark desires. The need for the role exchange between Rachel and Beatrix becomes clear through this duel; Henry can now control his desire by redirecting it toward a non-sexual and non-threatening object. Henry suggests the sexual suicide inherent in the duel by calling Beatrix "Herodias" (322) and blaming her for Hamilton's death (323). "'Herodias! you know not what you carry in the charger'" (322). Herodias is the name of Herod's wife and daughter (who is also known as Salome). Henry identifies Beatrix as mother *and* daughter, so desire for her is both Oedipal and sexual. Identifying Beatrix's "charger", a great silver tray embossed with Hamilton's coat of arms, with the tray bearing John the Baptist's head, Henry makes Beatrix's desire responsible for Hamilton's death.[38] Thus while the plot offers no obvious reason to blame Beatrix for the duel, Henry's accusation that she is to blame is symbolically appropriate. As Salome/Herodias, Beatrix's own desire as well as desire for her are marked as fatal, so Henry's desire for her necessitates radical repression to restore his ideal self-image. However, constructing an identity on the basis of such profound repression culminates in a symbolic suicide.

After Hamilton's death and Mohun's exile, the stage is now empty, to be filled by Henry himself, finally acting for himself. Henry will solidify his and Rachel's equality as mother and father and assume his place as domestic monarch by engineering Beatrix's downfall, exploiting her sexual ambition by means of the secret plot to restore James to the throne. Without acknowledging his power, Henry creates a situation that will free him from his passion for Beatrix. He disguises his own complicity by blaming Beatrix's downfall on "Fate": she "might well believe that a malignant fate watched and pursued her, tearing her prize out of her hand just as she seemed to grasp it" (326). This "fate" will be engineered by Henry, whose wariness of his own desire is justified by the immoral nature of the woman whose dangerous allure is strong enough to reveal the power of desire. Henry assumes the Duke of Hamilton's public allegiance to the Stuarts but will act it out privately as a family drama (342) – simultaneously reaffirming his knightly vow of fidelity.

> Years ago, a boy on that very bed, when [Rachel] had blessed him and called him her knight, he had made a vow to be faithful and never desert her dear service. Had he kept that fond boyish promise? Yes, before Heaven; yes, praise be to God! His life had been hers; his blood, his fortune, his name, his whole heart ever since had been hers and her children. (329)

This protestation of faith must sound peculiar coming from a man who has spent two hundred pages in paroxysms of desire for "her" daughter until we remember that this voice is the narrator recreating the thoughts of his younger self. He is now his own split, torn between his role as knight errant to Rachel and knight lover of Beatrix. The plot to restore the Pretender builds from these mixed desires and resolves them, leaving only one Henry. Henry the narrator casts his action as that of a "devoted knight" for Rachel, while Henry the character uses his plot as a last attempt to gain Beatrix: "'If I come back to you and bring you fame, will that please you? If I do what you desire most – what he who is dead desired most – will that soften you?'" (332). It turns out that Henry the narrator knows best. Beatrix "earns" her destruction by confessing that she is incapable of worship:

"I think I have no heart; at least I have never seen the man that could touch it; and had I found him, I would have followed him in rags, had he been a private soldier, or to sea, like one of those buccaneers you used to read to us about when we were children. I would do anything for such a man, bear anything for him: – but I never found one. You were ever too much a slave to win my heart; even my Lord Duke could not command it . . . . were I joined to you I should have the same sense of servitude, the same longing to escape." (333)

Beatrix, living in a world that demands that the female define herself by her worship of others, cannot submit to such self-annihilation. Paradoxically, her only power, her beauty, commits her to the life of a slave and her lovers to lives of the enslaved. The plot to restore the Stuarts exploits her entrapment as icon to destroy her iconicity. Her "active search for power" by means of her sexuality, will ultimately reveal that this sexuality has all along reduced her to the status of sexual object of "symbolic power exchange" between men (Sedgwick 158). The conditions of her defeat make it clear that she never really had any power in the first place, but as an object of value to be guarded and then discarded by men, Beatrix is a means to gauging the power-relations between Henry and young Frank and between Henry and James Edward.

James Stuart arrives in England playing the roles of king, servant, son, and brother. He is Henry's final rival and alter-ego and reveals the narcissism at the heart of Henry's desire for Beatrix. Frank, Beatrix's brother, has been compared with Beatrix in beauty, and when they entered society they were acknowledged as a "beautiful couple" (183). Thus the resemblance between Pretender and Frank (336) is also a resemblance between Beatrix and the Pretender, and the portrait of Stuart is likewise a "portrait" of Frank and Beatrix. James/Frank confronts Beatrix with a mirror of the masculine self she has wanted to be. A union with the Pretender would be the ultimate satisfaction for her social ambition and her self-definition – the self erotically joined to the self-as-other, a fulfillment of narcissus'desire.[39] Henry the character has claimed that such a "restoration" would fulfill Beatrix's deepest desire, and the union between the male and female selves does in fact fulfill a basic Romantic trope in which the male poetic voice seeks union with a figure of his ideal gendered as female (*Hyperion, Alastor, Endymion, Prometheus Unbound*, etc). The attraction between James Stuart and Beatrix is inevitable, and its consummation would surely move Beatrix beyond Henry's power. For although the union between Stuart and Beatrix would satisfy Beatrix's desires, she would still remain an object of desire for Henry. For Rachel to become a successful symbolic substitute, Henry must become disenchanted with the mirror which is Beatrix; his narcissistic ideal must be besmirched, shown unworthy of the worship it will not give him. Beatrix acting out the narcissistic union of self with self in her dual role as mother and beloved object, identifies Henry's desire as taboo, and forces him to desecrate his self-projection. On the eve of her destruction, Beatrix burns more brightly than ever in Henry's eyes:

> A light shone out of her eyes; a gleam bright enough to kindle passion in any breast. There were times when this creature was so handsome that she seemed, as it were, like Venus revealing herself a Goddess in a flash of brightness. She appeared so now, radiant and with eyes bright with a wonderful lustre. A pang, as of rage and jealousy, shot through Esmond's heart, as he caught the look she gave the Prince. (348)

Henry the narrator here uses the same image for Beatrix as Venus as he had upon his first view of Rachel as "dea certe". Her brilliance is directed toward the fullest realization of herself; she gradually identifies her speech with James' and relegates Henry to his father role as a family tyrant (363). But because his role as father has been acknowledged by all the family, he can act to separate Beatrix "for her own good" from the temptation his plot has introduced. This private authority is reinforced by Frank's sense that the Pretender "'is not like a King; somehow, Harry, I fancy you are like a King'" (345). And, in fact, Henry actually controls the "King" (347, 351). But while he uses this authority to separate Beatrix and James, his moral assurance is not necessarily disinterested. He feels "rage" at their behavior (351) and threatens James indirectly when he takes the opportunity of the Prince's advances toward his valet's sweetheart to ask "the Prince to consider what the effect of a single man's jealousy might be" (351). Moreover, he feels "ashamed" at ordering Beatrix away (363). By forcing Beatrix and Stuart apart, Henry ensures that they will come together in a union metaphorically both incestuous and autoerotic. (The crucial letter setting up the assignation is assumed by the servant to be from Beatrix to her brother [378]).

Henry claims that he sees Beatrix clearly when he sees her impure mind: "What mattered how much or how little had passed between the

Prince and the poor faithless girl? They were arrived in time perhaps to rescue her person, but not her mind" (382). His ultimate revelation is not of her moral "unworthiness" but that his desire for her is self love: "The treacherous heart within her had surrendered, though the *place* was safe: and it was to win *this* that he had given a life's struggle and devotion; *this*, that she was ready to give away for the bribe of a coronet or a wink of the Prince's eye" (emphasis mine; 382). The "place" is both Beatrix and Henry's body. His struggle to keep himself "pure" is implicitly derided by her willingness to barter her body, a willingness that mocks Henry's worship of her. In fact he had known this at least since she had engaged herself to Ashburnham.[40]   His response to her degradation and, parenthetically, the degradation of his desire for her, wins him equal footing with the would-be king. They cross swords, and then James offers to embrace Henry, a second "anointing" of King Henry. Upon achieving this position, Henry has no more need for Beatrix but he also "breaks his sword" (384). This action signals the simultaneous loss of his desire and loss of his family. He can still affirm his fidelity to his code because Beatrix, "who was served by me with ten years of such a constant fidelity and passion" refuses to be rescued (388). Her final rejection allows Henry to think of her with "disdain" (388). And his marriage to Rachel is a triumphant fulfillment of his knightly vow: "my dearest mistress felt that she was severed from her children and alone in the world – alone but for one constant servant [note the similarity of language] on whose fidelity, praised be Heaven, she could count" (388). Rachel is only too willing to be rescued and worship at the Esmond shrine.

Henry's success is a return to his first emotional relationship: Rachel's acceptance of the unnamed, unwanted little boy. However, the terms of the relationship are almost exactly reversed. Rachel, now homeless and unwanted, rejected by Beatrix and displaced by Frank's wife (388), worships Henry as the savior of her family's name and honor. The goddess is now a priestess, and the faithful knight rules a virgin Castlewood, carved out of untouched lands. He does, in fact, fulfill his desire to be "righted" by his "Mistress" where "Love reigns perpetual" (139). In this "new" Castlewood (389), untouched by time and old-world corruption, Henry can live out his chivalric ideal of Christian Love: "To have such a love is the one blessing, in comparison of which all earthly joy is of no value; and to think of her [Rachel], is to praise God" (388). But "man is of the earth, earthy" (I Corinthians 15:47). Bodies and desires we have while we live.

While this realization of the spiritual in the world of time has been the motive for Henry's autobiography, the creation of his life as a knight of the Holy Grail has its price. His struggle for self-regulation succeeds at the cost of his vitality. When he discovers Beatrix with James, Henry writes, "The love was dead within him" (382) (originally the manuscript read, "The love of life was dead within him"). Most telling is the juxtaposition between his acknowledgment that with this scene, "the drama of my own life was ended" (387) with the shoulder note in the first edition, "My crowning happiness", referring to his marriage to Rachel. The end of action in life is the end of living – hard to reconcile with "a crowning happiness". In the battle between the two Henrys, Rachel's knight errant has succeeded in destroying Beatrix's hero, only to find out that rejecting desire is a kind of suicide. Apollonius and old Ulysses live on in their husks, looking at a Grail which is sadly, and to them, inexplicably, empty. Perhaps Lancelot had the better life.

What do we learn from reading *Henry Esmond* this way? If we omit the traditional biographical interpretation of the novel as Thackeray's reaction to the Brookfield crisis – and I omit this not because I think it an invalid reading, but because it is only one reading of the novel – we can learn something of the need to see our own self-fashioning with Thackerayean skepticism. Autobiography as a genre shapes from the multiplicity of lived experience a coherent pattern of development culminating in the stable "I" of the character-writer. The frictions within Henry's narration and his narrative, the struggles to retain narrative authority that result in ambiguity and his sometimes almost inconceivable blindness, demonstrate that no "right line I" is flexible enough to contain the "multitudes" which constitute human character. But more specifically, Henry's intense desire to make his story work out *his* way, to *be* the character he believes himself to be results in solipsism. Ironically, Henry's devices to repress his egoism, such as speaking of himself in the third person and centering his morality in renunciation, create a narrative that is all ego. The frictions and ruptures lead us always back to Henry and his telling; nothing exists outside the world of his perspective. We have to read Henry Esmond skeptically to make sense of his story; Henry will not, perhaps cannot, overtly read himself at all skeptically. But reading with Henry as his narratorial audience, we become involved in his web of ambiguities; we are no longer outside observers because the powerful I-you rhetorical connection draws us in as participants in the way Henry constructs his history. Balancing between this intimate participation in Henry's telling and a skeptical awareness of the tensions characterizing his narrative practice makes us sense that Henry is always on the verge of knowing himself. A knowledge of his fallacies and dark desires, if he accepted them, would enable him to become a skeptical fideist: to live with questions and even self-doubt but not without hope. That he does not take this step and move into the Thackerayean game of language renders his story more poignant and contributes, perhaps, to the discomfort felt by many readers over the years. Henry chooses to live without questions but also without hope: "He submitted to life, rather than enjoyed it, and never was in better spirits than in his last hours when he was going to lay it down" (XVIII, 22).

The success of *The History of Henry Esmond*, as a novel, as a fictional autobiography, as the creation of being in language, is evidence of Thackeray's growing sense that subjectivity itself is constituted by language but that this concept of identity is no less meaningful than positing the existence of a metaphysical "self". In 1848, he wrote Jane Brookfield that changing handwriting, changing languages, changed the "I" who was writing (chapter 1). The very ruptures and secret history that make "Henry" seem not who he wants us to think he is only affirms the existence of his consciousness. To challenge "something", to undercut "something" is to assume that "something" is there. Hillis Miller argues that the Victorian novel "demonstrates in a 'safe' realm where nothing serious is at stake, the possibility of maintaining the fiction of selfhood in the teeth of a recognition that selfhood is a fictive projection, an 'interpretation' not a fact, and is always open to being dissolved by contrary interpretation – for example, that of the multiplicity or nonentity of the ego" ("Rhetorical Study" 213). From *Henry Esmond* onward, Thackeray's novels will use their story and narration to develop the possibilities of language for tellers and hearers as explorations of consciousness in action. The fullness of Henry's consciousness will develop in *The Newcomes* and *The Adventures of Philip* as Pen's expert language-games which will change the terms of our reading contract by exploiting the conventions of mimetic fiction and narration.

Notes

[1]   Mary Mason explicitly and William Spengemann, James Olney, and Regina Gagnier implicitly note that autobiography proper throughout the nineteenth century was a masculine genre. See Mason, "Autobiographies of Women Writers" in James Olney, *Autobiography* (Princeton: Princeton UP, 1980), 207-35; Spengemann, *The Forms of Autobiography* (New Haven: Yale UP, 1980), Olney, *Metaphors of Self* (Princeton: Princeton UP, 1972), and Gagnier, *Subjectivities: A History of Self-Representation in Britain 1832-1920* (New York: Oxford UP, 1991).

[2]   Catherine Peters, *Thackeray's Universe: Shifting Worlds of Imagination and Reality* (Boston: Faber and Faber, 1987), 206

[3]   "Time and Memory in Thackeray's *Henry Esmond*", *Review of English Studies* 13 (1962), 151.

[4]   A manuscript revision supports this reading. Henry asks, "What spectacle is more august than that of a great king in exile?" (4). The manuscript originally read "man" instead of "king", suggesting that Thackeray wanted to emphasize the rank. All the notes on alterations in the manuscript depend upon the textual apparatus in Edgar Harden's edition of *Henry Esmond*.

[5]   See Robert P. Fletcher, "Visual Thinking and the Picture Story in *The History of Henry Esmond*", *PMLA* 113 (May 1998), 379-94. Fletcher discusses Henry's "visual thinking", what I am calling his fixation on the frozen surface, and argues that these pictures do not present a unified self, but "scenes of pictures. . .of his own desires" which are "dissonant" (387).

[6]   Elaine Scarry, "Henry Esmond: The Rookery at Castlewood". *Thackeray, Hawthorne and Melville, and Dreiser*, ed. Eric Rothsheim and Joseph A. Wittreich Jr., *Literary Monographs*, vol. 7 (Madison: U of Wisconsin P, 1975), 3-43.

[7]   In the relevant passage (Harden 93), Thackeray's choice of the language of despotism was conscious: "helpmeet" was canceled and replaced by "drudge".

[8]   I cannot resist pointing out the literal meaning Henry's fortune gives to the bourgeois adage, " a man's home is his castle".

[9]   Paul Jay, citing de Man, suggests that this textual subjectivity is characteristic of all autobiographical writing: "The action proper to autobiography . . . is not historical but rhetorical". *Being in the Text* (Ithaca: Cornell UP, 1984), 18. But, actually, I would go further and agree with J. Hillis Miller that this sense of "personhood" created by the text is characteristic of mimetic fiction, not just autobiographical fiction. Miller writes of nineteenth-century readers "peopling" their world with characters they meet in fiction. "Rhetorical Study at the Present Time", *Theory Then and Now* (Durham: Duke UP, 1991), 212. Especially with serial publication, nineteenth-century readers felt – and this can be attested to by

reading almost any review of fiction in any periodical – that the characters in "realistic" fiction were "like us", people.   This sense of vivid presence is one reason the status of the novel was so hard-fought; mimetic fiction was felt to have real influence on people's lives and sense of self.

[10]   Ross Chambers, *Story and Situation: Narrative Seduction and the Power of Fiction* (Minneapolis: U. of Minnesota P, 1984), 51.

[11]   Chambers' narrative and narratorial authority is analogous to Garrett Stewart's theory of the "conscripted reader" who is taken into, or formed by, his or her reading by direct address, indirect free discourse, and "the broader level of plotted temporality, by the valorized inscription of delay, retardation, and forestalled achievement as well as disclosure — in short by the formalizing of emotional tenacity and deferred gratification". *Dear Reader,   The Conscripted Audience in Nineteenth-Century British Fiction* (Baltimore: The Johns Hopkins UP, 1996), 106.   My point is that these techniques act on different reading positions, from mimetic (inside the narrative) to narratorial (aligned with the narrator) to synthetic (outside the fiction).

[12]   J. Hillis Miller, *Fiction and Repetition* (Cambridge, MA: Harvard UP, 1982); .Marjorie Garson, "'Knowledge of Good and Evil': Henry and Rachel in *The History of Henry Esmond*", *English Studies in Canada* 9 (December 1983), 418-434.

[13]   Henry acknowledges his lingering desire for Beatrix: "I invoke that beautiful spirit from the shades and love her still; or rather I should say such a past is always present to a man; such passion once felt forms a part of his whole being and cannot be separated from it" (321) even though his love "fell down dead on the spot" when he catches Beatrix with the king (386).   But his lingering love can be simply more evidence of his code of fidelity: "Parting and forgetting! What faithful heart can do these?" (321.)

[14]   Some of the manuscript revisions suggest Thackeray revised for ambiguity. Here are three examples from early in the novel.   1.   When we first meet Rachel, she "looked" to be a girl was revised to she "seemed" to be a girl and is made to be younger: "scarce more than" twenty was revised to "scarce" twenty. Thackeray here is already allowing Rachel to be young enough in Henry's perception to justify their final union (9).   2.   That George Castlewood was concerned in "every one" of the plots against Cromwell was revised to the more uncertain "almost all" of the plots (12).   3.   That Frank is Isabella's junior by "ten" years was revised to "several" years (13). These seem minor, but, as Scarry points out, this pattern of vague language eventually puts a veil between us and any sense of "hard fact".

[15]   Again, Thackeray's revisions to the manuscript show this distancing to be his conscious strategy. After Isabella first meets Henry, she calls him "Master Henry" which is revised to the more formal and condescending "Page Esmond"

(23); and there is a distinct pattern of revision from "I" and "me" to "Esmond" and "Harry": on page 24, "whereof I" is revised to "whereof Esmond", on page 25, "tell me" is revised to "tell Harry", and so on.

[16] The pun here is, I suggest, intended. Henry's daughter Rachel describes his life as "truly noble" in her introduction (xxv).

[17] That these discrepancies derived from Thackeray's "sloppiness" and "carelessness" is the traditional canard, used to disambiguate Thackeray's intentions.   However, he took care with all his work, particularly in writing *Esmond*. He had a thousand-pound advance from George Smith in addition to income from his lectures. Although he was preoccupied with the Brookfield crisis during writing, his emotional roller-coaster seemed to send him deeper into his writing. See Harden's account of its composition in his edition of *Henry Esmond*, 391-405.

[18] This description of Henry in his later years is written by Pendennis in *The Virginians* (XVIII, 22).

[19] Thackeray's Henry Esmond (both author and "author") combine the autobiographical roles of Wordsworth in *The Prelude* and Carlyle in *Sartor Resartus* – both Thackeray's literary heritages: Romanticism and anti-romantic skepticism. "Wordsworth . . . writes his retrospective narrative to order himself into a renewed state of unity, while Carlyle ironically represents the impossibility of such an effort by creating a mystified autobiography of himself that explicitly disorders and disperses its subject. In so doing, *Sartor Resartus* questions the efficacy of the ordering and healing power of Wordsworth's poem and at the same time seeks to undermine the idea that the self is a 'homogenous little figure' that can be 'tightly articulated' in a biographical narrative" (Jay 34-35).

[20] Karen Chase, "The Kindness of Consanguinity: Family History in *Henry Esmond*", *Modern Language Studies* 16 (1986), 218.

[21] John Keats, *Lamia, The Complete Poems*, ed. Jack Stillinger (Cambridge, MA: Harvard UP, 1982), 358-59.

[22] *The Romantic Ventriloquists* (Seattle: U of Washington P, 1975), 161.

[23] Frederick Goldin, *The Mirror of Narcissus in the Courtly Love Lyric* (Ithaca: Cornell UP, 1967), 13.

[24] See Barbara Hardy, *The Exposure of Luxury. Radical Themes in Thackeray* (Pittsburgh: U of Pittsburgh P, 1972), 99. Hardy argues that Henry's desire is only for the surface; as my discussion will demonstrate, this surface is simply the mirror for Henry's desire.

[25] *Dante: The Poetics of Conversion* (Cambridge, MA: Harvard UP, 1986), 130-31).

[26] Garson (421) points out that when Henry was twelve he was Dick Steele's confident about Steele's amours and even had to pay off the village "wench" who did Steele's "laundry". Moreover, Henry accused Dr. Tusher of sexual games in

response to Tusher's criticism of Henry's flirtation with Nancy (Garson 422), so Henry cannot be sexually naïve as his own narration implies. However, Thackeray's revisions show he was concerned to minimize Henry's awareness of the erotic element in their relationship. In the first version, Henry writes, "I blush to think how often in my walks" he "happened" to meet Nancy. This self-consciousness of his youthful sexual motives is revised to "somehow in his walks and rambles it often happened that <<I>> he fell" in with Nancy. His "blush" is transferred to his memory of "poor Nancy" as a peasant girl who could not understand his poetry. Henry-narrator's self-consciousness becomes awareness of class not of sex (61).

[27]   Thackeray is very sensitive to the kind of love the twelve-year-old Henry conceives for Rachel. An early reflection on his passion says that her words "gave him a pleasure that amounted almost to anguish". The first version in the manuscript continues this erotic tone with the phrase, "If lads may be said to fall in love at" twelve; this phrase is canceled and replaced with "It cannot be called love, that a lad of" twelve . . . (55). The revision denies the love while keeping the suggestion of erotic attraction; it ambiguates Henry's feeling.

[28]   Garson argues that when Henry blurts out that Rachel is much changed (70) and Rachel looks and the mirror and cries, she cries not because she has lost her beauty but because Henry has insulted her. Thackeray's revisions introduce an ambiguity that supports this reading. The first version has Rachel look into the mirror, a look "which showed her that what the stupid boy said was only too true". Thackeray revised this to " which showed her, *I suppose*, that what . . ". (emphasis mine; 70). The qualification says that her tears only *may* be because of her loss of beauty; they could be a reaction to Henry's words. In fact, Thackeray introduced the description of Henry as "dumb-stricken" two lines later as if to emphasize this interpretation.

[29]   Thackeray again made Henry's interpretation more ambiguous in his revisions. After little Frank has told Henry of Rachel's reaction to the accident, a new paragraph started in the first version, "Musing upon this curious mistake. . . ". "mistake" is replaced by the vaguer "history", suggesting that Thackeray wanted to avoid Henry being over-aware that Rachel's scream, "Harry!" and faint is directed toward *him*.

[30]   A significant revision ensures that Henry can remain the innocent victim at this point. Originally, Thackeray had Henry awake from his "idol-worship" here, while he is in prison (148). The motive for this change was his life at Cambridge, "After two years of Cambridge and such a life as students had there", suggesting that Henry acquired a Pendennis-like sexual awareness at college. He also called the worship "this harmless childish flame". The revised passage, describing Henry seeing Rachel as "goddess no more" after he has been at war, keeps the love ambiguous, not childish, calling her mistress, sister, mother, and attributes the loss

of worship to Rachel's unjust treatment of him, her "weakness" not to Henry's sexual experience (173).

[31] Henry as narrator is quite explicit about this: "Esmond thought of his early time as a noviciate and of this trial as an initiation before entering into life" (2:1). The Henry/Ulysses sees quite clearly that his life with Rachel was a life of repressed desire ("noviciate") which would have trapped him in a pre-sexual existence.

[32] An interesting perspective on Rachel's love is that of her son, the younger Frank. He sees quite clearly that "mother's in love with you" (184) but sees nothing wrong with this, that is, does not find it incestuous or in any way improper except for *Henry's* "bar sinister" (184-85). The problem with Rachel and Henry becomes Henry's lack of status, not Rachel's guilty love. Frank Junior's pragmatic reaction dissolves Rachel's self-torturing into thin air and raises the question of whether or not Henry has been exaggerating these hints of sin and guilt so as to protect him from a union he does not want and from the fact that his renunciation of rank does really inhibit his success in the world.

[33] Thackeray revised this scene to de-sexualize Henry's and Rachel's love. He rewrote "only love lives after you" to "only True Love" to suggest the idealism of Rachel's love. Henry feels "thanksgiving" for her love instead of "adoration". He calls her, in the actual proposal, "dear lady" instead of "my dearest". And, most significantly, Thackeray added "a mother's" to qualify Rachel's "sweet plaintive tone". Given the fact that he always intended to marry them, these revisions suggest he wanted us to read between the lines and see Henry as forcing a platonic interpretation of this relation, which does not quite fit.

[34] In this Henry resembles Grifon in *Orlando Furioso* who is more miserable in his self-aware love for an unworthy object than the lover who is simply unrequited in his love: "Let him weep, though, who has enslaved himself to a pair of alluring eyes, a pretty head of hair, and, beneath it, a callous heart, compounded of a little gold and much dross. Such a man fain would escape, but, like a stricken hart, carries the arrow embedded wherever he goes. He is ashamed of himself and his love, but dares not avow it, and vainly longs to be healed. / Such is the case of young Grifon: he sees his error but cannot mend it; he sees how abject is his love for Orrigilla, a despicable, faithless woman; but evil habit has got the better of right reason; judgement has yielded place to appetite". Canto 16. 3 (trans. Guido Waldman [New York: Oxford UP, 1974], 166).

[35] *Between Men. English Literature and Male Homosocial Desire* (New York: Columbia UP, 1985), 152.

[36] Thackeray again stresses the incestuous overtones, revising one description of Rachel and Beatrix's similarity from "a pair of girls" to "a pair of sisters" (282).

[37] One sign of Beatrice's unsuitability for Henry is that she knows him all too

well; she is a mirror of his inner desires, first as displaced onto Mohun, and now predicting the actual closure, and not a mirror of his ideal of himself.

[38]   The exchange of roles between mother and daughter is complete by Hamilton's death. Beatrix in mourning "was older, paler, and more majestick than in the year before; her mother seemed the youngest of the two" (331).

[39]   *Orlando Furioso* also sees Grifon's entrapment by Orrigilla as an auto-erotic desire projected as incest. She deceives Grifon by explaining her lover as her brother until "Little by little Grifon traced out the situation to which Love had blinded him until this moment: to his intense dismay he realized that Orrigilla's companion was her bed-mate, not her brother". Canto 17. 115 (191). Beatrice pursues her "brother" who is really her bedmate but is also, because of his resemblance to Frank and her, is symbolically her brother, the male version of herself.

[40]   He says of himself at the end of volume two: "I blush even now, as I recal the humiliation of those distant days, the memory of which still smarts, though the fever of baulked desire has passed away more than a score of years ago. When the writer's descendants come to read this Memoir, I wonder will they have lived to experience a similar defeat and shame? Will they ever have knelt to a woman, who has listened to them, and played with them, and laughed at them, –who beckoning them with lures and caresses, and with "Yes", smiling from her eyes, has tricked them onto their knees; and turned her back, and left them? All this shame, Mr. Esmond had to undergo; and he submitted, and revolted, and presently came crouching back for more" (258).

6 Infinite Isolations

> Ah, sir – a distinct universe walks about under your hat and under
> mine – all things in nature are different to each – the woman we look
> at has not the same features, the dish we eat from has not the same
> taste to the one and the other – you and I are but a pair of infinite
> isolations, with some fellow-islands a little more or less near to us.
>
> Thackeray, *Pendennis* 1: 143

One of the most tantalizing aspects of Henry Esmond is that we never
know how aware he is of his manipulations and self-contradictions. We
know he manipulates his story of himself to ensure his heroism, but how
far does he succumb to Sternism and believe his own distortions? But this
ambiguity only appears to us if we read with the implied author, outside of
Henry's narration. Narratorial reading traps us within Henry's own
distortions. A skeptical reading suggests that Esmond's only way toward a
stable identity is to eradicate realities and passions that disrupt the integrity
of the identity created by his words. But the Thackerayean narrators in *The
Newcomes*, *The Virginians*, and *The Adventures of Philip* are not interested
in presenting stable narrative presences, if by that we mean a determinate
narrative persona. On the contrary, the play of narrative stances within the
narrative voice and between narrators and characters seems only to
emphasize the futility of essentialism as a philosophy of either narration or
characterization. These novels achieve their skepticism by exploiting the
very fixed sociolects that would seem to ensure the stability of the
characters. Fixed sociolects read against each other and against the
backdrop of the protean narration force us to read both narration and
sociolects skeptically because we experience both the efficacy and
inadequacy of language to describe and so create the world.

The critic-voice of *Vanity Fair* has become, by *The Newcomes*,
Pendennis, the master linguist, who knows his words are his realities. My
choice of pronoun is deliberate here, because not only is Pen a male, but he
is also "masculine" in his choice of sociolects, using primarily traditionally
masculine aesthetic categories. His free play with the conventions of

aesthetic realism and narrative positioning increasingly – from *The Newcomes* to *The Adventures of Philip* – collide with the insistent rhetorical stability of first-person narration.[1] Thackeray insists on Pen as the narrator of *The Newcomes* only to have Pen gleefully self-destroy his authority during the novel through his self-parody and conflicting authenticating devices. At the end of the novel, "Thackeray" finally enters to finish the demolition. *The Newcomes* pairs Laura's fixed sociolect with its male counterpart in Colonel Newcome to explore the consequences of such language when it actually can have power in the social world, while Pen's overt narrative artifices and conflicting claims for authenticity provide a skeptical context for the Colonel's and Laura's transcendental certainty. In a more pronounced fashion, Pen as the narrator of *The Adventures of Philip*, abandons any claims to narrative authority while he plays language games that directly counter Laura's providential version of Philip's story. Harlequin Pen in *The Adventures of Philip* is a masterwork of Thackeray's verbal imagination. George Levine describes Pen as

> Thackeray's survivor . . . the one who resists commitment as long as possible, who understands in the midst of commitment, the absurdity of it, who dallies with the most possibilities, and who makes the best terms with his own inevitable weaknesses and irrational desires. He can believe nothing intensely enough to attempt to impose it on others, and is therefore no revolutionary against prevailing beliefs. After all, although these are as absurd as their alternatives, they at least provide convenient modes of ordering, and antagonism to them would simply cause unnecessary pain. The great art becomes knowing the conventions and using them.[2]

While Pen is certainly not an idealist, he is not quite as defeated as Levine suggests. Levine's discussion of Pendennis in *The Realistic Imagination* searches in vain for a reading that leads beyond the skepticism he acknowledges (168) to a "satisfying place to locate authenticity" (177). Levine sees Pen moving toward a "modernist" skepticism (168); however, *Philip*, as self-parodic as both story and narration are, is not "empty" at the center, but transfers authenticity to our own reading process. One indication that this transfer of authority is deliberate is Thackeray's iconoclastic attack on the conventional closure of the "Victorian bower". Both *The Newcomes* and *Philip* present readers with debased romances that offer us unorthodox not to say unsatisfactory conclusions. One might say, to paraphrase Millamant in Congreve's *Way of the World*, we "dwindle" into closure. In the intervening novel, Pendennis conjures up from mythical letters, the wise voice of "Ulysses" in *The Virginians* to embroil himself in his self-conscious web of words to the point of abandoning his story to a first-person narrator equally as skeptical as himself of the ability of language to tell a referential story.[3] Analyzing how pertinent elements of narrative style interweave with an increasingly debased Thackerayean romance in these three novels leads this study toward a conclusion that considers pragmatically what Thackeray's skeptical romance actually *does* to the reader.

The most determinate totalizing perspective or fixed sociolect is a transcendental language, best evinced by Laura Pendennis. While Esmond's monologue cripples him, monologism does offer a potential union between language, act, and perception to create a stable sense of self if the frame of reference is displaced from the secular self to an Authority. Genuine religious belief, in contrast to historical truth (public or private), completely fixes linguistic and psychological meaning by restoring immutable referentiality to the Word. Laura Pendennis submerges her ego and desire for power in an other-directed discourse justified by religion. She succeeds in making the world conform to her vision and rejecting that part of the world that does not. Her vision, consequently, seems non-egoistic and non-skeptical. Laura inherits her language from Helen, who becomes after her death the primary linguistic reference for Laura. To mention Helen is to invoke God's Word, a reference system into which Laura re-incorporates Pendennis.

In her deathbed scene, Pen's mother transmits the power of the Word to him.

> Ever after, ever after, the tender accents of that voice faltering sweetly at his ear – the look of the sacred eyes beaming with an affection unutterable – the quiver of the fond lips smiling mournfully – were remembered by the young man. And at his best moments, at his hours of trial and grief, and at his times of success or well-doing, the mother's face looked down upon him, and blessed him with its gaze of pity and purity, as he saw it that night when she yet lingered with him; and when she seemed, ere she quite left him, an angel, transfigured and glorified with love . . . . (*P* 2: 188)

As Helen dies, Pen repeats with her the prayer she taught him as a child.

But after her death, "the great blank she left was in Laura's heart, to whom her love had been everything, and who had now but to worship her memory" (*P* 2: 190), while Pen returns to London and Blanche and represses the Word. At his crisis with Blanche, deciding whether to choose the worldly "right" or the morally "right" option, Pen obeys Laura's decisive instructions that I have discussed in chapter 3. Laura is adjudged right by Pen, Warrington, the narrator, and the poetic justice of the plot. His giving himself to her instruction returns him to his mother in symbolic form, his sister/ mother/lover Laura. His refusal to tell Laura about life in the public world allows Laura to keep her fixed perspective and retain an intact system of Word and reference.[4] This development is coterminous with Pen's growth into a narrator. He has a fixed system of reference in Laura's religious sociolect that sustains a system of absolute private value while he is free to play with languages in his public roles.

In *The Newcomes* and *Philip*, Laura's intuition and language remain decisive, consistent, and oblivious to gray areas. The Laura introduced to us in *The Newcomes* is still apart from the world, applying a standard which brooks no compromise.

> She had been bred to measure her actions by a standard, which the world may nominally admit, but which it leaves for the most part unheeded. Worship, love, duty, as taught her by the devout study of the Sacred Law which interprets and defines it – if these formed the outward practice of her life, they were also its constant and secret endeavours and occupation. She spoke but very seldom of her religion, though it filled her heart and influenced all her behaviour. Whenever she came to that sacred subject, her demeanour appeared to her husband so awful that he scarcely dared to approach it in her company, and stood without as this pure creature entered into the Holy of Holies. What must the world appear to such a person? Its ambitions, rewards, disappointments, pleasures, worth how much? Compared to the possession of that priceless treasure and happiness unspeakable, *a perfect faith*, what has life to offer? (emphasis mine; *N* 2: 117)

Note that it is a perfect "faith", not any real knowledge of truth that Pen/Thackeray attributes to her. Moreover, this perfect faith isolates Laura: she has "but to will, and as it were an invisible temple rises round her" (*N* 2: 181). But hers is not the isolation of selfish solipsism. Others can communicate with her if they adopt the role of humble worshipper, like Pen in the passage above, or of pupil like Ethel Newcome. Ethel uses the language she has learned from Laura to defy convention and release Lord Farintosh not because her family is disgraced by Clara's flight but because she cannot love him: "Farintosh, I could never make you happy; I know I could not: nor obey you as you are accustomed to be obeyed; nor give you such a devotion as you have a right to expect from a wife" (*N* 2: 210). This rhetoric of unselfish concern for Farintosh's happiness echoes Laura's language of female Christian Love – but it also disguises Ethel's assertion of will in the face of traditional male power. There is nothing Farintosh can do to sway her or make her feel in the wrong – because in this phrasing of the situation, Ethel cannot be wrong. At the same time that Ethel humbly submits to society's verdict that Farintosh jilted *her*, she gains tremendous moral power within her family, a moral authority which translates into an active ordering power over the lives of her niece and nephew, mother, and younger brother. Having entered Laura's world of religious authority, Ethel can condescend to the rascal Barnes, even though she has disgraced herself according to his code: "But Barnes has never forgiven me my refusal of Lord Farintosh. He is of the world still, Laura. Nor must we deal too harshly with people of his nature, who cannot perhaps comprehend a world beyond" (*N* 2: 269). As her evaluation suggests, Ethel, like Laura, has developed a sense of sight that interprets everything according to the light of divine justice. Pen's and Clive's aesthetic codes are culturally constructed while female religious language seems to be Transcendental because the faith implies an unconstructed, unrepresentable Reality that translates the world into a divine pattern. In the resulting circular vision, any event can be justified as "intended" – and, of course, as Thackeray well knew, in the conventions of the novel, the author as God does fulfill this divine vision. Thackeray exploits this conflation of divine justice with conventional plotting in the serendipitous ending of *The Newcomes*. The lost letter, written by their grandmother and hidden in a volume of Orme's *India*, gives Ethel the justification to restore Clive to financial security from her own fortune, rewarding her for her conversion by allowing her to manifest her new spiritual power in worldly terms (2: 339). She becomes Clive's benefactor but can call it "serving" him. She retains her feminine modesty by insisting that the money be named as coming from the "family" (2: 345), but it is her money and her decision and she is the one who tells Clive of his good fortune.

So, this transcendental sociolect is not divorced from human action. Laura and Ethel see concrete duties and factual truths not just general principles. Female action is private and hidden; female knowledge is intuition and dream: Laura intuits Rosey's unfittedness for Clive (*N* 2: 172), Clara's fatal moral weakness (e.g. *N* 2: 157, 162), and Barnes' brutality (chapters 46, 49). In fact, Laura tries to save Clara by using Jesus' method of the parable. She makes up a "dream" to scare Clara into staying in her loveless marriage:

> "'a bad spirit came and tore [your children] away from you: and drove
> you out into the darkness: and I saw you wandering about – quite lonely
> and wretched and looking back into the garden where the children were
> playing.'" (*N* 2: 183)

Except that Laura's parable seems divinely inspired: "'And I *had* the dream, Pen; it came to me absolutely as I was speaking to her'" (*N* 2: 183). The dream foreshadows Clara's elopement with Jack Belsize, the "bad spirit" who tears Clara from her children. Her dream and secret words ("'I took her hands, and I said more to her in this way, Arthur, that I need not, that I ought not to speak again.'") invite Clara into the Temple of female religious mystery, into which Ethel has been initiated (*N* 2: 183). Clara almost enters, but Barnes interferes. His rule of fear is temporary, however, and she runs away with Belsize. Female use of this language gives the users a sense of moral certainty and absolute meaning, but Laura and Ethel cannot impose their views to force change in others' behaviors; ultimately theirs is an "allowed power", with no ability to ensure its effect upon others.

When men use Laura's transcendental sociolect to pursue their own desires, catastrophe follows because males have effective power in the public world. Colonel Newcome's code of absolute Right and Wrong is based on a sense of Christian honor and chivalry that is the male version of Laura's code of love and purity. From the moment we meet him, the Colonel actively imposes his perspective upon the male world. Pen introduces us to him, significantly, in the all-male, late-night club, the Cave of Harmony. The "harmony" is a bawdy song sung by Costigan and interrupted by Newcome whose code of Christian domesticity condemns its sexual overtones:

"Silence! . . . .

"Does any man who has a wife and sisters, or children at home, say 'Go on' to such disgusting ribaldry as this? Do you dare, sir, to call yourself a gentleman, and to say that you hold the king's commission, and to sit down amongst Christians and men of honour, and defile the ears of young boys with this wicked balderdash?" (*N* 1: 10).

It works this time. Costigan stops singing, and everyone feels ashamed. But the Colonel immediately leaves, which suggests that his influence lasts only as long as his presence enforces it.

Applying his absolute standards to people causes discord, not harmony because his perspective can only be dogmatic, impervious to the truth-claims of other sociolects. Once convinced that Barnes has been a traitor to the his wish to unite Ethel with Clive, the Colonel's righteous indignation degenerates into a desire for revenge. What he cannot see is that hypocritical, opportunistic, cowardly Barnes is by the standards of "du monde" simply acting according to a code everyone knows *is* a code. Barnes combines the self-protective code of "society" (e. g. Lady Kew's not being "at home") with the commodification of human relations implicit in his business of banking. To live in Barnes's world as a "moral" person requires the separation of public and private ethics symbolized in Pen's and Laura's relation. Pen's ironic voice allows him to work within the mercantile relationships of the public world, including the trade of writing, while protecting his private Judeao-Christian definitions of right and wrong, voiced for him by Laura. The two codes never meet except in private conversation. Barnes has only public ethics, and the Colonel has only private ethics. The distinction between public and private would demand a self-awareness impossible for the Colonel, but his private ethics cannot succeed in the predatory world of the market place.

When Pen claims that, in seeking his revenge upon Barnes, "Our Colonel was changed, changed in his heart, changed in his whole demeanour towards the world, and above all towards his son", he is not entirely accurate (*N* 2: 240). The forbearance and charity that Laura claims the Colonel has lost (*N* 2: 242), he never has had. When his desires have failed to shape the world, the Colonel has always reacted violently – as a boy he sneaks out at night, as a man he storms out of the Cave of Harmony, or bursts into Barnes' office to give him the lie (2: 147), or persecutes

Barnes during his election. His actions pervert the code of Christian forgiveness and reflect an increasingly insular vision: "It is in the nature of such a simple soul as Thomas Newcome to see but one side of a question, and having once fixed Ethel's worldliness in his mind, and his brother's treason, to allow no argument of advocates of the other side to shake his displeasure" (2: 228). This is closer to Old Testament wrath and punishment than New Testament charity. The incompatibility of Laura's Christian code with his masculine action is symbolized in the military language with which the Colonel speaks of acting for his sense of Right. He speaks of a "war" with Barnes, and attaining "victory".[5] Clive rebukes the Colonel with his own professedly Christian code, asking for "peace" and "forgiveness" which the Colonel interprets as "retreat".

The militancy of the Colonel's Christian code reminds us that as a wealthy man he is empowered to make his subordinates act according to his own desires. His uncompromising perception creates roles for others as appendages to his vision of life, inhibiting any autonomous identity or action. As long as Clive is an unformed, malleable boy, their relation is intimate and harmonious. But as Clive grows into his own aestheticized perceptions, the Colonel is unable to revise his vision of his son. After forcing Clive into an unwanted material prosperity and an unwanted marriage, he still is blind to his own culpability.

> His life had been a sacrifice for that boy! What darling schemes had he not formed in his behalf, and how superciliously did Clive meet his projects! The Colonel could not see the harm of which he had himself been the author. Had he not done everything in mortal's power for his son's happiness, and how many young men in England were there with such advantages as this moody, discontented, spoiled boy? (*N* 2: 266)

The result is emotional torment for him: alienation from Clive and a sense of being betrayed by his family. He causes agony for others, especially Clive, who tries to live as his father desires but only succeeds in stunting his own development toward independence and growth as an artist. J. J. sadly observes that "they" (Colonel Newcome, his wife Rosey, and her mother Mrs. Mackenzie) have taken Clive's "art" away from him, that part of him that can unite private desire with public action. Clive's acquiescence also allows his father to inflict material damage: investing money in an

Indian bank and refusing to see its signs of financial weakness (*N* 2: 276), which actually robs Rosey of her settlement. The humility with which the Colonel bears his bankruptcy, his willingness to take *all* the blame, his descent into being an almoner at Gray Friars, simply extends the fixed perspective that created the disaster. As he was right in everything, so he must be wrong in everything. From complete dominator he must become complete victim (*N* 2: 328-29).

The argument might be made that the Colonel's fixed sociolect fails so miserably because its Christian referent requires it to be all-encompassing, that a less ambitious perspective – one based on the exigencies of living in the world – might succeed. But materialist perspectives, although they allow for survival, can only be counted partial successes. Major Pendennis' materialist vision "might not, perhaps, tend to a man's progress in another world, but it was pretty well calculated to advance his interest in this" (*P* 1: 85-86). He accurately interprets social class and social behavior, but weighing only social/material advantages deprives him of any intuitive moral judgment. His eyes, "somewhat dimmed by the constant glare of the pavement of Pall Mall" (*P* 1: 165), reduce all human relations to commodity considerations. McMaster points out that the contest between Helen and the Major for Pen is "a matter not just of ethics, but of perception" (67). The Major can see only the material world; Helen only the Invisible World. When seen in the context of each other, neither perception represents sufficient reality. Helen dies because she cannot accept Pen as a man with physical and material desires. Or rather, Pen's perception that human frailty mitigates absolute moral judgments kills her. The Major is as blind as Helen but blind about her moral reality; he cannot see that it is immoral to blackmail Sir Francis Clavering in order to put Pen on the road to material success.

> "No, begad, we've *fixed* you – and a man who's *fixed* to a seat in Parliament, and a pretty girl, with a couple of thousand a-year, is *fixed* to no bad thing, let me tell you," said the old man.
> "Great Heaven, sir!" said Arthur; "are you blind? Can't you see?"
> "See what, young gentleman?" asked the other.
> "See that rather than trade upon this secret of Amory's," Arthur cried out, "I would go and join my father-in-law at the hulks! See, that rather than take a seat in Parliament as a bribe from Clavering for silence, I would take the spoons off the table! See, that you have given me a felon's daughter for a wife; doomed me to poverty and

shame; cursed my career when it might have been – when it might
have been so different but for you! Don't you see that we have been
playing a guilty game, and have been over reached;   – that in
offering to marry this poor girl, for the sake of her money, and the
advancement she would bring, I was degrading myself, and
prostituting my honor?" (emphasis mine; *P* 2: 319)

The Major's perspective is flawed because it only sees the surface of
people and manners and views others as objects to be used. He cannot
succeed in reshaping Pen's world because Pen refuses to play the role the
Major has conceived for him. Unlike Clive, Pen will not annihilate himself
for another's vision.

Such materialist fixed perspectives are inevitably predatory and
potentially self-destructive, allowing the users to control their worlds and
anyone who succumbs to their vision. Barnes Newcome, Lady Kew, and
Mrs. Hobson-Newcome, and Mrs. General Baynes and Dr. Firmin (in *The
Adventures of Philip*) consciously use materialist sociolects in order to prey
upon others. However, to dismiss them as hypocrites is to ignore how
much they believe in their own versions of themselves and their own
constructions of reality. Barnes's image of himself as a man of business is
a self-conscious role that allows him to put Colonel Newcome consistently
in the wrong as a hot-headed brute, ignorant of the ways of the world.
However, his perspective cannot completely control his world. As his
brutality in private life demonstrates, the façade slips and others act outside
his control. But he survives as do all the predators. More successful is Dr.
Firmin who never lets his public and private self-projections of himself as
"doctor" and "father" falter. Firmin uses his victim-hood to steal sympathy
and money by using the language of these public and private roles and
relying on others to respect his presentation of himself (e.g., chapter 34).
Such predators differ from Laura, Rachel, Amelia, and Colonel Newcome
in that they project *consciously*, saying "I am" a man of business or a
woman of culture. Mrs. Hobson-Newcome presents herself as an
intellectual woman, but what the reader *sees* through Pen's descriptions is a
red-faced vulgarian. If, in *Philip*, Mrs. Baynes really *is* the protective
mother, why does she torment Charlotte into a serious illness and then
abandon her after she marries Philip? The gap between language and action
allows these characters to use language unethically, to disguise their
predatory natures by presenting themselves as harmless, virtuous, or even

victimized. One key to the predatory perspective is apparent in my own language. Instead of examining how these characters see the world, I have concentrated on how they make the world see them. The world is their mirror and their stage; their language creates a verbal identity that disguises their behavior by supplying a conventionally laudatory motivation for their predatory, selfish actions.

Since Barnes, Mrs. Mackenzie, and Dr. Firmin use language without reference to their actions or motivations, they can control their audience whether it believes them or not. If the other characters accept their self-presentations as businessman, long-suffering widow, or victimized doctor, they open themselves to manipulation by the callous, selfish beings behind the language. On the other hand, if the other characters reject these representations, the predators can dismiss them as non-human or, as with Mrs. Mackenzie and Dr. Firmin, cast those who reject them as the predators. Thus, the rapacity of the Thackerayean world – his many images of devouring, cannibalism, the slimy tail of the siren, the violence just below the surface of the sea or violence that takes place off stage (Woolcomb hitting Agnes Twysden, for instance; or Barnes striking Clara) – describes a predatory public world where those who cannot or will not participate in others' fixed perspectives can be regarded and treated as subhuman.

The irony is that the fixed perspective of a Dr. Firmin or a Mrs. Mackenzie is a triumph of the imagination: the self projects its image on the world to the extent that the distinctions between "world" and "self" are in danger of disappearing. For all who use fixed sociolects, language does acquire independent power; the Colonel, Laura, Ethel, Barnes, Mrs. Mackenzie, Dr. Firmin internalize their sociolects as "natural", not realizing – as the narrator forces us to realize – that their languages offer only versions of themselves and their worlds.

However, Pendennis as the narrator differs crucially from these characters: he knowingly *uses* the language; it has no power of its own. The inadequacy of the characters' worldviews is revealed by the narrator's contradictory assertions of empirical truth and self-conscious invention, in which he shows us how he constructs his sociolects. Pendennis himself as narrator of *The Newcomes* dramatizes the difference between a narrative attitude toward language – one that sees language as flexible and potential – and a mimetic or story-based attitude toward language – one that ties a language to a specific set of meanings. Pen's (and Thackeray's) narration in *The Newcomes* paradoxically incorporates traditional authenticating devices such as reference to other documents, conversations with characters, and topical allusions into the anti-realistic modes of theatre and fable. Versions of theater and fable install us in front of Pen's quizzical looking glass to watch him watching his material. For example, the initial meeting of Pen with Clive and the Colonel in the Cave of Harmony is presented by Pen as a piece of theater. Pen has gone to the club after the play; he immediately likens the Colonel to Don Ferolo Whiskerandos of Sheridan's *The Critic*; Hoskins, the entertainer, acts out all his songs; the Colonel's rendition of "Wapping Old Stairs" is compared to "Dr. Primrose preaching his sermon in prison";[6] and the confrontation between the Colonel and Captain Costigan (*N* 1: 10-11) is described in the dramatic present. The intricacies of the theater motif in this scene capture the paradox at the heart of theatricality in *The Newcomes*. While theatrical references push the reader out of the story by making us aware of its architectonics, at the same time, devices such as the dramatic present imply that the "story" is an actual event, occurring beyond the control of the narrator. Pendennis's insertions of himself as actor, evaluator, and observer constantly remind the reader that this "drama" is his creation, but he presents the underlying story as something he has not constructed – while his conflation of genres emphasizes the artifice.

Chapters 9 and 11 of volume 2 extend the interpenetration of theater and novel to the point where the conventions cancel each other's claims to authenticity. Chapter 9, relating the romance of Ethel and Clive under the watchful eye of Madame de Florac, emphasizes its theatricality in the title, "Contains Two or Three Acts of a Little Comedy", while Pen's peculiar introduction puts us in the position of "scientific" observers of the nonexistent:

> All this story is told by one, who if he was not actually present at the circumstances here narrated, yet had information concerning them, and could supply such a narrative of facts and conversations as is, indeed, not less authentic than the details we have of other histories. How can I tell the feelings in a young lady's mind, the thoughts in a young gentleman's bosom? – as Professor Owen or Professor Agassi takes a fragment of a bone and builds an enormous forgotten monster out of it, wallowing in primaeval guagmires, tearing down leaves and branches of plants that flourished thousands of years ago and perhaps may be coal by this time – so the novelist

puts this and that together: from the footprint finds the foot; from the foot the brute who trod on it, from the brute the plant he browsed on, the march in which he swam – and thus in his humble way a physiologist, too, depicts the habits, size, appearance of the beings whereof he as to treat – traces this slimy reptile through the mud and describes his habits filthy and rapacious; prods down this butterfly with a pin and depicts his beautiful coat and embroidered waistcoat; points out the singular structure of yon more important animal the megatherium of his history. (*N* 2: 80)

Pen's initial claim that his knowledge is incomplete but only as is other "scientific" knowledge implies that once complete knowledge did exist. This "story" occurred outside the knowable text, and Pen the paleontologist-novelist can build a scientifically accurate version. However, the fable-frame of the novel and the theatrical motifs have already suggested, if our understanding of "Pen" has not, that this "authenticity" is fictitious. The comparison between the "slimy reptile" with "habits filthy and rapacious" and the novelist's story of a young lady and young gentleman extends an odd tone to the ensuing romantic comedy. Is this a claim for archaeological accuracy or for fantasy? And what does Pen mean by saying he "could" supply an authentic narrative, or one "not less authentic" than other "histories"? Is he choosing to be inauthentic? Or, are these other histories (novels?) inauthenticity masquerading as authenticity, and Pen is simply refusing to play the game?

Of course he offers no solution to this puzzle, but simply moves to a scene design that complicates this ambiguity: "Suppose, then, in the quaint old garden of the Hotel de Florac, two young people are walking up and down a avenue of lime trees *which are still* permitted to grow in that ancient place" (emphasis mine; 2: 80). The first half of this sentence attaches the scene to the make-believe of theater while the relative clause extends it into our temporal reality. The distinction between window and stage has disappeared as has Pen as narrator, now reappearing as stage manager, and turning the conversation into stage dialogue complete with parenthetical directions for stage business. Why? To distance himself from an intimate sentimental scene? To be sure, artificial dialogue creates a kind of "veil" because we are forced to place Ethel and Clive as "characters", playing what Thackeray in *The Virginians* calls "the old story".[7] And Clive does propose to Ethel and is rejected. But similar to Pen's proposal to Emily, their "serious" romance is undercut by the formal characteristics of a play, which here includes a comic relief scene with the main characters' footmen, which emphasize the contrived nature of Clive and Ethel's "accidental" meeting.[8] In chapter 11 (volume 2) Pen puts himself and Laura in a play to discuss the worldly scandals of the Newcomes' world: the disaffection between Barnes and Clara, Ethel's campaign for Farintosh, and Jack Belsize's incipient pursuit of Clara. Both dramas create the world as a hardened, sophisticatd place in which characters act themselves out in "set" pieces, rehearsed and repeatable. Both chapters exchange the overt control of narrative commentary for the invisible direction of stage manager, yet the abruptness of the shift, marked so obviously in the typography, only emphasizes Pen as the playwright.

Exploiting the visible difference between "drama" and "novel" on the printed page, Pen displays his own ability to change roles and to change our responses to the characters. The dramatic mode moves us away, the novelistic engages us. Not surprisingly, Pen parodies his role as actor-manager in Charles Honeyman the fashionable preacher.[9] The "lay preacher" who acts out his sermon is cast as a "real" preacher whose identity is acting. Charles's incarnation as fashionable preacher in the Lady Whittlesea Chapel (which Pen compares to the Theatre Royal [1: 106]) is a religious version of a silver-fork narrator. Pen leaves us uncertain as to whether Charles knows he is acting but clearly identifies his role as the Man of Feeling, implying that narratorial sincerity is a rhetorical stance. Charles relies more on gesture than language to convey his emotions: "No man in London understood the ring business or the pocket-handkerchief business better, or smothered his emotion more beautifully" (1: 73). Pen's language suggests that Charles is fully aware ("understood") that he is acting ("business"). And, of course, the pun captures the moral problem at the heart of Charles's acting: Charles' stage business *is* his business; his mannerisms earn his "living" by enticing people to his chapel. So, too, the narrator's "stage business", his method of establishing a "confidential talk between writer and reader" (*P* 1: xv) is *his* business. In the preface to *Pendennis*, Thackeray grounds his test for the sincerity and integrity of the writer or preacher in the writer/speaker's motivations as experienced by the audience:

> And as we judge of a man's character . . . not by one speech, or
> by one mood or opinion, or by one day's talk, but by the tenor of his
> general bearing and conversation; so of a writer, who delivers

himself up to you perforce unreservedly, you say, Is he honest? Does he tell the truth in the main? Does he seem actuated by a desire to find out and speak it? Is he a quack who shams sentiment, or mouths for effect? Does he seek popularity by claptraps or other arts? (*P* 1: xv)

How can we tell whether the actor/narrator/stage-manager Pen and the actor/preacher Charles are "telling the truth in the main"? Both Pen and Charles use "claptraps": Pen's fable-frame and shifting modes are as much for "effect" as Charles's tears and pinky ring. What constitutes "truth" for Pendennis? Is he saved from insincerity and from Sternism because his self-conscious manipulation clearly suggests he knows what he is telling is only *his* version? And is it not more difficult to dismiss Charles as simply a charlatan when his later actions – marrying, going to India to preach, offering financial aid to the Colonel when he is ruined – belie easy ridicule?

Pen's first sentence in *The Newcomes*, "There once was a time when the sun used to shine brighter", should make us ask what kind of truth this narrator is desiring to find out and speak. What are the "truths" revealed by collapsing aesthetic realism into theatre within a fable-frame? The unreality of theatre and fable allow us to make an easy connection between the sudden discovery of Clive's grandmother's letter that allows Ethel to save Clive from poverty with the *deus ex machina* devices of melodrama. This easy unreality, however, ill befits Pen's numerous protestations that he is writing from actual sources: letters, memoirs, conversations, and his own participation. Thackeray further complicates the matter in Shandyean fashion by intervening in his "own" voice at the conclusion to tell us how and when he invented the story – how it was "revealed" to him – while still insisting that *Pen* controls it.

Is yonder line (– –) which I drew with my own pen [pun intended?], a barrier between me and Hades as it were, across which I can see those figures retreating and only dimly glimmering? Before taking leave of Mr. Arthur Pendennis, might he not have told us whether Miss Ethel married anybody finally? It was provoking that he should retire to the shades without answering that sentimental question. (*N* 2: 365)

In the subsequent passage, "Thackeray" calls Pendennis to account for mysterious knowledge that Pen could have gotten only from Ethel and for mistakes he made in the plot. This would seem to firmly settle Pendennis as the author except for the disturbing initial "I" and its claim for his own authority. "Thackeray" returns to the fable-land where "Pendennis" began but for a different purpose. Pen uses fables in chapter 1 to tell us that his world is predatory, that his story follows archetypal patterns, and that his moral will be the impossibility of discerning individual worth by material circumstances (1: 4-5). "Thackeray" uses fable to open up the story, to encourage the reader to subjectivize it as Pendennis has done:

> I, for my part, should like [Ethel] best without [children] and entirely devoted to little Tommy. But for you, dear friend, it is as you like. You may settle your fable-land in your own fashion. Anything you like happens in fable-land. (2: 366)

"Thackeray" ends by reclaiming authorship in the guise of "the Author" (2: 367). The conclusion to *The Newcomes* thus casts Pendennis as part of his own fable and mocks all of Pen's narrative power and protestations of authenticity. Thackeray's introduction of a self as the "I" who recasts Pen's novel as his own fable dispossesses Pen of final interpretive power, while undercutting its own authority. This "I" is elusive because whoever it is offers us only its own fantasy as closure. Ultimately what the "I" leaves us with is our own multiplicity of interpretations, transferring narratorial authority to the reader. We can accept this version or make up our own.

The fable-frame of *The Newcomes* suggests both that this story is not "true" and that it is timeless. Within this frame, Pen's constant reference to and inclusions from his sources – letters, memoirs, and conversations – gives us the novel as a textbook of aesthetic realism. Placing Ethel so firmly within the conventions of the art in which Clive has been schooled calls attention to the artifice of Pen's and Clive's own perceptions. Pen's plot and commentary are obviously a conglomeration of his and other's *readings*; so, too, Clive's infatuation with Ethel is obviously the fruit of his artistic training. These collisions between self-conscious artifice and the authenticating devices of aesthetic realism gradually shift the novel from narrative authority to narratorial authority. As "Pen" becomes more interested in *how* he is narrating, how a story is made, than *what* he is telling us, our mimetic reading is increasingly interrupted by an awareness of Pen's contrivances.

One consequence of this shift from story to narrative consciousness is that the dramatic protagonist becomes less relevant to us than the narrator who creates him in words. In Clive's case, his loss of intensity as actor is mirrored in his nature as an artist. Robert Colby has defined Clive as a quintessential Thackerayean artist:

> Clive may be said to represent the modern artist of the "bourgeois style," whose cause Thackeray had advanced in his art criticism, as well as the spirit of art itself domesticated and . . . accommodating itself to everyday life. Clive's conversion as an artist is illustrated on the title page of the second volume of *The Newcomes* (in its original format) where he is represented before the easel, his wife looking over his shoulder, his child at his feet playing with the sketches that have fallen on the floor.[10]

Colby's description captures the essence of Thackerayean "mediocrity". The setting of wife and child and "family-man" artist bespeaks no baptism in the fire of desire; indeed, Clive's greatest trials are after he is married to a child-woman. His "dragon" is not his own yearning but a tyrannical mother-in-law; and the "lady" he tries to save is his own father. Clive lacks the selfishness of Pen and self-consciousness of Henry; he is so ready to give himself away that he never claims himself.

Clive is better insulated from the dangers of his gaze because his training makes him see Ethel as a collection of formal qualities instead of an object of desire. His visions of Ethel are not nearly as sexual nor as agonized as Pen's of Emily or Henry's of Beatrix. But in terms of human experience, this greater safety means less intensity both for Clive and Ethel. Clive's dandyism corresponds with his absurd ambition to paint grandiose history paintings, not with his sexual desires. As a D'Orsay dandy, studying at Gandish's, he like a "young king" (1: 170):

> A florid apparel becomes some men, as simple raiment suits others; and Clive in his youth was of the ornamental class of mankind – a customer to tailors, a wearer of handsome rings, shirt-studs, mustachios, long hair, and the like; nor could he help in his costume or his nature being picturesque, and generous, and splendid. . . . Silver dressing cases and brocade morning gowns were in him a sort of propriety at this season of his youth. (1: 226-27)

His tender-hearted fondness for his father and children signify the absence of the egotism necessary for passion. When he finds himself falling in love with Ethel, he runs away to Rome where "Art exercised its great healing influence on his wounded spirit, which, to be sure, had never given in" (2: 3-4). His active role as desiring male is displaced onto Lord Kew who dismisses romantic love as "folly" in the face of the commodity marriages characteristic of the "real" world. It is Kew whose wild lifestyle separates him from his gentle, religious mother. It is Kew who gets embroiled with the aged siren Madame d'Ivry and fights a duel because of Ethel's behavior. And it is Kew whose wound in the duel develops into a raging fever, restoring him to his mother and purging him of his worldliness, including his desire to marry Ethel for her beauty and money (1: 359):

> His early impressions were such as his mother had left them, and he came back to her as she would have him, as a little child, owning his faults with a hearty humble repentance, and with a thousand simple confessions lamenting the errors of his past days. (1: 358-59)

Kew rejects Ethel because they do not love each other, prefiguring her rejection of Farintosh. While Ethel/Diana hunts Farintosh, Clive sublimates his passion for her into his pencil:

> He celebrated her with pencil and pen. He was for ever drawing the outline of her head, the solemn eyebrow, the nose (that wondrous little nose), descending from the straight forehead, the short upper lip, and chin sweeping in a full curve to the neck, &c. &c. &c. A frequenter of his studio might see a whole gallery of Ethels there represented. (2: 44-45)

Clive's passion challenges his phallic pencil. It is significant that it is his *"unsatisfied* longing" which "left him indifferent to all other objects of previous desire or ambition. The misfortune darkened the sunshine of his spirit, and clouded the world before his eyes. He passed hours in his painting-room, though he tore up what he did there" (emphasis mine; 2: 121). Ethel does not "dazzle" him; rather, his eyes are "darkened", suggesting that this yearning distracts him from what should be illuminating his vision, his art. Two mistresses, the earthly and the ideal, compete within Clive. That he cannot completely give in to either leads to the diminution of his art (2: 114-15). Unlike J.J. Ridley, Clive does not cultivate his artistic imagination; he cannot paint imagined scenes. Ironically, not being in danger of Sternism makes him capable only of portraiture, a re-presentation that fixes a surface identity. But Thackeray will not let Clive live in complacency, and creates an "Andrea del Sarto"-like awareness of his own aesthetic failure:

> "Look at him [J. J. Ridley]," Clive would say with a sigh. "Isn't he the mortal of all others the most to be envied? He is so fond of his art that in all the world there is no attraction like it for him. He runs to his easel at sunrise, and sits before it caressing his picture all day till nightfall. He takes leave of it sadly when dark comes, spends the night in a Life Academy, and begins next morning *da capo*. Of all the pieces of good fortune which can befall a man, is not this the greatest: *to have your desire, and then never tire of it*? I have been in such a rage with my own shortcomings that I have dashed my foot through the canvases, and vowed I would smash my palette and easel. Sometimes I succeed a little better in my work, and then it will happen for half-an-hour that I am pleased, but pleased at what? pleased at drawing Mr. Muggin's head rather like Mr. Muggins. Why a thousand fellows can do better; and when one day I reach my very best, thousands will be able to do better still. Ours is a trade for which nowadays there is no excuse unless one can be great in it; and I feel I have not the stuff for that . . . . I say, Pen, sir, why haven't I genius? There is a painter hard by, and who sends sometimes to beg me to come and look at his work. He is in the Muggins line too. He gets his canvases with a good light upon them: excludes the contemplation of all other objects, stands beside his pictures in an attitude himself, and thinks that he and they are masterpieces. Masterpieces! Oh me, what driveling wretches we are!" (emphasis mine; 2: 114-15)

Is Clive's lack of talent in fact the result of excising his passion from his art? Or of never having developed the consummate egoism which Thackeray attributed to geniuses like Michaelangelo? His inability to combine his sexual and aesthetic desires is partly at fault. But the nature of these desires is also significant. J. J. desires that which he *can* create and yet that which defies real completion; consequently, the completed paintings feed his imagination. His painting both satisfies his desire to achieve the ideal and sustains the potentiality that keeps the ideal unattainable. One painting leads to another; each vision strengthens his imagination. J. J.'s success contrasts with the failure of the ideal when it is reified as a female icon. His self-projections become independent creations instead of narcissistic mirrors.[11]   While Clive protects himself from entrapment by separating sexual and aesthetic desires, this very separation dooms him to mediocrity because the energy of pursuit for each is necessarily lessened.

If we remember that Pen's and Henry's intensity of vision derives from the nature and direction of the mother, we can begin to see why Clive's desire is vitiated. Helen and Rachel act as the transparent mirrors for Pen and Henry, pointing the way to moral perfection through their sacrifices. However, the mothers' sexual jealousy and desire for control help force the male into the world to strive for himself. Colonel Newcome, the tender-hearted, pure father, is a mother who accompanies the son into the world. Because the Colonel has both affective and effective power, Clive is never left to fend for himself until the very end of his story. The Colonel can act out his maternal desire to retain the son – to that end he finds Clive a wife and a house and a society. In order to create a sense of autonomous identity, Pen, and Henry must struggle to act as well as to be acted upon. Clive accedes to a choice that is not his and therefore cannot affirm his moral or social worth. Laura, with the clear perception of the angel, knows that Clive and Rosey are an ill-fitted couple:

> "If he were to marry little Rosey, I dare say he would be very good
> to her; but I think neither he nor she would be very happy. My dear,
> she does not care for his pursuits; she does not understand him when
> he talks." (2: 172)

Clive marries Rosey "to please the best father in the world" (2: 227). And Rosey becomes the loving female companion the Colonel never had; he chooses and decorates the house, escorts Rosey everywhere, acting as much like a besotted husband as her doting father-in-law (2: 247, 257). It is as if Pen married Laura the first time, to please his mother, when his heart was not engaged – with the difference, of course, that Pen's lack of love was due to his own self-absorption. At the end of *Pendennis*, Pen has recognized Laura's worth, his vanity has been moderated by his knowledge of the Major's blackmail, and he has come to love Laura – and his mother is dead. He recognizes Laura as a being separate from himself and freely chooses her, earning her by the self-sacrifice Laura has demanded.

Clive's lack of choice forces a premature closure to the protagonist's quest. A union lacking self-affirmation cannot create a private life to counter the dissension and contradiction of the public world. Clive and his father become alienated and Mrs. Mackenzie becomes the power within the house; Rosey is clearly destined to be child forever. With the mother and father still present, how can the romance hero ever attain his own status as father? This ideal union promotes separation:

> It seemed as if there were two parties in the house. There was Clive's set . . . . Then there was the great, numerous, and eminently respectable set, whose names were all registered in little Rosey's little visiting book. (2:234)

The Colonel's protestations of ignorance, his excuse that he was doing it all for his son, points up the problem: how can the errant knight ever err his way to selfhood if he is never allowed to err? Clive is caught by his own soft nature, "'If I differ from the dear old father, I wound him; if I yield up my opinion, as I do always, it is with a bad grace, and I wound him still. With the best intentions in the world, what a slave's life it is that he has made for me!'" (2: 255). Clive's story is as feminized as Ethel's in this captivity – as she is the Circassian slave sold in the marriage market, he is the household god turned subservient, never able to leave the role of son:

> "By Jove, Pen, I laugh when some of my friends congratulate me on my good fortune! I am not quite the father of my own child, nor the husband of my own wife, nor even the master of my own easel. I am managed for, don't you see! boarded, lodged and done for. And here is the man they call happy. Happy! Oh!!! why had I not your strength of mind? and why did I ever leave my art, my mistress?" (2: 227)

The softness of Clive's nature is contingent upon the split in his desire between art and Ethel, leaving him without the aggression to pursue either one. By the time Ethel has taken herself off the market and become a "mother" to Clara's children, and thus accessible to Clive, he has already accepted his defeat as a lover and married Rosey. If he had said "No" to the Colonel a little longer, he might have won his lady. And, instead of a Bower, Clive ends up in a House of Mammon dominated by a Dragon. The pastoral Bower is clearly parodied in the Newcome's townhouse, fitted up with the most garish flowered carpets and decorative porcelains that money can buy – a dwelling totally antithetical to Clive's aesthetics (*N* 2: 233).

When the Colonel's bad investments finally force Clive out of the home to work for himself, necessity cannot replace the driving desire for the ideal. Clive's artistic ambition has dwindled into mercantile hack work: "'I am pretty easy in my mind since I have become acquainted with a virtuous dealer. I sell myself to him, body and soul, for some half-dozen pounds a week. I know I can get my money, and he is regularly supplied with his pictures'" (2: 341). Clive cannot refuse this commodity relationship because he is prematurely hampered by a wife and by Mrs. Mackenzie, who accuses him of killing his Rosey by his neglect (2: 331). When Rosey dies and Mrs. Mackenzie finally leaves, Clive abandons any public ambitions, becoming the mother to his son and substituting the private capital of emotion for the actual capital his father had squandered.

> It was touching to see the eagerness and tenderness with which the great strong man now assumed the guardianship of the child, and *endowed* him with his entire *wealth* of affection. . . . My wife and I looked at them one morning as they were making their way towards the City [the financial center of London]. "He has inherited that loving heart from his father," Laura said; "and he is *paying over the whole property to his son.*" (emphasis mine; 2:362)

Pen/Thackeray is reversing his usual value system here. While he normally exposes the cupidity motivating the marriage market by using the vocabulary of money to describe women and their pursuit of men, here his collision of the languages of money and love validate Clive's emotions, especially because Laura uses this language to describe Clive's love. Just as Ethel saves herself from legal prostitution with Lord Farintosh by selling herself to be a wife, and instead becomes a virgin-mother, Clive meliorates his own artistic prostitution by subsuming it under his parental love. Ethel's secret gift of sanctified money liberates Clive from his slavery to the market, and he emerges as a feminized male, unscarred by any sexual passion or social ambition. Ethel has incurred more harm from her own social ambitions. In an ironic twist, she has acted out the social ambition of the protagonist while Lord Kew has suffered the fever and wounds from his sexual activity. Clive's torment has been one of impotency – inability to become master of his art, of his house, or of himself. Thus the "fable-land" conclusion of *The Newcomes* is a fable in part because the roles of lady and hero are reversed; Ethel, the reformed siren, has saved Clive the pure at heart. Her action has made their union superfluous; Clive's consistent anti-materialism has kept social ambition from ever luring him, and his sexual desire has been sublimated into an aesthetic ambition which was controlled by the premature marriage to Rosey and destroyed by his necessity to sell himself.

This "unnatural" romance is echoed in the perverse human world suggested by the actual fables Pen cites in the introduction. They anticipate the human error and despair at the heart of this, Thackeray's most brutal, story. *The Newcomes* contains domestic violence, one marriage torn apart by brutality leading to adultery and another marriage torn apart by bankruptcy, brutal quarreling, and emotional abuse. Some of the scenes in the Clive/Mackenzie household are painful to read (e.g., 2: 330-31). This violent world, however, is not Clive's story. Six chapters from the end of the novel, chapter 36 in volume 2, Clive "Begins the World". As "our history ends", Pen says, "poor Clive is but beginning the world" (2: 315). What has "Our History" been about if not the story of the hero? *The Newcomes* introduces us to a novel of discourse instead of a novel of event; the plot does not close with the conventional marriage, the narrator does not tie up the loose ends, and the narrator's fable-frame is revealed by another narrator to be an arbitrary device, which makes the readers responsible for closing the plot. Not allowed to be immersed in a supposedly self-sufficient story, the reader stands aloof from the cycle to see the artificiality of the pattern.

Edgar Harden's observation that the theatricality of Thackeray's characters increases as they age could also describe the development of Thackeray's own narration. Harden notes that "the passage of time not only reveals weakness and leads to artifice that is both more elaborate and more apparent, but it also changes the perspective in which the artifice is viewed".[12] As the individual behind the role becomes more and more disassociated from the role, role-playing tends toward caricature in Major Pendennis, and in *The Virginians* in Lady Maria, the Baroness Bernstein, and the Dowager Viscountess of Castlewood. These four characters play the role of youth: cracked make-up, wigs, stays, false teeth, caricaturing a reality long past. Similarly, Pen and Thackeray in *The Newcomes* become increasingly self-conscious about "formula" and the role-playing implicit in the conventions of the novel.

In *The Virginians*, the narrative façade cracks even more deeply when the narrator parodies his own parodic devices and abandons his story to one of the characters. The story is itself a parody of Thackerayean devices. Two brothers, George and Harry, are the twin grandsons of Henry Esmond. George, the elder by a half an hour, is taken prisoner on a disastrous expedition with General Braddock, but is presumed dead by his family. In sorrow, Harry travels to England to meet his maternal (Esmond) and paternal (Warrington) relatives. To put it simply, Harry is handsome, trustworthy, honest, but totally unread and naïve to the point of stupidity. After being taken in by his Esmond relatives, in particular his elderly cousin lady Maria and rascally cousin Will, Harry is rescued from a sponging house by his brother, miraculously returned from the dead. The rest of the novel describes the non-events leading to George's marriage to Theo Lambert and his decision to stay in England, while Harry returns to Virginia to marry Fanny Mountain, a pensioner of his mother. The brothers end on opposite sides of the Revolutionary War but reconcile after the war when George (now Sir George) is the means of returning the Virginia estate to Harry (now General Warrington) and his mother, whose papers of ownership were burnt during the War.

The narrator of chapters 1 to 71 is Pendennis, who tells us in chapter 1 that "a descendant of one of the brothers has shown their portraits to me, with many of the letters which they wrote, and the books and papers which belonged to them" (XVIII, 1). George Warrington has confided his family history to his friend, who abandons it abruptly in chapter 72 to the revolutionary-era George Esmond Warrington in his "Warrington MS". This manuscript abandons any pretense of narrative suspense, beginning with George referring to his "imprudent" marriage (XIX, 613) and to his wife whom the reader has already met as his "'dearest little Theo'"(XIX, 601).

Pendennis is much less evident as the persona "Pen" in this novel than he was in *The Newcomes* or will be in *Philip*, where his voice completely dominates the story. The greater impersonality of the voice does allow the story more independence but also makes his metafictional discourse seem harsher. While his disassociation from the story creates the temporal distance necessary to create the historicity of the narrative, his editorial commentary is more impatient and dismissive of both readers' and characters' illusion-making. This narrator uses the language of romance only to ridicule, never to suggest the intensity and danger of desire. Maria, Harry's older cousin and the siren-figure, is an "elderly Calypso" after a "young Telemachus", not a Ulysses (XVIII, 141). The fever of love is now a pool of "imbecility" (XVIII, 156). Maria is an "antique Andromeda" threatened by dragon-Lady Bernstein whom Perseus-Harry must rescue (XVIII, 193). But the "young knight" (XVIII, 171) tumbles ludicrously over the head of his broken-kneed Rosinante to be cured of his love (XVIII, 172). He is riding alongside their carriage on the way to Tunbridge Wells when his horse, a broken animal foisted upon him by his cousin Will in payment for a gambling debt, breaks down; Harry falls forward over the horse's head and is knocked out. He is taken in by the Lamberts, General and Mrs. Lambert and their two daughters, Hetty and Theo (there are sons at University whom we meet later). Of course the conventions of the novel dictate that Harry and one of the daughters fall in love. The narrator ridicules his own parody in chapter 22, by debunking this motif of the beautiful heroine and love at first sight. Theo "was not a particular beauty. Harry Warrington was not over head and ears in love with her at an instant's warning, and faithless to – to that other individual with whom, as we have seen, the youth had lately been smitten. Miss Theo . . . . was not a delicate or sentimental-looking person. Her arms, which were worn bare from the elbow like other ladies' arms in those days, were very jolly and red. Her feet was not so miraculously small but that you could see them without a telescope. There was nothing waspish about her waist" (XVIII, 186-87). Worse yet, when Harry first speaks he reveals himself as the good-natured but illiterate fellow he is, having never heard of Fielding and mistaking "Prussians" for "Persians". So, says the narrator, our expectations of "a knight with curling mustaches, a flashing scimitar, and a suit of silver" will find their reality in "a costermonger with his donkey and a pannier of cabbage!" (XVIII, 188-89). Such illusions persist in readers' and characters' minds because such expectations are the source of "story".

This parody corresponds with Harry's clunking performance as the Prince, particularly in his ignorance of literary romance. Harry never understands the cultural codes that would allow him to construct the world as a reflection of his identity. Pen, Henry, and Clive have imagined their loves and ambitions within traditional verbal and visual aesthetic contexts. Harry's ignorance of literary conventions and his (consequent) near inarticulateness make him so unself-consciousness that his life is a series of accidents. He falls in love and fulfills his position as elder brother in equal ignorance of Maria's age and schemes and George's imprisonment. He could not know that George was still alive and imprisoned by the French, but he could, if his perception had been trained, see through Maria's façade.

The subtext of gambling in *The Virginians* is the ironist's mirror of this haphazard hero. Everyone at Castlewood and Tunbridge Wells gambles; most of the Esmonds are mad for play. Henry plays and wins "because he does not care about losing" (XVIII, 166). "Gambling" is both the major social occupation and Thackeray's parody of the romance quest. Not only does Harry not know the object of his quest, he is unaware that he is on one or that he should be on one. The trial and error of the quest is here a trivial random game of chance, presented as an idle social activity that goes nowhere, does nothing, and thrives on empty craving. The worldly version of this "game", gambling, carries all the passion and danger of the actual romance quest possible within this world. Gambling like love is addictive– Maria, Lady Bernstein, Will, and Lord Castlewood, not to mention subordinate characters such as Lord March, passionately pursue the circular game of betting and playing, playing and betting, with no purpose, or "end" possible.[13] This game is inherently predatory: one wins only if one can make someone else lose. Henry is the innocent sheep fleeced by his own family of wolves. Maria "had taken unfair advantage of him, as her brother had at play. They were his own flesh and blood, and they ought to have spared him. Instead, one and the other had made a prey of him, and had used him for their selfish ends" (XIX, 404). No self-development is possible in this world, and people with any self-awareness, such as Colonel and Mrs. Lambert and their daughters Theo and Hetty, live out of it.[14]

So does George Warrington, who has the self-consciousness Henry lacks but has little visionary desire. George enters as St. George to save Henry from the bankrupt House of Mammon where he is imprisoned, itself a parodic image because the bailiff's house signifies the loss of all material goods. Moreover, Prince George has already attained the clear vision of Thackeray's mature protagonists. He is bookish, serious, although inclined to laugh at pretensions, "colder in his manner, and more mistrustful of himself and others than his twin-brother" as well as "sarcastic" (XIX, 493). He sees clearly how Henry has been duped (XIX, 456-57) and refuses to be duped himself. George has little ambition for worldly glory (XIX, 511) and is content to fall in love with the ordinary Theo. His only pretension is to overreach himself in his desire to write a tragedy. The narrator reminds us of the intensity of Thackeray's earlier young men who had merged sexual and aesthetic desire:

> Most young men pay their respects to the Tragic Muse first, as they
> fall in love with women who are a great deal older than themselves.
> Let the candid reader own, if ever he had a literary turn, that his
> ambition was of the very highest, and that however in his riper age
> he might come down in his pretensions, and think that to translate an
> Ode of Horace, or to turn a song of Waller or Prior into decent
> alcaics or sapphics, was about the utmost of his capability, tragedy
> and epic only did his green unknowing youth engage, and no prize
> but the highest was fit for him. (XIX, 533)

This is the voice of old Ulysses who now reduces the pursuit of the ideal to
a transient passion of youth. His nostalgic tone anticipates the sense of
failure George will feel when he has achieved his desire. The "obstacle"
hindering George and Theo is General Lambert's sense of insulted honor
when George's mother accuses Theo (and him) of gold-digging. But
George's "cause was won almost before he began to plead it" (XIX, 663),
and his mother's rejection of Theo "had not the least weight with me in
frightening me from my purpose" (XIX, 667). George and Theo overcome
their "cup and saucer" agony by simply marrying in secret when General
Lambert is offered the governorship of Jamaica. Although the tone of this
episode waxes melodramatic (all the females of the family conspire in the
marriage and everyone falls on their knees to confess in front of the
General), and George insists that the separation is severe (XIX, 642) but he
also ridicules his own emotional diatribes as overwrought and adolescent
(XIX, 659). The matter-of-fact solution hardly matches the intensity of
Henry Esmond's infatuation with Beatrix that left him "bankrupt". This
romantic crisis is contextualized as George and Theo telling its story to
their children; his position as the happy paterfamilias married to the
domestic goddess of his first choice deflates the intensity of what is
supposed to be the crisis in his story.

Chapter 18 of *The Virginians* suggests why Pendennis gives up his story
to this self-sufficient character. The title of the chapter, "An Old Story", is
a multiple pun: Lady Maria is too old for romance, her inveigling of Harry
is an oft-told tale of entrapment, and Thackeray has written many versions
of the love story. The narrator systematically destroys this version of the
story and his narrative process by discrediting everything he says after he
has said it. His standard sociolects of pastoral love and classical myth
reveal the arbitrariness of his story-telling and ridicule his reader for being
seduced by such empty discourse.

The narrator starts to undermine his novel and literary romance in his misapplication of Herrick's poem, "To the Virgins, To Make Much of Time", to Maria who has very little time to make much of. The chapter title, "An Old Story", emphasizes the urgency in the title of the facing illustration, "Gather Ye Rosebuds While Ye May", also, emphasized by the lines in Maria's face, while the headless cupid reflects Harry's lack of sight and thought (fig. 6.1). The third verse of the Cavalier poem offers Maria a satiric warning:

> That age is best which is the first,
>   When youth and blood are warmer,
> But being spent, the worse and worst
>   Times still succeed the former. (9-12)[15]

The narrator uses synecdoche to debunk idealized love by applying the language of pastoral love to superannuated Maria. She looks up from her tambour frame with "demure eyes", but the only innocence present is that of the "innocent violets and jonquils", innocent because they are mindless. The narrator "synechdocizes" Maria into "the eyes", emphasized in the illustration by Maria's gaze – with drooping lids – which has captured Harry (XVIII, 146). The ensuing dialogue follows the conventions of romantic fiction in its emotional expostulation; Harry, for instance, exclaiming, "'You said – when – when we walked in the terrace two nights since, – Oh Heaven!' with a voice trembling with emotion". Before the reader can become engaged in this language, the narrator's synecdoche destroys the ideal by reducing Maria to her stage property: "'Ah that sweet night, cousin.' cries the Tambour-frame" (XVIII, 146). Maria as embroidery frame suggests the woodenness of her emotion as well as the web she has woven to entrap Harry.

Her metaphoric lifelessness is confirmed by the episode of the rose, which recalls Herrick's lines, "And this same flower that smiles today, / Tomorrow will be dying". Sure enough, Maria acts out "To the Virgins" by giving Harry a rose, which to him is a rose but to the narrator is "a crumpled and decayed vegetable". And when he calls Maria "the Virgin", both poem and woman are discredited. Herrick's poem becomes a satire on itself when applied to a Maria whose age and open strategies reveal the illusion of the "naturalness" in Herrick's idealized love. (The romance is further undercut by Harry who, unlike a Cavalier swain, is inarticulate, "roars", and kicks spaniels.)

If we are somehow still reading mimetically, the narrator jolts us by renaming Maria "the spinster" (punning on her needlework), and having her inadvertently reveal her experience of other men – which Harry does not hear any more than he hears the Earl, Maria's brother, tell him Maria's age. Even when Maria, like most of Thackeray's actors, cannot sustain her role and begins name-calling and abusing her family, Harry does not really hear although he "is more and more amazed at the nymph's vehemence". Maria recovers her composure which makes Harry name her "'Angel.' . . . looking into her face with his eager, honest eyes" (XVIII, 148).

The scene stops here because the narrator can no longer tolerate the absurd picture his contradictory sociolects have produced. He parodies his own conflation of codes in a series of mixed metaphors that devalue one another. Maria's eyes become cold "fishpools" into which Harry "plunges", interpreting their coldness as "calm brightness".

> So that silly dog (of whom Aesop or the Spelling-book used to tell us in youth) beheld a beef-bone in the pond, and snapped it, and lost the bone he was carrying. Oh, absurd cur! He saw the beef-bone in his own mouth reflected in the treacherous pool, which dimpled, I dare say, with ever so many smiles, coolly sucked up the meat, and returned to its usual placidity. (XVIII, 148)

In this ridicule of narcissism, Harry seeing in Maria a projection of his own desire is recast here as simple greed and hunger. Harry's innocence is no excuse; he is a dog who wants more meat. The "treacherous pool" is the siren who, extending the siren image in *Vanity Fair*, becomes the sea in which her victims drown. "Do not some *very* faithful and unlucky dogs jump in bodily, when they are swallowed up heads and tails entirely? When some women come to be *dragged*, it is a marvel what will be found in the depths of them. *Cavete Canes*!" Harry the dog is also "silly Hylas", inveigled into the water by a "green-eyed Naiad", who feels no more pleasure in her prey than a "fisherman landing at Brighton does of one out of a hundred herrings". Any dignity the classical imagery might give to this situation is lost through its juxtaposition with Aesop's fables and contemporary commercial fishing. All the images stress some kind of annihilation by smothering – drowning, being devoured – being consumed in some way. And, in fact, they point outward to the way they themselves

Fig. 6.1 "Gather ye Rosebuds while ye may", Chapter 18, *The Virginians*
Photography courtesy of Elizabeth Huth Coates Library, Trinity University

make their own values disappear into their mixed codes. Significantly, the narrator blames the victim's cloudy sight, and no longer sympathizes with the idealism of youth as did the narrator of *Pendennis*.

> The last time Ulysses rowed by the Siren's bank, he and his men did not care though a whole shoal of them were singing and combing their longest locks. Young Telemachus was for jumping overboard: but the tough old crew could not hear his bawling or the sea-nymphs singing. They were dim of sight, and did not see how lovely the witches were. The stale, old leering witches! Away with ye! I dare say you have painted your cheeks by this time; your wretched old songs are as out of fashion as Mozart, and it is all false hair you are combing! (XVIII, 149)

However, Thackeray's illustration and the narrator have demonstrated that it is not Ulysses' sight which is "dim", but Telemachus's. The narrator identifies himself as the "lector Benevolus and Scriptor Doctissimus" who "figure as tough old Ulysses and his tough old Boatswain". But just as we seem to have reached a stable perspective from which to judge the pseudo-romance of Maria and Harry, and we have been taught to see the age of the "Virgin", the "decayed vegetable" underneath the rose, the "dog" behind Harry and Hylas, in short, when the disguises of pastoral love are revealed as disguises, the chapter changes tactics.

Suddenly, *readers* are addressed as "Brother Boatswain" (149) and asked to remember not our first love as we are asked to do in *Pendennis* but our "opera". In other words, the readers' own theatricalization of love is at the heart of this story. Thackeray identifies the readers' idealized love-play as Mozart's *Cosi Fan Tutte*, a comic opera in which two sets of lovers play deceptive roles. And we are returned to Herrick's rose with "Harry's faded vegetables" and "decomposing greens" now a sign of our own infatuations:

> Any man or woman with a pennyworth of brains or the like precious amount of personal experience, or who has read a novel, must, when Harry pulled out these faded vegetables just now, have gone off into a digression of his own, as the writer confesses for himself he was diverging whilst he has been writing the last brace of paragraphs. (XVIII, 149)

The narrator claims an independent existence from his narration, a life away from his story and his readers. But despite the falsity of the cavalier and classical sociolects, he still assumes that the experiences of the story are analogous to those of life. While he has just characterized "life" as opera, one of the most artificial art forms, "life" is present in the practical history of the symbol of love, the rose, when the narrator reminds us of "the market-gardener . . . the waterings, the clippings, trimmings, manurings, the plant has undergone" (XVIII, 150). The rose from the garden is also the commercial product of a Covent Garden. Real and ideal overlap without becoming reconciled. Love is art and life, opera and Cavalier poetry, commercial product and natural rose, Old Ulysses and green Telemachus, leering witches and green-eyed Naiads. "Is not one story as stale as the other? Are they not all alike? What is the use, I say, of telling them over and over?" (XVIII, 150). Love exists only in the naïve experience of it, only in Harry's transforming vision. No artistic code – Cavalier, classical, operatic or Thackerayean – can recreate that experience for the reader. All we will get is the form without the substance. But it is the readers' insistence on these conventions – our quasi-pragmatic reading – that perpetuates the false masquerade. The paradox that made us sympathize with Pen, that his illusion was at least real in his intense feeling, is not allowed for Harry. The narrator refuses to offer a version of this romance, implicitly blaming the reader for expecting it.

> Whole chapters might have been written to chronicle [how Maria came to give Harry the rose], but *a quoi bon?* The incidents of life and love-making especially, I believe to resemble each other so much, that I am surprised, gentlemen and ladies, you read novels anymore . . . . I suppose you will want me to say that the young fool kissed it next? (XVIII, 150)

The narrator immediately contradicts his self-conscious fictionality by excusing himself through a traditional authenticating device. He says he "cannot write this part of the story of our Virginians, because Harry did not dare to write it himself to anybody at home. . ". (150). Yet this narrator *could* have written "whole chapters" and, in fact, has just finished summarizing their whole courtship. Conventions of fiction and truth clash head on: the story is too familiar and boring *and* he does not know enough about this version. If it is too familiar to tell, then the plea of ignorance is inadmissible. If we accept his authenticating allusion to letters, then we have to accept this version as unique and not "too" familiar. We have just about moved into the realm of language-games; all these statements "mean" to us but, if language is fixed to any event or experience, they should not be able to mean simultaneously. And the narrator acknowledges his contradictions by dismissing his story: "What is the good of telling the story? My gentle reader, take your story: take mine. Tomorrow it shall be Miss Fanny's, who is just walking away with her doll" (XVIII, 150).

Abandoning his story to his readers is one method of giving up narrative and narratorial authorities. It is not that his tale is untellable; this narrator implies that it is all too easy to tell stories. But every story works by incorporating the reader into the narrator's world. (We should think here of Thackeray's fable of the Neapolitan story-teller in *Vanity Fair*.) The narrator of *The Virginians*, like the "I" of *The Newcomes*, invites us – forces us? – to become our own narrators. This speaker is not a "character" who worries about his own perception of reality but a teacher of the conventions of narration. The primary lesson, in chapters 59 to 60, again uses the theatre to explore how conventions of representation create authentic response. The Warrington brothers and the Lamberts attend a performance of John Home's tragedy *Douglas*. General Lambert and George ridicule the play, seeing only its exaggeration. The Lambert women, however, are genuinely affected by the tragedy. The narrator, introduces the discussion about the play by claiming that all representation can only be incidental: "The real business of life, I fancy, can form but little portion of the novelist's budget", meaning here that human occupations are, frankly, too tedious to represent. "All authors can do, is to depict men *out* of their business – in their passions, loves, laughters, amusements, hatreds, and what not" (XIX, 489). This statement contradicts his earlier claim that he cannot depict Harry's love, but functions as an *apologia* for the severely restricted focus on the obstacles hindering the union of George and Theo, and for the narrator finally eliminating himself from the tale altogether. If the business of fiction can only be the passions of men and women, the narrator must strive to represent these passions *authentically*, to "tell the truth. If there is not that, there is nothing" (*P* 1: xv). Yet, chapter 18 has demonstrated the narrator's inability to depict passion and love. Moreover chapters 59 and 60 show that only blind acceptance of representation evokes an authentic response, arguing that "quasi-pragmatic" reading is the most emotionally intense and engaged reading and produces the least self-conscious response.

And we have seen this in Pen's infatuation with Emily and Fanny Bolton's infatuation with Pen. However, this blind acceptance is essentially narcissistic and has little discrimination. Home succeeds with his public because he fits the audience's ideal of themselves:

> Say what you will about Shakespeare; in the works of that undoubted great poet . . . there were many barbarisms that could not but shock a polite auditory; whereas Mr. Home . . . knew how to be refined in the very midst of grief and passion; to represent death, not merely as awful, but graceful and pathetic; and never condescended to degrade the majesty of the Tragic Muse by the ludicrous apposition of buffoonery and familiar punning. (XIX, 495)

Home's formula drama feeds the audience's view of themselves as civilized. If we remember Thackeray's criticism of theatrical paintings, we can anticipate the judgment passed on *Douglas*. The narrator's absurd summary of the play emphasizes the unreality of the dramatic structure (e.g., myriad expositions unnecessary for the characters, so present only for the audience) and the hyperbole of Lady Randolph pining for her dead lover. General Lambert and George destroy the "magic of the scene" with their jokes and sarcasm. However, this artificial drama produces scenes that profoundly affect the ladies. Theo counters her father and George's criticism of the play's theatricality by pointing out the intense response it evokes.

> "Look, Papa! there is an answer to all your jokes!" says Theo, pointing toward the stage.
> At a part of the dialogue between Lady Randolph and her son, one of the grenadiers on guard on each side of the stage . . . could not restrain his tears, and was visibly weeping before the side-box.
> "You are right, my dear," says papa . . . .
> "Yonder sentry is a better critic than we are, and a touch of nature masters us all." (XIX, 499)

Yonder "critic" is no "critic" at all, however, but an unthinking receptor; his touch of nature is mimetic, absorbed reading. The narrator, the General, and George have represented the play to us as unnatural, contrived, and exaggerated. Either the emotional response of the individual is no longer a trustworthy gauge for aesthetic authenticity, any more than Harry's illusion of Maria's youth and virtue is an excusable illusion, or to experience art as "authentic" is necessarily to lose yourself in illusion, and we are at fault only when we misconstrue that illusion for "life". But if we are to lose ourselves in that illusion, we must be able to suspend our disbelief, which means blurring the distinction between art and life. That Thackeray has the General bow to Theo's "answer" and George feel "abashed" by her response argues for the paradoxical second of these propositions. However, neither the General nor George can bury their "skepticism", and end up "'laugh[ing] in the wrong place, and when [they] ought to have cried'"(XIX, 499, 501).

The basic problem uncovered in this episode is not the paradox that overtly artificial art can affect us as "real" (Thackeray is the man, after all, who loved melodrama at the Adelphi), but first, that "authenticity" in art is itself a meaningless criterion because it is an affect not a quality and, second, that education in the conventions of art – one of Thackeray's primary projects as critic and novelist – inhibits one's ability to lose oneself in this illusion. If one loses the ability to accept the finished surface, the art work loses its illusion of independent life, and its manipulative devices become obvious. The surface creates an illusion of stability that evokes a response that seems to be an interaction with something that is there. George and the General "were not inclined to weep, like the ladies, because we stood behind the author's scenes of the play, as it were. Looking close up to the young hero, we saw how much of him was rant and tinsel; and as for the pale, tragical mother, that her pallor was white chalk, and her grief her pocket-handkerchief" (XIX, 503). The very awareness – that of reading synthetically – the Thackerayean narrator desires to instill in his reader – as in chapter 18 – undermines the narrative's promise of mimetic truth.

The difficulty of reading *The Virginians* mimetically, as a conventional novel that invites sympathetic identification with characters acting out a story, has resulted in its legacy of hostile reader-response. Gordon Ray claimed Thackeray "reached an acme of formlessness in *The Virginians*" (*Age*, 373). Elizabeth Barrett Browning rightly saw the demise of straightforward story-telling: "He's clever always, but he goes round and round till I'm dizzy, for one, and don't know where I am. I think someone has tied him up to a post, leaving a tether" (Ray, *Age* 373). But when Ray criticized Thackeray for "derid[ing] the conventions of the novel in a fashion perversely destructive of fictional illusion" (*Age* 374), Ray evinced his own Jamesian, New Critical aesthetics. Moreover, Ray insisted upon reading the narrators in *The Virginians* and *Philip* as Thackeray: "The state of mind of his alter egos often reflects his own very exactly" (*Age* 375). To not read the novels as personal statements, and to reject, as this study has done, the pursuit of the unbroken illusion of aesthetic realism, can open the way to another way of reading – as an *aficionado* of the "conversation", as Richard Rorty called the languages that make up living. By debunking the artificiality of representation, *The Virginians* alerts readers to their own readiness to be seduced by reading. The question remains, then, the alerted reader may be able to see the seductions and avoid them – but to what end?

Notes

¹ Pendennis is also the editor of *The Virginians*, XVIII, 1-2.

² George Levine, *The Realistic Imagination* (Chicago: U of Chicago P, 1983), 169.

³ Thackeray's decision to move from third-person to first person was largely an effort to boost the sales of the novel in parts. *The Virginians* never appealed to the readers well; in December of 1857, Thackeray wrote John Blackwood that he "knock[ed] £50 a month off my pay" from Bradbury and Evans until the sales of the monthly numbers rose (*LPPS* 2: 835). And Bradbury and Evans did lose money by the novel. (*LPPS* 2: 996).

⁴ Baldridge sees this code of silence as keeping Laura from power (506-507) as indeed it does from a twentieth-century point of view. Her moral power is intensified, however, and even though Pendennis becomes increasingly ironic about her in *The Newcomes* and *Philip* as Ina Ferris has demonstrated, her linguistic strength never lessens. See Ferris' "The Demystification of Laura Pendennis", *Studies in the Novel* 13 (1981), 122-32.

⁵ Chapters 27, 28, and 29 in volume 2 are permeated with military language to emphasize the discordance of the Christianity of this military gentleman. My excerpts are all from these chapters.

⁶ This was only one scene from Oliver Goldsmith's *The Vicar of Wakefield* that was a favorite subject for Victorian genre painters and would have conjured up an immediate, sentimental image for his readers.

⁷ In *Henry Esmond,* Esmond finds all youth and young love to be similarly hypocritical.

> And so Nancy was gone; and Harry Esmond blushed that he had not a single tear for her, and fell to composing an elegy in Latin verses over the little rustic beauty. He bade the Dryad's mourn and the river-nymphs deplore her. As her father followed the calling of Vulcan, he said that surely she was like a daughter of Venus – though Sievewright's wife was an ugly shrew, as he remembered to have heard afterwards. He made a long face but in truth felt scarcely more sorrowful than a mute at a funeral. These first passions of men and women are mostly abortive: and are dead almost before they are born. Esmond could repeat to his last day some of the doggerel lines in which his muse bewailed this pretty lass; not without shame to remember how bad the verses were and how good he thought them; how false the grief and yet how he was rather proud of it. 'Tis an error, surely, to talk of the simplicity of youth: I think no persons are more hypocritical and have a more affected behavior to one another

than the young. They deceive themselves and each other with artifices that do not impose upon men of the world: and so we get to understand truth better, and grow simpler – as we grow older. (71)

[8] Pen continues his theatricalization of romantic love by titling the chapter in which Clive marries Rosey, "In which Benedick is a married man". The ironic structure and language inhibits any mimetic reading of these love affairs

[9] Charles' surname suggests his affiliation with novel-writing. He speaks "honey" just as a novelist serves up "sweets" to his public, as Thackeray was to characterize novels in the *Roundabout Paper*, "On a Lazy, Idle Boy".

[10] *Thackeray's Canvass of Humanity* (Columbus: Ohio State UP, 1979), 377.

[11] However, J. J.'s success is possible only in seclusion. Thackeray turns him into a physically feeble, monk-like character who, in *The Adventures of Philip*, knows he is forever celibate: "Low of stature, and of misshapen form, J. J. thought himself naturally out case from marriage and love, and looked in with longing eyes at the paradise which he was forbidden to enter" (XXI, 510).

[12] "Theatricality in *Pendennis*", *Ariel* 4 (1973), 83.

[13] In fact, Thackeray drew a full-page illustration for chapter 28, titled "The Ruling Passion", that shows the company seated at cards. The title's implicit punning, draws together the game of cards and the game of love-making.

[14] It is part of the tragedy of Beatrix that she is aware of the paltriness of her life but has willingly given into it.

[15] Robert Herrick, *The Poetical Works*, ed. L. C. Martin (Oxford: Clarendon Press, 1956), 84.

7 "The Abode of Bliss and the Halls of Prismatic Splendour"

"In wh. the Fairy descends from her Chariot"[1]
Thackeray, *The Adventures of Philip*, Ms

> Mr. Thackeray stands aloof from the entire race of novelists,. . . [setting] at defiance the tastes of those for whom he caters. It is true that he has a select band of worshippers, who swear by him without reserve; but the great mass of readers, though they cannot resist the temptation of his volumes, generally put them down at the end with a good growl at his expense, and with a demand for the novel of some smaller man.
>
> *The Times*, "Review of *The Adventures of Philip*" (5 December 1862)

The narrative "disclaimers" of *The Virginians*, that we are reading a novel which is not worth the reading, or that the narrator is inadequate to his task, or that the narrator is openly inventing his "real" story warn us of the "infinite trickiness of discourse", educating us not to believe either in the narrator or his narration.[2] Similarly in *The Newcomes*, Pen takes pains to inform us that he reports with *authority* things he does not or could not know.

> Also, no doubt, the writer of the book, into whose hands Clive Newcome's logs have been put, and who is charged with the duty of making two octavo volumes out of his friend's story, dresses up the narrative in his own way; utters his own remarks in place of Newcome's; makes fanciful descriptions of individuals and incidents with which he never could have been personally acquainted; and commits blunders, which the critics will discover . . . . the public must once for all be warned that the author's individual fancy very likely supplies much of the narrative; and that he forms it as best he may out of stray papers, conversations reported to him, and his knowledge, right or wrong, of the characters of the persons engaged. (*N* 1: 221-22)

Pen's openness can be interpreted as further authentication because such disclaimers imply the existence of a reality beyond his capacity for knowing. His version may be a construction, but it is a construction based on something other than his own consciousness. This assumption crumbles in the conclusion of *The Newcomes*, when, as I have pointed out, "Thackeray" steps in to claim Pen as *his* creation. Pen resorts to the same tactic in *The Adventures of Philip*, telling us his story is only a version of an unknowable but existing "truth".

> I could not, of course, be present at many of the scenes which I shall have to relate as though I had witnessed them; and the posture, language, and inward thoughts of Philip and his friends, as here related, no doubt are fancies of the narrator in many cases; but the story is as authentic as many histories, and the reader need only give such an amount of credence to it as he may judge that its verisimilitude warrants. (XX, 121)

By the end of the novel, Pen seems to be skeptical of his own decisions:

> People there are in our history who do not seem to me to have kindly hearts at all; and yet perhaps, if a biography could be written from their point of view, some other novelist might show how Philip and *his* biographer were a pair of selfish worldlings unworthy of credit . . . . I protest as I look back at the past portions of this history, I begin to have qualms, and ask myself whether the folks of whom we have been prattling have had justice done to them. (XX, 616-17)

Both are absurd statements because Pen's versions are the only versions. I suggest that "Pen" is performing the kind of critical interpretation that we are to be performing as we read. Earlier, Pen has asserted that the novelist does have access to the truth because he controls the creation of his object. After noting that we, in fact, live our lives among "stories" and construct our realities by means of "stories", none of which are reliable, Pen assures us that reliable stories are, paradoxically, fiction:

> It is only *our* histories that can't be contradicted (unless, to be sure, novelists contradict themselves, as sometimes they will). What *we* say about people's virtues, failings, characters, you may be sure

is all true. And I defy any man to assert that my opinion of the
Twysden family is malicious, or unkind, or unfounded in any
particular. (XX, 135).

Of course, Pen is right. Whatever a novelist writes is "true" in that it only
refers to *itself* and can only be known as the novelist has presented it. But
this makes mockery of the "lay preacher's" mission to speak the "truth" of
human nature. Pen's assertion of truth is accurate if we remember that this
is a *novel*, a construct of his own mind. But, as usual, Pen contradicts
himself: he insists on grounding his story in traditional authenticating
devices: letters, conversations with Philip, and his own eye-witness
memories; moreover, his picture of the Twysdens is malicious because, as
he admitted seven pages earlier, his picture of them stems from his anger at
their mistreatment of him and Laura (XX, 127-28). The "novelist who
knows everything about his people" (XX, 196) is difficult to reconcile with
the seemingly uncertain writer who admits to moral relativity and
incomplete vision (XX, 146).

Or, perhaps not. Ina Ferris has argued that we see a narrator at risk in
Philip and *Lovel*. Philip's story "becomes a way out of [Pendennis'] own
circular and chaotic consciousness, for Philip, at least, always moves in a
direct line. And his story enables Pendennis to impose a degree of order
upon language and technique".[3] Batchelor, the narrator of *Lovel* simply
"cannot find a way to tell his story".[4] But perhaps our experience of
narrative contradiction and circumlocution is the epistemological center of
Thackeray's later novels. What Ferris has described as "interiorization of
technique" ("Breakdown", 46) creates "stories" existing only in a narrating
consciousness that keeps insisting that the stories are both inside and
outside that consciousness. This "interiorization" in *Philip* is Thackeray's
process of theatricalizing telling and reading become complete. Pen's
contradictions, shifting voices, self-doubt, and playfulness make us acutely
aware of our own reading. Because the resulting theatrical archness is a
product of our interaction with Pen's self-conscious comments on his own
narration and his addresses to the readers, he (as narrator) and we (as
readers) avoid Sternism. We cannot be absorbed by either the narrator's
world as in *Henry Esmond* or by our own interpretation as does the young
Pendennis in *The History of Pendennis*. *Philip* successfully joins the
protean critical voice of *Vanity Fair* with the intimate right-line I of *Henry
Esmond*. And the narrative is sufficiently discontinuous to not require a

dislocating interlocutor such as "Thackeray" at the end of *The Newcomes*.

The story of *The Adventures of Philip* can be briefly summarized. It is a continuation of "A Shabby Genteel Story", published in *Fraser's Magazine* in 1840. Caroline Gann, a Cinderella figure, is seduced and abandoned by an upper-class scoundrel George Brandon. In *Philip*, Brandon reappears as the respectable Dr. George Brand Firmin who has married the niece of Earl Ringwood. Caroline reappears as the Little Sister, now a nurse, trained to that occupation by Dr. Goodenough. Philip's story starts with the Little Sister nursing him through a fever and her bedside recognition of Philip's father as her seducer, many years before. Two other families matter in the story, the Twysdens, Philip's aunt and uncle and competitors for Earl Ringwood's money, whose daughter Agnes is Philip's first love, but who jilts him for a wealthy mulatto Grenville Woolcomb. General Baynes is a trustee of Philip's fortune by his mother and his oldest daughter is Charlotte, destined to be Philip's wife. Dr. Firmin steals Philip's inheritance, tricking General Baynes into signing over Philip's maternal fortune, and runs away to New York. Philip could recoup his losses from the General but forebears. In gratitude, the General and Mrs. Baynes give their cognizance to the growing romance between Philip and Charlotte.

This blissful romance is disrupted when Earl Ringwood dies without, apparently, leaving Philip the fortune everyone thought would be his. Philip is a struggling journalist, and Mrs. Baynes tries to break the engagement after Philip has a public brawl with his cousin, Ringwood Twysden, at an embassy ball in Paris. Eventually they marry and struggle through poverty and illness until a carriage accident during Woolcomb's election to the old Earl's seat in Parliament reveals a hidden will, leaving Philip enough money so that he can retire to the country as the gentleman of leisure he was always supposed to be.

Both nineteenth and twentieth century critics of *Philip* have criticized the novel for its unlikeable protagonist, its formlessness, and have identified Pendennis with Thackeray.[5] But Pen's shifting narrative stances, his manipulation of his identity, and the structural games within the novel disassociate Pen from Thackeray and, instead, ask us to recognize that language is not a static product from a writer outside the text but an activity that creates an illusion of a consciousness by means of our reading. This solely linguistic interaction does not offer any "exterior standpoint [outside the interaction] from which to examine the problem of identity".[6] While Pen's narration is cognition in action, his consciousness is a social voice, one that is so inconsistent that its dramatization of "heteroglossia" recreates the basic principles of mimetic narration. In *Vanity Fair*, the social voice is overtly public, the critic's voice that in chapter 36 is an "'I'" . . . here introduced to personify the world in general" (*VF* 322). Pen's voice in *Philip* has interiorized the social voice to the extent that Pen's consciousness encompasses the world; or, rather, Pen's language structures his consciousness that then produces a world made out of that language. However plotless, *The Adventures of Philip* is a narratorial triumph; Thackeray used language so dexterously that he created the illusion of a consciousness in the act of creating.

The ambiguous presence of free indirect discourse in the manuscript and the struggles the compositors had to separate "Pen" from his characters suggests that Thackeray thought of this novel as an active consciousness. In at least 33 places, the manuscript is unclear as to whether passages are quoted character dialogue or thought or Pendennis's focalization into the character's mind and habits of speech.[7] Most of these passages were disambiguated by the compositors who, on their own authority, attributed thought and speech to characters.[8] One instance implies Thackeray's own intention in using indirect discourse because the serialization compositors and the first edition compositors disagree. At the end of chapter 7, Pen is wondering about the strange companionship between the fastidious Dr. Firmin and his dissolute drunken hanger-on, Tufton Hunt, who is the villain who married Caroline and Firmin and tries to blackmail Philip, only to be thwarted by Caroline in chapter 38. The manuscript reads:

> This philosophizing was all very well. It was good for a man not to desert the friends of his boyhood. But to live with such a cad as that; – with that creature low, servile, swaggering, *besotted – how* could his father, who had fine tastes, and loved grand company, put up with such a *fellow? asked* Phil. [emphasis mine]

The *Cornhill Magazine* reads:

> This philosophizing was all very well. It was good for a man not to desert the friends of his boyhood. But to live with such a cad as that; – with that creature low, servile, swaggering, *besotted – "How* could his father, who had fine tastes, and loved grand company, put up with such a *fellow?"* asked Phil. [emphasis mine]

And the first edition reads:

> This philosophizing was all very well. It was good for a man not to
> desert the friends of his boyhood. But to live with such a cad as that;
> – with that creature low, servile, swaggering, *besotted* – *How* could
> his father, who had fine tastes, and loved grand company, put up
> with such a *fellow? asked Phil.* [emphasis mine]

Thackeray did read proof for the first edition, so these revisions suggest
that he took out the quotation marks, preferring to have reported speech
rather than direct speech. Reported speech means that this is another of
Pen's versions of what Philip says; the statement does not have the
independent authority conferred by quotation marks. Most of the
ambiguous passages do not have a clear dialogue tag such as "asked Phil",
suggesting the possibility that Pen simply focalizes into or appropriates his
characters' speech, as well he might, since he has told us he is making it up
anyway.

The difference between reading the manuscript version (free indirect or
indirect discourse) and the *Cornhill* version (quoted speech or thought) is
that the former incorporates the characters into Pen's own thinking, really
suggesting that the narrator is imagining his character's habits, while the
latter punctuates Pen's consciousness with independent statements. As free
indirect or indirect discourse, the passages demonstrate Pen's capacity to
speak for his world, to use all its languages, and because they are so
distinct, that is one character cannot be mistaken for another, the narrator's
focalized passages can become parodies of the characters. For example, in
the following passage Pen speaks as Agnes Twysden, the "siren" who uses
"the same smiles, same eyes, same voice, same welcome" to captivate
Philip and his rival suitor, Grenville Woolcomb (XX, 195). The *Cornhill*
quotation marks are included in brackets in the passages.

> Meanwhile our boy and girl are prattling in the drawing-room.
>   About what? About everything on which Philip chooses to talk –
> There is nobody to contradict him but himself, and then his pretty
> hearer vows and declares he has not been so very contradictory. He
> spouts his favourite poems – ["]Delightful! Do, Philip, read us some
> Walter Scott – He is as you say the most fresh, the most manly, the
> most kindly of poetic writers – not of the first class, certainly – in
> fact he has written most dreadful bosh as you call it so drolly – and

so has Wordsworth though he is one of the greatest of men and has reached sometimes to the very greatest height and sublimity of poetry – but now you put it – I must confess he is often an old bore and I certainly should have gone to sleep during the Excursion, only you read it so nicely. You don't think the new composers as good as the old ones, and love mamma's old-fashioned playing? Well, Philip, it is delightful so ladylike, so feminine!["]Or perhaps Philip has just come from Hyde Park and says, ... (XX, 191-92)

In this next passage Pen performs Frederick Mugford, the *nouveau riche* newspaper proprietor:

I have heard him say that he only came [to Society entertainments] because Mrs. M. would have it – and frankly owned that ["]he would rather 'ave a pipe, and a drop of something 'ot, than all your ices and rubbish.["] (XX, 279)

In chapter 10, Pen becomes the Little Sister, proclaiming her father's right to "blood money," as it were, in repayment for her disgrace, when she accepts money from him to pay some of her father's bills:

Do you think she took money from him? As a novelist who knows everything about his people, I am constrained to say Yes. She took enough to pay some little bills of her weak-minded old father, and send the baliffs hand from his old collar. But no more. ["]I think you owe him as much as that,["] she said to the Doctor. (XX, 198)

In one instance the inserted quotation marks are clearly wrong, attributing a tone to a character that she could not have. Philip's legitimacy is questionable because Dr. Firmin had seduced Caroline (the Little Sister) into a "false" marriage before he married Philip's mother. Now, while Dr. Firmin claims the marriage was false, it was probably a legitimate Scotch marriage. The ceremony Hunt performed was not genuine, but Firmin and Caroline traveled in Scotland as husband and wife, long enough to make their marriage legitimate under Scottish law. Hunt is now blackmailing the doctor and, in a drunken fit calls Philip, "Bastard!" Caroline comes to Firmin to warn him, telling him that Philip has been brooding about the name-calling:

"Yes. He referred to it again and again – though I tried to coax him

> out of it. But it was on his mind last night and I am sure he will think of it the first thing this *morning.* " Ah yes, Doctor! Conscience will sometimes let a gentleman doze but after Discovery has come and opened your curtains, and *said,* "You desired to be called, *early"* there's little use in trying to sleep *much.* "You look very much frightened, Doctor F.," the nurse continues. "You haven't such a courage as Philip has, or as you had when you were a young man, and came a leading poor girls astray . . . ." (emphasis mine; XX, 221)

The *Cornhill* version reads as follows:

> "Yes. He referred to it again and again – though I tried to coax him out of it. But it was on his mind last night and I am sure he will think of it the first thing this *morning.* Ah yes, Doctor! conscience will sometimes let a gentleman doze but after discovery has come and opened your curtains, and *said,* 'You desired to be called, *early'* there's little use in trying to sleep *much.* You look very much frightened, Doctor F.," the nurse continues. "You haven't such a courage as Philip has, or as you had when you were a young man, and came a leading poor girls astray . . . ." (emphasis mine)

Such abstract rumination is completely outside Caroline's nature and ignores the meaning of the dialogue tag "continues". Attributing the sentence to her distances Pen from this exchange; whereas, moving from Caroline to Pen keeps us aware of his consciousness in as the active commentator. This elision of character dialogue into narrative discourse is one way of breaking down the distinction between story and discourse.

Philip becomes a novel of narrative dexterity rather than Ferris's narratorial nervousness if we read Pen's consciousness as a creation of Thackeray rather than identifying Pen's meandering polyphony with Thackeray. Pen's proximity to his characters changes his position in relation to his readers in ways that question any identification between Thackeray and Pendennis or the reader and the narrator. Thackeray places Pen both inside (as character and interlocutor) the novel and outside (as narrative "I" to the "dear reader's" you). Throughout the novel, Pen and Laura act as Philip's advisors and active participants in his life. Their many conversations with him are recorded in a conventional distanced past tense, with Pen subordinating his narrator's distance under his characterological role. But Pen also plays with the time-frame of conventional realism. Having told us that Philip is a grown man with children of his own in chapter 2, that is, that the story of this novel is over and done with, in chapter 12, Pen, anticipating Dr. Firmin's bankruptcy and flight, asks, "Why were these the last days son and father were to pass together?", saying, "Dr. Firmin is still alive. Philip is a very tolerably prosperous gentleman" (XX, 230). But Dr. Firmin is not "still alive" at the time of writing if Pen is still in the same narrating time as in chapter 2 because chapter 42 will tell us that he died after Phil has left poverty but before he is in the settled state Pen describes in chapter 2.[9] When he is a grown man in chapter 2 his father is already dead. Pen is narrating events both as they occur and after the fact, eliding "story" time with "narrative" time.

Chapter 34 merges past and present in Pen's narration; it opens in the past, with Dr. Firmin, now an exile in New York, stealing Philip's salary from his work for an American paper. Philip is falling into poverty and has an increasingly difficult time working for his vulgar publisher, Frederick Mugford. The narrative shifts time to "now" and from past tense into dramatic present, "Philip says", "Charlotte looks", (XXI, 527) and Pen moves into a meditation on "how do men live" that ends by taking us back to the past when "Tregarvan, the wealthy Cornish member of parliament" decided to start his own paper (XXI, 528). Then begins a standard passage of narrative description and report of dialogue in conventional mimetic past tense. Laura finagles a position for Philip on the new paper and attributes her manipulation to the workings of divine providence, accusing Pen of being an "atheist" if he does not believe it to be so. Pen then shifts to present tense, "I mention these points by the way, and as samples of lady-like logic. I acknowledge that Philip himself as he looks at his past career, is very much moved" (XXI, 529). This tense shift brings us back to current reflection on the past story. Philip's meditation brings him back to the past, remembering when his daughter was sick in the bedroom while he was trying to write an essay for Tregarvan's paper. Then, abruptly, Thackeray uses this shift into present tense to bring the reader into his narrative time, the same time as chapter 2:

> Here our conversation was interrupted by the entrance of a tall young lady, who says, "Papa, the coffee is quite cold: and the carriage will be here very soon, and both mamma and my godmother say they are growing very angry. Do you know you have

been talking here for two hours?"

Had two hours actually slipped away, as we sate prattling about old times? As I narrate them, I prefer to give Mr. Firmin's account of his adventures in his own words, where I can recal or imitate them. Both of us are graver and more reverend seigniors than we were at the time of which I am writing. Has not Firmin's girl grown up to be taller than her godmother? Veterans both, we love to prattle about the merry days when we were young – (the merry days? no, the past is never merry) – about the days when we were young; and do we grow young in talking of them, or only indulge in a senile cheerfulness and prolixity? (XXI, 531)

Pen also refers to the serialization itself, calling number 14, the "February number", and "this month's *Cornhill*". He ends chapter 31, in which Philip has managed enough employment to allow him to marry Charlotte and they rejoice in the prospect: "There was a pretty group for the children to see, and for Mr. Walker to draw!" – a reference, of course, to Frederick Walker, Thackeray's illustrator. And, the final paragraph of the novel has Pen, Clive, and Philip assembled with their families at Fairoaks, Pen's country estate. The combination, or I should say, collision, of positions makes it difficult to place Pen securely in one narrative time or to identify him with Thackeray. "Pen" did not hire Frederick Walker. "Thackeray" is not conversing in his study with Philip when Pen's eldest daughter, Helen, interrupts him. The elision of metafiction and fiction both invite and disallow narrator/author identification.

Pen's social voice and inconsistent positioning place him inside and outside of his story, one of and distant from his characters. This positioning is a kind of "intratextual" narration that mirrors the novel's original intertextual activity. *Philip* was Thackeray's only novel serialized in a magazine of which he was the editor. He was author, *quondam* illustrator, as well as the magazine editor who chose the essays and fiction of which his novel was a part. *Philip* was to be read as part of a 19-month conversation with other "professional gentlemen" writing for the *Cornhill Magazine*. Anne Horn argues for a theatrical presence throughout the early numbers of the periodical, that its professional writers were self-consciously aware of "the presence of a paying audience".[10] Pen's social voice articulates, criticizes, and performs conflicting variations of social practices, understandable in their own frames of reference but incompatible with each other.[11]   His I-you interpellation is self-consciously multiple, placing the reader into incompatible reading positions. Consequently, readers play between interpretation and control, constantly moving from mimetic to narratorial reading. In other words the stable but undogmatic readings Titmarsh made of Louis Trimolet's painting, *La Prière*, in 1841 is now the discursive center of the *Cornhill Magazine* (see chapter 2).

Philip and the other fiction in the *Cornhill* (Trollope's *Framley Parsonage*, Eliot's *Romola*, Stowe's *Agnes of Sorrento*) were the "sweets" complementing the "bread and butter" of the factual essays.[12]   *Philip* in particular spoke directly with the serious essays.[13]   For example, the climax of *Philip* in chapter 38, when the Little Sister chloroforms the villain in order to steal a forged bill that would bankrupt Philip if he had to pay, draws on Dr. Henry Thompson's essay "Under Chloroform" published in April of 1860. Part 2 of the novel in *Cornhill* 14 (February 1861), introduces the socially pretentious Twysden family whose father and son work in the Office of Powder and Pomatum. The same issue contains the essay, "Samples of Fine English", deriding pretentious "shopkeeper" English and an essay on "The Civil Service as a Profession". This theme of "seeming and being" introduces the Twysdens in chapter 4 (part 2) and develops as the struggle of the gentleman to maintain himself and his family's status in a commercial world. How can one be a gentleman if one has to earn a living? This is a crucial question for Philip, perhaps the question of his life, and it is a key theme in the *Cornhill* in essays such as "Keeping up Appearances" (September 1861), which argues, as Pen does in the novel, that financial security is essential to maintaining one's social status.[14]   *Philip* dramatizes what the *Cornhill* was about: the problem of maintaining one's identity as a gentleman in an increasingly predatory commercial world. Thackeray as a successful writer and editor who maintained his status wrote a novel narrated by a Pendennis whose eloquence cannot disguise the ineptitude of his subject in this struggle nor the rapacity of his world.[15]

This intra- and inter- textuality produce what Andrew Blake has called "realism": an ideology *in process* that offered no *a priori* moral system but one discussed and debated. Pieces of a story appearing each month in conversation with nonfiction prose "gave people a chance to discuss domestic ideology *in public* without touching on their own domestic secrets" (71). Blake also argues that Victorian "realism" was produced through "gentlemanly" writing (74), a trait, I have noted, always attributed to Thackeray even when his critics derided his lack of plot and repetition. But if even while calling *The Virginians* a failure, the *Saturday Review* could praise Thackeray for writing like a gentleman (19 Nov. 1859),[16] then how must his public have felt when confronted by Pen's stylish but unorthodox deconstruction of the "realistic" novel's conventional linear plot line and its stable moral center voiced by a consistent narrative persona?[17]   One response was anger. The *London Review and Weekly Journal of Politics, Literature, Art, and Society* identified Pen as Thackeray and waxed indignant at the narrative self-consciousness:

> Half the reviewer's task is superseded, for Mr. Thackeray criticizes himself as he goes along, mocks at what he considers to be the weak points of the narrative, and acknowledges that he is not unfrequently inexcusably garrulous . . . . Even while the performance is going on, we hear the manager's voice behind the stage, now jeering at the sentiment, now quizzing some theatrical conventionality, and now, with an indolent melancholy, confessing that the representation is a poor one, or excusing the non-production of some necessary scene by the statement that it has been acted before, and that the audience is perfectly able to imagine it for themselves. (192-93)

Pen's gentlemanly style gives us "gentlemen" who are a snob (Sir John Ringwood), a debauched aristocrat (Earl Ringwood), a swindling seducer (Dr. Firmin), a deceitful social climber (Twysden), and a "genteel atheist" (Pendennis). These gentlemen are forgers, drunkards, debauches, liars, and hypocrites. In this world, the greatest act of virtue is the Little Sister's robbery. If we step outside Pen's narration and read synthetically to recognize these "facts", we have to become skeptical of the entire theme of "gentlemanliness".

The narrative structure is just as unsettling as the story's major theme because Pen's and Laura's understanding of narrative sequence are incompatible. Laura's mode is an "argument from design", a "providential aesthetic", to use Thomas Vargish's term.[18] While her transcendental "textbook, admitting of no contradiction according to her judgment" (XXI, 572) reinforces Pen's Samaritan motif, his primary mode is one of empirical cultural construction, the voice of the man of the world accepting only situational contingencies. And both modes conflict with the pantomime mode that turns aesthetic realism into a fantastic comedy.

These collisions make it difficult for the reader to settle on any one way of reading because while no models are sufficient, they all have meaning.

And lest we try to ignore these contradictions, the novel denies reader expectations of plot – a series of connected actions unfolding to an end. Pen almost totally abandons narrative authority by chapter 2 when he tells us:

> [Philip] is not going to perish in the last chapter of these memoirs – to die of consumption with his love weeping by his bedside, or to blow his brains out in despair, because she has been married to his rival, or killed out of a gig, or otherwise done for in the last chapter but one. No, no; we will have no dismal endings. Philip Firmin is well and hearty at this minute, owes no man a shilling, and can enjoy his glass of port in perfect comfort. So, my dear miss, if you want a pulmonary romance, the present won't suit you. So, young gentleman, if you are for melancholy, despair, and sardonic satire, please to call at some other shop. (XX, 110)

The story of how Pen tells us Philip's history becomes the dramatization of skeptical epistemology. Pen's associations with set scenes organize the plot into a spiral of events organized by the movement of Pen's mind in, out, and around them, analogous to the near-far view and prism-vision of *The History of Pendennis*. The "direct" line of Philip's early story begins with Dr. Firmin's seduction and abandonment of Caroline Brandon, his later marriage to Philip's mother, Philip's youthful illness in which he discovers his father's betrayal of Caroline, and the subsequent estrangement and hostility between father and son. Pen loops this history into two consecutive spirals. He remembers one scene, a hostile conversation between Dr. Firmin and Philip, and had been told of another, a confrontation between Dr. Goodenough and Dr. Firmin at Philip's sickbed. These scenes seem to have no connection – except for Pen's persistent question "Why?" (XX, 104, 117). We, with Pen, Helen, and Dr. Goodenough discussing Philip's illness (XX, 99), move to the annual Founder's dinner at Grayfriars and then to the hostile conversation between Firmin and Philip (XX, 102-104). Then we return to the illness (XX, 106) and Philip's youth, move forward out of the story completely to narrative present (XX, 109), back to Dr. Firmin's history, forward to the deaths of Helen and Mrs. Firmin (XX, 116), back "yet farther in time to a period which I cannot precisely ascertain" (XX, 121) to the story of Caroline Brandon leading up to Philip's illness (XX, 124) which is at the end of chapter 3 *now* treated as a "discovery" scene and the cause of Philip's hostility toward his father. The only way to follow Philip's story is to immerse yourself in Pen's consciousness – there is no separation between teller and tale. The plot "progresses" by means of this wandering memory which is constantly qualified by Pen's (false ?) apologies for his method and uncertainty about his own attitudes. The conventional plot question, "What next?" is meaningless in *Philip* because Pen repeatedly tells us: "I tell you they are married; and don't want to make any mysteries about the business . . . but before they married, and afterwards, they had great griefs and troubles; as no doubt you have had, dear sir or madam, since you underwent that ceremony" (XXI, 375; cf. XX, 110).[19]

After the discovery scene in chapter 3, Pen gives up most of his narrative authority. His assurances that Philip's love affair with Agnes will come to nothing, that Philip and Charlotte will be married and that they still are happily married at the time of his writing eliminate any narrative suspense. But Pen does withhold knowledge of who "he" is. Would he really defend Nero (see pp. 272-73)? Are writer and readers really cannibals (see pp. 264-65)? From asking "what really happened" in *Henry Esmond* we change to asking, "who is he, really?".   Pen gleefully point readers to his own vagaries by parodying omniscient narration – no longer his but Laura's (and perhaps the reader's). He incorporates her Word of God into his own structural frame of the Good Samaritan, referring to the motif at least eleven times. But he conflates this frame with fairy-tale and theater motifs and a personal voice of increasing irony. One of her weapons is to withhold her language and to judge by *not* verbalizing, as when she disapproves of the Twysdens in chapter 8: "My wife exasperates me . . . in nothing more than in that obstinate silence, which she persists in maintaining sometimes when I am abusing people, whom I do not like, whom she does not like, and who abuse me" (XX, 181). Her silence is not the Christian code of charity but expresses her superior disassociation from "'you people' who are opportunistic" (XX, 182). But, as throughout this novel, Pen, the ironist, validates her perspective by arriving at the same conclusion. His language is that of the marketplace which describes Agnes' match with Woolcomb not as sin because loveless but as a sordid bargain (XX, 185). Laura's criteria is "woman's love", her "faith and purity" and the "world's most sacred subject" (XX, 182). The paradox of these two codes agreeing unsettles the reader – as Pendennis (and Thackeray) perhaps intend that it should: "This is what is called cynicism, you know. Then I suppose my wife is a cynic, who clutches her children to her pure heart, and prays gracious Heaven to guard them from selfishness, from worldliness, from heartlessness, from wicked greed" (XX, 185).

However, the novel is not advocating relativity. It is precisely the collision of such opposite perspectives that still can come to the same moral judgment that establishes a point of ethical stability – marrying for money is wrong. Readers can evaluate and make decisions to act rightly and wrongly, but they cannot depend upon any single system of representation to be an adequate guide for their judgment. Viewed negatively, Pen is John Henry Newman's "true gentleman" who "'carefully avoids whatever may cause a jar or a jolt in the minds of those with whom he is cast'".[20] Robin Gilmour concludes that this seeming tolerance disguises "a real selfishness; the gentleman will surrender the outworks of his personal convenience in order to preserve the citadel of his self-esteem intact" (91). What Ferris calls the "ethic of restraint", Gilmour sees as, and Pen acts as, a man "who refrains from doing" (Ferris "Narrative Strategy", 419; Gilmour 91). Pen's relativism demonstrates ironically the "social grace" that Fitzjames Stephen in his essay, "Gentlemen", sees as essential: ". . . when we speak of a gentleman we do not mean either a good man, or a wise man, but a man socially pleasant, and we consider his goodness and wisdom, his moral and intellectual qualities as relevant to his claims to be considered a gentleman only in so far as they contribute to his social pleasantness" (331).[21] Walter Bagehot saw this tolerance not as relativism or as cynicism but as a compromise that allows the gentleman to live in an ungentlemanly world. His praise of Thackeray's ability to "analyze most men as they stand before you" is a summary of Pen's "juste milieu" approach: "Do not be exaggerated, do not aim too low; do not take the worst of the world; extreme badness is as monotonous and of as few species as the best excellence" (*Critical Heritage* 309). Pen is graceful, witty, and noncommittal: "My dear young friend", he advises, "the profitable way in life is the middle way. Don't quite believe anybody, for he may mislead you; neither disbelieve him, for that is uncomplimentary to your friend. Black is not so very black; and as for white, *bon Dieu*! in our climate what paint will remain white long?" (XX, 164). The "gentlemanly style" for which the *Saturday Review* praises Thackeray is really a pose of "self-restraint, modesty, and honesty", a rejection of the egoism of authorship:

The commonplace, ill-bred, uneducated, literary gentlemen who take to writing novels almost always assume that they and their craft are not only the salt of the earth, but the natural rulers, guides, and lights of mankind. They almost always assume that to be able to write a popular tale is a gift so precious that its possessor has a right to stand towards the prosaic part of human society in the same sort of relation as that which the Hebrew Prophets assumed towards the Jewish Kings. . . . Mr. Thackeray is absolutely free from this monstrous presumption. (*Critical Heritage,* 299)

Laura, of course, rejects Pen's gentlemanly tolerance:

"The cowardice of you men, Pen, upon matters of opinion, of you masters and lords or creation, is really despicable, sir! You dare not have opinions, or holding them you dare not declare them and act by them. You compromise with crime every day because you think it would be officious to declare yourself and interfere. You are not afraid of outraging morals, but of inflicting *ennui* upon society, and losing your popularity . . . . It is not right to 'put your oar in' as you say in your jargon (and even your slang is a sort of cowardice, sir, for you are afraid to speak the feelings of your heart). . . . That is the language of the world." (XX, 243)

We know by now that to "speak" the feelings of your heart in Thackeray's world is to risk Sternism or, at the least, to become an unconscious performer. When Laura does "speak her mind, there [is] no mistaking her meaning" (XX, 257) because she is out of the world – as a consummate Victorian angel we hardly ever see her out of her house. Her absolute code not only identifies intended meaning with expressed meaning but also justifies that meaning as the only one possible. Her language has the miraculous power in *Philip* of creating a poetically just ending completely discordant with Pen's self-immersed, cynical, and self-aware narration. Laura not only speaks her meaning, but also makes the world of the novel conform to her language. After Philip and Charlotte fall in love, she first suggests the unlikely happy ending and rejects Pen's practical objections to their marriage.

"Do you suppose Heaven will not send him help at its good time, and be kind to him who has rescued so many from ruin? Do you suppose the prayers, the blessings of that father, of those little ones, of that dear child will not avail him? Suppose he has to wait a year, ten years – have they not time, and will not the good day come?"

Yes. This was actually the talk of a woman of sense and discernment when her prejudices and romance were not in the way, and she looked forward to the marriage of these folks some ten years hence, as confidently as if they were both rich, and going to St. George's tomorrow. (XX, 295)

Despite his denigration of Laura's belief in Providence, Pen's narration confirms Laura's prophecy which is repeated at least six more times (XX, 311; XXI, 474, 560, 572, 591, 611). The second time she is more certain: "Don't tell *me* sir. They *will* be provided for . . . *You* may call your way of thinking prudence. I call it *sinful worldliness*" (XX, 311). Pen's language of compromise opposes Laura's language of absolutes but *both* are "right", depending upon what priorities the reader chooses.

Evidently, Laura has not read Pen's novel because this voice of gentlemanly restraint has created a world imbued with definite moral values. It is as easy for the reader to find Caroline Brandon "good" as to condemn Dr. Firmin as a rascal. Such judgment is possible despite Pen's own vacillation. Dr. Firmin is "Dr. Fell" to Pen when he first meets him (XX, 106, 107) "though he was most kind to me" (XX,107). His double-vision of Dr. Firmin continues throughout the novel as the Doctor steals his son's patrimony, blames his own financial failure on his son's extravagance, and steals from his son while in exile. Even in the revelation of the Doctor's forgery, Pen, in the midst of his own indignation, tells us "'I can remember the soft white hand of the scoundrel, which has just been forging his own son's name, putting sovereigns into my own palms, when I was a schoolboy.' I always liked that man . . ." (XXI, 563). Liking the man for past kindnesses does not preclude seeing his moral turpitude. He does not excuse the Doctor but he does not, as does Laura, pigeon-hole him. Pen sees clearly, moreover, that his flexible language is a necessary protection from a perspective that would dominate him. "When my life partner speaks in a certain strain, I know that remonstrance is useless, and argument unavailing, and I generally resort to cowardly subterfuges, and sneak out of the conversation by a pun, a side joke, or some flippancy" (XX, 311). In other words, his dexterity with language allows him to avoid and thus deny the power of her intolerant perspective.

Ironically, the design Laura sees (or creates?) is just that which removes the "practical objections" of poverty that she so ignores. When Tregarvan,

Philip's publisher, finally sends Philip a remittance, she says, "Didn't I tell you it would be so?" (XXI, 560). When Philip is faced with his father's forgery, the covering of which will ruin him, Laura tells him to do the "right" thing, i.e., pay the debt and ruin his family. Goodness will reap its reward. "'In his time of trial Philip has met with wonderful succour and kindness,' Laura urged. 'See how one thing after another has contributed to help him! When he wanted, there were friends always at his need'" (XXI, 572). The Good Samaritan in this case is the Little Sister, who, disgusted with this Christian passivity, gets Tufton Hunt drunk and steals the bill. Ultimately, Laura insists that all evils are actually intended for Philip's good (XXI, 611), "that poverty, sickness, dreadful doubt, and terror, hunger and want almost, were all equally intended for Philip's advantage and would work out for good in the end" (XXI, 611).

While her language sustains the Good Samaritan motif in the novel, Pen's perspective reveals her "design" as the artifice of the artist. Lest we start to believe in Laura's Word, Pen writes the end of the novel as a fairy-tale pantomime. Pen, Philip, and J. J. are on a seaside holiday when they discover that Sir John Ringwood has put up the mulatto Woolcomb for a seat in Parliament. They decide to ridicule Woolcomb on election day, and confront Woolcomb in the old Earl's carriage with a mock-Woolcomb, a local mulatto driving a donkey cart. The carriage collides with the cart, and in the wreck, the sword case of the carriage breaks open to reveal – aha! – an old will of the Earl's that restores Philip to good fortune. It is difficult to accept Laura's perspective and see Philip's good fortune – especially finding the will – as divine providence when the final chapter is titled "The Realms of Bliss", a direct allusion to the transformation scene of the pantomime. When the "magic bat" is a hidden will, and when the brutal and stupid Woolcomb is "the fairy who was to rescue Philip" (XXI, 638) does the serendipitous closure affirm or ridicule Laura? The collision of codes reminds us that Laura's absolute language is as much a construction as is the pantomimic.

Pantomime or at least mock-romance characterizes Pen's view of Philip's courtship of Charlotte. Like Theo in *The Virginians*, Charlotte is not inherently unattainable; the obstacle to their union is Philip's own clumsiness. Philip does even less than Henry to pursue his Lady; he hangs around outside her door, goes to one ball where he disgraces himself, and waits. He and Charlotte are mock-heroically typed as "Una" and the "lion" (XXI, 19, 32). Philip alternately is a "Huron" (XXI, 21) and an "Iroquois"

(XXI, 22). Philip's anti-dandyism and willful disregard of "the ways of the world" are signs of his rejection of aesthetic traditions. Pen creates the gap between the real and ideal in his own mock-heroic and mock-romantic rhetoric. In chapter 20 (322) Pen compares Philip skipping a few dinners with his rich uncle, Lord Ringwood, to see Charlotte, to Leander swimming the Hellespont. Later, he extends into a melodramatic disaster a simple marital misunderstanding in which Charlotte spends five guineas on baby clothes when she and Philip are pressed for money (XXI, 34). This pattern of sensationalizing ordinary events suggests both the pettiness of Philip's story and Pen's mature skepticism that creates narrative episodes as experiences in infinite variety.

Philip's story is only a vehicle for Pen's pleasure in his verbal process. We see through "the fact of concealing that there is nothing behind one's discourse" (Chambers, *Story*, 125), that there is no narrator outside the language game. When we have learned to see through, to penetrate the facade of the right line I, narrative language can become "an art of displaying discourse for its own brilliant sake (the nothingness behind it then becoming the productive principle enabling the ongoing production of discursive 'smoke')" (Chambers 125). Ross Chamber's "smoke" is Richard Rorty's conversation, and conversational smoke is, paradoxically, the delightful substance of *Philip*. One extended example will point to the narrator's pleasure in his dexterity:

> I was in the company of an elderly gentleman, not very long since, who was perfectly sober, who is not particularly handsome, or healthy, or wealthy, or witty; and who, speaking of his past life, volunteered to declare that he would gladly live every minute of it over again. Is a man who can say that a hardened sinner, not aware how miserable he ought to be by rights, and therefore really in a most desperate and deplorable condition; or is he *fortunatus nimium* and ought his statue to be put up in the most splendid and crowded thoroughfare of the town? Would you, who are reading this, for example, like to live *your* life over again? What has been its chief joy? What are to-day's pleasures? Are they so exquisite that you would prolong them for ever? Would you like to have the roast beef on which you have dined brought back again to table, and have more beef, and more, and more? Would you like to hear yesterday's sermon over and over again – eternally voluble? Would you like to get on the Edinburgh mail, and travel outside for fifty hours as you

did in your youth? You might as well say you would like to go into the flogging-room, and take a turn under the rods: you would like to be thrashed over again by your bully at school: you would like to go to the dentist's, where your dear parents were in the habit of taking you: you would like to be taking hot Epsom salts, with a piece of dry bread to take away the taste: you would like to be jilted by your first love: you would like to be going in to your father to tell him you had contracted debts to the amount of $x + y + z$, whilst you were at the university. As I consider the passionate griefs of childhood, the weariness and sameness of shaving, the agony of corns, and the thousand other ills to which flesh is heir, I cheerfully say for one, I am not anxious to wear it for ever. No. I do not want to go to school again. I do not want to hear Trotman's sermon over again. Take me out and finish me. Give me the cup of hemlock at once. Here's a health to you, my lads. Don't weep, my Simmias. Be cheerful, my Phaedon. Ha! I feel the co-o-old stealing, stealing upwards. Now it is in my ankles – no more gout in my foot: now my knees are numb. What, is – is that poor executioner crying too? Good-bye. Sacrifice a cock to AEscu – to AEscula – . . . Have you ever read the chapter in Grote's *History*? Ah! When the Sacred Ship returns from Delos, and is telegraphed as entering into port, may we be at peace and ready! (XX, 296-97)

While narratorial authority is defined by Chambers as existing as long as we puzzle, I would add that it exists as long as we delight in such playful rhapsodies. Thackerayean seduction is our own pleasure in his theatrical language-play. Released from narrative authority, we are free to enjoy the sheer facility of the narrator's play.

That the narrator now sees language as a vehicle for his own enjoyment is also suggested by a shift in the moral reference characteristic of romance language in the novels up to *The Virginians*. Romance motifs fairly consistently place the reader at distinct moral vantage points from which to see the sirens or the dandies or the ladies in *Vanity Fair, Pendennis*, and *Henry Esmond*. But *Philip* muddies this moral clarity by assigning the language of the seductress to women like Laura. Calling her "Delilah" when she is wheedling Tregarvan into giving Philip a job, claiming she is "flattering, wheedling, humbugging him" could seem to call into question Laura's moral integrity (XXI, 34). However, in spite of the language, we read her action as "good" because she is Laura and she is "wheedling" for Philip's sake. Nonetheless, Laura's flattery is a social manipulation more characteristic of the siren. Pen's allusion to "Delilah" suggests the sexual play underlying such behavior whether Laura recognizes this or not. This diction unites the siren with the angel because both types manipulate men through male vanity. Laura and the Little Sister consistently coax and wheedle men for Philip's benefit. The Good Samaritan motif Laura stresses is in part a product of her own manipulation.[22]

In a sense, the plot in *Philip* parodies the entire idea of the "erring" knight – doing wrong in order to eventually win – because female manipulation acts for him: Madame Smolensk acting as intercessor, Laura using dinner parties and female conversational wiles to get him jobs, and especially the Little Sister saving him from the blackmail of Tufton Hunt. True, the "dragon" which he must defeat to win Charlotte is her mother, Mrs. Baynes, but Charlotte herself effects her own release by becoming hysterical which turns her father against her mother. Philip's "heroic" invasion of the boarding house happens after Charlotte, scarcely conscious, screams wildly, forcing Mrs. Baynes to acknowledge that "she had gone too far" (XXI, 435).

That the action of this quest is the action of women suggests not so much that they have usurped the quest, as that Philip has never really had the ability to act. As a child, Philip discovers sexual duplicity through his father and in hating his father for it, comes to hate his own inheritance of male sexual action and potency. When Philip witnesses the recognition scene between the Little Sister and Dr. Firmin in chapter three, he is seeing a metaphoric primal scene. Dr. Firmin enters the sickroom and speaks to Philip. The Little Sister "turned round once, and fell down like a stone by the bedside" (XX, 125). Dr. Goodenough accuses Dr. Firmin of being the "villain" who seduced the Little Sister many years before. Philip is silent but awake; he has spoken just before this scene. Pen calls Dr. Firmin "bluebeard" and presents him as a wife-killer (XX, 107-108, 119). Philip's "fever", significantly, is not caused by any infatuation and is the cause of his discovery of his father's sexual activity with a symbolic mother. The Little Sister by name is sister, but a mother by function. When he is sick, the Little Sister cares for Philip as his nurse, but, as the novel progresses, she comes more and more to fancy she is his mother.

The consequence is both estrangement and entanglement; as Philip develops, he can never escape his father because he never grows beyond the role of "son", but he hates everything his father stands for. This early discovery stunts Philip's own growth into desire; he cannot desire the imaginary because he has already been exposed to the real. It is logical, therefore, that his desire fixes upon a pre-sexual, safe, child-woman who may be won through passive waiting. "Winning" is too strong a term for this courtship. Philip says, "'My dear friends, what have I done in life that I am to be made a present of a little angel?'" (XXI, 508). He has grown into maturity with male egotism but no social ambition:

> He had a childish sensibility for what was tender, helpless, pretty, or pathetic; and a mighty scorn of imposture wherever he found it. He had many good purposes, which were often very vacillating, and were but seldom performed. . . . What he liked he would have. (XX, 164)

Caroline and Mrs. Mugford are "disappointed at his want of spirit" (XXI, 486), but Philip cheerfully accepts his own mediocrity, "'I am not at all a clever fellow, you see; and I haven't the ambition and obstinate will to succeed which carry on many a man with no greater capacity than my own'" (XXI, 485). Pen complains that Philip cannot be got to moderate his rough manners even to protect his job: "As if moderation and common sense could be got to move that mule of a Philip Firmin; as if any persuasion of ours could induce him to do anything but what he liked to do best himself!" (XXI, 323). But he wants to do nothing: "'My dear friends, don't you see how modest I am? There never was a man less likely to get on than myself'" (XXI, 485).

Philip's lack of ambition protects him from self-corruption but condemns him to failure in a world almost obsessed with money-making. One of Dr. Firmin's parental crimes is swindling Philip out of his inheritance; Pen's constant chorus is that Philip and Charlotte cannot marry because they have no money; Mrs. Baynes' objection to the marriage is Philip's poverty; and Laura's machinations are all to secure Philip's employment. The story's preoccupation with money-getting mirrors Pen's own fascination with the translation of his language into sustenance, a subversive image of the word made flesh:

> Ah! how wonderful ways and means are! When I think how this very line, this very word, which I am writing represents money, I am lost in a respectful astonishment. A man takes his own case, as he says his own prayers, on behalf of himself and his family. I am paid, we will say, for the sake of illustration, at the rate of sixpence

per line. With the words, "Ah, how wonderful," to the words "per line," I can buy a loaf, a piece of butter, a jug of milk, a modicum of tea, – actually enough to make breakfast for the family; and the servants of the house; and the charwoman *their* servant, can shake up the tea-leaves with a fresh supply of water, sop the crusts, and get a meal *tant bien que mal*. Wife, children, guests, servants, charwoman, we are all actually making a meal off Philip Firmin's bones as it were. (XXI, 537)

Language is money; language represents money (as in the forged bill); language gets money. The process of writing holds all the dangers and possibilities earlier figured in the romance quests of the young Pen and Henry Esmond. The siren Agnes Twysden no longer represents wealth and power; the title-page to *Pendennis* of nymph with carriage and cornet no longer applies. The danger of being "devoured" by one's passion is rewritten as the very process of living in the capitalist world – getting a job, doing the work, receiving the pay, buying and consuming goods. Consumer relations are sexual relations. Women like Laura and the Little Sister use their female arts to seduce men like Tregarvan or Mugford into creating jobs or giving payment to another man. The sexuality of this cycle would not be nearly so evident if Pendennis were agitating on behalf of his friend. That it is Pen's vision which sexualizes the process suggests that the desire Pen once felt for the siren is now channeled toward the language which lures him on to write for money. By "making a meal" of Philip's bones, Pen is eating himself, for his language has created the word as flesh which he then sells in order to consume. Pen the narrator is now Hylas looking into the pool where the nymphs of his own language beckon him and pull him in.

The pantomime, fairy-tale conclusion of *Philip* takes on new significance in this light. Certainly it signifies the failure of Philip as knight errant to achieve his own independence; certainly it calls attention to the artifice of the fiction; but its abrupt unreality also functions to jerk both narrator and reader out of a narrative which might otherwise never end because Thackeray has created a protagonist who will never be able to complete his story and a narrator who has no need to. Pen has realized his Harlequin function in an earlier incarnation as Pedrolino in *commedia dell'arte*. Pedrolino keeps the play moving . . . . through capricous design" while his counterpart, Arlechino, here Philip, furthers the plot "through witless inadvertence".[23]

The narration has appropriated the semantics of the romance, leaving the syntax, the structure, to falter along on its own. In Thackeray's skeptical version, the romance quest has proven only a qualified success. While the protagonist does make the "right" choice of the right woman and so joins with the ideal that affirms his identity, marrying the ideal woman means the end of potentiality. The example of J. J. offers an option for the artist that Thackeray demonstrates through Pendennis' narration. Language, like paint, is always potential. The semantic possibilities always tempt the writer to say it another way, to refashion and revise. Complete meaning always seems possible in the next paragraph or novel. The narration in *The Virginians* and *Philip* redefines desire as the pursuit of language, the concern with and love of language. The novels tell us eminently unsatisfactory stories written in eminently satisfying language.

The stock plot and characters of Thackeray's later romances show their diminution.[24] To typify ancient Lady Maria and obvious Agnes Twysden as "sirens" is to debase the notion of the siren while ridiculing the characters. The siren is stripped for the reader before she ever has clothes. To type boisterous, bewildered Harry Warrington as a Pen, a Henry Esmond, or even a Clive is to show us how paltry the knight errant can be. And Philip, actually pursuing child-like Charlotte as the lady of his dreams, reifies in the pettiness of his quest-object the anti-heroism suggested by his anti-dandy blundering manners and dress.

Just as romance characters become self-parodies, the romance quest dwindles into passive waiting and serendipitous closure, emphasizing the knight's lack of volition. The vitality of the descent/struggle pattern, or trial and error pattern, is displaced into the narration. The tortuous windings of the first chapters of *Philip* elaborates the simple redoubling of *Vanity Fair*, but always returns to the beginning. Our differing perspectives on Philip's story come not from stylistic parodies but from accumulating versions of Pen's narrative reflection. The oxymoron implied in the last phrase is deliberate; *Philip* has annoyed generations of readers by its refusal to "move on".[25] Overt narrative warnings, such as "Phil chose to fall in love with his cousin; and I warn you that nothing will come of that passion, except the influence which it had upon the young man's character" (XX, 183) obviate the necessity for even telling the story. However, the conventions of the nineteenth-century novel demand that language must work to tell the story.[26] The desire for language to become self-sufficient while retaining potentiality, that is to realize a kind of active ideal union, needs plot to act upon. While the narrator cannibalizes his romance story to internalize the quest in his act of telling, he needs the plot to pursue this quest. A narrator cannot tell us nothing; the conventions of both the novel and language demand process and meaning. So the reader follows, fascinated, the fluent language dragging around the Marleyesque ball and chain of the story which has been sucked dry of desire, leaving us to ask, as did even Thackeray's greatest fans, why are we reading?

Here I would like to follow the implications of my own analysis, to become, in the words of Frank Kermode, one of the "skeptical clerisy", or a reader trained by reading Thackeray.[27] To scrutinize the fictions I have made of Thackeray's fictionalizing I begin with his own endings in the context of the conclusion of his last complete novel. Like Thackeray, I feel compelled to close but without secure finality.

Pendennis in *Philip* seems to be aware that his closure is the closure for all the social novels, and he insists upon the claustrophobic intimacy of his pastoral community:

> The mothers in Philip's household and mine have already made a match between our children. We had a great gathering the other day at Roehampton, at the house of our friend, Mr. Clive Newcome (whose tall boy, my wife says, was very attentive to our Helen), and, having been educated at the same school, we sat ever so long at dessert, telling old stories, whilst the children danced to piano music on the lawn. Dance on the lawn, young folks, whilst the elders talk in the shade! What? The night is falling: we have talked enough over our wine; and it is time to go home? Good-night. Good-night friends, old and young! The night will fall: the stories must end: and the best friends must part. (XXI, 640).

Laura's silent voice silences Pen, guiding what and how much he can reveal in public. Thackeray gives us a version of the archetypal union between seen and unseen, heard and unheard. The unorthodox endings that enable the hero and heroine to retire from public view deny the normative Victorian sexual contract wherein the woman relinquishes economic and sexual power to the man in return for protection. Pen and Laura retire to Fairoaks with little mention of money; he has his inheritance (increased by the sale of some of his property to the railroad) and she had earlier given him her fortune. Clive and Ethel subvert the contract because she gives him money without sexual fulfillment while maintaining sovereignty over his heart. Henry is feminized in his moral authority by giving up the male prerogatives of title and land but nonetheless receiving female worship – this rewrites the contract as a kind of role reversal. Philip and Charlotte live in poverty until the pantomimic *deus ex machina* saves them both. These unorthodox closures emphasize the necessity for economic security but ridicule any idea that the "business" of life has a place in the conventions of romance that dictate the closures.[28]

The novels' thematic emphasis on money but avoidance of the actual pragmatics of getting it (until Pen's exploration of the market-place in *Philip*) accords with his statement in *The Virginians* that novels cannot deal with the "real business" of life. This "real" business is male business; what is left to the novelist is the female world of emotions. Accordingly, Nancy Armstrong claims that Thackeray's view is "bound by . . . an imperative to draw authority from the female domain of knowledge".[29] However, Thackeray's narrators write themselves as men. They, especially Pen, most emphatically do not analyze emotions or enter into domestic secrets. They exteriorize the personal by filtering it through traditionally masculine codes of imagery, allusion, and satire, thus maintaining a masculine posture toward stories which are increasingly the property of women – and which are driven by women within the novels themselves. So the tension between romance and realism is a gender-generic battle. While Armstrong sees the Victorian happy ending as a "division and balance" between separate spheres of masculine and feminine qualities (41-42), Thackeray's masculine codes verbalize feminine closures. One powerful symbol of this self-sufficient female world is Laura's habit in *The Newcomes* and *Philip* of enclosing her children within her arms when she is confronted by a worldly truth. This gesture captures the children within her "bower" exclusive of Pen.[30]

Instead of an independent subjectivity which triumphs over narcissism, Thackeray offers identity through union with these "invisible" or "transparent" women who reflect the way to moral perfection. But this solution strips the protagonist of the "I will" so crucial to the modern sense of identity in the realistic novel. Submitting to the order of the domestic woman demands not just control of sexual desire, burnt out by the infatuation with the siren, but, finally, the eradication of all desire. The sociolect of "love", espoused by Laura Pendennis, represents the triumph of the literally creative woman over the symbolically creative man. The quick production of children by Laura, Charlotte, and Ethel, with no mention of sexual desire or even male presence (and in the case of Ethel, no sexual action), gives procreation entirely to the women. Female creativity triumphs when woman escapes from the male gaze to become an invisible mother, and she usurps the male symbolic power by becoming a purveyor of the Word. The domestic woman subsumes the objectivizing protagonist into her world.

Correspondingly, the protagonists seem to evince frustration and dissatisfaction with their happy endings. I have already commented on Henry's "bankruptcy", and Ina Ferris has noted that Pen seems to direct his dissatisfaction into sarcastic attacks on Laura ("Narrative Strategy") and through his circular method of narration. Clive's discontent may be surmised from his awareness of his own artistic mediocrity. Even George Warrington, the paragon of limited desire, feels discontent. As he tells us, he is moody, often silent for days, and falls asleep at dinner:

> What admission is this I am making [after telling us the above]? Here was the storm over, the rocks avoided, the ship in port and the sailor not over-contented? Was the Susan I had been sighing for during the voyage, not the beauty I expected to find her? . . . . There came a period in my life, when having reached the summit of felicity I was quite tired of the prospect I had there: I yawned in Eden, and said, "Is this all? What, no lions to bite? No rain to fall? no thorns to prick you in the rose-bush when you sit down? – only Eve, for ever sweet and tender, and figs for breakfast, dinner, and supper, from week's end to week's end!" Hearken! Well, then, if I must make a clean breast of it. (XIX, 731)[31]

But George's confession will forever be unknown because, as Pen, the editor, tells us, three pages are (supposedly) missing from the manuscript. Even unambitious Philip remembers his days of struggle for Charlotte with a sense of something lost and goes away from his wife now and then even though he "is perfectly happy" with her, to "enjoy the luxury of living over our old days" (XXI, 459).

These bowers of bliss that appear to deny autonomy seem perilously close to bowers of indolence. The Garden of Adonis, whose porter is Genius, is a place of natural (self-generating) fertility.

> Ne needs there Gardiner to set, or sow,
>   To plant or prune: for of their owne accord

All things, as they created were, doe grow,
And yet remember well the mightie word,
Which first was spoken by th'Almightie lord,
That bad them to increase and multiply:
Ne doe they need with water of the ford,
Or of the clouds to moysten their roots dry;
For in themselves eternall moisture they imply.
(*FG.* III.vi.34)

The self-renewing fertility suggested by the name "Adonis" and described in Spenser's stanza is both sexual and aesthetic – the porter in this true bower is Genius, the spirit of the place and the spirit of inspiration. The fertility derives from an original, once-spoken, never repeated divine "Word". Here growth is constant even though the substance of things does not change – a symbolic expression of the perfect ideal, both possessed and potential (an ideal which recalls J. J. Ridley's absorption in his painting).

Spenser opposed to the Garden of Adonis a false bower, the Bower of Bliss, whose porter is the parodic "genius", Idleness, who opens the door to indolent pleasure (*FQ* II.xii.47-48). Instead of the flourishing foliage of natural genius, the Bower of Bliss flaunts "all the ornaments of *Floraes* pride. / Wherewith her mother Art, as halfe in scorne / Of niggard Nature, like a pompous bride / Did decke her" (II.xii.50). In the Bower of Bliss lives the siren Acrasia who, as does any good siren, devours her lovers (II.xii.73). Thackeray combined these bowers in a paradox. While the over-decorated artifice of Acrasia's bower and its invitation to sexual indulgence recalls the parodic pastoral townhouses of Blanche Amory and Rosey Mackenzie and the artifice of Becky and Beatrice, the self-conscious artistry of Pen flourishes in the "natural" bowers controlled by Laura. Why?

George's allusion Eden and to Theo as "Eve" implies one answer. He lives in an unfallen world, an Eden without desire. "Eating figs", George swallows or represses his desire – and his self-conscious irritation suggests he is at least aware that this passive completion is in fact incomplete for him. So, George tells us, he cannot finish his writing, both *Travels in Europe* and *History of the American War* go uncompleted – we are so told by the "editor" as if to impress upon us George's loss of ambition (XIX, 782). But George does write his part of the novel; just as Pen writes himself into his novels and Henry writes his autobiography. In other words, their renunciation of ambitious self-fashioning and public discourse leaves them able to publicize a private discourse, a discourse of the "I" – much like the "humble" sublime Thackeray advocated for modern painters. This is a discourse that in its very rejection of heroic posturing affirms the presence of an independent ego.

So, freeing oneself from enthrallment by the surface is represented by Thackeray as a triumph of the heart, a transfer from the outer to the inner, which facilitates a certain kind of representation. But the price is eradication of the yearning for the ideal. Herein lies another paradox. To compare Pen, Henry, and Clive with Harry, George, and Philip is to conclude that a desire for the unrealizable ideal awakens one's consciousness and leads one to attempt autonomy. Because this desire sparks the separation of the male from the mother, it pushes the protagonist into the world of convention and the Symbolic. The degree and nature of their separation from the mother – Pen from Helen, Clive from Colonel Newcome, Henry from Rachel, and George from Rachel Warrington – differs. However, they all do move away enough to transform her literal presence into a symbolic absence only to find themselves defined by the symbolic orders they have adopted. Their language delimits their possibilities of definition and action. It is not accidental, then that these protagonists become true romance narrators: interpreters who cannot act but know.[32]

The cost of what control and dexterity they do achieve can be profound. By eradicating desire through the destruction of the self-projected-as-object, Henry, for example, lapses into an unchallenged repression so complete as to finish his effective life. In a very real way he dies. He represses his knowledge of his desire and of the other when he claims not to know "what infatuation of ambition urged the beautiful and wayward woman to follow the Pretender to France" (*HE* 388). Marriage to Rachel is a marriage of two husks: "noble" Henry who has renounced all "self" and "beatific" Rachel who has ruthlessly excised her own desires. Henry's description of their final union sedulously avoids any suggestion of intimacy.

> I found my mistress one day in tears, and then besought her to confide herself to the care and devotion of one who, by God's help, would never forsake her. And then the tender matron, as beautiful in her autumn, and as pure as virgins in their spring, with blushes of love and "eyes of meek surrender," yielded to my respectful

> importunity, and consented to share my home. (*HE* 388)

This marriage is an "ascension", almost inhuman in its purity. Henry's mastery of himself was acquired by repudiating his most vital experience. He has completed himself by eliminating ambiguity. But my analysis argued that another history existed in the same events as the one he acknowledges. So the act of fixing meaning is itself an illusion. To write as Henry does is to become a censor, to keep oneself from knowing one's own contradictions and complexities, incurring, perhaps, a greater discomfort than the tension-filled state of desire. While the older Henry's criticism of himself as a character hinders readers from identifying with the character, the narrator's own mistakes and willful blindness to the incestuous nature of his union with Rachel distances the reader from his voice. Henry himself cannot be disinterested because his single voice is both subject and object. But his contradictions create distancing echoes for the reader. If we reject either character or narrator, we repeat the narrator's own censoring operations, we willfully reduce the text to a transparent mirror. Reading *all* of *Henry Esmond* requires us to accept – not reconcile – the character, the narrator's version of the character, and the narrator. We must cultivate disinterest alongside our engagement.

The Virginians and *Philip* resist *Esmond*'s censorship but transfer Henry's problems with interpretation to the readers. Ferris argues that by admitting the unreality of his endings, Thackeray preserved the dialectic of realistic narrative, its sense of process that implies there is no "end"but "a continuing process of redefinition, so rendering provisional, partial, and vulnerable each definition arrived at on the way" (Ferris, "Realism" 294). Thackeray's endings allow this process to go on outside the text, transferring the narrator's skepticism of conventions of representation to the reader. The novels' very resistance to elaborating upon their story and their focus on the meandering telling, repudiate any semantic stability in the symbolic. All languages work, all sociolects speak. To turn to generic conventions or the narrative "I" for the Real is to become captive to another's intentions. Reading and writing connect us but this connection is in the language itself, not an extra-linguistic relation signified by language.

> At that time of my life, being young and very green, I had a little mischievous pleasure in infuriating Square-toes, and causing him to pronounce that I was "a dangerous man." Now, I am ready to say

that Nero was a monarch with many elegant accomplishments, and considerable natural amiability of disposition. I praise and admire success wherever I meet it. I make allowances for faults and short-comings, especially in my superiors; and feel that, did we know all, we should judge them very differently. People don't believe me, perhaps, quite so much as formerly. But I don't offend: I trust I don't offend. Have I said anything painful? Plague on my blunders! I recall the expression. I regret it. I contradict it flat. (XX, 146)

Pen gleefully disavows meaning and responsibility for his language even while his "I" insists upon his presence in text. We may do what we like with his story; he will not do anything *to* us. The sense of triumph here is not unconnected to the protagonists' renunciations. All Thackeray's novels show us a society full of predatory violence; to condemn the bower in this context is paradoxical. Why should Pen or Clive pursue goals that have been exposed to us as harmful? Why should we want them to stay in worlds where "success" means the inability to develop emotional ties? What if they are less discontent than cunning in their removal of themselves? The unorthodox mechanisms of closure and the refusal to close in *The Newcomes* make fun of our belief that novels offer a literal escape from the world. You can do in novels what you cannot do in life. The protagonists do escape the trap the novels leave all others in; their wives show them a mirror of moral life that counters the cannibalism inherent in the art-market. Consequently, they avoid worshipping themselves or their art works as idols. No romantic egoism here. Their more mundane social individuality is presented literally in the closing passage from *Philip*; each protagonist is part of a community of the others and none depend upon Transcendental epiphanies for direction.

This alternative view is as true as the vision of the Bower as repressive and annihilating; both views hold simultaneously. Both may be traced to Thackeray himself, to finally invoke the biographical context I have been avoiding. The traditional way to deal with the narrative disavowals and uncertain closures is to ascribe them to Thackeray's dissatisfaction with novel-writing as "inadequate vehicles for the significance he wants them to carry, and he, as a result, stands estranged from the products of his own labor".[33] This conclusion ignores the alternative vision and the fact that these men do write, do function socially and responsibly. As Ferris points out about *Philip*, the tension and discordance, and, I would add, the vibrant narration, suggest more than "mere boredom with novelistic convention"

(Ferris, "Narrative Strategy", 453). But Ferris describes this as self-annihilation in *Lovel* evocative of Thackeray's developing insecurity about "reality".

> The speculative irony of narrative comment, the experimental use of allusive sequences, and the constant exploration and modification of convention forced an increasing recognition of the inadequacy of conventional narrative strategies (including the classic anti-conventional strategy of realism) to account for a reality that investigation revealed as ever more uncertain, subjective, and empty. ("Breakdown", 44).

Thus the later Pendennis and Batchelor convey a kind of helplessness and the world becomes a place of "death, murder, violence, horror".[34] Juliet McMaster's vision of Philip's world as a thin veneer covering a reality of predatory social relationships accords with Ferris' argument that the desire for self-destruction lies at the heart of Pen's narration. Certainly, Thackeray presents the novelist as just another cannibal; the author as "Ogre" devours his story and his reader and is left with an excruciating sense of consciousness of non-existence because he has no referent outside himself to convince himself of his identity.[35] And the only tool by which the novelist can create himself is language, which his narration demonstrates to be non-referential. To escape this circularity, Ferris argues that *Philip* projects the story of Philip, the unthinking, blindly self-assertive character, who enacts a linear, progressive self that Pen himself cannot realize. Pen's self-deprecation and awareness of his own cannibalism enact a fantasy of self-destruction, "to destroy his own consciousness in an attempt to escape its burdens" ("Narrative Strategy", 454).

Dislodging language from fixed meanings by discovering the arbitrary nature of literary and social languages originally seemed to free the perceiving self to invent and maintain multiple ways of patterning reality. The imaginative freedom of the artist seems to have become a trap: vision becomes solipsistic when the narrator discovers that all these perspectives are his own creation and are thus projections of a self itself indistinct from the perspectives. That the reader can be trapped in this circularity accounts for the critical estimate that *The Virginians, Philip,* and *Lovel the Widower* "fail" as novels. The multi-directioned irony and patterns of commentary that discredit the narrative authenticity leave the reader with no certain "place" in which to join the narrator. Ferris defines *Lovel* as *Thackeray's* failure "to create an implied author in the text to guide response" ("Breakdown", 50). Implicitly, this judgment, echoing those by McMaster and Ray, depends upon identifying Thackeray with his *narrators*. These critics are paradoxically searching for a stable reading of avowedly unstable texts.

If we avoid the seduction (admittedly strong in Thackeray's case) of this identification, we may attempt an alternative approach. In Thackeray's late novels, readers are no longer certain when they are reading "with" the narrator. However, the very idea of "joining" the narrator or implied author necessitates subsuming the reading self into the novel, being "devoured" by it.[36] The intricate relations between perspectives and events from *The Virginians* forward radically disengage the reader from both story and narration, encouraging the reader to see the narrator-story relation as a relation. We do not have to "identify" with Batchelor, Pendennis, the characters, or the reader-roles encoded in the text. Thackeray's favorite motif, "de te fabula", see yourself in the story, links the "man" not to his protagonists but to the entire web of narrator-story relations, to the master-manipulations which keep the narration self-qualifying and the story unsatisfying. The "breakdown" of plot structure in Thackeray's late novels *is a representation* of the inadequacy of conventional techniques to represent subjective reality. Convention, *The Virginians* points out, represents only convention, not experience. Thackeray's treatment shows the reader that all that can be represented is language itself and that our positions exist within this language. Language creates both itself and the speaking self. If so, then the "right line I" exists only in language and is beyond the control of the speaking self because that self depends upon language for its identity.

If we accept Thackeray's language play, we move beyond the world of the novels; "reality", "experience", and "authenticity" shift from object to reader. Watching the protagonists negotiate between the unpalatable necessities of the novels' world – to live silently in isolation is to not exist, but to live publicly in language is to masquerade and thus still be isolated – offers the reader the power to recognize and avoid the seduction of language and the predation of language users.[37] Thackeray's method insists on an existence, or a reality, which language can neither describe nor affirm.

Ever since Augustine, the Middle Ages insisted upon the link between Eros and language, between the reaching out in desire for what mortals can never possess and the reaching out of language toward the significance of silence. To refuse to see in human desire an incompleteness that urges the soul on to transcendence is to remain within the realm of creatures, worshipping them as only the Creator was to be worshipped. Similarly, to refuse to see language and poetry as continual askesis, pointing beyond themselves, is to remain within the letter, treating it as an absolute devoid of Spirit which gives meaning to human discourse.[38]

To be absorbed into the representing surface is to become part of a cycle of manipulation. The predatory siren whose deceptive voice and appearance seduce her "wretched pickled" victims under the surface for her to devour is analogous to the imaginary novelist writing imaginary stories that seduce his readers into buying his work. In turn, the novelist-as-cannibal mirrors his mercantile society whose money system destroys the intrinsic value of labor and objects. To discern these identities is to be freed to use language and read novels without being trapped in them.

Even Henry Esmond contradicts his belief that he will fix his identity by recording himself. In a discussion with Addison, he sees that language will necessarily generalize the "slimy tail" of experience into convention. He confronts Joseph Addison who heroicizes war in his poem *The Campaign* with his truth about war:

"I admire your art: the murder of the Campaign is done to military music, like a battle at the Opera, and the virgins shriek in harmony, as our victorious grenadiers march into their villages. Do you know what a scene it was? . . . . what scenes of shame and horror were enacted, over which the commander's genius presided, as calm as though he didn't belong to our sphere? You talk of the 'listening soldier fixed in sorrow,' the 'leader's grief swayed by generous pity'; to my belief the leader cared no more for bleating flocks than he did for infants' cries, and many of our ruffians butchered one or the other with equal alacrity. I was ashamed of my trade when I saw those horrors perpetrated, which came under every man's eyes. You hew out of your polished verses a stately image of smiling victory; I tell you 'tis an uncouth, distorted, savage idol; hideous, bloody, and barbarous. The rites performed before it are shocking to think of. You great poets should show it as it is – ugly and horrible, not beautiful and serene." (*HE* 211)

Addison responds that both his audience and his language require social discourse. One must never mistake the discourse for the experience – to do so is to become a performer.

Thackeray's narration offers the alternative of freely creating language (free within the conventions of meaning). Narrating is the constant renewal of desire, the becoming always possible in language, the constant extension of "I am" as a social being because "you" must be there. What thus seems to be failure in *Philip* is not: events recede because narration triumphs over the finality inherent in "story". Our discomfort is a liberation of sorts which we can turn into a mirror empowering us to be self-creating, verbal adepts, extending the model of Pendennis into our own discourse of desire. "There is novelistic genius", wrote Rene Girard, "when what is true about others becomes true about the hero, in fact, true about the novelist himself".[39]

If the "author function" actually controls what meanings can be produced and sets the limits of transgression, if the "author"/ "reader" subjectivities "sustain the existing cultural order" then what order does Thackeray's disruption sustain?[40] What do we produce? The insistent "I"- "you" discourse combined with the increasing demystification of textual authority asserts, paradoxically, the idea of essential identity. Not only do we witness the narrators' epistemological struggles, but we also struggle with their vagaries toward our own interpretations. Interpretation confirms the presence of a consciousness "out there", beyond the text, ultimately not dependent upon it. We will not become Fanny Bolton or Blanche Amory. But neither will we become Laura Pendennis or Henry Esmond. Perceiving the narrator-story relations allows us to avoid their circularity and solipsism. As Ross Chambers described the empowering function of La Fontaine's "The Wolf and the Lamb", the reader who aligns himself with characters, narrator, or implied narrator reinforces the "wolfishness of the world" by joining the closed system of victim and predator.[41] The Thackerayean "story" shows us again and again characters swimming in the sea of predatory commodity-relations; some sink, some tread water, and some survive by building a raft of a public languages. The reader is offered another option, to see the irony of the narrative method itself and so to understand that the very multiplicity of the narration is a means of avoiding predatory commodity relations. "Only the reader . . . capable of *producing* the text as ironic . . . can *learn* from it how to survive in a wolfish world without becoming wolfish herself" (Chambers, "'Narrative'" 36).

Forcing readers to perceive the dexterity and delight of the play of language and its arbitrariness fluency frees them from the idolatry of their reading, from being seduced by the narrators' versions of the world. The novels' "failures" dramatize the necessity to constantly be aware of one's own habits of interpretation, to recognize that interpretation is a matter of habit. Thackeray grew to use the self-consciousness of his criticism to teach his readers not how to read a painting or a novel but to see from the outside what reading is. The novels shatter the mirror of self which interpretation imposes upon the text and force the readers out of art into life (Steiner 73). Without the actual sense of failure conveyed by the fictional narrators' own frustration with their stories these novels would never point readers beyond themselves – an ambiguity, so Thackerayean, intended.

Notes

[1]   This chapter title and epigraph are manuscript titles for the last chapter of *The Adventures of Philip*. "The Abode of Bliss and Halls of Prismatic Splendour" was canceled; "In wh. the Fairy descends from her Chariot" was not. The chapter title in the serial in *The Cornhill Magazine* was "The Realms of Bliss".

[2]   The phrase is from Ross Chambers, "'Narrative' and 'Textual Functions'", *Reading Narrative: Form, Ethics, Ideology*, ed. James Phelan (Columbus: Ohio State UP, 1989), 36.

[3]   Ina Ferris, "Narrative Strategy in Thackeray's *The Adventures of Philip*", *English Studies in Canada* 5 (1979), 452.

[4]   Ina Ferris, "The Breakdown of Thackeray's Narrator: *Lovel the Widower*", *Nineteenth Century Fiction* 32 (1976), 38.

[5]   Walter Bagehot said of *The Adventures of Philip* in the *Spectator*, that "Mr. Thackeray is evidently trying to baffle his critics. They have said very often that he could never make a plot. He is now trying to show that he can . . . . Nevertheless as far as 'plot' is concerned, *Philip* is a failure". Reprinted in *Thackeray: The Critical Heritage*, eds. Geoffrey Tillotson and Donald Hawes (New York: Barnes & Noble, 1968), 306. The *Daily News* also complained about the absence of narrative suspense: "He tells us beforehand how everything will end, gives us hints in abundance of the coming happiness or misery" (4 September 1862, 2). The *London Review and Weekly Journal of Politics, Literature, Art, and Society* did not even think that Philip was a novel: "'Philip' is hardly more than a gigantic series of 'Roundabout Papers' strung upon the slender thread of the biography of a young gentleman, who suffers no more exceptional fate than to be ruined early in life" (30 August 1862, 192).

[6]   I borrow this phrase from Daniel Frank Chamberlain in *Narrative Perspective in Fiction: A Phenomenal Mediation of Reader, Text, and World* (Toronto: U of Toronto P, 1990), 7-8. Chamberlain is writing about the self-containment of language in general, but the concept applies equally well to a narrative voice overtly fashioned by language play.

[7]   I make this claim on the basis of missing both opening and closing quotes in the relevant passages in the manuscript, not passages with either open or close quotes. Moreover, there are at least three instances of clear free indirect discourse retained in the printed versions.

[8]   See Peter L. Shillingsburg, "Editing Thackeray: A History", *Studies in the Novel* 27:3 (1995), 370, for a discussion of "disambiguation" in compositor's practices.

[9]   Such shifts also reflect the reading time of Thackeray's audience. During *Philip*, Pen alludes to Philip "traveling abroad" just now or to "the author" being

out of town when the serial is going to press. These illusions of life-process align the novel to the serial reading habits of his audience, who go through similar changes in their 19-month reading process. See Linda K. Hughes and Michael Lund for a discussion of the correspondences between reading-time and narrative-time in *The Victorian Serial* (Charlottesville, VA: UP of Virginia, 1991), 1-14, especially.

[10]   "Theatre, Journalism, and Thackeray's 'Man of the World' Magazine", *Victorian Periodicals Review* 32 (Fall 1999), 224.

[11]   Andrew Maunder makes a similar point about Trollope's narrative voice in *Framley Parsonage*, the serialized novel that inaugurated the *Cornhill Magazine*. Where Maunder sees Trollope as endorsing a set of behaviors, I see Pen's voice undermining any single set of practices. All are flawed because all are limited by their conventions. ("'Discourses of Distinction': The Reception of the *Cornhill Magazine*, 1859-60". *Victorian Periodicals Review* 33 (Winter 2000), 44-64. See also Maunder's "'Monitoring the middle-classes': Intertextuality and Ideology in Trollope's *Framley Parsonage* and the *Cornhill Mazagine*", *Victorian Periodicals Review* 33 (Spring 2000), 44-64.

[12]   So Thackeray referred to fiction in his letter to Anthony Trollope (*LLPS* 2: 908) and his first *Roundabout Paper*, "On a Lazy, Idle Boy" in the first issue of the *Cornhill Magazine*, January 1861.

[13]   Andrew Blake notes that the conversation went two ways. Trollope's *Framley Parsonage* not only dramatized concerns discussed elsewhere in the *Cornhill*, but Lord Lufton and Lucy Robart's courtship provided a frame of reference for courtship in the real world. *Reading Victorian Fiction* (New York: St. Martin's Press, 1989), 89-96, *passim*.

[14]   That the *Cornhill* was fundamentally concerned with the relation between gentlemanly status and the need to earn money is widely acknowledged, and, indeed, part of their own philosophy. See the special issues of *Victorian Periodical Review*, 32 (Fall 1999) and 33 (Spring 2000) and Judith L. Fisher, "Thackeray as Editor and Author: *The Adventures of Philip* and the Inauguration of the *Cornhill Magazine*", *Victorian Periodicals Review* 33 (Spring 2000), 2-21 which takes this tension between earning money and retaining one's station as its thesis.

[15]   The genuineness of the discussion of the "gentleman" is made clear in Gordon Ray's account of the Edmund Yates/Thackeray imbroglio that emphasizes clear that Thackeray was incensed against Yates's attack on his character as a gentleman (Ray, *Age*, 280), and that Thackeray was concerned throughout the quarrel with the necessity to define and maintain the definition of gentlemanly circumspection.

[16]   Reprinted in *Critical Heritage*, 297-304. The praise for Thackeray's style was fairly general. The *North British Review* said, in 1863, "His style, for directness, high-bred ease, continual flexibility and grace, and adaptation to the

matter in hand, is perhaps the most perfect of any contemporary writer" (3 [February 1863]: 176). The *Weekly Dispatch* said of *Philip* in particular: "In style it is among the author's best; in construction it is on a level with his worst" (10 August 1862, 6). The *London Review* claimed Philip was only "endurable" because of the "real charm of Mr. Thackeray's style" (30 August 1862, 193).

[17] It is suggestive that Blake and Andrew Maunder deal with *Framley Parsonage* and not *Philip* when they discuss how fiction works reflexively with middle-class culture to model ways of living.

[18] *The Providential Aesthetic in Victorian Fiction* (Charlottesville: UP of Virginia, 1985), see especially the "Introduction".

[19] George Warrington similarly eliminates conventional suspense in his portion of *The Virginians* by assuring us of the successful outcome of his courtship: "Looking across the fire, towards *her* accustomed chair, who has been the beloved partner of my hearth during the last half of my life, I often ask . . . whether two young people ever were more foolish and imprudent than we were, when we married, as we did, in the year of the old King's death?" (XIX, 613).

[20] John Henry Newman, "Knowledge Viewed in Relation to Religion", qtd in Robin Gilmour, *The Idea of the Gentleman in the Victorian Novel* (London: George Allen & Unwin, 1981), 90.

[21] Fitzjames Stephen, "Gentlemen", *Cornhill Magazine* 5 (March 1862), 327-42. See also Stephen's "Keeping Up Appearances", *Cornhill Magazine* 4 (September 1861), 305-18.

[22] In fact, Deborah Thomas makes the point that all the "Samaritans" in *Philip* "pervert truth" on Philip's behalf. *Thackeray and Slavery* (Athens, OH: Ohio UP, 1993), 178.

[23] Robert F. Storey, *Pierrot: A Critical History of a Mask* (Princeton: Princeton UP, 1978), 13.

[24] The anonymous reviewer in the *Saturday Review* complains of the novel: "in the first place, he uses up at random the characters of almost all his former compositions. We have the later days of Pendennis and Mrs. Pendennis, of Clive Newcome, of the Ravenswing, and of poor little Caroline Gann. All these old favourites are trotted out, and made to jog once more over the course for our amusement. 'If people,' the author seems tacitly to say, 'really want my old characters tossed up again, they shall have as many as they like'" (*Critical Heritage* 310-311). The *Athenaeum* told Thackeray to "look to his laurels" because his readers "will at last get tired of being led down alley after alley of 'Vanity Fair.'—the lamps in all the alleys are the same: the toys in the booths are the same" ("New Novels", 9 August 1862, 174). To be fair, however, not all the reviews were negative. *John Bull*, for example, wrote, "we think that 'Philip' will prove to be one of the works by which Mr. Thackeray will be best known to posterity" (9 August 1862, 557). And the *British Quarterly Review* said that only

"mistaken criticism" saw the lack of plot as a defect, and that *Philip* had "all its author's characteristic excellencies" (36 [October 1862]: 467).

[25]   F. R. Leavis in *The Great Tradition* accuses Thackeray of only going on and on and not getting anywhere: "nothing has been done by the close to justify the space taken" (London: Chatto and Windus, 1969), 21.

[26]   After observing that the "story" was boring, Walter Bagehot commented, "Mr. Thackeray evidently feels this himself. He has not great impulse to tell us what happened to his characters. He must have a story, he knows, to tell us, and, therefore, he concocts or adapts a story, and involves his characters in it as best he may, . . . he can do no more. . . . His characteristic exclamation is, 'Story! God bless you, I have one to tell you, Sir; but do not ask me to tell it, Sir; it *is* such a bore, Sir'" (*Critical Heritage* 307)

[27]   *The Sense of an Ending* (New York: Oxford UP, 1967), passim.

[28]   These closures that paste a romance ending onto a realistic plot exemplify the difficulty nineteenth-century novelists in general had with endings. As Ina Ferris has pointed out, most aesthetic realists abandoned their realism when it came to the demands for a "happy ever after" (290). She sees Thackeray's endings as "in effect . . . questions about ending" "Realism and the Discord of Ending: The Example of Thackeray", *Nineteenth-Century Literature* 33 (1983), 292.

[29]   *Desire and Domestic Fiction: A Political History of the Novel* (Oxford: Oxford UP, 1987), 44.

[30]   The full-page illustration opening chapter 8 of *Philip* in the August 1861 *Cornhill Magazine* visualizes this motif. Called "Laura's Fireside", the illustration shows Pen leaning against the mantle, and Laura, with her back to him, sitting with one child encircled within her arms and the other child looking intently at her. No one looks at Pen, who gazes at Laura with a slight frown.

[31]   Thackeray added this passage, suggesting that he wanted to make sure his readers felt George's dissatisfaction.

[32]   Wendy Steiner, *Pictures of Romance* (Chicago: U of Chicago P, 1988), 53.

[33]   Andrew Miller, "*Vanity Fair* through Plate Glass", *PMLA* 105 (1990), 1043.

[34]   Catherine Peters notes this helplessness, *Thackeray's Universe: Shifting Worlds of Imagination and Reality* (Boston: Faber and Faber, 1987), 258. See, for example, Juliet McMaster, "Funeral Baked Meats: Thackeray's Last Novel", *Studies in the Novel* 13 (1981), 133-55; my quote is from George Levine, The Realistic Imagination (Chicago: U of Chicago P, 1983), 151.

[35]   Thackeray describes himself sitting down to write in this *Roundabout Paper*, "Ogres" as coming to a meal. But more importantly for my argument, he describes as "ogres" men "wicked, false, rapacious, flattering; cruel hectors at home, smiling courtiers abroad" (*Cornhill Magazine*, August 1861, 251-57 in XXIII, 312).

³⁶ Walter Reed's comments about the conclusion to Part Two of *Don Quixote* apply equally to Thackeray's representation of novelist as ogre: readers' interpretations "should center on the loss of control that the literary author experiences when his printed book enters the public domain, and on the way in which reading can become a means of asserting control over others instead of a means of recreating oneself". (*An Exemplary History of the Novel* [Chicago: U of Chicago P, 1981], 84].

³⁷ Kelly J. Mays offers a more complete analysis of the Victorian perception of reading as a craving, addiction, or devouring. See "The Disease of Reading and Victorian Periodicals", *Literature in the Marketplace, Cambridge Studies in Nineteenth-Century Literature and Culture* 5, eds. John O. Jordan and Robert Patten (Cambridge: Cambridge UP, 1995),165-94 *passim*.

³⁸ John Freccero, *Dante: The Poetics of Conversion* (Cambridge, MA: Harvard UP, 1986), 13.

³⁹ Rene Girard, *Deceit, Desire, and the Novel*, trans. Yvonne Freccero (Baltimore: The Johns Hopkins UP, 1965), 38.

⁴⁰ Kaja Silverman, *The Subject of Semiotics* (Oxford: Oxford UP, 1983), 237.

⁴¹ Ross Chambers, "'Narrative' and 'Textual' Functions (with an Example from La Fontaine)", *Reading Narrative: Form, Ethics, Ideology,* James Phelan, ed. (Columbus: Ohio State UP, 1989,) 38.

Bibliography

Alghieri, Dante (see Dante).

Ariosto, Ludovico. *Orlando Furioso*. Trans. Guido Waldman. New York: Oxford UP, 1974.

Armstrong, Nancy. *Desire and Domestic Fiction: A Political History of the Novel*. Oxford: Oxford UP, 1987.

Avery, Gillian. *Nineteenth-Century Children: Heroes and Heroines in English Children's Stories, 1780-1900*. London: Hodder and Stoughton, 1965.

Bakhtin, Mikhail. *The Dialogic Imagination*. Ed. Michael Holquist. Trans. Caryl Emerson. Austin: U of Texas P, 1981.

Baldridge, Cates. "The Problems of Worldliness in *Pendennis*". *Nineteenth Century Fiction* 44 (1990), 492-513.

Beer, Gillian. *Darwin's Plots: Evolutionary Narrative in Darwin, George Eliot, and Nineteenth-Century Fiction*. London: Routledge and Kegan Paul, 1983.

Berman, Jeffrey. *Narcissism and the Novel*. New York: New York UP, 1990.

Blake, Andrew. *Reading Victorian Fiction*. New York: St. Martin's Press, 1989.

Bloomfield, Morton. "Authenticating Realism and the Realism of Chaucer". *Thought* 34 (1964), 335-58.

Booth, Wayne. *The Company We Keep. An Ethics of Fiction*. Berkeley: U of California P, 1988.

Bostetter, Edward. *The Romantic Ventriloquists*. Seattle: U of Washington P. 1975.

Brewer, Derek. *Symbolic Stories*. Totowa, NJ: Rowman and Littlefield, 1980.

Bulwer-Lytton, Edward. *England and the English*. 1833. Chicago: U of Chicago P, 1970.

Burton, Richard, trans. *The Book of the Thousand Nights and a Night*. Burton Club: n. d. Vol. 1.

Carlisle, Janice. *The Sense of An Audience: Dickens, Thackeray, and George Eliot at Mid-Century*. Brighton, Sussex: Harvester Press, 1982.

Chamberlain, Daniel Frank. *Narrative Perspective in Fiction: A Phenomenal Mediation of Reader, Text, and World*. Toronto: U of Toronto P, 1990.

Chambers, Ross. "'Narrative' and 'Textual' Functions (with an example from La Fontaine)". *Reading Narrative: Form, Ethics, Ideology*. Ed. James Phelan. .Columbus: Ohio State UP, 1989, 27- 39.

—. *Room To Maneuver*. Chicago: U of Chicago P, 1991.

—. *Story and Situation: Narrative Seduction and the Power of Fiction*. Minneapolis: U. of Minnesota P, 1984.

Chase, Karen. "The Kindness of Consanguinity: Family History in *Henry Esmond*," *Modern Language Studies* 16 (1986), 213-26.

Chatman, Seymour. *Story and Discourse*. Ithaca: Cornell UP, 1978.

Clarke, Micael. *Thackeray and Women*. DeKalb: Northern Illinois UP, 1995.

Colby, Robert. Thackeray's *Canvass of Humanity*. Columbus: Ohio State UP, 1979.

Dante Alighieri, *Purgatory*. Trans. Mark Musa, Bloomington: Indiana UP, 1981.

Delany, Sheila. *Chaucer's House of Fame. The Poetics of Skeptical Fideism*. Chicago: U of Chicago P, 1972.

Dowling, Linda. *The Vulgarization of Art*. Charlottesville: UP of Virginia, 1996.

Dyer, Gary. "The 'Vanity Fair' of Nineteenth-Century England: Commerce, Women and the East". *Nineteenth-Century Literature* 46 (1991), 196-222.

Ennis, Lambert. *Thackeray: The Sentimental Cynic*. Evanston: Northwestern UP, 1950.

Ferris, Ina. "The Breakdown of Thackeray's Narrator: *Lovel the Widower*". *Nineteenth Century Fiction* 32 (1976), 36-53.

—. "The Demystification of Laura Pendennis". *Studies in the Novel* 13 (1981), 122-32.

—. "Narrative Strategy in Thackeray's *The Adventures of Philip*". *English Studies in Canada* 5 (1979), 448-56.

—. "The Reader in the Rhetoric of Realism: Scott, Thackeray and Eliot". *Papers of the Aberdeen Scott Conference*. Eds. J. H. Alexander and David Hewitt. Aberdeen: Association for Scottish Literary Studies, 1983, 383-92.

—. "Realism and the Discord of Ending: The Example of Thackeray". *Nineteenth Century Fiction* 33 (1983), 289-303.

Fetterley, Judith. *The Resisting Reader*. Bloomington: Indiana UP, 1978.

Fisher, Judith. "Image Versus Text in the Illustrated Novels of William Makepeace Thackeray". *Victorian Literature and the Victorian Visual Imagination*. Eds. Carol T. Christ and John O. Jordan. Berkeley: U of California P, 1995, 60-87.

—. "Thackeray as Editor and Author: *The Adventures of Philip* and the Inauguration of the *Cornhill Magazine*". *Victorian Periodicals Review* 33 (Spring 2000), 2-21.

Fletcher, Robert P. "Visual Thinking and the Picture Story in *The History of Henry Esmond*". *PMLA* 113 (May 1998), 379-94.

Freccero, John. *Dante: The Poetics of Conversion*. Cambridge, MA: Harvard UP, 1986.

Fried, Michael. *Absorption and Theatricality: Painting and the Beholder in the Age of Diderot*. Berkeley: U of California P, 1980.

Frye, Northrup. *The Secular Scripture. A Study of the Structure of Romance*. Cambridge, MA: Harvard University Press, 1976.

Gagnier, Regina. *Subjectivities: A History of Self-Representation in Britain 1832-1920* . New York: Oxford UP, 1991.

Garrett, Peter. *The Victorian Multiplot Novel*. New Haven: Yale UP, 1980.

Garson, Marjorie. "'Knowledge of Good and Evil': Henry and Rachel in *The History of Henry Esmond*". *English Studies in Canada* 9 (December 1983) 418-434.

Gay, Peter. *The Naked Heart, The Bourgeois Experience Victoria to Freud.* Vol. IV New York: W.W, Norton, Inc. 1995.

Gilmour, Robin. *The Idea of the Gentleman in the Victorian Novel.* London: George Allen & Unwin, 1981.

Girard, Rene. *Deceit, Desire, and the Novel. Self and Other in Literary Structure.* Trans. Yvonne Freccero. Baltimore: The Johns Hopkins UP, 1965.

Goldin, Frederick. *The Mirror of Narcissus in the Courtly Love Lyric.* Ithaca: Cornell UP, 1967.

Guerin, Wilfred L. et. al. *A Handbook of Critical Approaches to Literature.* New York: Oxford UP, 1992.

Hankins, John Erskine. *Source and Meaning in Spenser's Allegory: A Study of the 'Faerie Queene.'* New York: Oxford UP, 1971.

Hannah, Donald. "'The Author's Own Candles': The Significance of the Illustrations to *Vanity Fair*". *Renaissance and Modern Essays Presented to Vivian de Sola Pinto.* London: Routledge and Kegan Paul, 1966, 119-27.

Harden, Edgar. "The Discipline and Significance of Form in *Vanity Fair*". *PMLA* 82 (1967), 530-41.

—. "Theatricality in *Pendennis*". *Ariel* 4 (1973), 74-94.

Hardy, Barbara. *The Exposure of Luxury. Radical Themes in Thackeray.* Pittsburgh: U of Pittsburgh P, 1972.

Harvey, J. R. *Victorian Novelists and their Illustrators.* New York: New York UP, 1971.

Herrick, Robert. *The Complete Poems.* Ed. L. C. Martin. Oxford: Clarendon Press, 1968.

Hill, Jonathon. "Cruikshank, Ainsworth, and Tableau Illustration". *Victorian Studies* 23 (1980), 429-59.

Homans, Margaret. *Bearing the Word: Language and Female Experience in Nineteenth-Century Women's Writing.* Chicago: U. of Chicago P, 1986.

Horace, "The Art of Poetry". *Satires, Epistles, Ars Poetica.* Trans, H. Rushton Fairclough, *Loeb Classical Library.* Cambridge, MA: Harvard UP, 1947.

Horn, Anne. "Theatre, Journalism, and Thackeray's 'Man of the world' Magazine," *Victorian Periodicals Review* 32 (Fall 1999), 223-38.

Houfe, Simon. *The Dictionary of British Book Illustrators and Caricaturists 1800-1914.* London: British Library, 1978.

Hughes, Linda K. and Michael Lund. *The Victorian Serial.* Charlottesville, VA: UP of Virginia, 1991.

Hume, David. *A Treatise of Human Nature.* 1978. Ed. L. A. Selby-Bigge. Rev. P. H. Nittitch. Oxford: Clarendon Press, 1988.

Jay, Paul. *Being in the Text.* Ithaca: Cornell UP, 1984.

Keats, John. *Complete Poems.* Ed. Jack Stillinger. Cambridge, MA: Harvard UP, 1982.

Kermode, Frank. *The Sense of an Ending.* New York: Oxford UP, 1967.

Lambert, Miles. "The Dandy in Thackeray's *Vanity Fair* and *Pendennis*, an Early

Victorian View of the Regency Dandy". *Costume: The Journal of the Costume Society* 22 (1988), 60-69.

Langland, Elizabeth. "Domestic Ideology in the Victorian Novel". *PMLA* 107 (1992), 290-304.

Leavis, F. R. *The Great Tradition*. London: Chatto and Windus, 1969.

Lester, John. "Thackeray's Narrative Technique". *PMLA* 69 (1954), 392-409.

Levine, George. *Darwin and the Novelists*. 1988. Rpt. Chicago: University of Chicago Press, 1991.

—. *The Realistic Imagination*. Chicago: U of Chicago P, 1983.

Lewis, Sarah. *Women's Mission*. London, 1840.

Loofbourow, John. *Thackeray and the Form of Fiction*. Princeton: Princeton UP, 1964.

Lund, Michael. *Reading Thackeray*. Detroit: Wayne State UP, 1988.

MacIntyre, Alasdair. *After Virtue: A Study in Moral Theory*. South Bend: Notre Dame UP, 1981.

"Magazines". *John Bull*. 9 August 1862, 557.

Mander, Raymond and Joe Mitchenson. *Pantomime*. London: P. Davies, 1973.

Marin, Louis. "Poussin's *The Arcadian Shepherds*". *The Reader in the Text*. Eds. Susan R. Suleiman and Inge Crosman. Princeton: Princeton UP, 1980, 293-324.

Mason, Mary. "Autobiographies of Women Writers". *Autobiography*. Ed. James Olney. Princeton: Princeton UP, 1980, 207-35.

Mays, Kelly. "The Disease of Reading and Victorian Periodicals". *Literature in the Marketplace. Cambridge Studies in Nineteenth-Century Literature and Culture* 5. Eds. John O. Jordan and Robert Patten. Cambridge: Cambridge UP, 1995,165-94.

Maunder, Andrew. "'Discourses of Distinction': The Reception of the *Cornhill Magazine*, 1859-60". *Victorian Periodicals Review* 33 (Winter 2000), 44-64.

—. "'Monitoring the middle-classes': Intertextuality and Ideology in Trollope's *Framley Parsonage* and the *Cornhill Mazagine*". *Victorian Periodicals Review* 33 (Spring 2000), 44-64.

McMaster, Juliet. *Thackeray. The Major Novels*. Toronto: U of Toronto P, 1971.

—. "Funeral Baked Meats: Thackeray's Last Novel". *Studies in the Novel* 13 (1981), 133-55.

McMaster, R. D. *Thackeray's Cultural Frame of Reference. Allusion in The Newcomes*. Montreal & Kingston: McGill-Queen's UP, 1991.

Meisel, Meisel, *Realizations, Narrative, Pictorial, and Theatrical Arts in Nineteenth-Century England*. Princeton: Princeton UP, 1983.

Miller, Andrew. "*Vanity Fair* through Plate Glass". *PMLA* 105 (1990), 1042-54.

Miller, J. Hillis. *The Disappearance of God*. Cambridge, MA: Harvard UP, 1963.

—. *Fiction and Repetition*. Cambridge: Harvard U P, 1982.

—. "Rhetorical Study at the Present Time". *Theory Then and Now*. Durham: Duke UP, 1991.

Moers, Ellen. *The Dandy: Brummell to Beerbohm*. Lincoln: U of Nebraska P, 1960.

Mueller-Vollmer, Kurt. *The Hermeneutics Reader. Texts of the German Tradition from the Enlightenment to the Present*. New York: Continuum Publishing, 1985.

Nash, Henry. *Higher Criticism of the Bible*. London: Macmillan & Co., Ltd., 1900.

"New Novels". *Athenaeum* . 9 August 1862, 174.

"New Novels". *Daily News*. 4 September 1862, 2.

"Novels". *British Quarterly Review*. 36 (October 1862), 467-68.

"Novels." *London Review and Weekly Journal of Politics, Literature, Art, and Society* 30 August 1862, 192.

"Novels". *North British Review* 3 (February 1863), 176.

Oakeshott, Michael. "The Fortunes of Skepticism". *Times Literary Supplement*. No. 4850 (15 March 1996), 14.

Olney, James. *Autobiography*. Princeton: Princeton UP, 1980.

—. *Metaphors of Self*. Princeton: Princeton UP, 1972.

Parker, Patricia. *Inescapable Romance: Studies in the Poetics of a Mode*. Princeton: Princeton UP, 1979.

Peck, John. "Thackeray and Religion: The Evidence of *Henry Esmond*". *English* 40 (1991):217-35.

Perkin, J. Russell. "The Implied Theology of *Vanity Fair*". *Philological Quarterly* 77 (Winter 1998), 79-106.

Peters, Catherine. *Thackeray's Universe: Shifting Worlds of Imagination and Reality*. Boston: Faber and Faber, 1987.

Phelan, James. *Reading People, Reading Plots*. Chicago: U of Chicago P, 1989.

—. *Narrative as Rhetoric*. Columbus: Ohio State UP, 1996.

Pinchbeck, Ivy and Martha Hewitt. *Children in English Society*. 2 vols. Toronto: U of Toronto P, 1969.

Popkin, Richard. *A History of Skepticism from Erasmus to Spinoza*. Berkeley: U of California P, 1979.

Rabinowitz, Peter J. *Before Reading, Narrative Conventions and the Politics of Interpretation*. Ithaca: Cornell UP, 1987.

Rawlins, Jack. *Thackeray's Novels: A Fiction That is True*. Berkeley: U of California P, 1974.

Ray, Gordon. *Thackeray: The Uses of Adversity*. New York: McGraw-Hill, 1955.

Reed, John. *Punishment and Forgiveness, Dickens and Thackeray*. Athens, OH: Ohio UP, 1995.

Reed, Walter. *An Exemplary History of the Novel.*.Chicago: U of Chicago P, 1981.

Robertson, David. *Sir Charles Eastlake and the Victorian Art World*. Princeton: Princeton UP, 1978.

Rogers, Winslow. "Thackeray's Self-Consciousness". *The Worlds of Victorian Fiction*. Ed. Jerome Buckley. *Harvard English Studies 6*. Cambridge: Harvard UP, 1975. 149-63.

Rorty, Richard. *Philosophy and the Mirror of Nature.* Princeton: Princeton UP, 1979.

Russell, Norman. *The Novelist and Mammon, Literary Responses to the World of Commerce in the Nineteenth Century.* Oxford: Clarendon Press, 1986.

Saintsbury, George. *Thackeray: A Consideration.* London: Oxford UP, 1931.

Scarry, Elaine. "Henry Esmond: The Rookery at Castlewood". *Thackeray, Hawthorne and Melville, and Dreiser.* Eds. Eric Rothsheim and Joseph A. Wittreich Jr. *Literary Monographs.* Vol. 7. Madison: U of Wisconsin P, 1975, 3-43.

Sedgwick, Eve Kosofsky. *Between Men. English Literature and Male Homosocial Desire.* New York: Columbia UP, 1985.

Segal, Elizabeth. "Truth and Authenticity in Thackeray". *Journal of Narrative Technique* 2 (1972), 46-59.

Shillingsburg, Peter L. *Pegasus in Harness: Victorian Publishing and W. M. Thackeray.* Charlottesville: U of Virginia P, 1992.

—. "Editing Thackeray: A History," *Studies in the Novel* 27 (1995), 363-74.

"Short Notice," *Weekly Dispatch.* 10 August 1862, 6.

Siddons, Henry. *Practical Illustrations of Rhetorical Gesture and Action.* 1822. New York: Benjamin Blom, 1968.

Siegle, Robert. *The Politics of Reflexivity, Narrative and the Constitutive Poetics of Culture.* Baltimore: The Johns Hopkins UP, 1986.

Silverman, Kaja. *The Subject of Semiotics.* Oxford: Oxford UP, 1983.

Spengemann, William. *The Forms of Autobiography.* New Haven: Yale UP, 1980.

Spenser, Edmund. "The Faerie Queene," *Poetical Works.* Eds. J. C. Smith and E. de Selincourt. Oxford: Oxford UP, 1969.

Steiner, Wendy. *Pictures of Romance.* Chicago: U of Chicago P, 1988.

Stephen, Fitzjames. "Gentlemen". *Cornhill Magazine* 5 (March 1862), 327-42.

—. "Keeping Up Appearances". *Cornhill Magazine* 4 (September 1861), 305-18.

Stewart, Garrett. *Dear Reader. The Conscripted Audience in Nineteenth-Century British Fiction.* Baltimore: The Johns Hopkins UP, 1996.

Stevens, Joan. "Thackeray's Pictorial Capitals," *Costerus* n.s. 2 (1974), 113-40.

—. "Thackeray's 'Vanity Fair,'" *Review of English Literature* 6 (1965), 19-38.

Stierle, Karlheinze. "The Reading of Fictional Texts". *The Reader in The Text.* Eds Susan Suleiman and Inge Crosman. Princeton: Princeton UP, 1980, 83-105.

Stonehouse, J. H. *Catalogue of the Libraries of Charles Dickens and W. M. Thackeray.* London, 1935.

Storey, Robert F. *Pierrot: A Critical History of a Mask.* Princeton: Princeton UP, 1978.

Sudrann, Jean. "The Philosopher's Property: Thackeray and the Use of Time". *Victorian Studies* 10 (1967), 358-87.

Sweeney, Patricia. "Thackeray's Best Illustrator," *Costerus* n.s. (1974), 83-112.

Talon, Henri. "Time and Memory in Thackeray's *Henry Esmond*," *Review of*

English Studies 13 (1962), 147-56.

Taube, Myron. "Contrast as a Principle of Structure in *Vanity Fair*". *Nineteenth-Century Fiction* 28 (1963), 119-35.

—. "Thackeray and the Reminiscential Vision". *Nineteenth-Century Fiction* 18 (1963), 247-59,

Taylor, George. *Players and Performances in the Victorian Theatre.* Manchester: Manchester UP, 1989.

Thackeray. W. M. *The Adventures of Philip.* (1862). *Works*, XX-XXI.

—. "Caricature and Lithography in Paris". *The Paris Sketchbook* (1839), *Works*, IX, 142-65.

—. *Catherine.* Ed. Sheldon Goldfarb. Ann Arbor: U of Michigan P, 1999.

—. "Charity and Humour" (1852). *Works*, XIV, 715-25.

—. *The English Humourists and the Four Georges* (1851, 1855), *Works*, XIV, 423-710.

—. "An Essay on the Genius of George Cruikshank". *Westminister Review* 34 (June 1840), 4-59. *Works*, XXIV, 284-319.

—. "Exhibition Gossip". *Ainsworth's Magazine* 1 (June 1842), 319- 22.

—. *Henry Esmond.* Ed. Edgar F. Harden. New York: Garland Publishing, 1989.

—. *The History of Pendennis.* Ed. Peter L. Shillingsburg. New York: Garland Publishing, 1991.

—. "John Leech, *Pictures of Life and Character*". *Quarterly Review* 96 (December 1854), 75-86. *Works*, XXV, 480-92.

—. *The Letters and Private Papers of William Makepeace Thackeray.* 4 vols. Ed. Gordon Ray. Cambridge, MA: Harvard UP, 1945-50.

—. *The Letters and Private Papers, A Supplement to Gordon N. Ray, The Letters and Private Papers of William Makepeace Thackeray.* 2 vols. Ed. Edgar F. Harden. New York: Garland Publishing, Inc., 1995.

—. "May Gambols, or Titmarsh in the Picture Galleries". *Fraser's Magazine* 29 (June 1844), 700-17. *Works*, XXV, 419-45.

—. *The Newcomes.* Ed. Peter L. Shillingsburg . Ann Arbor: U of Michigan P, 1996.

—. *Novels By Eminent Hands. Punch* (1847), *Works*, XII, 467-537.

—. "On the French School of Painting". *Fraser's Magazine* 20 (Dec. 1839), 679-88. *Works*, IX, 41-57.

—. "On Men and Pictures, A Propos of a Walk in the Louvre". *Fraser's Magazine* 24 (July 1841), 98-111. *Works*, XXV, 361-83.

—. "Picture Gossip". *Fraser's Magazine* 31 (June 1845), 713-24. *Works*, XXV, 446-464.

—. "Review of William Tait's *Life and Correspondence of David Hume. Morning Chronicle*, 23 March 1846. *Contributions to the Morning Chronicle.* Ed. Gordon Ray. Urbana: U of Illinois P, 1966, 113-118

—. *Roundabout Papers. Cornhill Magazine* (1860-63), *Works*, XXII.

—. "Royal Academy". *Morning Chronicle*, 5 May 1846. *Contributions to the*

Morning Chronicle. Ed. Gordon N. Ray. Urbana: U of Illinois P, 1966, 142-45.

Thackeray, W. M. "Royal Academy, Third Notice". *Morning Chronicle,* 11 May 1846. *Contributions to the Morning Chronicle*. Ed. Gordon N. Ray. Urbana: U of Illinois P, 1966, 149-53.

—. "A Second Lecture on the Fine Arts". *Fraser's Magazine* 19 (June 1839), 743-50. *Works*, XXIV, 272-84.

—. *Sketches After English Landscape Painters* .London: David Bogue, 1855.

—. "Strictures on Pictures". *Fraser's Magazine* 17 (June 1838), 758-64. *Works*, XXIV, 261-71.

—. *Vanity Fair*. Ed. Peter L. Shillingsburg. New York: Garland Publishing, 1989.

—. *The Virginians*. (1859) *Works*, XVIII-XIX.

—. *The Works of William Makepeace Thackeray*. *Special Biographical Edition*. 26 vols. Intro. Anne Ritchie. New York: Harper and Bros., 1903.

Thomas, Deborah. *Thackeray and Slavery*. Athens, OH: Ohio UP, 1993.

Tillotson, Geoffrey. *Thackeray the Novelist*. New York: Barnes and Noble, 1974.

—. *A View of Victorian Literature*. Oxford: Clarendon Press, 1978.

Tillotson, Geoffrey and Donald Hawes, eds. *Thackeray: The Critical Heritage*. New York: Barnes & Noble, 1968.

Unger, Roberto. *Passion: An Essay on Personality*. New York: Free Press (Macmillan), 1984.

Vargish, Thomas. *The Providential Aesthetic in Victorian Fiction*. Charlottesville: UP of Virginia, 1985.

Vinge, Louise. *The Narcissus Theme in Western* Literature. Trans. Robert Dewsnap. Lund: Gleerups, 1967.

Wajngot, Marion, Helfer. *The Birthright and the Blessing. Narrative As Exegesis In Three of Thackeray's Later Novels. Stockholm Studies in English XCI.* Stockholm: Almqvist & Wiksell International, 2000.

Westburg, Barry. *The Confessional Fictions of Charles Dickens*. Dekalb: Northern Illinois UP, 1977.

Whalley, Joyce and Tessa Rose Chester. *A History of Children's Book Illustration*. London: John Murray, 1988.

Wilkinson, Ann. "The Tomeavesian Way of Knowing the World: Technique and Meaning in *Vanity Fair"*. *English Literary History* 32 (1965), 370-387.

Williamson, Jerry. "Thackeray's Mirror". *Tennessee Studies in Literature* 22 (1977), 133-53.

"Wit without Money, or, How to Live Upon Nothing" by "Vampyre Horseleech, Esq". *Punch*. December 1841, 38.

Index

Addison, Joseph 276, 277
    The Campaign 276
Adelphi Theatre 239
Adventures of Philip, The, see
Thackeray, William
Aeneid, see Thackeray, William
Aesop 233
Agg, John 158
    "The London Bazaar, or, Where
      to Get Cheap Things" 158
Ainsworth, William Harrison 44
    Ainsworth's Magazine 44
Alastor, see Shelley Percy Bysshe
Alberti, Leon Batista 49
    De Pictura 49
Algihieri, Dante 156, 180
    Purgatory, The 156, 180
Annuals 21
Arabian Nights; see *Thousand and
    One Nights, A*
Ariosto
    Orlando Furioso 203n, 204n
Armstrong, Nancy 268
Athenaeum 281n
authenticating devices, *see* narrative;
    Thackeray, William
autobiography 169, 171, 197; *see
    also* Thackeray, William
    autobiographical fiction 103,
      176, 177

Bagehot, Walter 257, 279n
Bakhtin, Mikhail 8, 86
Baldridge, Cates 126
bazaars, charity 157-58
Beeton, Isabella 151
    *Book of Household Management,
    The* 151
Bible, higher criticism of 10-11
    Jeremiah 168

bildungsroman 24, 90, 103; *see also*
    Thackeray, William
Blake, Andrew 253
Booth, Wayne 9
    The Company We Keep 9
Bostetter, Edward 179
bower, *see* Victorian idyll
Boydell, John 58
British Quarterly Review 281n-282n
Bronte, Charlotte
    Jane Eyre 103
Brookfield crisis, see Brookfield,
    Jane
Brookfield, Jane 14, 197, 198
Browning, Elizabeth Barrett 239
Bulwer-Lytton, Edward 38n, 45,
    81, 115
Buonarroti, Michel Angelo
    [Michelangelo] 139, 167n, 223
Byron, George Gordon, Lord 47,
    110, 137
    Byronic hero 110

Carlisle, Janice 7
Carlyle, Thomas 201n
    Sartor Resartus 201n
Cary, Joyce 37
Catherine, see Thackeray, William
Cavalier poetry 236
Chambers, Ross 165, 173, 261, 262,
    277
    Story and Situation 173
Chapman, John 10
Chase, Karen 178
Chaucer, Geoffrey 15
Cimabue 55
"Civil Service as a Profession, The",
    see Cornhill Magazine
Clarke, Micael 1
    Thackeray and Women 1

codes, *see* sociolect; representation
Colby, Robert 1, 12, 15, 36, 77, 221
    Canvass of Humanity 1, 12
Coleridge, Samuel Taylor 17
    "Eolian Harp" 17
commedia dell 'arte 265
Commission on the Fine Arts 56,
    92n
    "Exhibition of Decorative Works
        for the New Houses of
        Parliament" 56, 92n
Congreve, William 207
    Way of the World, The 207
conscripted reader, *see* reading
Cope, Charles West 54, 56, 57
    Charity 54
Cornhill Magzine 252, 253; *see also*
    Thackeray, William
    "Civil Service as a Profession,
        The" 253
    "Samples of Fine English" 253
Cousin, Victor 12, 36
Covent Garden 236
Creswick, Thomas 13
Cruikshank, George 91n, 151, 158
    "A Bazaar" 158

Daily News 279n
Danby, Francis 13
dandy 81, 115, 262; *see also*
    Thackeray, William
Dante, *see* Alighieri, Dante
Darwin, Charles 40n
David Copperfield, see Dickens,
    Charles
Delany, Sheila 15
Dickens, Charles 2, 38n, 45
    David Copperfield 174
    Oliver Twist 2-3, 46
    Nicholas Nickleby 24
    Our Mutual Friend 24
Dilthey, Wilhelm 11
Disraeli, Benjamin 81

D'Orsay, Alfred 81, 82, 115
Dyer, Gary 157

Egan, Pierce 59
    Life in London 59
egoism 18, 23, 67, 45, 223; *see also*
    narrator; Thackeray, William
    Romantic 137, 273
Eliot, George (Marian Evans) 2, 8,
    45, 150, 253
    Middlemarch 24
    Romola 253
Endymion, see Keats, John

Fairie Queene, The, *see* Spenser,
    Edmund
Ferris, Ina 8, 245, 250, 257, 269,
    272, 273, 274, 275
Fielding, Henry 70, 229
Fraser's Magazine 246
Freccero, John 180
Frye, Northrup 24

Gadamer, Hans-Georg 11
Garrett, Peter 63, 77
Garson, Marjorie 174, 181, 184
Gay, Peter 45
    The Naked Heart 45
Gillray, James 58, 60, 61
Gilmour, Robin 257
Giotto 55, 57
Girard, Renè 277
Goethe 132n
    Sufferings of Young Werther, The
        132n
Goldin, Frederick 112, 114
Gothic Revival 55, 56
Gros, Antoine, Baron 12

Harden, Edgar 35, 63, 139, 227
Harding, James 48
Hardy, Barbara 151, 158
Harvey, J. R. 77

Haydon, Benjamin 167n
"Hedgehog, Humphrey", see Agg, John
hermeneutics, see Schleiermacher; skepticism
Herrick, Robert 232, 235
    "To the Virgins, To Make Much of Time" 232
History of Henry Esmond, The, see Thackeray, William
History of Pendennis, The, see Thackeray, William
Home, John 237, 238
    Douglas 237, 238
Horace 135
Horn, Anne 252
Hugo, Victor 118
    Le Roi s'Amuse 118, 133n
Hume, David 12, 14, 17
    Essays and Treatises 12
Hunt, William Henry 159
Hyperion, see Keats, John
interpretive community 2, 137

Iser, Wolfgang 22

Jane Eyre, see Bronte, Charlotte
Jeremiah, see Bible
John Bull 281n

Keats, John 31, 179
    Lamia 178-79
    Endymion 194
    Hyperion 194
"Keeping up Appearances", see Stephen, Fitzjames
Kermode, Frank 267
Kotzebue, August von 111
    The Stranger 111

La Fontaine, Jean de 277
Lambert, Miles 81
Landseer, Charles 48

Charles I before the Battle of Edge Hill 48
Lawrence, Sir Thomas 48
Leech, John 57-62
    Life and Character 57
Lefond, Charles 12
Lemon, Mark 8
Leslie, Charles Robert 49-50
    Twelfth Night 49
    Roderick Random 50
Lester, John 63
Levine, George 7, 206
    Realistic Imagination, The 206
Lewes, George Henry 63
Lewis, Sarah 153
Linwood, Mary 58
London Review 281n
London Review and Weekly Journal of Politics, Literature, Art, and Society 254, 279n
Loofborow, John 15
Lund, Michael 22, 97

Maclise, Daniel 52
    Play Scene in Hamlet 52
McMaster, Juliet 63, 96, 104, 109, 213, 274, 275
McMaster, R.D. 15, 39n
Marlborough, John Churchill, Duke of 170, 171, 181
Martin, John 167n
Marvy, Louis 12
    Sketches After English Landscape Painters 12
medievalism, see Victorian medievalism
Medusa 180
Meisel, Martin 46, 137, 153
Michel Angelo, see Buonarroti, Michel Angelo
Miller, J. Hillis 25-26, 174, 175, 181,198
Moers, Ellen 82

Montaigne, Michel Eyquen, seigneur de 12
    Essays 12
Moore, Thomas 110
Mozart, Wolfgang Amadeus 235
    Cosi Fan Tutte 235

Narcissus 27
narcissism 111-112, 139, 140, 180, 194-95, 233, 238, 268; *see also* Thackeray, William
narrative; *see also* sociolects; Thackeray, William
    authority 173, 174, 220, 255, 256, 262
    authenticating devices 18, 21, 42n, 216, 220, 237, 245
    consciousness, *see* Thackeray, William
    multiple languages of, *see* sociolects
    perspective, fixed 20, *see also* sociolects
    strategies 18-19
narrator 4, 174, 243-44; *see also* Thackeray, William
    egoism of 6, 13, 17, 67
    intrusive 4
    masks 7, 13, 126, 128
    master-linguist 5, 36, 176, 205-206, 215
    voice 7, 16, 45, 247
Nash, Henry 11
Nazarenes 55
Newcomes, The, see Thackeray, William
Newman, John Henry 57, 257
North British Review 280n-281n

Oliver Twist, see Dickens, Charles
Orlando Furioso, see Ariosto
Orme, Robert 209
    India 209

Our Mutual Friend, see Dickens, Charles
pantomime 86, 127, 254; *see also* Thackeray, William
    Harlequin Crochet and Quaver 86, 127
Parker, Patricia 31
Peck, John 40n
Perkins, J. Russell 12, 40n
perspective, *see* sociolects
Peters, Catherine 95
Phelan, James 3, 9, 16
    Reading People, Reading Plots 3
Popkin, Richard 10
Poussin, Nicholas 139, 164, 167n
Pretender, The, *see* Stuart, James Edward
Proctor, Adelaide 14
Prometheus Unbound, see Shelley, Percy Bysshe
Punch 61
    "Literary Recipes" 63
Pyrro 40n

Quarterly Review 57

Rabinowitz, Peter 1, 3
Raphael 55, 56
Rawlins, Jack 7
Ray, Gordon 239, 275
reading 1, 3-4, 22, 51, 175, 176, 177, 197, 220, 233, 237-38, 239; *see also* sociolects
    conscripted reader 200n
    skeptical 8, 62, 165, 175, 205
realism 6, 8, 15-16, 21, 22, 49, 77, 121, 140, 220, 240, 253-54, 272
Redgrave, Richard 20-21
    Marriage Morning 20-21
Reed, John 1
    Punishment and Forgiveness 1
representation; *see also* sociolects
    codes of 13, 15, 211, 229, 236

conventions of 14, 41n, 137
traditions of 15, 19, 140-41, 275
Reynolds, Sir Joshua 48
Rogers, Winslow 7
romance 2, 6, 16, 21, 24, 26, 31,
    113, 140, 158, 173, 206, 227,
    229, 266, 271; *see also*
    Thackeray, William
  language 262; *see also*
    sociolects; Thackeray, William
  settings of 31
  skeptical 25, 207, 266
  splits in 27-28, 185; *see also*
    Thackeray, William
Romanticism 13, 17, 31, 47, 201n
  tropes of 194
Rorty, Richard 11, 20, 240, 261
Rousseau, Jean Jacques 45
  Confessions 45
Rowlandson, Thomas 58, 60, 61

"Samples of Fine English", *see*
    Cornhill Magazine
Sass Henry 12
satire 60-61
Saturday Review 254, 257, 281n
Scarry, Elaine 171, 174, 175
Schleiermacher, Frederich 11, 91n
Scott, Sir Walter 8, 56, 110, 137
Sedgewick, Eve 190
Segal, Elizabeth 77
Shelley, Percy Bysshe
  Alastor 194
  Prometheus Unbound 194
Sheridan, Richard Brinsley 216
  Critic, The 216
Shillingsburg, Peter 8
  Pegasus in Harness 8
Siddons, Henry 73
  *Practical Illustrations of
    Rhetorical Gesture and Action*
    73
skepticism 2, 36, 40n-41n; *see also*

Thackeray, William
  fideism 15, 125, 198
  hermeneutic of 9, 15, 17
  mitigated 10, 14
  Pyrrhenic 10, 28
Smith, George 201n
social individual 14, 19, 36
sociolect 4-5, 15, 19-20, 21, 23, 137,
    147, 160, 164, 166, 205, 268,
    272
  arbitrary nature of 274
  collision 5, 8, 19, 20-21, 22, 220,
    254, 260
  collusion 6, 8, 19, 52, 54, 62
  ethics of 9, 257
  fixed 20, 62, 205, 206, 207, 213-
    215; *see also* Thackeray,
    William
Spectator, The 279n
Spenser, Edmund 29,147, 155,156
  Fairie Queene 24, 29, 147, 155,
    156, 269-70; *see also*
    Thackeray
Stephen, Fitzjames 257
  "Gentlemen" 257
  "Keeping up Appearances" 253
Sterne, Laurence 35, 47
Sternism, *see* Thackeray, William
Stevens, Joan 74, 77, 86
Stewart, Garrett 177
Stierle, Karlheinz 51, 110, 139
Stowe, Harriet Beecher 253
  Agnes of Sorrento 253
Stuart, James Edward 170,
    characterization in *Henry
    Esmond* 194, 195-96
Sudrann, Jean 96
sublime 139, 167n, 271
Sweeney, Patricia 77

Talon, Henri 170
Taube, Myron 63, 96
Taylor, Tom 133n

Fool's Revenge, The 133n
textual authority 173; *see also*
    narrator
Thackeray, Harriet (Minny) 9
Thackeray, Isabella 39n
Thackeray, William Makepeace
    ambiguity of 86
    art criticism of 12, 23, 48-57, 63,
        96, 177-78
    rhetorical strategies in 54-62
    as art student 12
    closure in novels of 267-75; *see
        also* Victorian idyll
    criticism of works of 7-8
    cynicism of 8
    illustrations in work of 20, 22, 45
    irony in works of 277-78
    marriage-market in works of 23,
        139, 165, 225-26
    narrative strategies of 18-19
    narrative voice of 2, 5, 6, 7, 16;
        see also narrator; narrative
    pronominalization in writing 8,
        22, 35, 44-45, 52, 58, 61, 175,
        220, 237
    protagonists of 24, 26-34, 115-
        116, 271
    realism in 8
    religious beliefs of 9-10, 40n
    skepticism 2, 10, 11, 13-14, 25-
        26, 37, 47, 108, 197, 205, 272
    siren in works of 34, 84, 116,
        131, 135-68, 169, 171, 262,
        266, 276
        as metaphors for text 131,
            137, 161, 164
        stripping of 154-56, 164
    sociolects in works of 19-20, 23,
        205
    "Sternism" in works of 35, 46,
        47, 136, 153, 205, 219, 223,
        245, 258
    women, types of in work of 28,

34, 151, 268
Works
    Adventures of Philip, The 6,
        7, 8, 13, 17, 19, 22, 23, 24,
        27, 36, 38n, 47, 128, 173,
        198, 205, 206, 208, 214,
        228, 240, 243-68
        Authenticating devices in
            245
        closure in 267, 272
        criticism of 246, 254, 257,
            266, 274, 279n, 280n,
            281n, 282n
        "gentleman" in 252-54,
            257-58
        Good Samaritan motif in
            24, 254, 256, 260, 263
        illustrations in 252
        manuscript of 247
        manuscript compared to
            Cornhill Magazine 247-
            51
        narrative consciousness in
            246, 255-56
        narrative structure of 254-
            56
        pantomime in 254, 260, 265
        Pendennis as narrator of
            244-45, 246, 251-53, 261-
            62, 272-73
        plot structure in 266-67
        "providential aesthetic in"
            254, 258-59
        sociolects in 256
        siren in 158-59, 163-64,
            165, 248, 265
    Book of Snobs 8, 25-26
    "Caricatures and Lithography
        Paris" 70
    Catherine 2-3, 38n
    "Charity and Humour" 93n
    English Humourists, The 35
    "Essay on the Genius of

George Cruikshank" 44
*History of Henry Esmond,
The* 1, 6, 18, 22, 27, 29-
30, 31, 33, 96, 103, 131,
164, 169-204, 205,
245, 256, 262, 265, 276
Aeneid in, 29
Arthurian motif in 31, 171,
179, 197
autobiography in 173, 177,
189, 197, 198
closure in 271-72
contradictions in codes 173
history in 170
manuscript revisions in
199n, 200n-201n, 202n-
203n
narrative consciousness in
177
narrative technique in 174,
175
Oedipal overtones 192
ruptures in 174, 177, 197,
198
splits in 178-79, 185, 188,
192, 193
siren in 142-43, 154, 161,
162, 165, 179, 184, 190
History of Pendennis, The 14,
18, 19, 22, 23, 27, 28, 31,
46, 90, 95-134, 136-37,
164, 170, 171, 190, 205,
207, 213-14, 235, 245,
262, 265, 272-73
dandy 104, 115, 116-117
Fairie Queene in 24, 29,
109-110, 111-113, 117,
121, 122, 123-24, 125,
150, 151
illustrations in 22, 98, 102,
109, 112-113, 119, 126
narrative consciousness 96,
97, 106

narrative strategies in 95,
96, 97, 102, 103, 108-109,
255
pantomime in 104, 126-27
romance in 113, 117, 121,
123
siren in 98, 117, 137-39,
140-41, 149-51, 154, 161,
164
skepticism in 108, 125
sociolects in 98, 102, 108,
213
structure of 106
theatricality in 103, 116,
117, 128
Lovel the Widower 245, 274,
275
"May Gambols" 54-57
Newcomes, The 6, 12, 13, 18,
19, 22, 24, 39n, 128, 151,
158, 164, 198, 205, 206,
209, 211-213, 214, 216-
217, 228, 237, 243, 246,
268
authenticating devices in
216, 220
Christian code in 209, 212
closure 273
code of "society" 211
dandy in 221
fables in 227
fable-frame in 16, 219-220,
226
Pendennis as narrator of
215-216, 219, 243-44
siren in 141-42, 143-46,
153, 159-60, 161, 162-63,
165, 227
sociolects in 206, 208
fixed 206, 208-209, 213
transcendental 210-211
Thackerayean artist in 221
theatricality in 216-217,

218
"On Men and Pictures" 52, 143
"On the French School of Painting" 143, 164
"Picture Gossip" 48
"Review of John Leech's 'Life and Character'" 57-62
Roundabout Papers 8
  "On a Lazy Idle, Boy" 35
"Shabby Genteel Story, A" 246
Vanity Fair 1, 6, 7, 10, 12, 16, 18, 22, 36, 47, 49, 62-90, 96, 126, 128, 158, 205, 233, 237, 245, 247, 262
  critic's voice in 36, 63-64, 95, 102, 205
  dandy in 81-83, 84
  illustrations in 62, 68-81, 86
  narrative strategies in 66-67, 77, 80-81, 85-86, 266
  modes of reading in 67
  puppet motif 63, 86
  Romance in 84
  siren in 85, 148-49, 151, 152-53, 155, 156-57, 161, 165
  sociolects in 62-63, 87
  structure of 63, 266
Virginians, The 6, 7, 8, 22, 128, 154, 164, 179, 205, 207, 217, 227-42, 243, 260, 262, 266, 268, 269-70
  authenticating devices in 237
  closure in 272
  criticism of 239-40, 254, 274

cultural codes in 229
gambling motif in 230
illustration in 232, 235
narrative strategies in 228, 232-37, 275
Pendennis as narrator of 228, 232-36
sociolects in 231, 233, 236
siren in 154, 228, 233
theatricality 47-50, 227; *see also* Thackeray, William
Thomas, Deborah 95
  Thackeray and Slavery 95
Thompson, Henry, Dr. 253
  "Under Chloroform" 253
Thousand and One Nights, A 36, 83
Tillotson, Geoffrey 6, 7, 38n
Times, The 243
Trimolet, Louis 52-54, 253
  La Prière 52-54, 253
Trollope, Anthony 253
  Framley Parsonage 253
Trotter, John 157
Turner, Joseph Mallord William 97

Unger, Robert 25

Vanity Fair, see Thackeray, William
Vargish, Thomas 254
Vestris, Madame Eliza 48
Victorian idyll 25, 206, 225, 268-70, 273
Victorian medievalism 55
Vigo Bay 188
Virginians, The, see Thackeray, William

Walker, Frederick 252
Watt, Isaac 12
  Logic; or, the Right Use of Reason 12
Webb, General 170, 171, 181
Weekly Dispatch 281n

West, Benjamin 59
Westburg, Barry 137
Wilkinson, Ann 77

Williamson, Jerry 73, 86
Wordsworth, William 17, 31, 201n
    Prelude, The 17, 31, 201n

.